Contents

OPPOSITE THE LÁNCHÍD AND ST STEPHEN'S BASILICA **PREVIOUS PAGE** GELLÉRT BATHS

Introduction to
Budapest

With a wonderful natural setting straddling the River Danube, beautiful architecture and flavoursome Magyar cuisine, Budapest is one of the most rewarding cities in Europe to visit. Its magnificent bridges and boulevards and its grand riverside views invite comparisons with Paris, Prague and Vienna – as do many features of its cultural life, from coffee houses and a love of music to its restaurants and its wine-producing tradition, while it has recently acquired a new modern edge all its own, with cool boutique hotels and its hip bars springing up in artfully decaying buildings. The city is also distinctively Hungarian, its inhabitants displaying fierce pride in their Magyar ancestry. Their language, too, whose nearest European relative is Finnish, underlines the difference – that can represent a challenge to visitors but is no barrier to enjoyment of this most cosmopolitan of European cities.

Fundamental to the city's layout and history, the **River Danube** (Duna) – which is seldom blue – separates **Buda** on the hilly west bank from **Pest** on the eastern plain. Until 1873 these were separate cities, and they still retain a different feel. Buda is older and more dignified: dominated by the Vár (Castle Hill), a mile-long plateau overlooking the Danube, it was the capital of medieval monarchs and the seat of power for successive occupying powers. Built during the city's golden age in the late nineteenth century, with boulevards of Haussmann-like apartment blocks sweeping out from the old medieval centre, **Pest** holds most of the capital's magnificent Art Nouveau edifices and has a noisy, bustling feel. Following construction of the first permanent bridge between the two cities in 1849, power gradually moved across the river, culminating in the building of the grandiose Parliament on the Pest side. The two halves of the city still retain their differences, but as a whole Budapest is a vibrant place today, never in danger of being overwhelmed by tourism but nonetheless offering plenty for visitors to enjoy.

One of Budapest's strongest suits is its **restaurants**, which have made Budapest one of the new gastronomic destinations of Europe. There are places to suit all pockets and

ABOVE MILLENNIUM MONUMENT, HŐSÖK TERE

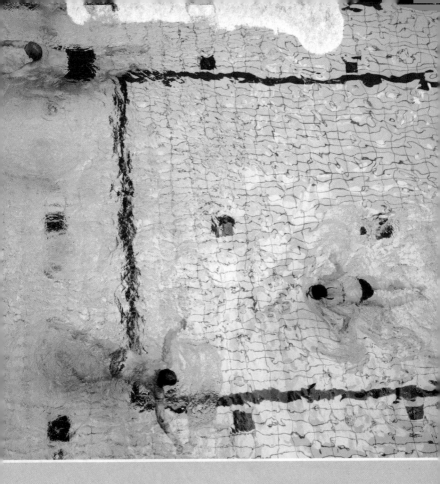

THE ROUGH GUIDE TO

Budapest

DISCARDED

written and researched by

CHARLES HERBERT AND DAN RICHARDSON

with additional co

Norm Longley

013656899 X

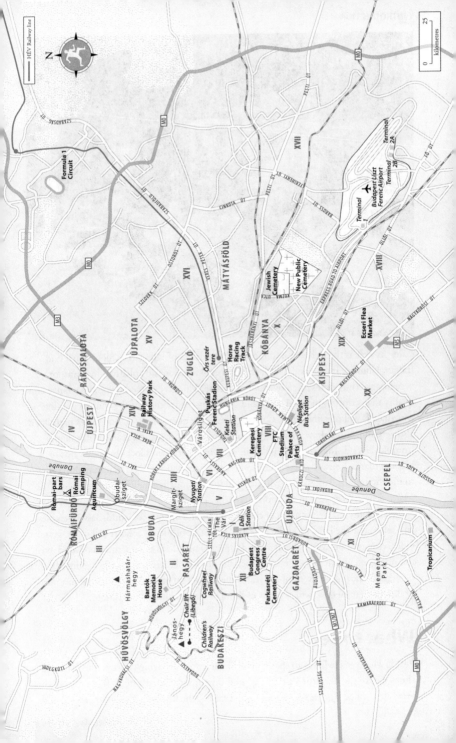

tastes: as well as the richly sauced meat and fish dishes of Hungarian food, you'll find Indian, Chinese, Italian and Middle Eastern cooking alongside plenty of options for vegetarians. Though it's often overlooked abroad, Hungary's superb **wine** has a range and quality that surprises many visitors, and exploring the produce of the country's young winemakers will pay dividends. Catering for a wide range of tastes, Budapest's **nightlife** is also very much of a draw. Generally trouble-free, welcoming and accessible, it ranges from the city's distinctive "ruin pubs" in decaying apartment blocks or courtyards to *tánchaz* (dance houses) where Hungarians of all ages perform wild stamping movements to the rhythms of darkest Transylvania, and internationally renowned artists such as Márta Sebestyén appear in an informal setting.

There's plenty to offer in terms of **classical music and opera**, too: world-class ensembles and soloists can be enjoyed in the Palace of Arts' state-of-the-art concert hall or the grander, older settings of the Music Academy and Opera House. Fans of **pop, rock** and **world music** can discover a wealth of local talent, especially on the folk scene, alongside big international names, but the biggest event of the year is the **Sziget Festival**, held on an island just north of the centre in August, which is one of Europe's largest musical celebrations.

What to see

Pest is where you're likely to spend most of your time, enjoying the streetlife, bars and shops within the **Belváros** (Inner City) and the surrounding districts. These surrounding areas are defined by two semicircular boulevards – the **Kiskörút** (Small Boulevard) and

ABOVE MŰVÉSZ COFFEE HOUSE

Itineraries

DAY 1

Mátyás Church and Fishermen's Bastion
Begin in the Vár, walking its cobbled streets to the
Mátyás Church and Fishermen's Bastion (p.89).

National Gallery Wander along to the Royal
Palace, which houses this collection of works by
Hungary's finest artists (p.96).

Sikló funicular Hop on the Sikló funicular, and
enjoy a great view of the city as you ride down to
the riverside (p.101).

Lunch Head for *Baldaszti's*, at the foot of the
castle, where the eclectic menu offers a
tantalizing range of flavours (p.170).

Budapest Zoo Cross the Lánchíd and catch the
Underground Railway to Hősök tere and visit the
Zoo, great for both animals and architecture (p.73).

Széchenyi Baths Nip over the road to the baths
to wallow in the hot pool and steam rooms in
palatial splendour (p.196).

Dinner Head back to the Belváros for supper at
the *Bock Bisztró*, and enjoy traditional Hungarian
food with a modern take – and with very good
local wine (p.167).

DAY 2

Coffee house Set yourself up for the day at one
of these local institutions, such as the *Centrál*, to
eat, drink and people-watch (p.173).

Museum of Ethnography The #2 tram offers
the best views of Buda, so ride up the bank to see
this fascinating display on Hungarian folk art (p.54).

Great Market Hall Ride the #2 back down to
the Great Market Hall, to browse among the
salamis and paprikas (p.81).

Lunch Have lunch in Borbíróság behind the
Market Hall. The "Wine Court" serves Hungarian-
style tapas – and, of course, top wines (p.169).

Applied Arts Museum The flamboyant building
is as much an exhibit as the displays inside (p.82).

Dinner Make for *Café Kör*, a small, buzzy
restaurant, beside the basilica (p.165).

Drink Walk into the old Jewish Quarter for a drink
at one of the district's atmospheric "ruin pubs"
such as the *Instant* (p.178).

FROM TOP FISHERMEN'S BASTION; CENTRÁL KÁVÉHÁZ;
APPLIED ARTS MUSEUM

A TRIBAL NATION

As a small, landlocked country whose language sets it apart from its neighbours, Hungary is a tribal nation, whose citizens still identify with their ancestors, pagan Magyar tribes who conquered the Carpathian Basin in 896 AD. Since the epochal Christmas Day when the Magyar ruler Vajk was baptized and crowned as King Stephen by a papal envoy, Hungary has identified itself with Europe while simultaneously remaining aware of its "otherness" –a sentiment reinforced by successive foreign occupations and the loss of much of its territory to neighbouring states.

The symbol of statehood is **St Stephen's Crown**, whose bent cross – caused by it being squashed in the eighteenth century – is a cherished sign of the vicissitudes that Hungary has endured, and features on the national **coat of arms** that you'll see everywhere in Budapest. The shield beneath the crown bears a Catholic cross of Lorraine, and the red and white "Árpád stripes" of the early Magyar tribal kings; today, the latter signify far-right loyalties, having formerly been employed as the flag of the Fascist Arrow Cross. With the fall of Communism, St Stephen's Crown returned to the coat of arms, but not to the national **flag** – which is a simple red, white and green tricolour.

the **Nagykörút** (Great Boulevard) – and radial avenues such as Andrássy út and Rákóczi út. Exploring the area between them can easily occupy you for several days. In the financial and government centre of **Lipótváros**, interest lies in St Stephen's Basilica and the monumental Parliament building, which rivals the grand structures across the Danube. In **Terézváros**, Andrássy út leads out past the grandiose Opera House and the House of Terror to Hősök tere (Heroes' Square), a magnificent imperial set piece where the Fine Arts Museum displays a first-rate collection of old European masters. Beyond, the **Városliget** (City Park) holds one of the finest zoos in Europe, both in terms of its animals and its architecture, as well as the hugely popular Széchenyi Baths, served by its own thermal springs.

Of Pest's remaining inner-city districts, **Erzsébetváros** and **Józsefváros** hold the most appeal. The former is Budapest's old Jewish quarter, with a rich and tragic history that's still palpable in the bullet-scarred backstreets behind the great synagogue on Dohány utca. But its old apartment blocks have also spawned a new genre of bars, the "ruin pubs", which have become a popular destination for younger Budapestis. From here, it's not far to the National Museum, a well-presented introduction to Hungarian history, and to the Great Market Hall, further round in **Ferencváros**, whose hinterland harbours the Applied Arts Museum, Holocaust Memorial Centre and the major new cultural centre of the Palace of Arts.

The **Vár** (Castle) on the **Buda** side was once the seat of Hungary's monarchs, and its palace, museums, churches and Baroque streets offer some absorbing sightseeing; the historic Turkish baths along the banks of the Danube are also well worth experiencing. There's more history to the north in **Óbuda**, with its extensive Roman remains. In fine weather, people flock to **Margit-sziget**, the large, leafy island mid-river between Buda and Pest, to swim and sunbathe at the enormous lido and party through the night. Encircling the city to the west, the **Buda Hills** have a different kind of allure, with fun rides on the Cogwheel and Children's railways and chairlift, and intriguing caves to be visited. **Further out**, the steam trains of the Hungarian Railway History Park and the redundant Communist monuments within the Memento Park rate as major attractions.

There is plenty to see on **excursions** from Budapest. Szentendre is a picturesque artists' colony with a superb open-air ethnographic museum. Further upriver, the Danube Bend offers gorgeous scenery, a Renaissance palace and citadel and an amazing treetop zip-ride at Visegrád, while Esztergom boasts its basilica and a remarkable Turkish relic, while on the east bank of the Danube sits Vác, with its well-preserved Baroque centre.

Classical-music lovers will also enjoy concerts in the former Habsburg palace of Gödöllő, to the east of Budapest, while Székesfehérvár has a fine collection of museums in its very pleasant Belváros.

When to go

The best times to visit Budapest are **spring** (late March to the end of May) and **autumn** (Sept–Oct), when the weather is mild and there are fewer tourists (though things tend to get busy during the **Budapest Spring Festival** in late March/early April). The majority of visitors come in the summer, when many residents decamp to Lake Balaton and those who remain flock to the city's pools and parks to escape the heat and dust. Though some concert halls are closed over summer, there are all kinds of outdoor events to compensate – and also major international events such as the Sziget Festival and Formula One Grand Prix, both in August. Winter is cold and may be snowy, but you can still enjoy all the city's sights and cultural attractions (as well as trying roasted chestnuts from street vendors), while the thermal baths take on an extra allure. It's wise to book accommodation in advance for Christmas, New Year, the Spring Festival and Grand Prix.

ABOVE THE PARLIAMENT BUILDING

22

things not to miss

It's not possible to see everything that Budapest has to offer in one trip – and we don't suggest you try. What follows is a selective taste of the city's highlights: magnificent Art Nouveau treasures, unique thermal baths, and world-class concerts and festivals. All highlights have a page reference to take you straight into the Guide, where you can find out more. Coloured numbers refer to chapters in the Guide

1 THERMAL BATHS
Page 193

Bathe in splendour at the city's spas, which are fed by hot springs.

2 FOLK MUSIC
Page 187

Catch the irrepressible sounds of Hungary's folk and Gypsy fiddlers in Budapest's lively music scene.

3 WINE
Page 168

Hungary's vineyards turn out excellent wines – taste them at the Budapest Wine Festival in September, or all year round in the city's top-class restaurants.

4 #2 TRAM RIDE
Page 25 and 42

This route past Parliament and along the Pest embankment affords some of the best views of the city.

8

5 BUDAPEST ZOO
Page 73

Feed the giraffes, tickle the rhinos and marvel at the magnificent Art Nouveau buildings – the Elephant and Palm Houses are particularly impressive.

6 CLASSICAL CONCERTS
Page 168

High-class musicianship throughout the year, often in dramatic venues.

7 HUNGARIAN NATIONAL GALLERY
Page 96

Showcased in the imposing Royal Palace, this is Hungary's premier collection of home-grown art, from Gothic altarpieces to Art Nouveau and Abstract Expressionism.

8 COFFEE HOUSES
Page 172

Ponder the world over a coffee and cake – after all, it's an old Central European tradition.

9 MEMENTO PARK
Page 125

Lenin and his comrades in Communist statuary are now laid out in a park on the outskirts of Budapest.

9

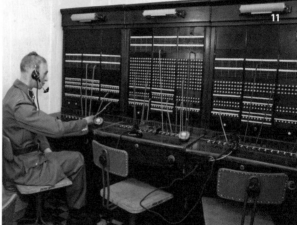

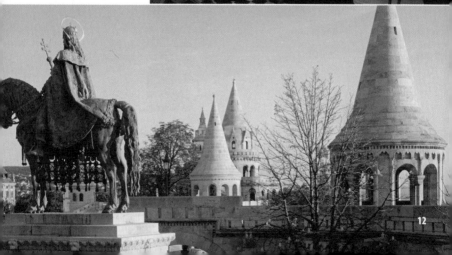

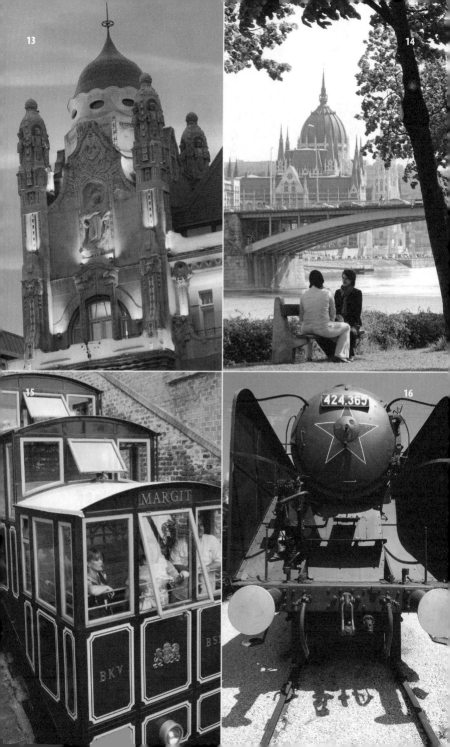

CYCLING PAST THE PARLIAMENT BUILDING

Basics

Getting there

Budapest is easy to reach by air, with a number of budget airlines flying from several UK airports, in addition to the established carriers, British Airways and the Hungarian national airline Malév. There are also nonstop flights from the US. Travelling overland from the UK is another option, though this inevitably takes much longer and usually works out far more expensive.

To get the very cheapest fares advertised by the budget airlines, you'll need to book weeks, if not months, in advance. Fares with Malév and other major airlines tend to be more expensive and seasonal, with the highest fares from June to September, Christmas and New Year. You'll get the best prices during the low season, November to February.

Most airlines prefer you to book online these days, and you can find some great deals, but always check the small print as most budget airlines are non-changeable and non-refundable. Another option is to contact a general flight or **travel agent** – these have similar deals on flights and services, and some are particularly geared towards youth, student and independent travel. Other specialist **tour operators** can book you onto a variety of city breaks or themed tours in Budapest.

Flights from the UK and Ireland

Flying time to Budapest from the UK or Ireland is between two and a half and three hours, depending on your departure airport.

There are currently three budget airlines flying from the UK to Budapest: easyjet (W easyjet.com), which flies from London Gatwick and Luton; Wizz Air (W wizzair.com), which flies from Luton; and Jet2 (W jet2.com), which flies from Manchester and Edinburgh. Tickets with these airlines can be obtained from as little as £50 return, including tax.

British Airways (W britishairways.com) and Malév (W malev.com) fly direct daily from Heathrow and Gatwick. Economy-class return fares with both start around £180 high season and £100 low season, though the earlier you book, the more likely you are to get even lower prices than these. Moreover, both offer good-value promotional deals.

From **Ireland**, Aer Lingus (W aerlingus.com) and Malév fly daily between Dublin and Budapest – flights take three hours. Fares start at around €150 in low season.

Flights from the US and Canada

The only airline to fly nonstop from North America to Budapest is American Airlines (W aa.com), which flies from New York JFK. Flying time is around nine and a half hours. European-based airlines (like Air France (W airfrance.com), British Airways (W britishairways.com) and Lufthansa (W lufthansa .com) can also get you to Budapest from elsewhere in the US and Canada, though you'll be routed via their respective European hubs.

Fares from New York to Budapest are around US$900 high season and US$550 low season, and from the west coast around US$1200 high season and US$850 low season. From **Canada**, fares rise from Can$1000 to at least Can$1600 in high season.

Flights from Australia, New Zealand and South Africa

There are no direct flights to Budapest from Australia, New Zealand or South Africa; the best option is to fly to a western European gateway and get a connecting flight from there. A standard return **fare** to Budapest with Qantas from eastern **Australia** via Frankfurt is around Aus$2600 in low season, rising to Aus$3500 in high season. From **New Zealand**, a standard return ticket via London with Air New Zealand costs around NZ$3500 in low season, NZ$4000 in high season. Flying from **South Africa**, you can get return flights for ZAR8900 in low season and ZAR9600 in high season.

A BETTER KIND OF TRAVEL

At Rough Guides we are passionately committed to travel. We feel that travelling is the best way to understand the world we live in and the people we share it with – plus tourism has brought a great deal of benefit to developing economies around the world over the last few decades. But the growth in tourism has also damaged some places irreparably, and climate change is exacerbated by most forms of transport, especially flying. All Rough Guides' trips are carbon-offset, and every year we donate money to a variety of charities devoted to combating the effects of climate change.

City breaks and tours

Budapest is an extremely popular city-break destination and this is reflected in the growing number of operators offering the city as a destination in itself or as part of a two- or three-centre trip, usually combined with Prague and Vienna.

AGENTS AND OPERATORS

Cox & Kings UK ☎ 020 7873 5000, ⓦ coxandkings.co.uk. Upmarket cultural trips to Budapest staying in five-star hotels such as the Four Seasons and the Corinthia Royal: three-night breaks starts at around £425 including flights and transfers. There are also luxury and private group tours aboard the Danube Express, which either start at, or pass through, Budapest.

Kirker Holidays UK ☎ 020 7593 1899, ⓦ kirkerholidays.co.uk. Three-night cultural breaks in four- and five-star hotels from around £450 per person, including flights and transfers. They can reserve opera tickets and arrange walking tours of the city.

Martin Randall Travel UK ☎ 020 8742 3355, ⓦ martinrandall.com. Well-respected art, architecture and music tours led by a lecturer covering, for example, the Spring Festival and Budapest at Christmas. Prices for a seven-day trip start at around £2000, which includes flights from the UK, hotels, transfers, excursions, concert tickets and some meals.

North South Travel UK ☎ 01245 608 291, ⓦ northsouthtravel .co.uk. Friendly, competitive travel agency, offering discounted fares worldwide. Profits are used to support projects in the developing world, especially the promotion of sustainable tourism.

Osprey City Holidays UK ☎ 0131 243 8098, ⓦ ospreyholidays .com. Two-night breaks in one of several three- and four-star hotels, from £255 per person, including flights and transfers.

Page & Moy UK ☎ 0116 217 8006, ⓦ pageandmoy.com/ motorracing. Eight- to twelve-day rail and river cruises taking in Budapest as part of a three- or four-centre trip, typically with Austria, Germany and Slovakia. From £1260.

Regent Holidays UK ☎ 0117 921 1711, ⓦ regent-holidays .co.uk. Central and Eastern European specialists offering three-night city breaks from £245 and Christmas market breaks from £300 (including flights from the UK), as well as tailor-made itineraries.

Stag Republic UK ☎ 0845 686 0619, ⓦ stagrepublic.co.uk. A Budapest-based operation that arranges stag packages that can include Trabant treks, quad biking, visits to the baths and stag dinners. Prices start at £59 per person for a two-night hostel stay, on top of which you add the various activities.

STA Travel UK ☎ 0871 2300 040, US ☎ 1 800 781 4040, Australia ☎ 134 782, New Zealand ☎ 0800 474 400, South Africa ☎ 0861 781 781; ⓦ statravel.co.uk. Worldwide specialists in independent travel; also student IDs, travel insurance, car rental, rail pass and more. Good discounts for students and under-26s.

Thermalia Spas UK ☎ 01843 864 688, ⓦ thermaliaspas.co.uk. Spa holiday specialists offering stays centred around health and fitness at four-star thermal resorts in Budapest. Prices from around £400 for three nights and £720 for seven nights, including flights from the UK and Ireland.

Trailfinders UK ☎ 0845 054 6060, Ireland ☎ 021 464 8800, Australia ☎ 1300 780 212; ⓦ trailfinders.com. One of the best-informed and most efficient agents for independent travellers.

By rail

Getting to Budapest by **train** is likely to be considerably more expensive than flying, though it's a great deal more fun. First stop should be ⓦ seat61.com, an excellent website that provides route, ticket, timetable and contact information for all European train services.

The quickest and most straightforward option from the UK is to take the **Eurostar** from London's St Pancras International via the Channel Tunnel to Paris, and then continue from Gare de l'Est via Munich or Vienna, both of which take around nineteen hours. A standard second-class **return ticket** on this route costs around £300, but booking ahead can reduce it to less than £200. Going via Brussels and Cologne is slightly cheaper: it involves more changing trains and takes up to 24 hours but the views along the Rhine Valley are delightful. There are discounts for students, and those under 26 or over 60.

A **train pass from** InterRail (ⓦ interrail.net.com) or Eurail (ⓦ eurail.com) – both cover Hungary – makes it convenient to take in the country as part of a wider rail trip around Europe.

RAIL CONTACTS

European Rail UK ☎ 020 7619 1083, ⓦ europeanrail.com.
Eurostar UK ☎ 0843 218 6186, ⓦ eurostar.com.
Rail Europe UK ☎ 0844 848 4064, US ☎ 1 800 622 8600, Canada ☎ 1 800 361 7245; ⓦ raileurope.co.uk.

By bus

Eurolines (ⓦ eurolines.co.uk) operates three **buses** a week directly from London to Budapest, which take around 26 hours. Otherwise, you can change in Vienna. A standard return fare costs around £120, though advance deals and special offers can bring this down considerably. Eurolines buses are air-conditioned and have on-board toilets. The usual route is to take the ferry across the Channel to Calais and then on via Brussels and Vienna.

Driving to Budapest

Driving to Hungary from the UK can be a pleasant proposition, particularly if you want to make stops in other places along the way. It's about 1500km from London to Budapest, which, with stops, takes two days to drive. To plan your route, try **motoring organizations** such as the AA (W theaa.com), the RAC (W rac.co.uk) and Via Michelin (W viamichelin.com).

The most common cross-Channel options are the **ferry** links between Dover and Calais or Ostend. However, the quickest way of crossing the Channel is to go via the **Eurotunnel** service (W eurotunnel .com), which operates drive-on drive-off shuttle trains between Folkestone and Calais/Coquelles. The 24-hour service runs every twenty minutes throughout the day.

Once across the Channel, the most direct route to Budapest is via Brussels, Aachen, Cologne, Frankfurt, Nürnberg, Linz and Vienna. To avoid the long queues at Hegyeshalom, consider entering Hungary from Deutsch-Kreutz, just south of Einstadt, instead. The main cause for any queues is the need to buy a motorway **vignette** (sticker; *matrica*) – compulsory if you are driving on Hungarian motorways. A four-day vignette costs 1650Ft, while a ten-day one costs 2750Ft; see W motorway.hu for details. You can buy the vignette online ahead of travelling, or at one of the petrol stations in Austria before you cross the border, which should reduce any waiting. A system of mobile patrols and electronic number-plate readers enforces the scheme, and there are steep fines for those travelling on a motorway without one. See p.25 for information on driving in Budapest.

FERRY CONTACTS

P&O Ferries UK ☎ 08716 642 121, International ☎ 01304 863 000, W poferries.com.
Sea France UK ☎ 0871 423 7119, W seafrance.com.
Stena Line UK ☎ 0844 770 7070, W stenaline.co.uk.

Arrival

Other than the airport, all points of arrival are fairly central and most within walking distance or just a few stops by metro from downtown Pest. Budapest's excellent public transport system ensures that few parts of the city are more than thirty minutes' journey from the centre; many places can be reached in half that time. The city's three metro lines and three main roads meet at the major junction of Deák tér in Pest, making this the main transport hub of the city; there's a transport map at the back of this book.

By air

Liszt Ferenc International Airport (☎ 1 296 9696, W bud.hu), 20km southeast of the centre in Ferihegy (which it is still sometimes known as), has three passenger terminals. Terminal 1 exclusively serves the no-frills airlines. Terminals 2A and 2B are ten minutes' drive further out: Terminal 2A serves countries covered by the Schengen Agreement, while 2B serves all non-Schengen destinations (UK, the US etc). Terminal 1 handles both Schengen and non-Schengen traffic. Before leaving, it is worth checking which terminal you're flying from, as the Schengen divide might be subject to revision. There are **ATMs**, exchange facilities, tourist information desks and car-rental offices in all the terminal buildings.

The easiest – but most expensive – way to get into the centre is an **airport taxi**. Run by Fótaxi (☎ 1 222 2222), these charge a fixed fee to different zones (you'll pay around 5300Ft or €19 to the centre).

Another option is the **Airport Shuttle** minibus (☎ 1 296 8555, W airportshuttle.hu), which will take you directly to any address in the city. Tickets (2990Ft/€10 for one person, 4490Ft/€16 for two) can be bought in the luggage claim hall while you are waiting for your bags, or in the main concourse; you give the address you're heading to and then have to wait five to twenty minutes until the driver calls your destination.

Far cheaper is public transport; bus #200E departs every fifteen minutes from the stop between terminals 2A and 2B via terminal 1 to Kőbánya-Kispest metro station; from here, you switch to the blue metro line to get to the centre. Total journey time is about thirty minutes from terminal 1 and 45 minutes from 2A and 2B. Both bus and metro tickets cost 320Ft each if bought from the newsagents in the terminals or from the machine by the bus stop. Buying a bus ticket from the driver on board will cost you 400Ft. With a Budapest Card (see p.30), it's free to travel on the bus from the airport.

Alternatively you can catch a train from the station across the road from terminal 1, which takes you to Nyugati Station in around twenty minutes. A single ticket costs 370Ft. You buy tickets at the Tourinform desk inside the terminal building, and trains go at least every half-hour. Trains from Nyugati Station to the airport leave regularly. You can get tickets from the ticket offices by platform 13; the information window should be able to say which platform to go to. You'll want a train to Monor, Cegléd and Szolnok; the airport is the stop after Kőbánya-Kispest.

By train

The Hungarian word *pályaudvar* (abbreviated "*pu.*" in writing) is used to designate a **train station**. Of the six in Budapest, only three are important for tourists, but note that their names, which are sometimes translated into English, refer to the direction of services handled rather than their location.

Most international trains terminate at Pest's **Keleti Station**, on Baross tér in the VIII district. It's something of a hangout for thieves and hustlers – particularly people offering currency exchange – and there are occasionally police about checking ID. By far the best source of information here is the Mellow Mood agency (daily: June–Aug 7am–10pm; Sept–May 7am–7pm; ☎1 343 0748, ⓦmellowmood.hu), whose offices are to the right of the big glass doorways at the far end of the station. It can also book accommodation and organizes transport to its hostels. There are 24-hour left-luggage lockers situated underneath the platforms (400Ft or 600Ft for 24hr depending on bag size).

Avoid all offers of a **taxi** either inside or outside the station – you'll almost certainly be ripped off. Instead, look out for taxis from the companies listed on p.25, such as Fótaxi. Better still, call one.

Nyugati Station, north of central Pest in the VI district, is the main-line link to the airport. It has left-luggage lockers (400Ft or 600Ft for 24hr) next to the international ticket office. To reach Deák tér, take the blue metro line two stops in the direction of Kőbánya-Kispest.

Some trains from Vienna arrive at **Déli Station**, 500m behind the Vár in Buda, which has left-luggage lockers but no tourist office. It's four stops from Deák tér on the red metro line.

By bus or hydrofoil

International buses and services from the Great Plain and Transdanubia terminate at the modern **Népliget bus station**, 5km southeast of the centre at Üllői út 131 in the IX district. The international ticket counters are on the main concourse, where there's a travel centre, with domestic ticket counters located downstairs, which is where you'll also find the left-luggage office (daily 6am–9pm; 300ft). An underpass links the bus station to metro line #3 (blue), from where it's just six stops to Deák tér in the centre.

Of the other bus stations, the **Újpest Városkapu** in the XIII district (on the blue metro line) is the jumping-off point for buses to and from Szentendre and the Danube Bend; the **Stadion bus station** in the XIV district (on the red metro line) serves the Northern Uplands and the **Etele tér bus station** in the XI district (take bus #7 or #7E to the centre) serves the Buda hinterland. None of the city's bus stations has any tourist facilities.

Hydrofoils (operated by Mahart; ☎1 484 4013, ⓦmahartpassnave.hu) from Vienna (May–Sept) dock at the **international landing stage**, on the Belgrád rakpart (embankment), near downtown Pest.

By car

Most drivers enter Budapest along the M1 motorway from Vienna via Hegyeshalom, which is a busy road, heavily policed to fine speeding foreigners. It approaches Budapest from the southwest, and goes straight through to Erzsébet híd in the centre, with turn-offs signed to Petőfi híd in the south of the centre, and Széll Kálmán tér and Margít híd to the north.

Getting around

Budapest's well-integrated transport system comprises the metro, buses, trams and trains, all of which reach most areas of interest to tourists, while the outer suburbs are well served by the overground HÉV rail network. Services operate generally between 5am and 11pm, and there are also night-time buses covering much of the city.

There is a whole array of **tickets** available for use on public transport, but since validating your ticket can be complex and is easy to forget, it's best to get a **travel pass** if you're staying for more than half a day. The local transport authority, the **Budapest Transport Company** (BKV; ⓦbkv.hu) has a useful website with full timetable and ticket information.

Tickets and passes

Standard single **tickets** (*Vonaljegy*) valid for the metro, buses, trams, trolleybuses, the Cogwheel Railway (see p.120) and suburban HÉV lines (up to the edge of the city) cost 320Ft per journey and are sold at metro stations, newspaper kiosks and tobacconists. There are also an increasing number of coin-operated vending machines at bus and tram stops. Metro tickets also come in a variety of other types, depending on whether you are changing trains and how many stops you want to go: a short section metro ticket (*Metrószakasz*; 260Ft) takes you three stops on the same line; a metro transfer ticket

BUDAPEST ADDRESSES

Finding your way around Budapest is easier than the welter of names might suggest. Districts and streets are well signposted, and those in Pest conform to an overall plan based on radial avenues and semicircular boulevards.

Budapest is divided into 23 districts, numbered using Roman numerals. Except when addressing letters, a Budapest **address** always begins with the district number, a system used throughout this book. On letters, a four-digit **postal code** is used instead, the middle two digits indicating the district (so that 1054 refers to a place in the V district). For ease of reference, we list below the district numbers you're most likely to encounter, along with the areas within those districts that you'll probably spend most time in.

I	The Vár and Viziváros	X	Kőbánya
II	Rószadomb and Hűvösvölgy	XI	The area south and east of
III	Óbuda and Aquincum		Gellért-hegy
IV	Újpest	XII	The area from the Vár west into
V	Belváros and Lipótváros		the Buda Hills
VI	Terézváros	XIII	Újlipótváros and Angyalföld
VII	Erzsébetváros	XIV	Városliget and Zugló
VIII	Józsefváros	XXII	Budafok and Nagytétény
IX	Ferencváros		

As a rule of thumb, **street numbers** ascend away from the north–south axis of the River Danube and the east–west axis of Rákóczi út/Kossuth utca/Hegyalja út. Even numbers are generally on the left-hand side as you head outwards from these axes, odd numbers on the right. One number may refer to several premises or an entire apartment building, while an additional combination of numerals denotes the floor and number of individual **apartments** (eg Kossuth utca 14.III.24). Confusingly, some old buildings in Pest are designated as having a half-floor (*félemelet*) or upper ground floor (*magas földszint*) between the ground (*földszint*) and first floor (*elsőemelet*) proper – so that what the British would call the second floor, and Americans the third, Hungarians might describe as the first. This stems from a nineteenth-century taxation fiddle, whereby landlords avoided the higher tax on buildings with more than three floors.

(*Atzállójegy*; 490Ft) is valid for as many stops as you like with one line change. Tickets bought on board buses, trams and trolleybuses cost 400Ft.

The standard single ticket is not valid on night buses: you have to buy a 350Ft *helyszini vonaljegy* separately – on board or from a ticket machine – unless you have a day or weekly pass. Books of ten standard single tickets (*tíz-darabos gyüjtőjegy* – 2800Ft) are also available – these are still valid if torn out of the book but cannot be used on night services.

Tickets must be **validated** when you use them. On the metro and HÉV you punch them in the machines at station entrances (remember to validate a new ticket if you change lines, unless you have a metro transfer ticket); on trams, buses and trolleybuses, you punch the tickets on board in the small red or orange machines.

Day **passes** (*napijegy*) cost 1550Ft and are valid for unlimited travel from midnight to midnight on the metro, buses, trams, trolleybuses, the Cogwheel Railway and suburban HÉV lines; three-day passes cost 3850Ft and weekly passes 4600Ft. **Season tickets** cost 6500Ft for two weeks and 9800Ft for a month, and are available from metro stations, but you'll need a passport photo for the accompanying photocard; there are photo booths inside the entrance of Deák tér and Széll Kálmán tér stations.

Children up to the age of 6 and EU citizens over the age of 65 travel free on all public transport, though in both cases some form of official documentation must be shown if challenged by inspectors.

Pickpockets operate on the metro, buses and trams. Gangs distract their victims by pushing them or blocking their way, and empty their pockets or bags at the same time. Also beware of bogus ticket inspectors "working" the transport system and demanding money from passengers. Genuine inspectors wear blue armbands and usually work in twos or threes.

The metro

The second oldest underground system in the world after London, the Budapest **metro** has three lines, usually referred to by their colour and shown on the colour map at the end of this book; they intersect at Deák tér in downtown Pest. Line #1 – also known as the Millennium Underground railway – was the first to be constructed, and in 2002 it was listed as a UNESCO World Heritage Site. A fourth line is under construction, though it's not expected to be completed until 2014 at the earliest. Trains run at two- to twelve-minute intervals. There's little risk of going astray once you've learned to recognize the signs *bejárat* (entrance), *kijárat* (exit), *vonal* (line) and *felé* (towards). The train's direction is indicated by the name of the station at the end of the line, and drivers announce the next stop between stations, though these are barely audible, so you're better off looking out for the signs at each station.

Buses, trams and trolleybuses

There is a good **bus** (*autóbusz*) network across the city, especially in Buda, where Széll Kálmán tér (on the red metro line) and Móricz Zsigmond körtér (southwest of Gellért-hegy) are the main terminals. Bus stops are marked by a picture of a bus on a white background in a blue frame, and have timetables underneath; most buses run every ten to twenty minutes (*utolsó kocsi indul …* means "the last one leaves …"). On busier lines express buses – with an E at the end of the number – run along the same route making fewer stops: for example, the bus #7E that runs along most of the route of the #7. **Night buses** have three-digit numbers beginning with a 9 and run every hour or half-hour from around midnight or whenever the service they replace finishes.

The network of yellow (or the newer orange) **trams** (*villamos*) is smaller, but they provide a crucial service round the Nagykörút and along the Pest embankment. **Trolleybuses** (*trolibusz*) mostly operate northeast of the centre near the Városliget. Interestingly, their route numbers start at 70 because the first trolleybus line was inaugurated on Stalin's 70th birthday in 1949. Trolleybus #83 was started in 1961, when Stalin would have been 83.

HÉV trains

The green overground **HÉV trains** provide easy access to Budapest's suburbs, running roughly three to five times an hour between 4.30am and 11.30pm. As far as tourists are concerned, the most useful line is the one from **Batthyány tér** (on the red metro line) out to **Szentendre**, which passes through Óbuda, Aquincum and Rómaifürdő. The other lines originate in Pest, with one running northeast from **Örs vezér tere** (also on the red metro line) to **Gödöllő** via the Formula One racing track at Mogyoród; another southwards from Boráros tér at the Pest end of Petőfi híd to Csepel; and the third from **Közvágóhíd** (bus #23 or #54 from Boráros tér) to **Ráckeve**.

Ferries and other transport

Although ferries play little useful part in Budapest's transport system, they do offer an enjoyable ride. From May to September there are boats along the Danube between Boráros tér (by Petőfi híd) and Batthyány tér up to Margit-sziget, Rómaifürdő and Pünkösdfürdő near Szentendrei-sziget. These run every ninety minutes between 8am and 6pm, and cost between 250Ft (for going from Pest across to the Margit-sziget) and 900Ft. Ferry tickets can be obtained from kiosks (where timetables are posted) or machines at the docks.

In the Buda Hills, there's also the **Cogwheel Railway** (Fogaskerekűvasút, now officially designated as tram #60), the **Children's Railway** (Gyermekvasút), and the **chairlift** (*libegő*) between Zugliget and János-hegy; see Chapter 9 for details. Note that BKV tickets and passes are valid only for the Cogwheel Railway – for the others, you'll need to buy tickets at the point of departure or on board.

Taxis

Budapest's **taxis** have a reputation for ripping off foreigners, who are often seen as easy prey. Make sure your taxi has a meter that is visible and **switched** on when you get in, and that the rates are clearly displayed. **Fares** begin at 300Ft, and the price per kilometre is around 250Ft.

Taxis can be flagged down on the street, and there are **ranks** throughout the city; you can hop

USEFUL BUS, TRAM AND TROLLEYBUS ROUTES
(LISTED WITH KEY STOPS)

BUSES

#7 Bosnyák tér–Keleti Station–Móricz Zsigmond körtér (via Ferenciek tere, Rudas Baths, *Gellért Hotel*).

#16A Dísz tér (Castle District)–Széll Kálmán tér.

#16 Deák tér–Dísz tér (Castle District)–Bécsi kapu tér–Széll Kálmán tér.

#26 Margit-sziget–Árpád híd metro station.

#65 Kolosy tér–Pálvölgyi Caves–*Fenyőgyöngye* restaurant at the bottom of Hármashatár-hegy.

#86 Southern Buda–Gellért tér–Batthyány tér–Margit Bridge–Flórián tér (Óbuda).

#105 Apor Vilmos tér–Lánchíd–Deák tér–Oktogon–Gyöngyösi utca.

#116 Fény utca market–Széll Kálmán tér– Dísz tér (Castle District).

NIGHT BUSES

#906 Széll Kálmán tér–Margit-sziget–Nyugati Station–Nagykörut (Great Boulevard)–Móricz Zsigmond körtér.

#907 Örs vezér tere–Bosnyák tér–Keleti Station–Erzsébet híd–*Gellért Hotel*–Etele tér (Kelenföld).

#914 and **#950** Kispest (Határ út metro station)–Deák tér–Lehel tér–Újpest, along the route of the blue metro and on to the north and south.

TRAMS

#2 Margit Bridge (Jászai Mari tér)–Belgrád rakpart (along embankment)–Petőfi híd–Vágóhíd ter.

#4 Széll Kálmán tér–Margit-sziget–Nyugati Station–Nagykörut (Great Boulevard)–Petőfi Bridge–Október 23 utca.

#6 Széll Kálmán tér–Margit-sziget–Nyugati Station– Nagykörut (Great Boulevard)–Petőfi Bridge–Móricz Zsigmond körtér.

#19 Batthyány tér–the Víziváros–Kelenföld Station.

#47 Deák tér–Szabadság híd–*Gellért Hotel*–Móricz Zsigmond körtér–Budafok.

#61 Móricz Zsigmond körtér–Villányi út–Déli Station–Széll Kálmán tér–Huvősvölgy.

TROLLEYBUSES

#72 Arany János utca metro station–Nyugati Station–Zoo–Széchenyi Baths–Hermina út.

#74 Dohány utca (outside the Main Synagogue)–Városliget.

---

into whichever cab you choose – don't feel you have to opt for the one at the front of the line if it looks at all dodgy. For a slightly cheaper rate, order a cab by phone. Avoid unmarked private cars, and drivers hanging around the stations and airport. There are also a few fake Fő and Citytaxis, sporting poor copies of their logos.

TAXI COMPANIES

Citytaxi ☎ 1 211 1111
Fótaxi ☎ 1 222 2222
Volantaxi ☎ 1 433 3322

Driving

All things considered, **driving** in Budapest can't be recommended. Road manners are nonexistent, parking spaces are scarce and traffic jams are frequent, while the Pest side of the Lánchíd (Chain Bridge) and the roundabout before the tunnel under the Vár are notorious for collisions – and

careering trams, bumpy cobbles, swerving lane markings and unexpected one-way systems make things worse. In addition, access to the Castle District and parts of the Belváros are strictly limited.

If you do decide to take the plunge, the most important **rules** to bear in mind are: you must give way to cars on your right if there are no road markings to indicate otherwise; at night, many traffic lights go into flashing orange mode, which means that priority is given to the right; drinking and driving is totally prohibited, as is the use of a hand-held mobile phone. The speed limit in built-up areas is 50kph (30mph), and 90kph (60mph) outside built-up areas. On main roads, it's 110kph (68mph), and on motorways 130kph (80mph).

In terms of **parking**, you might be better off leaving your car outside the centre and using public transport to travel in – there are park and ride facilities at most metro termini. If you must park in the centre, the best options are the underground car parks in Szent István tér by the Basilica and underneath Szabadsag tér, both in Lipótváros. Parking on the street in the central districts costs 120–440Ft – you get a ticket from the nearest machine.

Renting a car is easy provided you're 21 or older and hold a valid driving licence that's at least one year old. Rental **costs** are not particularly cheap – expect to pay around €50–60 upwards for a day's rental (unlimited mileage) and upwards of €250 per week. When checking prices make sure the price quoted includes the twenty-percent ÁFA (VAT). Before signing, check on mileage limits and any other restrictions or extras, as well as what you're liable for in the event of an accident.

CAR RENTAL COMPANIES

All these companies have offices at the airport.
Avis V, Szabadság tér 7 ☎ 1 318 4240, Ⓦ avis.hu.
Budget Hotel Mercure Buda, I, Krisztina körút 41–43 ☎ 1 214 0420, Ⓦ budget.hu.
Europcar V, Erzsébet tér 7–8 ☎ 1 505 4400, Ⓦ europcar.hu.
Hertz V, Váci utca 135–139 ☎ 1 237 0407, Ⓦ hertz.hu.
Regina X, Regina köz 1 ☎ 1 319 9999, Ⓦ reginaauto.hu.

Cycling

Cycling is finally catching on in Budapest, with rising numbers of cyclists and the emergence of dedicated cycle lanes. That said, it isn't easy riding: drivers are only beginning to be aware of **cyclists** and you also have to contend with sunken tramlines and bumpy cobbles and bad air pollution. **Cycle routes** are still patchy and don't link up to form a network yet, though there are good routes out of town, such as along the Buda bank of the Danube to Szentendre and on up towards Slovakia. Tourinform has free cycling maps of Budapest. Bicycles can be carried on HÉV trains and the Cogwheel Railway for the price of a one-way ticket, but not on buses or trams. For trail-biking in the Buda Hills, see p.120.

There are several excellent bike-rental outfits in the city, as well as a number of bike shops that do repairs, including Nella Bikes, off Bajcsy-Zsilinszky út at V, Kálmán Imre utca 23 (☎ 1 331 3184, Ⓦ nella.hu).

BIKE RENTAL

Expect to pay around 2000Ft for half a day's rental and 2500–3000Ft for a full day's rental, including a lock and helmet.
Bikebase VI, Podmaniczky utca 19 ☎ 1 269 5983, Ⓦ bikebase.hu. Excellent operation near Nyugati Station, with friendly staff who dole out maps and advise on cycling routes. Repair service available too. March to mid-Nov daily 9am–7pm.
Budapest Bike VII, Wesselényi utca 13 ☎ 30 944 5533, Ⓦ budapestbike.hu. Bike rental and bike tours. Mid-March to mid-Oct daily 10am–7pm.

Yellow Zebra VI, Lázár utca 16 ☎ 1 269 3843, Ⓦ yellowzebrabikes.com. See below.

City tours

There are now a wide range of city tours available in Budapest. If you're hard-pressed for time, you might appreciate one of the city's bus tours. These generally take you past the Parliament, along Andrássy út, across to the Várhegy and up to Gellért-hegy for panoramic photo opportunities.

Most of Budapest's backstreets and historic quarters are eminently suited to walking, and this is much the best way to appreciate their character. Traffic is restricted in downtown Pest and around the Vár in Buda, and fairly light in the residential backstreets off the main boulevards, which are the nicest areas to wander around. The Budapest Card (see p.30) entitles you to two free guided walks, one of Buda, one of Pest.

BIKE TOURS

Yellow Zebra VI, Lázár utca 16 ☎ 1 269 3843, Ⓦ yellowzebrabikes.com. Excellent outfit offering both scheduled and private cycling tours of the city. The standard bike tour (6000Ft, 5000Ft with your own bike) departs from Deák tér daily at 11am between mid-March and mid-November, and there's an addition tour at 5pm in July and August. The same office also offer segway tours, city sightseeing on the strange-looking, two-wheel segway bikes (from €48).

BUS TOURS

Budapest Sightseeing ☎ 1 317 7767, Ⓦ programcentrum.hu. Hop-on hop-off city tour taking in all the major sights. The bus departs from Erzsébet tér every thirty minutes and takes around two and a half hours from start to finish. Tickets (5000Ft), though, are valid for 24 hours. April–Oct.
Giraffe Hop On Hop Off VI, Andrassy utca 2 ☎ 1 374 7070, Ⓦ citytour.hu. In a similar vein, this hop-on hop-off bus tour takes in all the key city sights, but on red double decker buses. There are two lines; red departing every thirty minutes from József Nádor tér, and yellow departing hourly from Erzsébet tér. Tickets (4500Ft) are valid on both lines for 24 hours. They also do a hop-on hop-off cruise departing hourly from Vigadó tér (2500Ft). April–Oct.

WALKING TOURS

Absolute Walking Tours VI, Lázár utca 16 ☎ 1 269 3843, Ⓦ absolutetours.com. Run by the same team as Yellow Zebra (in the Discover Budapest office). Aside from the standard city and historical walks (4500Ft), Absolute offer a terrific range of themed tours, such as Food & Wine (7500Ft) and Hammer & Sickle (6200Ft), as well as an evening pub crawl (4000Ft). Tours depart from Deák tér and last around three hours.

Free Budapest Tours ☎ 20 534 5819, **Ⓦ** freebudapesttours.hu.
Aimed at backpackers, Budapest city tours daily at 11am (from in front of the Opera House) and 2pm (from in front of *Gerbeaud Café* on Vorosmarty tér), each one lasting around three hours. It's free, though tips are welcome.
Jewish Heritage ☎ 1 317 2754, **Ⓦ** ticket.info.hu. Three tours of the Jewish quarter, ranging from one and half hours (3900Ft) to four hours (9900Ft), though all include a guided visit of the Dohany synagogue. Daily except Sat, either at 10am or 2pm (and 11am on Sun). Advance booking required.

RIVER TOURS

RiverRide ☎ 1 332 2555, **Ⓦ** riverride.com. Jump aboard the floating bus for a slightly more unorthodox sightseeing tour; starting in Széchenyi tér, the bus takes in all the main sights in Pest before splashing into the Danube and continuing down to the Chain Bridge and winding up in Buda. Departures daily at 10am, noon, 3pm and 5pm. 7500Ft.

The media

Hungary has a long tradition of lively print media, and there are several broadsheets available, in addition to a handful of local English-language papers. Television differs little from that in other European countries, with foreign cable and satellite television dominating the airwaves.

Newspapers and magazines

There are several Budapest-based English newspapers, including the very readable *Budapest Times* (**Ⓦ** budapesttimes.hu), which also has good cultural content; the monthey *Time out Budapest* magazine; and the *Budapest Business Journal* (**Ⓦ** bbj.hu), which covers mainly business and politics. You can often find them for free in the lobbies of larger hotels. The best source of in-depth information about Hungary and its culture is *The Hungarian Quarterly* (**Ⓦ** hungarianquarterly.com), a periodical that has presented Hungarian literature and essays to English readers for more than seventy years.

The best place to find foreign newspapers and magazines are the newsagents (such as Relay) at stations and shopping malls, though all the major bookshops should have a decent stock of foreign-language material; the best of these is Bestsellers (see p.203).

Listings magazines

There are several sources of English-language **listings information**: the fortnightly *Budapest Funzine*, distributed free in cafés and bars, is aimed at the expat market and has comprehensive information on all the city's nightlife, as well as background information on other happenings in Budapest. The free monthly magazine *Where Budapest* has information on current events, while the online butapestsun.com has listings information. The widely available Hungarian-language listings bible *Pesti Est* has extensive details of film and music events, and sometimes has an English section in the summer.

Television

Hungarian **television** is not particularly exciting, with state TV (MTV) screening a dreary diet of gameshows and low-budget soaps from morning to night. In addition, there are numerous commercial channels such as TV2, the RTL Klub and Duna TV, a state-supported channel geared to Hungarian minorities abroad, though these are little better. For this reason many Hungarians subscribe to satellite channels, with whole apartment blocks sharing the cost of installation. The majority of hotels have satellite TV, though the programming is dominated by German channels or those from neighbouring countries. Most, though, will also feature the likes of BBC World or CNN.

Festivals

Whatever time of the year you visit Budapest, there's almost certain to be something happening. The two biggest events by far are the Spring Festival in March and the Autumn Festival in October, both of which feature world-class music, film and drama. Indeed, music is a constant theme throughout the festival year, with none bigger than the mega Sziget Festival in August.

Many theatres, concert halls and dance houses close down during the long, hot months of July and August, when open-air performances are staged instead. The city's population returns from the countryside for the fireworks on August 20, and life returns to normal as school starts the following week. The new arts season kicks off in the last week of September with a rash of music festivals and political anniversaries. Great fun, too are the several food festivals that take place throughout the year.

JANUARY AND FEBRUARY

Farsang Jan 6 to Ash Wednesday. Held in the run-up to Lent, this Hungarian carnival sees revellers taking to the streets in fancy dress, parading across the Lánchíd and down to Vörösmarty tér. Unfortunately the inclement weather at this time of year often dampens the event's spirit.

Mangalica Festival First weekend in Feb. A pig-out in every sense of the word, as the nation's favourite curly-haired swine is celebrated in the grounds of Vajdahunyad Castle in City Park; hog roasts aside, there are cooking competitions and a stack of other foodie treats.

MARCH AND APRIL

Declaration of Independence of 1848 March 15. A public holiday in honour of the 1848 Revolution, which began with Petőfi's declaration of the National Song from the steps of the National Museum. Budapest decks itself out with Hungarian tricolours (red, white and green), and there are speeches and gatherings outside the museum and by Petőfi's statue on Marcius 15 tér. The more patriotic citizens wear little cockades in the national colours pinned to their lapels.

Budapest Spring Festival (Budapest Tavaszi Fesztivál) Mid- to late March; W btf.hu. The city's most prestigious arts festival is an intensive, two-week jamboree of classical music, with orchestral, chamber and operatic performances taking place in venues across the city. There's also theatre, cinema, exhibitions (including the World Press Photos show) and dance, including a big folk dance gathering and market (*Országos Tánchztalálkozó és Kirakodóvásár*; W tanchaz.hu).

Easter (Húsvét) Late March/early April. Easter has strong folk traditions in Hungary. In the city this is limited to some processions in churches Easter Saturday, while on Easter Monday *locsolkodás* (splashing) takes place, when men and boys visit female friends to spray them with cologne in a tamer version of an older village tradition involving a bucket of water. Kids get a painted egg or money in return for splashing, while the men receive *pálinka* (schnapps). The weeks preceding Easter see arts and craft fairs in the Museum of Ethnography (p.54) and the Hungarian Open-Air Museum in Szentendre (p.134), with traditional folk skills like egg painting on display; and performances of the Bach Passions in the big, yellow Lutheran church on Deák tér.

Titanic International Film Festival Mid-April; W titanicfilmfest.hu. Superb ten-day programme of independent films from all over the world, with separately themed categories. See p.188.

MAY, JUNE AND JULY

Labour Day May 1. These days, Budapest's citizens are no longer obliged to parade past the Lenin statue that once stood behind the Műcsarnok; instead, the major trade unions put on a big do in the park, with shows, games, talks and food and drink in large quantities.

Pálinka Festival Early May; W budapestipalinkafesztival.hu. Held in the grounds of Buda Castle, this colourful four-day event features some two dozen distilleries offering several hundred variations on the quintessential Hungarian tipple, alongside sausages, cheese and the like.

Book Week (Könyvhét) Early June. Established in 1929, and as popular as ever, Book Week sees Hungarian writers from all over the world gather around stalls on Vörösmarty tér and Szent István tér in front of the Basilica. There are signings – politicians have now joined the book circus – as well as dancing on the temporary stages in the two squares.

Athe Sam Roma Arts Festival Mid-June; W athesam.hu. Big international event in the *Gödör Klub* in central Pest (see p.45) that showcases Roma music, art, theatre and film. "We are Here", as the festival translates in Romany, has grown rapidly and now attracts some of the biggest Roma artists in the world. Better still, most events are free.

Duna Party End June. The commemoration of the building of the Lánchíd in the 1840s marks the start of Summer on the Chain Bridge, a two-month long festival that sees the Lánchíd closed to cars each weekend until the middle of Aug to make way for music, food and craft stalls and jugglers and dancers. Each weekend has a different theme, from theatre to world music or jazz.

Budapest Pride Mid-June. The largest event in the gay calendar, this is a week-long celebration of gay and lesbian culture, with particular emphasis on film. The week culminates in a march along Andrássy út to the Városliget. See p.182.

AUGUST

Sziget Festival Mid-Aug; W sziget.hu. A stamina-sapping eight days long, Sziget is now firmly established as one of Europe's biggest rock and pop festivals. Staged on Óbudai sziget, an island north of the centre, it features a stellar line-up of rock, pop and world music acts, alongside dance, theatre, films and children's events. See p.185.

Festival of Crafts (Mesterségek Ünnepe) In the days leading up to Aug 20, the Vár is taken over by a huge festival of traditional crafts, accompanied by folk music and dancing.

Red Bull Air Race Aug 19 & 20; W redbullairrace.com. The Budapest leg of the international race sends the daredevil pilots speeding under the Danube bridges.

St Stephen's Day Aug 20. A public holiday in honour of Hungary's national saint and founder, with day-long rites at his Basilica, and a spectacular fireworks display fired off between the Erzsébet and Margit bridges at 9pm, watched by over a million people who line the Danube; the traffic jam that follows is equally mind-blowing. Restaurants are packed that night, so book well ahead if you want to eat out.

Jewish Summer Festival End Aug; W jewishfestival.hu. Vibrant, week-long jamboree, attracting an international range of classical, jazz and klezmer music performances, films and exhibitions.

SEPTEMBER AND OCTOBER

Budapest Wine Festival (Budapest Bor Fesztivál) Early Sept; W winefestival.hu. The country's top producers set out their wares on the terrace of the Royal Palace in the Castle District: for the price of a day ticket (2500Ft, 7000Ft for a five-day pass) you get unrestricted access, a glass and a glass holder. Individual tasting tickets are available once inside.

Budapest Autumn Festival (Budapest Őszi Fesztivál) Mid-Oct; W bof.hu. Slightly smaller than its spring counterpart, the autumn version is stronger on contemporary music and also features an excellent programme of film, dance and photography.

Budapest Music Weeks (Zenei hetek) Late Sept to late Oct. City-wide music events, courtesy of the Budapest Philharmonic, starting around the anniversary of Bartók's death on Sept 25.

Music of Our Time Early Oct. Two weeks of contemporary music concerts from Hungarian and foreign artists.

Anniversary of the Arad Martyrs Oct 6. Commemoration of the shooting of the thirteen Hungarian generals in 1849 in Arad (Nagyvárad) in present-day Romania, when the 1848 revolution was crushed by the Austrians with Russian help. Wreaths are laid at the Eternal Flame.

Commemoration of the 1956 Uprising Oct 23. A national holiday to mark the 1956 Uprising and the declaration of the Republic in 1990. Ceremonies take place in Kossuth tér, by the nearby Nagy Imre statue, and at Nagy's grave in the New Public Cemetery. Bear in mind that 1956 has left a divided inheritance and tempers can flare.

NOVEMBER AND DECEMBER

All Saints' Day (Mindenszentek napja) Nov 1. Cemeteries stay open late and candles are lit in memory of departed souls, making for an incredible sight as darkness falls.

St Nicholas's Day (Mikulás) Dec 5 & 6. On Dec 5, children clean their shoes and put them in the window for "Mikulás", the Santa Claus figure, to fill with sweets; naughty children are warned that if they behave badly, all they will get is *virgács*, a gold-painted bunch of twigs from Mikulás's little helpers.

Christmas (Karácsony) Dec 24 & 25. The main celebration is on Dec 24, when the city becomes eerily silent by late afternoon. Children are taken out while their parents decorate the Christmas tree (until then the trees are stored outside, and on housing estates you can often see them dangling from windows). When the kids return home, they wait outside until the bell rings, which tells them that "little Jesus" (Jézuska) has come. Inside, they sing carols by the tree, open presents, and start the big Christmas meal, which traditionally includes spicy fish soup. In the preceding weeks there are Christmas fairs in several locations around town, the best being in the Museum of Ethnography, where traditional crafts are demonstrated.

New Year's Eve (Szilveszter) Dec 31. Revellers gather on the Nagykörút during the evening, engaging in paper trumpet battles at the junction with Rákóczi út.

Culture and etiquette

Forty years of Communism swept away Hungary's archaic semi-feudal society but you can still find remnants of the old ways, for instance in the language. As a foreigner, you are not obliged to know these details, but Hungarians will love it if you can get them right.

Hungarians preserve certain formalities in meeting and greeting. Young people will go usually straight into the informal form of address with each other (the Hungarian equivalent of the French "*tu*" is to use the second person), but with their elders or in the more formal settings of work or school they would use the formal mode, talking to people in the third person, until invited to use the **informal** mode. So "*Hogy vagy?*" is the informal "how are you?", "*Hogy van?*" is the **formal** – and then to be awfully polite, talking to someone's granny for instance, you can say "*Hogy tetszik lenni?*" (literally, "How does it please you to be?").

When introduced to someone you shake hands and say your name. You would usually **shake hands** when meeting people, though between friends kissing on both cheeks is the norm – between men, too. Some older men still bow to kiss a woman's hand – but it looks rather affected when anyone else does it, so it is best not to try. You will hear an echo of this social convention in the greeting "*Csókolom*", which means "I kiss [your hand]". Children will say this to adults and adults will say it to elderly ladies – responding in kind is an easy error to make and will provoke much laughter.

The formal salutation – to say hello or goodbye – is "*Jó napot*" (or "*Jó reggelt*" before 9am) while with friends "*Szia*", "*Szervusz*" or even "*Helló*" is normal. For more on language see p.224.

A sense of social formality is preserved in other ways too. When visiting someone at home, taking flowers is always acceptable: there are many complex rules and codes in flower-giving that you need not worry about – but do take an odd number of flowers (not 13, though).

Two other useful points when visiting: it is common to take off your shoes when you go into people's houses; and if eating at someone's house it is customary to compliment the host(ess) on the food early on after the first couple of mouthfuls.

Smoking is pretty universal in Budapest – though in someone's home, of course, it is polite to ask if it is permitted. A smoking ban in restaurants and bars came into being in 2012 although it remains to be seen whether this will be fully enforced. Smoking is also banned on all public transport.

Travel essentials

Admission charges

The majority of the city's museums charge between 500Ft (€2) and 800Ft (€3), though the showpiece ones, such as the Museum of Fine Arts and the House of Terror cost around 1600–2000Ft (€6–7.50). There's usually a reduction or free entrance if you show a student, youth or senior citizen card. If you're planning on visiting multiple museums, consider buying the Budapest Card (see p.30), which offers excellent savings. For details of admission charges to Budapest's baths, see p.194.

Climate

Budapest has quite distinct seasons; summers can be extremely hot with prolonged periods of sunshine and temperatures regularly reaching the mid-30s (°C). Winters, by contrast, can be bitterly cold, with snow common in the months either side of Christmas – though this can make for a wonderful sight around the festive season, particularly with the markets in full flow. The most reliable seasons are spring and autumn, which are generally pretty mild; spring is invariably beautiful, and it's not uncommon for the city to experience long days of sunshine throughout March and April, though May can get showery. The sun, meanwhile, often lingers well into September, and even October. This makes the city a perfect time to visit for the prestigious Spring and Autumn Festivals respectively.

Costs

Although Budapest is not the bargain destination it once was, it's still very good value, especially when compared to cities in Britain, France or Italy, for example.

If you're not staying in a hostel, the main drain on your resources will be hotel accommodation; while rates fluctuate wildly according to season and demand, expect to pay around €60 a night for a double room in a three-star hotel, and somewhere in excess of €100 for a four-star. A two-course lunch or dinner with a glass of wine in one of the better restaurants should set you back around 4000Ft (€15) – for more information on dining out, see p.163. Public transport is cheap, with a one-day pass covering all modes of transport costing 1550Ft (€5.50).

Foreigners are easy targets for overcharging, so it is always worth checking the price of what you are buying ("*Mennyibe kerül?*" means "how much is it?"). One hidden extra is the ÁFA or sales tax (the equivalent of VAT in Britain) of up to 25 percent, which can hike up the cost of rental cars and hotels, for example: look out for the phrase "*az árak nem tartalmaznak Áfát*", meaning "prices do not include tax". There is also a three percent tourist tax on hotel prices, and it is

worth checking that both taxes are included in any prices quoted. The simplest way to ask is "*Ez az ár bruttó vagy nettó?*" – "Is this price with or without tax?".

Crime and personal safety

Hungary is one of the safest European countries, and there's little reason to worry about your personal security while visiting. Violent crime is extremely rare, though petty theft is common, with downtown Budapest a prime area for pickpocketing and scams directed at tourists.

The Hungarian **police** (*rendőrség*) have a milder reputation than their counterparts in other Eastern Bloc states, and are generally keen to present a favourable image. During the summer, **tourist police** patrol the streets and metro stations mainly to act as a deterrent against thieves, and to assist in any problems tourists may encounter. Most Hungarian police have at least a smattering of German, but rarely speak any other foreign language. To contact the police, call ❶107, or ❶112,

---

THE BUDAPEST CARD

If you're doing a lot of sightseeing, the **Budapest Card** (ⓦ budapest-card.com) represents great value. It's available for 24hr (5000Ft), 48hr (6900Ft) or 72hr (8300Ft), and grants free public transport in the city, free entrance to three museums (Museum of Fine Arts, Museum of Ethnography and the Budapest History Museum), and two free guided walking tours. In addition, there are discounts of between ten and fifty percent on lots of other attractions, including some of the baths, plus shops and restaurants. The card is available online, from tourist offices, hotels, central metro stations and at the airport, and comes with a booklet explaining where it can be used.

BUDAPEST CLIMATE

	Jan	Feb	Mar	Apr	May	Jun	Jul	Aug	Sep	Oct	Nov	Dec
AVERAGE DAILY TEMPERATURE												
Avg Minimum C˚(F˚)	-4 (25)	-2 (28)	2 (36)	7 (45)	1 (52)	15 (59)	16 (61)	16 (61)	12 (54)	7 (45)	3 (37)	-1 (30)
Avg Maximum C˚(F˚)	1 (34)	4 (39)	10 (50)	17 (63)	22 (72)	26 (79)	27 (82)	27 (82)	23 (73)	16 (61)	8 (46)	4 (39)
AVERAGE RAINFALL												
mm	37	44	38	45	72	69	56	47	33	57	70	46

SCAMS AND STAYING SAFE

Parts of Budapest, notably Váci utca in the Belváros, are notorious for **"consume girls"**, who target solo male foreigners. A couple of attractive young women (they're not difficult to spot) will approach you, get talking and, without wasting any time, "invite" you to a bar of their choice. A few drinks later, you'll find yourself presented with a bill somewhat bigger than you bargained for and be strong-armed into paying up. The bars, and the waiters who work in them, are an integral part of the scam, so bids for escape or complaint are futile, but if ever you do find yourself caught up in such a situation then report it to the police.

Even if you disregard pick-ups and avoid places offering the "companionship of lovely ladies", there's a risk of **gross overcharging** at restaurants or bars which don't list their prices. Always check how much things cost before ordering. If you get stung, try insisting that you'll only pay in the presence of the police. Elsewhere, be on your guard on public transport, which is where you're most likely to be relieved of your belongings.

which is also the number for the ambulance and fire services. Alternatively, Tourinform has a 24-hour English-speaking service on ☎ 1 483 8080.

Electricity

The Hungarian system runs on 220 volts. Round two-pin plugs are used. A standard continental adapter allows the use of 13-amp square-pin plugs.

Entry requirements

Hungary is part of the Schengen Agreement, so citizens of the other Schengen states can enter Hungary with just an ID card and stay for up to ninety days. Citizens of the UK, Ireland, US, Canada, Australia and New Zealand, and most other European countries, can enter Hungary with just a passport and stay for the same period. South African citizens will need to apply to their local Hungarian consulate for a visa, though note that visas valid for another Schengen country are also valid for Hungary.

FOREIGN CONSULATES IN BUDAPEST

Australia XII, Királyhágó tér 8–9 ☎ 1 457 9777, ⓦ hungary .embassy.gov.au.
Canada II, Ganz utca 12–14 ☎ 1 392 3360, ⓦ kanada.hu.
Ireland V, Szabadság tér 7, Bank Center, seventh floor ☎ 1 301 4960, ⓦ embassyofireland.hu.
South Africa II Gárdonyi Géza út 17 ☎ 1 392 0999.
UK V, Harmincad utca 6 ☎ 1 266 2888, ⓦ britishembassy.hu.
US V, Szabadság tér 12 ☎ 1 475 4400, ⓦ usembassy.hu.

Health

No inoculations are required for Hungary and standards of public health are good. The **European Health Insurance Card** gives EU citizens access to Hungary's national health service (OTBF) under reciprocal agreements. While this will provide free or reduced-cost medical care in the event of minor injuries or emergencies, it won't cover every eventuality – so **travel insurance** is essential (see below).

Budapest has plentiful **pharmacies** (*gyógyszertár* or *patika*), which normally open Monday to Friday from 8am to 7 or 8pm, and on Saturday from 8am until noon or 1pm; signs in the window give the location or telephone number of the nearest all-night (*éjjeli* or *ügyeleti szolgálat*) pharmacy.

In **emergencies**, dial ☎ 104 for the Mentok ambulance service (or ☎ 112, the central number for emergencies), or get a taxi to the nearest **hospital** (*kórház*). For non-urgent treatment, tourist offices can direct you to a local **medical centre** or doctors' surgery (*orvosi rendelő*), and your embassy in Budapest will have the addresses of foreign-language-speaking **doctors** and **dentists**, who will probably be in private (*magán*) practice.

Sunburn (*napszúrás*) and insect bites (*rovarcsípés*) are the most common **minor complaints** for travellers, so take plenty of sunscreen and repellent. Mosquitoes can be annoying, but the bug to beware of in forests around Budapest is the *kullancs*, a tick which bites and then burrows into human skin, causing inflammation of the brain. The risk of one biting you is fairly small, but if you get a bite that seems particularly painful, or are suffering from a high temperature and stiff neck following a bite, have it checked out as quickly as possible.

HOSPITALS AND CLINICS

FirstMed Center I, Hattyu utca 14 ☎ 1 224 9090.
MAV Hospital VI, Podmaniczky utca 109–111 ☎ 1 475 1800.

Insurance

You should take out a comprehensive insurance policy before travelling to Budapest, to cover

ROUGH GUIDES TRAVEL INSURANCE

Rough Guides has teamed up with WorldNomads.com to offer great travel insurance deals. Policies are available to residents of over 150 countries, with cover for a wide range of adventure sports, 24hr emergency assistance, high levels of medical and evacuation cover and a stream of travel safety information. Roughguides.com users can take advantage of their policies online 24/7, from anywhere in the world – even if you're already travelling. And since plans often change when you're on the road, you can extend your policy and even claim online. Roughguides.com users who buy travel insurance with WorldNomads.com can also leave a positive footprint and donate to a community development project. For more information go to ⓦroughguides.com/shop.

against loss, theft, illness or injury. A typical policy will provide cover for loss of baggage, tickets and – up to a certain limit – cash or travellers' cheques, as well as cancellation or curtailment of your journey.

If you need to make a **claim**, you should keep receipts for medicines and medical treatment, and in the event you have anything stolen, you must obtain an official statement from the police.

Internet

Budapest is saturated with **internet cafés**, though the speed of connections varies and not many have keyboards labelled in English. Such competition means that prices are cheap; expect to pay 150–250Ft per hour online. Nearly all youth hostels provide free internet access, as do most hotels (either cable connection or wi-fi). Outside hotels, wi-fi is fairly widespread in cafés and bars, though you will be obliged to buy a drink for using this facility. The website ⓦhotspotter.hu/en lists places offering access both for free (*ingyenes*) and for a fee (*térítéses*),

Kids

Budapest is a child-friendly city, with plenty to entertain young ones – see chapter 20 for details. Hungarians tend to be welcoming to kids without making them the centre of attention as you might find in, say, Italy.

Facilities are a bit patchy, though; while the network of playgrounds is marvellous, nappy-changing facilities (*pelenkázó*) are hard to find – they're mostly concentrated in big shopping malls. Buildings don't tend to be very accessible if you're pushing a buggy, but help is usually quickly forthcoming when you're trying to negotiate stairs. On public transport people will readily give up seats to pregnant women and to parents with babies. They will also happily chat to children – the flipside is that old ladies may also loudly

berate parents for not looking after their babies "properly", such as for not putting a hat on a baby even in the mildest of weather.

The malls are also the best bet for nappies, baby toiletries and clothes, while many also have indoor play areas. Restaurants usually have high chairs, and although there isn't a culture of whole families dining out in the evening, waiting staff (even in smart places) are usually accommodating. In many places you can ask for a small child's portion –*kisadag*.

Laundry

There are very few self-service launderettes (*mosoda*) in Budapest, but you could try the following: Laundromat Mosómata at VI, Ó utca 24–26 (Mon–Fri 9am–7pm, Sat & Sun 10am–4pm) near the Basilica; Liliom Szalon, IX, Liliom utca 7–9 (Mon–Fri 8am–8pm, Sat 8am–noon); the Electric Café, VII, Dohány utca 37 (daily 9am–midnight). Expect to pay around 1800Ft for a wash and dry. Otherwise, most youth hostels have laundry facilities, with a small fee payable; hotels will charge considerably more.

Living in Budapest

Teaching English has traditionally been the main opportunity for **work** in Hungary, and it remains a big business, with many native speakers working in Budapest and a number of schools in and around the capital. The most reputable **language school** is International House, whose Budapest branch is at I, Vérmező út 4 (❶1 212 4010, ⓦih.hu); its minimum requirement is a CELTA or TESOL qualification, and preferably one year's experience. It offers a range of teacher training qualifications in Budapest. There are also teaching opportunities at the British Council, VI, 1075 Madách Imre út 13–14 (❶1 483 2020, ⓦbritishcouncil.org).

Another possibility is teaching in a **primary or secondary school.** Although it pays much less, the

HUNGARIAN NAMES

Surnames precede forenames in Hungary, to the confusion of foreigners. In this book, the names of historical personages are rendered in the Western fashion, for instance, Lajos Kossuth rather than Kossuth Lajos (Hungarian-style), except when referring to the names of buildings, streets, etc. The Hungarian order has a clear logic: in Hungarian the stress in any word always comes on the first syllable; since Hungarian, like most other languages, puts the main stress on the family name when saying a person's name, that means putting the family name first.

deal usually includes subsidized or free accommodation. Expect to teach around twenty 45-minute periods a week, with a timetable that may also include exam preparation, marking, invigilation and the like. Primary schools may take anyone whose native language is English and who seems capable and enthusiastic, though you are likely to require at least a certificate in TEFL and/or a PGCE.

Study programmes

Several schools in Budapest cater for foreigners wishing to **learn Hungarian**, the best of which is the Hungarian Language School at VIII, Bródy Sándor utca 4 (❶1 266 2617, ⓦmagyar-iskola.hu). The school runs a comprehensive range of short- and long-term courses, from beginners to advanced, as well as organizing cultural programmes and workshops. The Debrecen Summer School also runs year-round courses in Budapest (V, Báthory utca 4.II.1 ❶1 320 5751, ⓦsummerschool.hu/bp).

Lost property

For items left on public transport go to the BKV office at VII, Akácfa utca 18 (Mon 8am–8pm, Tues–Thurs 8am–5pm, Fri 8am–3pm; ❶1 258 4636). Lost or stolen passports should be reported to the police station in the district where they were lost.

Mail

Post offices (*posta*) are usually open Monday to Friday 8 or 9am to 5pm, though these following main offices keep longer hours: V, Petőfi Sándor utca 13 (Mon–Fri 8am–8pm, Sat 8am–2pm); by Keleti Station at VIII, Baross tér 11c (Mon–Fri 7am–9pm, Sat 8am–2pm); by Nyugati Station at VI, Teréz körút 51 (Mon–Fri 7am–8pm, Sat 8am–6pm); at the Mammut Mall by Széll Kálmán tér (Mon–Fri 8am–8pm, Sat 9am–2pm); while the branch in the Tesco at XIV, Pillangó utca 15 near the Pillangó utca stop on the red metro is open 24 hours a day. **Stamps** (*bélyeg*) can be bought at tobacconists or post offices, though the latter are usually pretty crowded and very few staff speak English. Stamps cost 220Ft for postcards within Europe, 250Ft for further afield, while stamps for letters up to 20g cost 240Ft and 270Ft respectively. Note that letters and postcards have different rates, so don't buy a job lot of stamps.

Maps

The maps in this guide, together with the small freebies supplied by tourist offices and hotels, should be sufficient to help you find your way around. Larger folding maps are sold all over the place, but their size makes them cumbersome. For total coverage you can't beat the wire-bound **Budapest Atlasz**, available in bookshops in a range of sizes, which shows every street, bus and tram route, and the location of restaurants, museums and such like. It also contains enlarged maps of the Vár, central Pest, Margit-sziget and the Városliget, plus a comprehensive index.

Money

Hungary's unit of currency is the **forint** (Ft or HUF), with notes issued in denominations of 200, 500, 1000, 2000, 5000, 10,000 and 20,000 forints, and coins in denominations of 5, 10, 20, 50 and 100 forints. At the time of writing, the **exchange rate** was around 300Ft to the pound sterling, 270Ft to the euro and around 200Ft to the US dollar. You might be able to buy forints at some banks or exchange offices, or in the UK at post offices, but you will probably have to order them in advance.

By far the easiest way to get money is to use your bank **debit card** (or credit card) to withdraw cash from an ATM, found all over the city. All major credit cards are accepted in hotels, restaurants and shops, though not necessarily in some of the smaller ones.

As a rule, you're best off changing money in **banks**, which are normally open Monday to Thursday from 8am to 4 or 5pm, and on Friday from 8am to 3pm, although the ubiquitous private exchange offices offer similar rates; neither banks nor exchange offices levy a commission. Large hotels will change most hard currencies and **travellers' cheques**. Although it may not be required in all instances, make sure you have your passport when changing travellers' cheques or cash.

If taking cash, and you are not able to obtain forints in advance, a modest amount of low-denomination euros is advisable, although pound sterling and dollars are widely accepted. Avoid anyone who approaches you on the street or at stations offering to exchange money – you will almost certainly be fleeced.

Opening hours and public holidays

Shops are generally open Monday to Friday from 10am to 6pm, and on Saturdays from 10am to 1pm; grocery stores and supermarkets open slightly longer hours at both ends of the day. The shopping malls are open Monday to Saturday 10am to 8pm or 9pm, and Sunday 10am to 6pm. There are also a growing number of 24-hour shops (signed "non-stop", "0–24" or "*éjjel-nappali*").

Museums are generally open Tuesday to Sunday 10am to 6pm, and in winter 9 or 10am to 4 or 5pm. Budapest's **thermal baths** are usually open daily from 6 or 7am to 8pm. Office hours are usually Monday to Friday from 8am to 4pm.

Most things in Hungary shut down on the **public holidays** listed below. When these fall on a Tuesday or Thursday, the Monday before or the Friday after may also become a holiday, and the previous or next Saturday a working day to make up the lost day.

Phones

Telephone numbers in Budapest have seven digits, and the area code for all landline phone numbers is 1. To make a call to another part of Hungary, dial

PUBLIC HOLIDAYS
January 1 New Year's Day
March 15 Independence Day
March/April (variable) Easter Monday
May 1 Labour Day
August 20 St Stephen's Day
October 23 National holiday
November 1 All Saints' Day
December 25 Christmas. (Since celebrations start on Christmas Eve, many shops will be closed the whole day, and by the afternoon everything closes down.)
December 26

☎06 (which gives a burring tone), followed by the area code and the subscriber's number. Hungarian mobile numbers have nine digits, and begin with 20, 30 or 70, depending upon the network.

If you want to use your home mobile phone in Budapest, check with your phone provider whether it will work in Hungary, and what the call charges will be; US cell phones need to be tri-band to work. If you plan on staying in Budapest for a while, you might want to consider buying a Hungarian pay-as-you-go **SIM card**; T-Mobile or Vodafone are the most ubiquitous outlets. and both have pay-as-you-go offers.

To call Hungary from abroad, dial your international access code, then 36 for Hungary, then the area code (omitting the initial zero where present) and the number. If the Hungarian number begins with 06, omit these two digits. **Within Hungary**, directory enquiries is on ☎198, international directory enquiries on ☎199.

Religion

The majority of the Hungarian population is officially Roman Catholic, with the remainder comprising Calvinists, smaller numbers of Lutherans and Jews and even smaller groups such as Serb and Greek Orthodox.

As in other former eastern bloc countries, the church was very strong before World War II, and some people believe it should once again be a powerful force. In Hungary, their number is small: there has been a steady rise in religious interest, with the church playing a more visible role in everyday life, although, Christmas and Easter aside, it's rare to see churches full.

Hungary has a rich Jewish heritage and is today the focus of huge donations aiming to build up communities and restore buildings that were devastated in the Holocaust. Budapest still retains a sizeable and increasingly active Jewish community, which is far more visible than it was before 1989.

Getting into **churches** may be problematic: the really important ones charge a small fee to see their crypts and treasures, and may prohibit sightseeing during services (*mise* or *istentisztelet*, or *Gottesdienst* in German). Visitors are expected to wear "decorous" dress – that is, no shorts or sleeveless tops. Several churches offer religious services in English: Anglican: Sunday 10.30am, VII, Almássy utca 6 ☎06 23 452 023; Baptist: Sunday 10.30am, International Baptist Church, II, Törökvész út 48–54 (Móricz Zsigmond Gimnázium) ☎1 319 8525; Roman Catholic: Saturday 5pm, Pesti Jézus Szíve Templom, VIII, Mária utca 25 ☎1 318 3479.

Time

Hungary is one hour ahead of GMT, six hours ahead of Eastern Standard Time and nine ahead of Pacific Standard Time. A word of caution: Hungarians express time in a way that might confuse the Anglophone traveller. As in German, 10.30am is expressed as "half eleven" (written 1/2 11 or f11), 10.45am is "three-quarter-eleven" (3/4 11 or h11), and 10.15am is "a quarter of eleven" (1/4 11 or n11).

Tipping

Tipping is standard practice in most restaurants; ten percent or thereabouts is fine, unless the service was not worth it. Note that ten percent may have quietly been added to the bill, in which case you don't have to leave more, though restaurant menus really should state whether a service charge is included. Otherwise, include the tip when you are paying the bill – say the amount you want to pay and they will give you the change – or give the tip to the staff rather than leaving it on the table. Taxi drivers usually get around five percent, more if they have helped you with bags or been similarly useful. It's also customary to tip bath attendants who unlock your cubicle (100–200Ft is usual). In all cases, when tipping be warned that if you expect change back, don't say *köszönöm* (thank you) when handing over payment, as it will be assumed that you want the change to be kept.

Tourist information

The best source of **tourist information** in Budapest is Tourinform (𝕎 tourinform.hu), the National Tourist Office, which has three offices split between Buda and Pest, as well as desks at the three airport terminals (daily 8am–8pm). There are also a couple of independent tourist offices providing similar information. The official Budapest Tourism website (𝕎 budapestinfo.hu) has a wealth of information on the city.

INFORMATION OFFICES

Tourinform V, Sütő utca 2, by the Deák tér metro (daily 8am–8pm; ☎ 1 438 8080); VI, Liszt Ferenc tér 11 (daily: May–Sept noon–8pm; Oct–April 10am–6pm; ☎ 1 322 4098); Szentháromság tér 6, in the Castle District (daily 10am–6pm; ☎ 1 488 0475). The main office on Sütő utca has free maps and plenty of material, though it's often packed.
Discover Budapest VI, Lázár utca 16 (daily 9.30am–6pm, June–Aug till 8pm; ☎ 1 269 3842, 𝕎 discoverbudapest.com).

Housed in the same building as Yellow Zebra Bikes (see p.26), just behind the Opera House, this friendly, well-equipped office has stacks of information to hand, can book accommodation and also organizes various tours of the city.
Mellow Mood Keleti train station concourse (daily: June–Aug 7am–10pm; Sept–May 7am–7pm; ☎ 1 343 0748, 𝕎 reservation.hu). A very handy source of information if arriving at Keleti, the young team here can also arrange accommodation and organize sightseeing tours.

HUNGARIAN TOURIST OFFICES ABROAD

UK Hungarian National Tourist Office, 46 Eaton Place, London SW1 8AL ☎ 020 7823 1055, 𝕎 hungary.com. There is also a free tourist hotline with information on the city (☎ 0800 360 0000).
US Hungarian National Tourist Office, 447 Broadway, Fifth Floor, New York, NY 10013 ☎ 212/695 1221, 𝕎 gotohungary.com.

USEFUL WEBSITES

𝕎 **caboodle.hu** English-language news and listings website aimed at the expat community.
𝕎 **hungary.org.uk** The website of the Hungarian Cultural Centre in London is a useful place to keep up Hungarian links after your visit.
𝕎 **met.hu** Daily weather bulletins and forecasts.
𝕎 **pestiside.hu** Irreverent but informed expat-run website on the Budapest scene.

Travellers with disabilities

Hungary has been painfully slow to acknowledge the needs of the disabled traveller, and while progress is being made, don't expect much in the way of special facilities. However, the rapid growth of new hotels in Budapest has meant much better access for those with disabilities, with particular emphasis on specially designed rooms. Moreover, an increasing number of museums are providing ramps for wheelchairs.

The website of the **Hungarian Disabled Association** or Meosz, III, San Marco utca 76, 1032 Budapest (☎ 1 388 5529, 𝕎 meosz.hu), has useful – though not always up-to-date – information about access to museums, cultural and historical sites, baths and some restaurants. For information on public transport accessibility, check the "Passengers with disabilities" section of the Budapest transport website, 𝕎 bkv.hu, which lists routes where modern low-floored buses operate. The only accessible trams are the #4 and #6 on the Nagykörút. The Airport Shuttle from the airport is also accessible. Meosz also operates its own special transport service in Budapest whereby, for a fixed payment, a bus equipped with a lift or ramp can take you to your chosen destination.

ART NOUVEAU MOSAIC, SZERVITA TÉR

The Belváros

Abuzz with pavement cafés, street artists, vendors, boutiques and nightclubs, the Belváros or Inner City is the hub of Pest and, for tourists at least, the centre of what's happening. Commerce and pleasure have been its lifeblood as long as Pest has existed, first as a medieval market town and later as the kernel of a city whose *belle époque* rivalled that of Vienna. Since their fates diverged, the Belváros has lagged far behind Vienna's Centrum in prosperity, but the gap is fast being narrowed, at least superficially. It's now increasingly like any Western city in its consumer culture, but you can still get a sense of the old atmosphere, especially in the quieter backstreets south of Kossuth utca, where café life fans out in the shadow of some dramatic architecture.

The **Kiskörút** (Small Boulevard; comprising Károly körút, Múzeum körút and Vámház körút) that surrounds the Belváros follows the course of the medieval walls of Pest, showing how compact it was before the phenomenal expansion of the nineteenth century. However, little remains from further back than the eighteenth century, as the "liberation" of Pest by the Habsburgs in 1686 left the town in ruins. Some Baroque churches and the former Greek and Serbian quarters attest to its revival by settlers from other parts of the Habsburg empire, but most of the **architecture** dates from the era when Budapest asserted its right to be an imperial capital, between 1860 and 1918. Today, first-time visitors are struck by the statues, domes and mosaics on the Neoclassical and Art Nouveau piles, which are reflected in the mirrored banks and luxury hotels that symbolize the post-Communist era.

After a stroll along **Váci utca** from **Vörösmarty tér** and a look at the splendid view of the Vár from the **embankment**, the best way to appreciate the Belváros is by simply wandering around. People-watching and window-shopping are the most enjoyable activities, and though prices are above average for Budapest, any visitor should be able to afford to sample the **cafés**. Shops are another matter – there are few bargains – and nightclubs are a trap for the unwary.

Vörösmarty tér

Vörösmarty tér, the leafy centre of the Belváros, is a good starting point for exploring the area. Crowds eddy around the portraitists, conjurers and saxophonists, and the craft stalls that fill the square at Christmas and at festivals throughout the year, such as the Book Week in June. While children play on the Lion fountain, teenagers lounge around the **statue of Mihály Vörösmarty** (1800–50), a poet and translator whose hymn to Magyar identity, *Szózat* ("Appeal"), is publicly declaimed at moments of national crisis. Its opening line "Be faithful to your land forever, Oh Hungarians" is carved on the statue's pedestal. Made of Carrara marble, the statue has to be wrapped in plastic sheeting each winter to prevent it from cracking. The black spot below the inscription is reputedly a "lucky" coin donated by a beggar towards the cost of the monument.

Gerbeaud patisserie

Gerbeaud cukrászda • V, Vörösmarty tér 7 • Daily 9am–9pm • ☎ 1 429 9000, ⓦ gerbeaud.hu

On the north side of Vörösmarty tér is the **Gerbeaud patisserie**, Budapest's most famous confectioners. Founded in 1858 by Henrik Kugler, it was bought in 1884 by the Swiss confectioner Emile Gerbeaud, who invented the *konyakos meggy* (cognac-cherry bonbon) – still a popular sweet with Hungarians. He sold top-class cakes at reasonable prices, making the *Gerbeaud* a popular rendezvous for the middle classes. Now the prices are astronomical by Hungarian standards, but it still has an undeniable appeal. Emile's portrait hangs in one of the rooms, whose gilded ceilings and china recall the *belle époque*.

Underground Railway

From the terrace outside the *Gerbeaud* patisserie you can observe the entrance to the **Underground Railway** (Földalattivasút, the yellow #1 metro line), whose vaguely Art Nouveau cast-iron fixtures and elegant tilework stamp it as decades older than the other metro lines. For its centenary in 1996, the line's stations were restored to their original decor. If you're curious to know more about its history, visit the Underground Railway Museum at Deák tér (see p.44). The Underground Railway's route along Andrássy út is covered in Chapter 3, with Hősök tere described in Chapter 4.

Bershka store and former Bank Palace

Directly behind Vörösmarty's statue stands the **Bershka store**, its 1911 facade adorned with bronze panels with plant motifs. In the Communist era the Luxus Áruház, as it was then known, was *the* place to get your Western-style clothes. Now it sells the real

■ ACCOMMODATION		● RESTAURANTS, CAFÉS & BARS					
Astoria	6	Action	16	Mélypont	14	Emilia Anda	5
Best Western Hotel Art	9	Amstel River Café	6	Nobu	3	Ernst Galéria	10
Cosmo Fashion	8	Astoria Kávéház	10	Rézkakas	13	Holló Folk Art Gallery	8
Gerlóczy	5	Azték	9	Spoon	1	Intuita	12
Green Bridge	7	Babel	17	Trattoria Toscana	15	Kodály Zoltán Zeneműbolt	14
Kempinski Corvinus	1	Capella	11	Vapiano	4	Libri	4
La Prima Fashion	3	Centrál Kávéház	12			Malatinszky	1
Le Méridien	2	Fresh Factory	8	● SHOPS		Red Bus	6
Peregrinus	10	Gerbeaud	2	BÁV	2	Rozsavölgyi Zeneműbolt	3
Red Bus	4	Gerlóczy	7	Bio ABC	13	Valéria Fazekas	11
Zara Boutique	11	La Cucina	5	Eclectick	9	Vass	7

thing, Western clothes as produced by the Spanish fashion company and aimed at the younger market.

Another early twentieth-century building, the former **Bank Palace**, stands at the southern end of the square on the corner of Váci utca. When the Budapest **Stock Exchange** reopened its doors in 1990, this was its new home. Built in the heyday of Hungarian self-confidence, by Ignác Alpár, who also designed the prewar Stock Exchange on Szabadság tér (see p.150), it has now been turned into a major retail centre.

Váci utca and around

Váci utca has been famous for its shops and **korzó** (promenade) since the eighteenth century. During the 1980s, its vivid street life became a symbol of the "consumer socialism" that distinguished Hungary from other Eastern Bloc states. Over the past thirty years it has become a tourist haunt, with endless souvenir sh.ops and rip-off bars where unsuspecting visitors would be tricked into paying huge bills.

Today the northern half of the street, down to Ferenciek tere, has at least gained a touch of style from a number of outlets for big Western fashion names such as Zara. A few landmarks along the way might catch your eye: the scantily clad **Fisher-girl fountain** on **Kristóf tér**; the **Pest Theatre** (no. 9) on the site of the *Inn of the Seven Electors*, where the 12-year-old Liszt performed in 1823 – note also the gorgeous Art Nouveau florist's and the former **Auction House** (no. 11a), with its neo-Gothic facade of majolica tiles and toothy wrought-ironwork.

An underpass further south brings you out on Március 15 tér, where a weird stone **monument** resembling a giant cactus flower commemorates the 125th anniversary of the unification of Buda and Pest. Beyond here, the pedestrianized continuation of Váci is infested with tourist-trap restaurants and shops, but retains some imposing architecture: worth a look are the prewar **Officers' Casino** (no. 38) guarded by statues of halberdiers (now a bank's headquarters), and the sculptural **plaque** on the wall of no. 47, commemorating the fact that the Swedish king Charles XII stayed here during his lightning fourteen-day horseride from Turkey to Sweden, in 1714. Further along at nos. 62–64 looms the griffon- and majolica-encrusted **Budapest City Hall**, where the city council still meets.

Serbian Orthodox Church

Szerb Ortodox templom • V, Szerb utca 2–4 • Daily 10am–5pm if staff are available to open it • 300Ft • High Mass on Sun 10am

A left turn off Váci utca into Szerb utca brings you to the **Serbian Orthodox Church**, built by the Serbian artisans and merchants who settled here after the Turks were driven out. Secluded in a high-walled garden, it's best visited during High Mass on Sunday, when the singing of the liturgy, the clouds of incense and flickering candles create an unearthly atmosphere.

A block or so south of the church, part of the **medieval wall** of Pest can be seen behind a children's playground on the corner of Bástya utca and Vernes Pálné utca. There is more of the wall near the eastern end of Bástya utca, tucked away inside the bank at Kecskeméti utca 19, on the corner of Kalvin tér.

1

Petőfi Literary Museum

Petőfi Irodalmi Múzeum • V, Károlyi Mihály utca 16 • Tues–Sun 10am–6pm • 600Ft • ⓦ pim.hu

A short walk up Kecskeméti utca from the **Serbian Orthodox Church** lies Egyetemi tér, where tables spill across the wide pavements in the shadow of the Law Faculty of the university, giving the square a real buzz. On the northeast corner stands the Károlyi Palota, the birthplace of Count Mihály Károlyi, the liberal politician who briefly led the government after World War I. Today the palace houses the **Petőfi Literary Museum**, which has a permanent exhibition on the life of the personal effects of Sándor Petőfi, the nineteenth-century revolutionary poet (see box, p.43). The information sheet in the first room offers a little background about his life. There are regular temporary displays with a literary connection, but the captions are often in Hungarian only. During the summer you may be able to see round the rest of the palace rooms (separate entry fee).

The mansion's garden, the **Károlyi-kert**, is a delightful green haven in the centre of the city, and has a children's playground. It was here that Lajos Batthyány, head of the independent Hungarian government following the 1848 revolution, was arrested in 1849, and General Haynau, the "Butcher of Vienna", signed the death warrants of Batthyány and other rebel leaders after finishing his morning exercises.

Ferenciek tere

Running north from the Petőfi Literary Museum is Károlyi Mihály utca, which leads into **Ferenciek tere** (Franciscans' Square) – though it's more L-shaped than square, and is dominated by the network of roads approaching the Erzsébet bridge. Yet even the six-lane highway that runs across the top of the square cannot detract from the magnificence of the buildings. At the top of Károlyi Mihály utca to the left is the **Centrál Kávéház**, one of Pest's grand old coffee houses where, in the early twentieth century, writers and intellectuals lingered day and night, while to the right rises the coloured dome of the university library.

Párisi Udvar

The most notable building on Ferenciek tere is the **Párisi Udvar**, a flamboyantly eclectic shopping arcade on the square's north side that was completed in 1915. Its fifty naked statues above the third floor were deemed incompatible with its intended role as a savings bank, symbolized by images of bees throughout the building, though they might fit in better with its proposed transformation into a luxury hotel. Certainly the neglected arcade, as ornate as an Andalusian mosque, with its hexagonal dome designed by Miksa Róth, desperately needs restoration and should come out of it glowing.

The Klotild Palaces

The traffic roars into the western end of Ferenciek tere between a pair of imposing *fin-de-siècle* office buildings – designed by Flóris Krob and Kálmán Giergl, the same team behind the Bershka department store building (p.37) and the Music Academy (p.60). Named the **Klotild Palaces** after the Habsburg princess who commissioned them, the northern one is home to the luxury hotel, while Egon Ronay's father owned a restaurant in the southern palace. After it was nationalized in 1946, the young Ronay moved to London where he was appalled by cooking standards.

Kossuth Lajos utca

Heading out the eastern end of Ferenciek tere, the road seamlessly becomes **Kossuth Lajos utca**, where the noise and the fumes deter the visitor from lingering. Immediately

1

on the right is the **Franciscan Church** that gave the square its name. The relief on the church's wall recalls the great flood of 1838, in which over four hundred citizens were killed; it depicts the heroic efforts of Baron Miklós Wesselényi, who personally rescued scores of people in his boat.

Some 200m further along, the junction of Kossuth Lajos utca with the Kiskörút is named after the **Astoria Hotel** on the corner, a prewar haunt of spies and journalists that was commandeered as an HQ by the Nazis in 1944 and the Soviets after the 1956 Uprising. Today, its Neoclassical coffee lounge is redolent of Stalinist chic.

Szervita tér

North from Ferenciek tere Petőfi Sándor utca leads up to **Szervita tér**, a square containing the best and the worst of twentieth-century architecture. Three remarkable buildings from the golden age of Hungarian architecture line its western side. No. 3, the former Turkish Bank House dating from 1906, has a gable aglow with a superb **Art Nouveau mosaic** of *Patrona Hungariae* (Our Lady) flanked by key figures from Hungarian history, one of the finest works of Miksa Róth (see p.66). No. 2 (1908) is one of the earliest Modernist buildings in Budapest, with its geometric motifs and its decorative screws, while on the other side at no. 5 the **Rózsavölgyi Building** (1911–12) was built by the "father" of Hungarian Modernism, **Béla Lajta**, whose earlier association with the National Romantic school is evident from the majolica bands on its upper storeys, typical of the style. The Rózsavölgyi music shop on the ground floor is one of the oldest in the city – sadly Lajta's interior fittings were lost in a fire in 1955.

Servite Church

Szervita Templom • V, Szervita tér 6 • Daily 10am–1.30pm & 2–6pm • Free; concerts Wed noon, donations accepted

Szervita tér is named after the eighteenth-century Servite Church (Belvárosi Szent Anna templom is the full name), whose facade bears a relief of an angel cradling a dying horseman, in memory of the Seventh Kaiser Wilhelm Hussars killed in World War I. The interior is standard Baroque fare. The attached monastery was damaged in World War II and in 1964 was replaced with the brutalist communications centre that now hems in the church. Both this and the ugly car park/office block on the north side of the square are slated for demolition.

Along the embankment

The riverbank bore the brunt of the fighting in 1944–45, when the Nazis and the Red Army exchanged salvos across the Danube. As with the Vár in Buda, postwar clearances exposed historic sites and provided an opportunity to integrate them into the environment – but the magnificent **view** of the Royal Palace and Gellért-hegy is hardly matched by the row of modern hotels on the Pest side. While such historic architecture as remains can be seen in a fifteen-minute stroll between the Erzsébet híd and the Lánchíd, tram #2 enables you to see a longer stretch of the waterfront between Szabadság híd and Kossuth tér in the north, interrupted by a tunnel at the Lánchíd.

Erzsébet híd

The bold white pylons and cables of the **Erzsébet híd** (Elizabeth Bridge) are as dominant a feature of the panorama as the stone Lánchíd to the north or the wrought-iron Szabadság híd to the south. Of all the Danube bridges blown up by the Germans as they retreated to Buda in January 1945, the Erzsébet híd was the only one not rebuilt in its original form. In fact it was not replaced until 1964 – and even then had to be closed down immediately due to faulty engineering.

Belváros Parish Church

Belvárosi Főplébánia Templom • V, Március 15 tér 2 • Mon–Sat 7am–7pm, Sun 8am–7pm • Free

In the shadow of the approach ramp, the grimy facade of the **Belváros Parish Church** masks its origins as the oldest church in Pest. Founded in 1046 as the burial place of St Gellért (see p.107), it was rebuilt as a Gothic hall church in the fifteenth century (his remains had long been shipped off to Venice), turned into a mosque by the Turks and then reconstructed as a church in the eighteenth century. This history is reflected in the interior, and after Latin Mass at 10am on Sunday you can see the Gothic sedilia and Turkish *mihrab* (prayer niche) behind the high altar, which are otherwise out of bounds. The vaulted nave and side chapels are Baroque.

Március 15 tér and Petőfi tér

On the square beside the Belváros Parish Church, you can peer down through the glass covers at the remains of **Contra-Aquincum**, a Roman fort that was an outpost of the settlement at Óbuda at the end of the third century. More pertinently to Hungarian history, the name of the square, **Március 15 tér**, refers to March 15, 1848, when the anti-Habsburg Revolution began, while the adjacent **Petőfi tér** to the north is named after Sándor Petőfi, whose poem *National Song* – the anthem of 1848 – and romantic death in battle the following year made him a patriotic icon (see box, below). Erected in 1882, the square's **Petőfi statue** has long been a focus for demonstrations as well as patriotic displays – especially on March 15, when the statue is bedecked with flags and flowers.

Cathedral of the Dormition

Nagyboldogasszony magyar ortodox székesegyház • V, Petőfi tér 2 • Wed & Fri 3.30–5pm, Sat 3–6pm, Sun noon–3pm; services Mon–Fri 5pm, Sat 6pm, Sun 8, 9 & 10am • Free

On the eastern side of Petőfi tér looms the Greek Orthodox **Cathedral of the Dormition**, built by the Greek community in the 1790s and, more recently, the object of a tug-of-war between the Patriarchate of Moscow that gained control of it after 1945 and the Orthodox Church in Greece that previously owned it. One of the church's towers was lost in the siege of Budapest in 1944, but a temporary replacement was recently erected, signifying the intention to rebuild it. The cathedral has services in Hungarian, Church Slavonic and Greek, according to the make-up of the congregation, accompanied by singing in the Orthodox fashion. The big feast here is on August 28, the Dormition of Mary (the Assumption) in the Orthodox calendar.

Marriott Hotel and Duna-korzó

Just north of Petőfi tér, the unattractive **Marriott Hotel** is situated between the embankment and the street running parallel, Apáczai Csere János utca. Inaugurated as

---

SÁNDOR PETŐFI

Born on New Year's Eve, 1822, of a Slovak mother and a southern Slav butcher-innkeeper father, **Sándor Petőfi** was to become obsessed by acting and by poetry, which he started to write at the age of 15. As a strolling player, soldier and labourer, he absorbed the language of working people and composed his lyrical poetry in the vernacular, to the outrage of critics. Moving to Budapest in 1844, he fell in with the young radical intellectuals who met at the *Pilvax Café* (its modern embodiment on Pilvax utca, off Váci utca, fails to capture the rebellious spirit), and embarked on his career as a revolutionary hero. He declaimed his *National Song* from the steps of the National Museum on the first day of the 1848 Revolution, and fought in the War of Independence with General Bem in Transylvania, where he disappeared during the Battle of Segesvár in 1849. Though he was most likely trampled beyond recognition by the Cossacks' horses (as predicted in one of his poems), Petőfi was long rumoured to have survived as a prisoner. In 1990, a Hungarian entrepreneur sponsored an expedition to Siberia to uncover the putative grave, but it turned out to be that of a woman.

1

the *Duna Intercontinental* in 1969, it was the first hotel in the Eastern Bloc managed in partnership with a Western firm and the model for others on the embankment.

On the Danube side of the *Marriott*, the concrete esplanade is a sterile attempt at recreating the prewar **Duna-korzó**, the most informal of Budapest's promenades, where it was socially acceptable for strangers to approach celebrities and stroll beside them. The outdoor cafés here, which boast wonderful views, charge premium rates.

Vigadó tér

Vigadó tér is an elegant square named after the **Vigadó** concert hall, whose name translates as "having a ball" or "making merry". Inaugurated in 1865, this Romantic pile by Frigyes Feszl is encrusted with statues of the Muses and plaques recalling performances by Liszt, Mahler and Wagner and other renowned artists. Badly damaged in World War II, it didn't reopen until 1980, such was the care taken to recreate its sumptuous decor. It closed again in 2004, but the new administration may well push to get it reopened.

Little Princess

On Vigadó tér it's easy to miss the statue of the impish **Little Princess**, which has been sitting on the railings by the tram line since 1990. After dusk, you'll hardly notice that she isn't a person, if you notice her at all. By day, she looks like a cross-dressing boy in a Tinkerbell hat. Prince Charles was so taken by her that he invited her creator, László Marton, to hold an exhibition of his work in Britain.

Deák tér

Three metro lines and several important roads meet at **Deák tér,** to form a jumping-off point for the Belváros and Lipótváros. However, finding local addresses can be confusing since Deák Ferenc tér merges seamlessly into the far larger **Erzsébet tér** to the north. Two landmarks mark out the sides of Deák tér: the vast mustard-coloured **Anker Palace** to the east and the **Lutheran Church** to the west.

Anker Palace

The **Anker Palace** (Anker palota) is one of several imposing edifices in the centre of Budapest built for a foreign insurance company, in this case the Viennese Insurance Company. Its design by Ignác Alpár, the man behind the former Stock Exchange and the National Bank on Szabadság tér, was widely admired for its clever use of an awkward plot. Not everyone was impressed: when it opened in 1910, Alpár's wife said, "Oh Ignác, aren't you ashamed of yourself? What have you done here?"

Lutheran Church and Museum

Deák téri Evangélikus Templom & Evangélikus Múzeum • V, Deák tér 4 • Tues–Sun 10am–6pm • 500Ft • ⓦ evangelikusmuzeum.hu

The large **Lutheran Church**, which looms over the metro pavilion on the edge of the Belváros, hosts some excellent concerts that include regular free Sunday evening organ recitals and Bach's *St John Passion* over the fortnight before Easter. Next door, the **Lutheran Museum** displays a facsimile of Martin Luther's last will and testament, and a copy of the first book printed in Hungarian, a New Testament from 1541.

Underground Railway Museum

Földalattivasút Múzeum • V, Deák tér underpass by the entrance to the metro station • Tues–Sun 10am–5pm • 320Ft or one BKV ticket

Accessible via the upper sub-level of Deák tér metro, the **Underground Railway Museum** extols the history of Budapest's original metro. The exhibits include three old wooden carriages (one used up until 1973) and period fixtures and posters, which enhance the museum's nostalgic appeal.

The metro's genesis was a treatise by Mór Balázs, proposing a steam-driven tram network starting with a route along Andrássy út, an underground line being suggested as a fallback in case the overground option was rejected. Completed in under two years, it was inaugurated in 1896 – in time for the Millennial Exhibition – by Emperor Franz Josef, who agreed to allow it to bear his name, which it kept until 1918. The metro was the first on the European continent and the second in the world (after London's Metropolitan line), and originally ran from Vörösmarty tér as far as the Millennial Exhibition grounds at Hősök tere.

Erzsébet tér

Once the site of a cemetery beyond the medieval city walls, **Erzsébet tér** has gone through many names since then, notably Sztálin tér from 1946 until 1953, when it became Engels tér, before getting its older name back. The statue in the middle of the park is of **Old Father Danube** with his three tributaries, the Dráva, Száva and Tisza, and was designed in 1880 by Miklós Ybl.

On the east side of the square a small **skateboard park** attracts youngsters keen to perfect their skills. They also use the long, low functionalist building next door, a former bus station protected by a conservation order and so unable to be demolished, much to the ire of locals.

Gödör Klub

V, Erzsébet tér • Mon–Thurs & Sun 10am–2am, Fri & Sat 10am–4am • ☎ 1 201 3868, ⓦ godorklub.hu

The area on the east side of the old bus station was the scene of a political squabble in the 1998, when the city's plan to build a new National Theatre in the square was thwarted by the incoming government, leaving a vast pit dubbed the "National Hole" (Nemzeti Lyuk). It now houses the **Gödör Klub** (the Pothole Club), a bar and underground cultural centre, visible from above through a glass-bottomed pool. It has become one of the most popular places to gather on summer evenings, as the crowds spill out across the square.

Lipótváros and Újlipótváros

Lipótváros (Leopold Town), lying to the north of the Belváros, started to develop in the late eighteenth century, first as a financial centre and later as the seat of government and bureaucracy. Several institutions of national significance are found here, including Parliament, St Stephen's Basilica, the National Bank and the Television headquarters. Though part of the V District, as is the Belváros, Lipótváros has quite a different ambience, with sombre streets of Neoclassical buildings interrupted by squares flanked by monumental Art Nouveau or neo-Renaissance piles. However, the area has undergone a transformation recently as the streets around the Basilica have been pedestrianized. Bars now sprawl across Szent István tér and Zrinyi utca, and Sas utca has attracted some of the best restaurants in the city.

Across the Nagykörút lies Újlipótváros (New Leopold Town; the XIII district), stretching from the bustling Pozsonyi út through quieter residential streets to another focus of activity, **Lehel tér**.

ARRIVAL AND GETTING AROUND

Lipótváros It makes sense to start a Lipótváros visit either with Széchenyi István tér (until recently called Roosevelt tér), by the Lánchíd, or St Stephen's Basilica, two minutes' walk from Deák tér. Most of the streets between them lead towards the set-piece expanse of Szabadság tér, whence you can head on towards Parliament – though the Kossuth tér metro station or tram #2 along the river will provide quicker access.

Újlipótváros The way to get here is either by tram #4 or #6 along the Nagykörút or on the blue #2 metro line to the Lehel tér stop.

Széchenyi Istvan tér

At the Pest end of the Lánchíd, **Széchenyi István tér** is named after "the greatest Hungarian", the man responsible for building the bridge (see p.101). Blitzed by traffic crowding on and off the bridge, it's also dominated by huge trees – including one propped-up acacia said to be the oldest tree in the city – that make it hard to get a feel for this historic square. It was here that the Austrian emperor Franz Josef was crowned King of Hungary in 1867 – paradoxically symbolizing Hungary's increasing independence within the Habsburg empire. Soil from every corner of the nation was piled into a Coronation Hill, on the site of the present square. The emperor flourished the sword of St Stephen and promised to defend Hungary against all its enemies – a pledge that proved almost as ephemeral as the hill itself. In 1947 the square was renamed **Roosevelt tér** in honour of the late US president – a rare example of Cold War courtesy that survived until 2011 when the new mayor determined to sweep away the old Communist names. To soothe American feelings, he promised to honour Roosevelt elsewhere in the city – one rumoured choice being Szabadság tér in front of the US embassy.

Gresham Palace

Unquestionably the finest building on **Széchenyi István tér** is the magnificent Art Nouveau **Gresham Palace** on its eastern side. Commissioned by a British insurance company in 1904, it's named after the financier Sir Thomas Gresham, the author of Gresham's law that bad money drives out good, whereby the circulation of coins of equal face value but different metals leads to those made of more valuable metal being hoarded and disappearing from use.

The building was in an awful state when it was acquired by the Four Seasons hotel chain in 2001, but fears of a crass refurbishment were dispelled by a loving restoration: authentic materials and even the original workshops were sought out to do the job. Today you can once again see Gresham's bust high up on the facade, and members of the public may walk in to admire the subtle hues of the tiled lobby and glass-roofed arcade, with wrought-iron peacock gates and stained-glass windows by Miksa Róth.

Hungarian Academy of Sciences

Magyar Tudományos Akadémia • V, Széchenyi István tér 9 • Mon & Fri 1–4pm • Free

Statues of Count Széchenyi (see p.101) and Ferenc Deák, another major nineteenth-century politician who helped to forge Hungary's agreement with the Austrians in 1867, stand at opposite ends of Széchenyi István tér. The statue of the former isn't far from the **Hungarian Academy of Sciences**, founded after Széchenyi pledged a year's income from his estates towards its establishment in 1825 – as depicted on a relief on the wall facing Akadémia utca. The only part of the Academy that is open is its small collection of paintings, mainly portraits but including the odd Munkácsy landscape.

LIPÓTVÁROS AND ÚJLIPÓTVÁROS

Margit Sziget

River Danube (Duna)

Buda & Moszkva tér

Wallenberg

Szent István Park

VICTOR HUGO UTCA

IPOLY UTCA

Lehel market

CSANÁDY UTCA

VÁCI ÚT

BALZAC UTCA

ÚJLIPÓTVÁROS

Lehel tér

RADNÓTI MIKLÓS UTCA

RAOUL WALLENBERG UTCA

TÁTRA UTCA

PANNÓNIA UTCA

HEGEDŰS GYULA UTCA

VISEGRÁDI UTCA

LEHEL TÉR

Ferry Docks

KATONA JÓZSEF UTCA

JÁSZAI MARI TÉR

FERDINÁND HÍD

MARGIT HÍD

West End Center

VÁCI ÚT

SZENT ISTVÁN KÖRÚT

Vígszínház

RESTAURANTS, CAFÉS, AND BARS

Bedő Ház	7
Borkonyha	15
Briós	1
Café Kör	14
Le Café M	9
Csarnok	8
Duran Sandwich Bar	13
Europa	3
Firkász	2
Govinda	12
Momotaro	10
Okay Italia	5
Pomo D'Oro	11
Szalai	6
Tokaji Borozó	4

BALASSI B. UTCA

BALATON UTCA

FALK MIKSA U.

HONVÉD UTCA

SZEMERE UTCA

NAGY UTCA

NYUGATI TÉR

Nyugati pu

Nyugati Station

EIFFEL TÉR

PODMANICZKY UTCA

Károlyi

Kossuth

Museum of Ethnography

Eternal Flame

KOSSUTH LAJOS TÉR

ALKOTMÁNY UTCA

VADÁSZ UTCA

TEREZ KÖRÚT

TOKAI UTCA

Parliament

KÁLMÁN IMRE UTCA

Rákóczi

BÁTHORI UTCA

Eternal Flame

Glass House

NAGYMEZŐ UTCA

TERÉZVÁROS

József

Kossuth tér

Bedő House

US Embassy

State Treasury

Market Hall

HAJÓS UTCA

Nagy Reagan

SZABADSÁG TÉR

HOLD U.

NAGYSÁNDOR J. U.

Holocaust Memorial

TV Building

Soviet Army Memorial

General Bandholtz

BÁNK UTCA

Opera House

National Bank

Arany János utca

Opera

AKADÉMIA UTCA

SZÉCHENYI U.

Academy of Sciences

ARANY JÁNOS UTCA

Bank Center

HERCEGPRÍMÁS U.

JÓZSEF RAKPART

ZRÍNYI UTCA

VIGYÁZÓ F. UTCA

CEU

OKTÓBER 6. UTCA

SZENT ISTVÁN TÉR

St. Stephen's Basilica

Bajcsy-Zsilinszky út

ANDRÁSSY ÚT

Gresham Palace

SZÉCHENYI ISTVÁN TÉR

MÉRLEG UT.

JÓZSEF ATTILA UTCA

JÓZSEF NÁDOR TÉR

ERZSÉBET TÉR

KIRÁLY UTCA

LÁNCHÍD

JANE HANNING RAKPART

DOROTTYA UTCA

Vigadó tér

Deák tér

N

SHOPS
Bestsellers	5
Bortársaság	4
CEU	6
Katti Zoób	3
Ómama Bizsúja	1
Wladis Galéria	2

CLUB
Trocadero Café	1

ACCOMMODATION
Four Seasons	1
Starlight Suiten	2

0 ————— 250
metres

Castle District

River Danube (Duna)

St Stephen's Basilica

Szent István-Bazilika • **Basilica** Mon–Sat 9am–7pm, Sun 1–6pm • Free but donations encouraged • Mass on weekdays 7am & 6pm, Sun 8.30am, 10am, noon & 6pm. **Chapel** Mon–Sat 10am–4pm, Sun 1–4.30pm • Free • **Panorama Tower** Daily: April–June 10am–4pm; July–Oct 10am–7pm, closing earlier in bad weather • 500Ft • **Treasury** Same hours as tower • 500Ft

St Stephen's Basilica took so long to build that Budapestis once joked, when borrowing money, "I'll pay you back when the basilica is finished". Work began in 1851 under the supervision of József Hild, continued after his death under Miklós Ybl, and was finally completed by Joseph Krauser in 1905. At the inaugural ceremony Emperor Franz Josef was seen to glance anxiously at the dome, whose collapse during a storm in 1868 had set progress back. At 96m, it is exactly the same height as the dome of the Parliament building – both allude to the putative date of the Magyars' arrival in Hungary (896 AD). After recent restoration work that seemed to take as long as the original construction, the basilica looks very grand today. Its beauty lies in the combined effect of the frescoes, marble and gilded stucco rather than in any particular works of art, though the **organ** above the doorway is splendid.

2

In the second chapel to the right is a painting of King Stephen offering the Crown of Hungary to the Virgin (see p.92), while a statue of him haloed as a saint (but with a sword at his side) forms the centrepiece of the altar.

In a **chapel** to the left at the back is the gnarled **mummified hand of St Stephen**, Hungary's holiest relic. The Szent Jobb (literally, "holy right") is paraded with great pomp through the surrounding streets on August 20, the anniversary of his death, but at other times you can see it in the chapel by inserting 200Ft to illuminate the casket. There is also a display offering a brief history of the saint's life.

Another name that recurs throughout the basilica is that of Cardinal Mindszenty, the head of the church who is much honoured for his challenge to the Communist regime (see p.142).

You shouldn't miss the grand **view** over the city from the Panorama Tower (Körkilátó) reached by two lifts to the base of the cupola; the lift – or the 302 stairs – are to the right of the entrance. On the way down you can pop into the **treasury** (*kincstár*) when it reopens in its new home upstairs, though it is paltry compared to that in Esztergom's basilica (see p.141).

The square around the basilica is packed with bars spilling onto the streets, a great place for people-watching. The fine Art Nouveau frontage at no. 15, down the north side of the basilica, is due to become yet another luxury hotel.

Bajcsy-Zsilinszky út

While Stephen is revered as the founder and patron saint of Hungary, the pantheon of national heroes includes a niche for **Endre Bajcsy-Zsilinszky** (1866–1944), after whom the avenue that runs past the Basilica is named. Originally a right-winger, he ended up an outspoken critic of Fascism, was arrested in Parliament and shot as the Russians approached. **Bajcsy-Zsilinszky út** is the demarcation line between the Lipótváros and Terézváros districts, running northwards to **Nyugati Station**, an elegant, iron-beamed terminal built in 1874–77 by the Eiffel Company of Paris.

Szabadság tér and around

For more than a century, Lipótváros was dominated by a gigantic barracks where scores of Hungarians were imprisoned or executed, until this symbol of Habsburg tyranny was demolished in 1897 and the site redeveloped as **Szabadság tér** (Liberty Square). Invested with significance from the outset, it became a kind of record of the vicissitudes of modern Hungarian history, where each regime added or removed **monuments**, according to their political complexion. For an excellent vantage point from which to admire the square's buildings, head to the café pavilion in the centre of the square. (Following the street name changes in 2011 there was talk of the name Roosevelt tér being bestowed on all or part of Szabadság tér.)

The Stock Exchange

In the early twentieth century, Hungary's burgeoning prosperity was expressed by two monumental temples to capitalism on opposite sides of Szabadság tér. To the west stands the former **Stock Exchange**, one of the grandest buildings in Budapest. Designed by Ignác Alpár, it has blended motifs from Greek and Assyrian architecture and is crowned with twin towers resembling Khmer temples. After the Communists closed down the Exchange in 1948, it became the **headquarters of Hungarian Television**. During the riots of 2006 protesters broke into the building, but generally it is closed to the public.

National Bank

Magyar Nemzeti Bank • V, Szabadság tér 8 • Visitor Centre Mon–Fri 9am–4pm, open till 6pm Thurs • Free • ⓦ lk.mnb.hu

Ignác Alpár, the man behind the former Stock Exchange, also designed the **National Bank** on the eastern side of Szabadság tér, which still functions as such and is notable for the bas-reliefs on its exterior, representing such diverse aspects of wealth creation as Magyars ploughing and herding, ancient Egyptians harvesting wheat, and Vikings loading longships with loot. The stones for its columns were hauled all the way from Transylvania by oxen. The main entrance on the south facade of the building leads to a stylish **Visitor Centre** featuring curiosities like the "Kossuth" banknotes that were issued in America during the politician's exile after the failed War of Independence, and notes denominated in trillions of forints from the period of hyper-inflation in 1946. (The bank also has some fine stained-glass windows on the stairs, but you can only see these during European Heritage Days in September.) Across the way outside, the mirrored-glass and granite **Bank Centre** is a triumphant affirmation of the fact that Hungary has rejoined the capitalist system.

The US embassy

The northern neighbour of the National Bank on the eastern side of Szabadság tér is the imposing **US Embassy** (now cordoned off for security); for fifteen years, the latter sheltered Cardinal Mindszenty, the Primate of Hungary's Catholic Church, in the aftermath of the 1956 Uprising. Later, however, the US became embarrassed by his presence, as did the Vatican, which finally persuaded him to leave for Austria in 1971 (see box, p.142).

In front of the US embassy, the stocky figure of **General Harry Bandholtz** commemorates the US general who intervened with a dogwhip to stop Romanian troops from looting the Hungarian National Museum in 1919. The statue was erected in the 1930s, removed after World War II, and reinstated by the Communists prior to President George Bush's visit in 1989.

Hungarian State Treasury

Right behind the US embassy lies a fine example of Hungarian Art Nouveau. The tiled facade of the **Hungarian State Treasury** is patterned like a quilt, with swarms of bees symbolizing thrift – this was originally the **Post Office Savings Bank** (Postatakarékpénztár). The polychromatic roof with its beehives and dragon tails is the wildest part of the building. Its architect, Ödön Lechner, once asked why birds shouldn't enjoy his buildings too, and amazing roofs are a feature of his other masterpieces in Budapest, the Geological Institute (p.74) and the Applied Arts Museum (p.82). The interior is only open to the public on European Heritage Days sometime in September, but a small display of photographs of the interior gives you a taste of the design in the foyer, accessible during banking hours.

The Hold utca market hall

Vásárcsarnok • V, Hold utca 13 • Mon–Thurs 6.30am–5pm, Fri 6.30am–6pm

Diagonally across the street from the State Treasury is a wrought-iron **market hall** one of five opened on a single day in 1896, and which still serve the centre of Pest; it's much less touristy than the Great Market Hall on Vámház körút (see p.81). Its rear entrance will bring you out on Vadász utca, not far from one of Budapest's least-known memorials to the Holocaust.

Glass House Memorial Room

Üvegház Emlékszoba • V, Vadász utca 29 • Daily 1–4pm • Free, donations accepted • ☎ 1 242 6964, ⓦ uveghaz.org

The **Glass House Memorial Room** was named both for the extensive use of glass in its Modernist design and for its erstwhile role as a glass showroom. From 1944 to 1945, it was one of many properties in Budapest that was designated as neutral territory by the Swiss consul Carl Lutz serving as a refuge for 3000 Jews and the underground Zionist Youth organization. An **exhibition** (to the right in the courtyard) explains how Lutz and other "Righteous Gentiles" managed to save thousands of Jews from the SS and Arrow Cross death squads by issuing Schutzpasses to Jews, attesting that they were Swiss or Swedish citizens – a ruse subsequently used by Wallenberg. After the war Lutz was criticized for abusing Swiss law and, feeling slighted, proposed himself for the Nobel Peace Prize. While their co-religionists from the provinces were transported en masse to Auschwitz, the Jews of Budapest faced random executions in the heart of the capital, within full view of Parliament (see p.53) and their Gentile compatriots, who seemed more offended by the bloodshed than outraged by their murder. Inside is also the shattered marble tablet to Artur Weisz, the owner of the Glass House who was shot in 1944: it stood on the wall outside until it was smashed by neo-Nazis a few years ago.

Soviet Army Memorial

From 1921 to 1945, Szabadság tér was dominated by the Monument to Hungarian Grief – consisting of a flag at half mast and four statues called North, South, East and West – in protest at the 1920 Treaty of Trianon, which awarded two-thirds of Hungary's territory and a third of its Magyar population to the "Successor States" of Romania, Czechoslovakia and Yugoslavia. After World War II, this was replaced by a **Soviet Army Memorial** commemorating the liberation of Budapest from the Nazis, with bas-reliefs of Red Army troops and tanks advancing on Ferenciek tere and Parliament. Today, the Soviet obelisk is fenced off to protect it from vandalism by right-wing nationalists, who periodically erect a tent nearby, emblazoned with "Give us back our flag!", coyly neglecting to mention the revanchist impulse behind the original monument. István Tarlós's victory as mayor in 2010 must increase the chances of the memorial being shipped back to Moscow.

Statue of Ronald Reagan

The statue of **Ronald Reagan** was set up to mark the 100th anniversary of the former US president's birthday in 2011. The 2m-high statue, which presents him striding from Parliament into the square (he never visited the city), was erected in recognition of his role in ending the Cold War.

The Bedő House

Bedő Ház, or Magyar Szecesszió Háza • V, Honvéd utca 3 • Mon–Sat 10am–5pm • 1500Ft • ☎ 1 269 4622, ⓦ magyarszecessziohaza.hu

Behind the Soviet Army Memorial, look out for the pistachio facade of the **Bedő House**, a superb example of Hungarian Art Nouveau architecture, built by Emil Vidor in 1903. Restored after decades of neglect, it now holds the **Museum of Hungarian Art Nouveau**, displaying a private collection of furniture, graphics and interior design (check out the toilets in the basement), and with a shop selling reproduction and original pieces and a pleasant café.

The Batthyány and Nagy monuments

Two monuments off the northern corners of Szabadság tér recall very different historical figures. To the northeast at the far end of Aulich utca, a lantern on a plinth flickers with an **Eternal Flame** commemorating **Count Lajos Batthyány**. The Prime Minister of the short-lived republic declared after the 1848 War of Independence, Batthyány was executed by the Habsburgs on this spot on October 6, 1849. As a staunch patriot – but not a revolutionary – he is a hero for conservative nationalists, and his monument is the destination of marches on October 6.

To the northwest of Szabadság tér at the far end of Vécsey utca a figure stands on a footbridge in Vértanuk tere (Martyrs' Square), gazing towards Parliament. This is **Imre Nagy**, the reform Communist who became Prime Minister during the 1956 Uprising and was shot in secret two years afterwards. With his raincoat, trilby and umbrella hooked over his arm, Nagy cuts an all-too-human, flawed figure – and is scorned by those who pay homage to Batthyány.

Kossuth tér

The apotheosis of the government district and Hungary's romantic self-image comes at **Kossuth tér**, with its colossal Parliament building and memorials to national heroes and epic moments in Hungarian history. The square is named after **Lajos Kossuth**, the leader of the 1848 Revolution against the Habsburgs (see box, below), who was originally represented by a sculptural tableau showing him and his ministers downcast by their defeat in 1849. However, the Communists replaced it with a more "heroic" **statue** of Kossuth rousing the nation to arms, by Kisfaludy-Strobl (see p.109). The dramatic equestrian statue is of **Prince Ferenc Rákóczi II**, an earlier hero of the struggle for Hungarian independence, whose plinth is inscribed with the words "The wounds of the noble Hungarian nation burst open!" This is a reference to the anti-Habsburg war of 1703–11, but also perfectly describes the evening of October 23, 1956, when crowds filled the square, chanting anti-Stalinist slogans at Parliament – the prelude to the Uprising that night. To the right of the main entrance, a black pillar upholds an **Eternal Flame** (sometimes extinguished), in memory of those who died on Kossuth tér on October 25, when ÁVO snipers opened fire on a peaceful crowd that was fraternizing with Soviet tank-crews. There is another smaller monument to the massacre on the other side near the equestrian Rákóczi statue.

LAJOS KOSSUTH

Lajos Kossuth was the incarnation of post-Napoleonic bourgeois nationalism. Born into landless gentry in 1802, he began his career as a lawyer, representing absentee magnates in Parliament. His Parliamentary reports, which advocated greater liberalism than the Habsburgs would tolerate, became widely influential during the Reform era, and he was jailed for sedition. While in prison, Kossuth taught himself English by reading Shakespeare. Released in 1840, he became editor of the radical *Pesti Hírlap*, was elected to Parliament and took the helm during the 1848 Revolution.

After Serbs, Croats and Romanians rebelled against Magyar rule and the Habsburgs invaded Hungary, the Hungarians proclaimed a republic with Kossuth as de facto dictator. After the Hungarians surrendered in August 1849, Kossuth escaped to Turkey and later toured Britain and America, espousing liberty and trying to win support for the Hungarian cause. So eloquent were his denunciations of Habsburg tyranny that London brewery workers attacked General Haynau, the "Butcher of Vienna", when he visited the city. One man who did his best to undermine Kossuth's efforts was Karl Marx, who loathed Kossuth as a bourgeois radical and wrote hostile articles in the New York *Herald Tribune* and the London *Times*.

As a friend of the Italian patriot Mazzini, Kossuth spent his last years in Turin, where he died in 1894. His remains now lie in the Kerepesi Cemetery (see p.81).

Statue of Attila József

Immediately south of Parliament, close to the river, sits the brooding figure of
Attila József, one of Hungary's finest poets, who was expelled from the Communist
Party for trying to reconcile Marx and Freud, and committed suicide in 1937 after
being rejected by his lover. His powerful, turbulent verse has never lost its popularity,
and he earns his place here for his poem *By the Danube*.

Holocaust Memorial

Right on the riverbank 200m south of Parliament is a poignant **Holocaust Memorial**:
dozens of shoes cast in iron, marking the spot where hundreds of Jewish adults and
children were machine-gunned by the Arrow Cross and their bodies thrown into the
Danube. Before being massacred, they were made to remove their coats and footwear,
which were earmarked for use by German civilians. (Access from Parliament is
dangerous as it means crossing the busy embankment road; the nearest crossing is
down by the tram stop before the Lánchíd.)

2

Parliament

Országház • V, Kossuth Lajos tér • Tours in English daily at 10am, noon & 2pm; tours in other major languages at different times; the ticket
office opens at 8am (tickets sell fast) at Gate X; queue for tickets by the Eternal Flame to be admitted by guard; visitors with tickets wait
nearby • Free for EU citizens with passport, otherwise 3400Ft • ⓦ parlament.hu

The Hungarian **Parliament** building makes the Houses of Parliament in London look
humble, its architect Imre Steindl having larded Pugin's Gothic Revival style with
Renaissance and Baroque flourishes. Sprawling for 268m along the embankment, its
symmetrical wings bristle with finials and 88 statues of Hungarian rulers, surmounted
by a dome 96m high (alluding to the date of the Magyar conquest; see p.67). Though
most people are impressed by the building, the poet Gyula Illyés once famously
dismissed it as "no more than a Turkish bath crossed with a Gothic chapel" – albeit one
that cost 38,000,000 gold forints. One weakness in the design was the white limestone
of the exterior, which has been degraded by the elements and pollution; since 1925 it
has required almost constant cleaning and replacement.

For centuries, Hungarian assemblies convened wherever they could, and it wasn't
until 1843 that it was resolved to build a permanent "House of the Motherland" in
Pest-Buda (as the city was then called). By the time work began in 1885, the concept of
Parliament had changed insofar as the middle classes were now represented as well,
though over ninety percent of the population still lacked the right to vote. Gains were
made in 1918, but they were soon curtailed under the Horthy regime, just as the
attainment of universal adult suffrage in 1945 was rendered meaningless after 1948 by
a Communist dictatorship. The introduction of multiparty democracy in 1990 was
symbolized by the removal of the red star from Parliament's dome and the replacement
of Communist emblems by the traditional coat of arms featuring the crown of King
Stephen – whose Coronation Regalia is now on show in the building's Cupola Hall.

The interior – and the Coronation Regalia

Having passed through a security check, the extent to which the interior is accessible
depends on Parliament's activities, but you can be sure of seeing the main staircase, the
Cupola Hall and the Lords Chamber, if nothing else.

Despite its archaic style the building was high-tech for its time, being air-conditioned
via blocks of ice in the basement that kept it at the constant temperature of 25°C
which the architect reckoned was most conducive to thought – since modern
airconditioning was installed, MPs have complained of back pains. Statues, carvings,
gilding and mosaics are ten a penny, lit by lamps worthy of the Winter Palace – but
there are also cosy touches such as the individually numbered brass ashtrays where
peers left their cigars smouldering in the lounge while they popped back into the
chamber to hear someone speak; a good speaker was said to be "worth a Havana".

2

ST STEPHEN'S CROWN

The much revered **St Stephen's Crown**, the jewel of the Coronation Regalia on display in the Parliament building, consists in fact of two crowns joined together: the cruciform crown that was sent as a gift by Pope Sylvester II to Stephen for his coronation in 1000, and a circlet given by the Byzantine monarch to King Géza I. The distinctive bent cross was caused by the crown being squashed as it was smuggled out of a palace in a baby's cradle. At other times it has been hidden in a hay-cart or buried in Transylvania, abducted to Germany by Hungarian Fascists and thence taken to the US, where it reposed in Fort Knox until its return home in 1978, together with Stephen's crystal-headed sceptre, a fourteenth-century gold-plated orb and a sixteenth-century sword made in Vienna, used by his successors. Under the Dual Monarchy, Habsburg emperors ruled Hungary in the name of St Stephen, and travelled to Budapest for a special coronation ceremony, traditionally held in the Mátyás Church in the Vár.

Guards holding drawn sabres flank the **Coronation Regalia**, whose centrepiece, **St Stephen's Crown** (see box, above), has symbolized Hungarian statehood for over a thousand years. Don't be surprised to see loyal citizens prostrating themselves in its sacred presence. On a humbler note, you'll be shown a **scale model** of Parliament made of 100,000 matchsticks, built by a patriotic family over three years.

Statue of Mihály Károlyi

In the park just north of the Parliament is another statue, that of **Mihály Károlyi**, the Social Democratic Prime Minister after World War I (see p.210), portrayed standing below an arch. Right-wing politicians talk of removing him from this prestigious place, blaming him for Hungary's ensuing troubles.

Museum of Ethnography

Néprajzi Múzeum • V, Kossuth Lajos tér 12 • Tues–Sun 10am–6pm • 1000Ft • ⓦ neprajz.hu

Across the road from Kossuth's statue stands a neo-Renaissance building housing the **Museum of Ethnography**. Little visited by tourists, it's actually one of the finest museums in Budapest, originally built as the Palace of the Supreme Court; petitioners would have been overawed by its lofty, gilded main hall, whose ceiling bears a fresco of the goddess Justitia surrounded by allegories of Justice, Peace, Revenge and Sin.

The museum's permanent exhibition on Hungarian folk culture occupies thirteen rooms on the first floor (off the left-hand staircase) and is fully captioned in English, with an excellent catalogue available. Exhibits from all over the Carpathian Basin, including a reconstructed church interior, bear traps, painted furniture and plentiful photos, are well presented under headings such as "Institutions" and "Peasant Work", but there's only occasional reference to the range of ethnic groups who lived in Habsburg-ruled Hungary. Though few of the beautiful costumes and objects on display are part of everyday life in Hungary, you can still see them in parts of Romania, such as Maramureş and the Kalotaszeg, which belonged to Hungary before 1920.

Temporary exhibitions (on the ground and second floors) cover anything from Hindu rituals to musical instruments from around the world, while over Easter and Christmas there are **concerts** of Hungarian folk music and dancing, and **craft fairs**.

Újlipótváros

Szent István körút, the section of the Nagykörút running from Nyugati Station to the Danube, marks the end of Lipótváros – but there are a few sights further out in **Újlipótváros** (the XIII District) that are worth a mention.

Holocaust memorials

Running up from the *körút* parallel to the river is Pozsonyi út, a bustling tree-lined street leading to **Szent István Park**, the prewar social hub of a wealthy Jewish neighbourhood. The park is an apt site for a **monument to Raoul Wallenberg**, who gave up a playboy life in neutral Sweden to help the Jews of Budapest in 1944 (see p.63). The monument was constructed in the 1950s but "exiled" to Debrecen in eastern Hungary before being stashed away for decades, only taking its rightful place in Budapest in 1999.

There is another less well-known Holocaust memorial some 100m north in the riverside Vizafogó park at the end of Vező utca. The **Martyrs' Memorial**, by the Greek sculptor Agamemnon Makrisz, is a copy of the composition he made earlier for the Mauthausen concentration camp, and has nine figures standing with their arms upraised. Erected in 1986, this was the first major public memorial to the wartime murder of the Jews – and typically it was hidden away up here.

2

Lehel tér market hall

Lehel Csarnok • XIII, Lehel tér • Mon 6am–5pm, Tues–Fri 6am–6pm, Sat 6am–3pm

Heading 500m eastwards along Csanádi utca will take you to **Lehel tér**, notable for its picturesque 1930s reconstruction of the ruined **Romanesque church** at Zsámbék, west of Budapest. Beyond lies the **Lehel tér market hall**, which may look like a stylistic mishmash but has a great set of stalls selling vegetables, sausages and the like.

Terézváros and Erzsébetváros

Terézváros (Theresa Town, the VI District) is home to the State Opera House, the Academy of Music and the Hungarian equivalent of Broadway, making it one of the most vibrant parts of the city. Its main thoroughfare, Andrássy út, marking the border between it and Lipótváros, is Budapest's longest, grandest avenue, running in a perfect straight line for two and a half kilometres up to Hősök tere and the Városliget, covered in Chapter 4. With its coffee houses and grey stone edifices laden with dryads, not to mention the Opera House, the avenue retains something of the style that made it so fashionable in the 1890s, when "Bertie" the Prince of Wales drove its length in a landau, offering flowers to women as he passed.

To the south of Király utca, the mainly residential **Erzsébetváros** (Elizabeth Town, the VII District) is composed of nineteenth-century buildings whose bullet-scarred facades, adorned with fancy wrought-ironwork, conceal a warren of dwellings and leafy courtyards. There is certainly no better part of Pest to wander around, soaking up the atmosphere. The old buildings have made the district popular for a distinctive form of nightlife in the "ruin gardens": bars set up in derelict plots or old houses awaiting development or demolition.

This is also the old **Jewish quarter** of the city, which was transformed into a ghetto during the Nazi occupation and almost wiped out in 1944–45, but has miraculously retained its cultural identity. Its current resurgence owes much to increased contacts with international Jewry, and a revival of interest in their religion and roots among the eighty-thousand-strong Jewish community of Budapest, which had previously tended towards assimilation, reluctant to proclaim itself in a country where anti-Semitic prejudices linger.

ARRIVAL AND GETTING AROUND

3

Terézváros The stretch of Andrássy út up to the Oktogon – where it meets the Nagykörút (Great Boulevard) – is within walking distance of Deák tér, and the whole length of the boulevard is served by the metro. Trams circle the Nagykörút night and day, and several trolleybus lines run through the two districts out to the Városliget.

Erzsébetváros The obvious starting point for exploring the area is the Dohány utca Synagogue, a short walk down the Kiskörút from the metro interchange at Deák tér.

Terézváros

Laid out in the late nineteenth century, **Terézváros** was heavily influenced by Haussmann's redevelopment of Paris, and at that time it was one of the smartest districts in the city. Under Communism, the area became pretty run-down, but the appeal of the old apartment blocks lining its streets is now bringing in the middle classes; luxury brands such as Gucci and Louis Vuitton have moved in, the villas near the park have recovered their value and café society flourishes around Liszt Ferenc tér.

Andrássy út was inaugurated in 1884 as the Sugár (Radial) út, but was soon renamed after the statesman Count Gyula Andrássy, and it was this name which stayed in popular use throughout the years when this was officially Stalin Avenue (1949–56) or the Avenue of the People's Republic (1957–89).

Post Office Museum

Posta Múzeum • VI, Andrássy út 3 • Tues–Sun 10am–6pm • 750Ft • Ⓦ postamuzeum.hu

At the beginning of Andássy út stands the **Post Office Museum**, which occupies a fabulous old first-floor apartment complete with parquet floors, marble fireplaces, Venetian mirrors and frescoes by Károly Lotz; its owners fled to the US in 1938. Besides offering a window into how wealthy Budapestis lived before World War II, it also features a wealth of postal exhibits including a compressed-air mail tube, vintage delivery vehicles and a display on the inventor and telephone pioneer Tivadar Puskás, a colleague of Thomas Edison, with English information sheets in each room. Press #10 on the entry-phone to gain access to the building – note the magnificent decorations on the stairway up to the museum.

The State Opera House

Állami Operaház • VI, Andrássy út 22 • English-language tours of the interior daily 3pm & 4pm • 2900Ft • Ⓦ opera.hu (for programmes), Ⓦ operavisit.hu (for tours)

The **State Opera House** was founded by Ferenc Erkel, the composer of Hungary's national anthem, and occupies a magnificent neo-Renaissance pile built in 1875–84 by Miklós Ybl. It can boast of being directed by Mahler (who was driven out by the anti-Semitism he experienced in the city), hosting performances conducted by

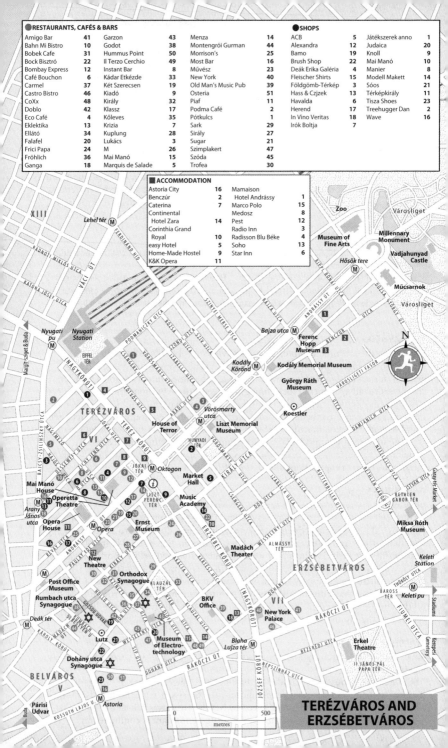

RESTAURANTS, CAFÉS & BARS

Amigo Bar	41	Garzon	43	Menza	14
Bahn Mi Bistro	10	Godot	38	Montengrói Gurman	44
Bobek Cafe	31	Hummus Point	50	Morrison's	25
Bock Bisztró	22	Il Terzo Cerchio	49	Most Bar	16
Bombay Express	12	Instant Bar	8	Művész	23
Café Bouchon	6	Kádár Etkézde	33	New York	40
Carmel	37	Két Szerecsen	19	Old Man's Music Pub	39
Castro Bistro	46	Kiadó	9	Osteria	51
CoXx	48	Király	32	Piaf	11
Doblo	42	Klassz	17	Podma Café	2
Eco Café	4	Kőleves	35	Pótkulcs	1
Eklektika	13	Krizia	7	Sark	29
Ellátó	34	Kuplung	28	Sirály	27
Falafel	20	Lukács	3	Sugar	21
Frici Papa	24	M	26	Szimplakert	47
Fröhlich	36	Mai Manó	15	Szóda	45
Ganga	18	Marquis de Salade	5	Trofea	30

SHOPS

ACB	5	Játékszerek anno	1
Alexandra	12	Judaica	20
Bamo	19	Knoll	9
Brush Shop	22	Mai Manó	10
Deák Erika Galéria	4	Manier	8
Fleischer Shirts	15	Modell Makett	14
Földgömb-Térkép	3	Sóos	21
Hass & Czjzek	13	Térképkirály	11
Havalda	6	Tisza Shoes	23
Herend	17	Treehugger Dan	2
In Vino Veritas	18	Wave	16
Irók Boltja	7		

ACCOMMODATION

Astoria City	16	Mamaison	
Benczúr	2	Hotel Andrássy	1
Caterina	7	Marco Polo	15
Continental		Medosz	8
Hotel Zara	14	Pest	12
Corinthia Grand		Radio Inn	3
Royal	10	Radisson Blu Béke	4
easy Hotel	5	Soho	13
Home-Made Hostel	9	Star Inn	6
K&K Opera	11		

TERÉZVÁROS AND ERZSÉBETVÁROS

0		500
	metres	

Otto Klemperer and Antal Doráti, and sheltering two hundred local residents (including Kodály) in its cellars during the siege of Budapest. The 1260-seat auditorium was the first in Europe to feature an iron fire curtain (installed after a blaze at the Vienna Opera House), underfloor heating and air conditioning. Its chandelier weighs three tonnes, and 2.7 kilos of gold were used to gild the fixtures. To the left of the stage is the box used by Emperor Franz Josef's wife, Sisi (see p.149), who loved Hungarian opera as much as he detested it. The upstairs reception rooms and downstairs foyer are equally lavish, festooned with portraits and busts of Hungarian divas and composers. Tickets for tours are available from the shop to the left in the foyer; see p.186 regarding tickets for performances.

New Theatre

Új Színház • VI, Paulay Ede utca 35 • W ujszinhaz.hu

Tucked behind the old Ballet Institute on the opposite side of Andrássy from the Opera House, stands the **New Theatre**, whose blue and gold Art Deco facade and foyer (by Béla Lajta in 1909) look superb. However, in 2011 a new nationalist team, was appointed to the theatre; its members, among them playwright and former far-right politician István Csurka, talk about rescuing Hungarians from the yolk of the "sickly liberal hegemony".

Nagymező utca

Continuing from the Opera House along Andrássy you'll pass one of Budapest's venerable coffee houses on the right-hand side, the *Művész* (no. 29), where the magnificent interior is more enticing than the cakes or service.

The next major junction is **Nagymező utca** – nicknamed "**Broadway**" because of its theatres and nightclubs. Outside the Operetta Theatre at no. 17 take a look at the **statue** of the composer **Imre Kálmán**, lounging on a bench. Better known to the world as Emmerich Kalman, he penned such operetta favourites as *The Gypsy Princess* and *Countess Maritsa* – it's a genre that wins Hungarian hearts with its combination of music and melodrama. Strangely, the statue has a bronze computer beside it: the idea was that you could look at the theatre's website on it, but that did not account for vandals.

Mai Manó House (Hungarian House of Photography)

Mai Manó Ház (Magyar Fotográfusok Háza) • VI, Nagymező utca 20 • Mon–Fri 2–7pm, Sat, Sun & holidays 11am–7pm • 700Ft • W maimano.hu

During the interwar years, the best-known club on Nagymező utca was the Arizona at no. 20: "the most glamorous nightclub I have ever visited," said Patrick Leigh Fermor, who went there on his way across Europe. It was run by Sándor Rozsnyai and his wife, Miss Arizona. However, he was sent to a concentration camp and she was murdered by the Arrow Cross in 1944 (which inspired Pál Sándor's 1988 film, *Miss Arizona*, starring Hanna Schygulla and Marcello Mastroianni). The bottle-green-tiled building was the former home of the Habsburg court photographer **Mai Manó**, which made it a fitting choice for the photography museum that occupies it today. It hosts temporary exhibitions in three separate galleries, and an excellent photographic bookshop on the first floor – the café on the ground floor does great pastries.

Ernst Museum

Ernst Múzeum • VI, Nagymező utca 8 • Tues–Sun 11am–7pm • 700Ft • W mucsarnok.hu

On the far side of Andrássy the first-floor **Ernst Museum** is a venue for temporary contemporary art exhibitions, affiliated to the Műcsarnok on Hősök tere (see p.68). It's worth a peek inside to see the Art Nouveau features by József Rippl-Rónai and Ödön Lechner; take a look at the Art Deco lobby of the Tivoli Theatre next door, too.

Miklós Radnóti statue

Across Nagymező utca, outside the theatre at no. 11 that takes his name, lounges a statue of one of Hungary's finest poets, **Miklós Radnóti**, whose most powerful poems were written while serving in a Jewish labour brigade in the war. When his body was exhumed eighteen months after he was shot in 1944 a notebook of his last poems was discovered in his pocket.

Paris Department Store

A couple of doors up from Nagymező utca is the striking Art Nouveau frontage of Budapest's first department store, with a glass facade that soars up five floors. When the **Paris Department Store** opened in 1911 it boasted a roof terrace and even an ice rink. Today it is a large bookstore, but it's worth having a look inside to see how the recent restoration has preserved the sweeping lines of the interior. There is a surprising contrast on the first floor at the back of the shop: the **Lotz terem**, which was a ballroom dating from 1885 in a neighbouring casino, is magnificently decorated in frescoes by Károly Lotz, and today holds a café with comfy armchairs.

Jókai Mór tér and Liszt Ferenc tér

Close to the Oktogon, two elongated squares stretch out on either side of Andrássy út, lined with pavement **cafés**. On the left is **Jókai Mór tér**, with a large statue of the novelist Mór Jókai, while on the right is **Liszt Ferenc tér**, crammed with the terraces of bars and restaurants. In the middle of the square, the composer Liszt hammers an imaginary keyboard with his vast hands, blind to the drinkers and diners surrounding him. At the far end, the **Music Academy** that bears his name (no. 8) contains a magnificent Art Nouveau entrance hall designed by Aladár Körösfői Kriesch, and two gilded auditoriums whose glorious decor matches the quality of the music there – at least when it opens its doors in 2013 after a major reconstruction.

The Oktogon

Andrássy út meets the Nagykörút at the **Oktogon**, an eight-sided square flanked by eclectic buildings. With 24-hour fast-food chains ensconced in two of them, and trams and taxis running along the Nagykörút through to the small hours, the Oktogon never sleeps. During the Horthy era it rejoiced in the name of Mussolini tér, while under the Communists it was called November 7 tér after the date of the Bolshevik revolution.

The House of Terror

Terror Háza • VI, Andrássy út 60 • Tues–Sun 10am–6pm • 1800Ft • Ⓦ terrorhaza.hu

You can't miss the **House of Terror**, due to the ominous black frame that surmounts the building, once the dreaded headquarters of the secret police. Dubbed the "House of Loyalty" by the Fascist Arrow Cross during World War II, it was subsequently used for the same purpose by the Communist ÁVO (see box, p.61). When captured by insurgents in 1956, no trace was found of the giant meat-grinder rumoured to have been used to dispose of corpses; after the re-imposition of Soviet rule, the building was thoroughly sanitized before being handed over to the Communist Youth organization.

Opened in 2002 as a cross between a museum and a memorial, the House of Terror has been criticized for its selective approach to terror. Its public treatment of the Stalinist years is much needed but terror in twentieth-century Hungary extended far further. The fleeting reference to the Holocaust and the irrelevant introductory film about the break-up of Hungary after World War I rob this powerful exhibition of the respect it should merit.

The moment you step in through the spooky automatic door you're bombarded with funereal sounds and powerful images, starting with a Soviet tank and photos of ÁVO victims in the courtyard, while the video in the lobby repeatedly plays the image of a man weeping at the execution of 1956 insurgents, saying, "this was their socialism". An audio-guide (1000Ft) can save you the trouble of reading the English-language sheets

THE ÁVO

The **Communist secret police** began as the Party's private security section during the Horthy era, when its chief, **Gábor Péter**, betrayed Trotskyites to the police to take the heat off their Stalinist comrades. After World War II it became the 9000-strong Államvédelmi Osztály or **ÁVO** (State Security Department), its growing power implicit in a change of name in 1948 – to the State Security Authority or **ÁVH** (though the old acronym stuck). Ex-Nazi torturers were easily persuaded to apply their skills on its behalf, and its network of 41,000 informers permeated society. So hated was the ÁVO that any members caught during the Uprising were summarily killed, and their mouths stuffed with banknotes (secret policemen earned more than anyone else).

in each room, but the latter pack far more information. The displays begin on the second floor (you take the lift, then work downwards). The murder of 600,000 Jews and Gypsies is summarily dealt with in a room or two, before you get to the main subject of the museum: the Soviet "liberation", deportations of "class enemies", rigged elections, collectivization and other themes. The most harrowing part is the **basement**, with its reconstructed torture chamber and cells, where the music mercifully stops and the exhibits are allowed to speak for themselves.

Hunyadi tér

Crossing Andrássy út from the House of Terror brings you to **Hunyadi tér**, which has a fine old market hall (*vásárcsarnok*) that has not yet been modernized, and some fruit and vegetable stalls under the trees in the square itself.

The Liszt Memorial Museum

Liszt Ferenc Emlékmúzeum • Andrássy út 67 • Mon–Fri 10am–6pm, Sat 9am–5pm; closed on national holidays • 900Ft • Concerts every Sat at 11am, 900Ft, which includes entry to the museum; Budapest Card covers entry to the museum but not concert tickets • ⓦ lisztmuseum.hu

Returning to Andrássy from Hunyadi tér and turning right, you come to the Old Music Academy. This harbours the **Liszt Memorial Museum**, entered from Vörösmarty utca 35, where the composer – who was the first president of the Academy – lived from 1881 until his death in 1886. His glass piano and travelling keyboard are the highlights of an extensive collection of memorabilia and scores. Young pianists perform concerts here every Saturday.

Kodály körönd

Kodály körönd, named after the composer Zoltán Kodály, is one of Budapest's most elegant squares, flanked by four neo-Renaissance mansions that are finally getting a much-needed restoration. During World War II the *körönd* (circus) was named Hitler tér, prompting the émigré Bartók to vow that he would not be buried in Hungary so long as anywhere in the country was named after Hitler or Mussolini.

Kodály Memorial Museum

Kodály Emlékmúzeum • VI, Kodály körönd 1 • Wed–Fri 10am–noon & 1.30–4.30pm by prior appointment only on ☎ 1 352 7106 or ✉ kodalym@enternet.hu • 900Ft • ⓦ kodaly-inst.hu

In the northeast corner of Kodály körönd, the ground-floor flat where Zoltán Kodály lived until his death in 1967 now houses the **Kodály Memorial Museum**, preserving his library, salon, dining room and folk-art collection – press #11 buzzer to get in.

Ferenc Hopp Museum

Hopp Ferenc Múzeum • VI, Andrássy út 103 • Tues–Sun 10am–6pm • 1000Ft • ⓦ hoppmuzeum.hu

Two fine displays of Asian art lurk just beyond the Kodály körönd. The **Ferenc Hopp Museum** presents temporary displays of works from the vast collection of more than 20,000 items amassed by optician and art collector Ferenc Hopp (1833–1919), with pieces from Japan, China, India, Korea, Indonesia and Vietnam. One item on permanent display is the imposing Chinese moon gate standing in the garden.

György Ráth Museum

Ráth György Múzeum • VI, Városligeti fasor 12 • Open by appointment only: ask at the Ferenc Hopp Museum (see p.61) three days in advance or ring ☎ 1 456 5110 or email ✉ hoppmuzeum@imm.hu • 600Ft

In an Art Nouveau villa on Városligeti fasor, which runs parallel to Andrássy and is lined with even finer mansions, the **György Ráth Museum** displays artefacts from the same collection as the Ferenc Hopp Museum (see p.61). The statue in the garden of a Buddhist monk actually depicts Sándor Kőrösi-Csoma, a Hungarian who achieved fame by compiling the first English–Tibetan dictionary, though his real goal was a vain search for the ancestors of the Hungarian people. Highlights include an early fourteenth-century lacquer Water-Moon Guanyin Bodhisattva in the Chinese collection, a seventeenth- to eighteenth-century gilt bronze Buddha in the Mongolian collection, and a fifteenth-century Kalachakra mandala in the Tibetan Collection.

Erzsébetváros

One of the centres of the new cool Budapest is **Erzsébetváros**, separated from **Terézváros** by the narrow **Király utca** (the main road through the area before Andrássy út was built). The vibrant "ruin garden" (*romkert*) movement that has spread through the city started here among the decaying apartment blocks and empty plots of the old **Jewish quarter** (see box, below). The run-down stock of the district is also attracting big money in housing and retail developments such the **Madách sétany**, cutting swathes through the old city, or doing up older parts such as the Gozsdu-udvar or Kazinczy utca.

The Dohány utca Synagogue

Dohány utcai Zsinagóga • VII, Dohány utca 2–8 • March–Oct Mon–Thurs & Sun 10am–5.30pm, Fri 10am–3.30pm; Nov–Feb Mon–Thurs & Sun 10am–3.30pm, Fri 10am–1.30pm • 2000Ft including the Jewish Museum • 🌐 greatsynagogue.hu

The splendid **Dohány utca Synagogue** (also known as the Great Synagogue, Nagy Zsinagóga) is one of the landmarks of Pest. Located only five minutes' walk from Deák tér, just off Károly körút, it is Europe's largest synagogue and the second biggest in the

---

THE JEWISH QUARTER

In the streets fanning out to the east of Károly körút lies Budapest's old **Jewish quarter**. After Josef II's reforms in 1783 allowed Jews back into Pest for the first time since the defeat of the Turks, they were invited to live in the grounds of Count Orczy's house between Király utca and Madách tér. Thereafter they flourished, and the Pest community grew from eight percent of the population in 1800 to twenty-three percent in 1920. In April 1944 this was chosen by the Nazis as the location of Budapest's Jewish **ghetto** – a sign on Wesselényi utca by the synagogue marks where the ghetto gate stood. All Jews living outside the ghetto were compelled to move in. As their menfolk had already been conscripted into labour battalions intended to kill them from overwork, the 70,000 inhabitants of the ghetto were largely women, children and old folk, crammed into 162 blocks of flats, with over 50,000 of them (in buildings meant for 15,000) around Klauzál tér alone.

JEWISH QUARTER WALKING TOURS

English-language guided walking tours of the area, run by Aviv (Sip utca 12 ☎ 1 462 0477, 🌐 aviv.hu), depart from the Dohány utca Synagogue (daily except Sat at 10.30am, 11.30am, 12.30pm & 1.30pm; April–Oct also 2.30pm & 3.30pm). The cheapest tour (2650Ft) simply covers the synagogue and memorial garden; another (3000Ft) includes the Jewish Museum, while the most expensive (3650Ft) also features the Rumbach utca Synagogue. For a fascinating personalized walking tour of the entire quarter, contact Eszter Gömöri (✉ bp.cityguide@gmail .com), who charges €20 an hour.

world after the Temple Emmanuel in New York, with 3600 seats and a total capacity for over 5000 worshippers. It belongs to the **Neolog** community, a Hungarian denomination combining elements of Reform and Orthodox Judaism. Today, eighty percent of Hungarian Jewry are Neologs, but their numbers amounted to only twenty percent before the Holocaust, which virtually wiped out the Orthodox and Hassid communities in the provinces. Neolog worship includes features that are anathema to other denominations, not least organ music during services.

Designed by a Viennese Gentile, Ludwig Förster, the building epitomizes the so-called Byzantine-Moorish style that was popular in the 1850s, and attests to the patriotism of Hungarian Jewry – the colours of its brickwork (yellow, red and blue) being those of Budapest's coat of arms. In the 1990s the synagogue was restored at a cost of over $40 million; the work was funded by the Hungarian government and the Hungarian-Jewish diaspora, notably the Emmanuel Foundation, fronted by the Hollywood actor Tony Curtis who was born of 1920s emigrants.

The interior
You have time to admire the gilded onion-domed towers while waiting to pass through a security check, before entering the magnificent **interior** by Frigyes Feszl, the architect of the Vigadó concert hall. Arabesques and Stars of David decorate the ceiling, the balconies for female worshippers are surmounted by gilded arches, and the floor is inset with eight-pointed stars. The layout reflects the synagogue's Neolog identity, with the *bemah*, or Ark of the Torah, at one end, in the Reform fashion, but with men and women seated apart, according to Orthodox tradition. On Jewish festivals, the place is filled to the rafters with Jews from all over Hungary, whose chattering disturbs their more devout co-religionists. At other times, the hall is used for concerts of classical or klezmer music, as advertised outside.

The Jewish Museum
Heading up to the second-floor **Jewish Museum** (Zsidó Múzeum), to the left of the main synagogue entrance, note a relief of Tivadar (Theodor) Herzl, the founder of modern Zionism, who was born and taught on this site. (The square in front of the museum, Herzl Tivadar tér, commemorates him.) In the foyer is a gravestone inscribed with a menorah (seven-branched candlestick) from the third century AD – proof that there were Jews living in Hungary six hundred years before the Magyars arrived. The first three rooms are devoted to Jewish festivals, with beautifully crafted objects such as Sabbath lamps and bowls for the Seder festival, some from medieval times. The final room covers the Holocaust in Hungary, with chilling photos and examples of anti-Semitic propaganda. Oddly, the museum says nothing about the huge contribution that Jews have made to Hungarian society, in every field from medicine to poetry.

The cemetery and Heroes' Temple
The **cemetery** beside the synagogue only exists at this spot because the Nazis forbade Jews from being buried elsewhere – one of many calculated humiliations inflicted on the Jewish quarter (by then a walled ghetto) by the local SS commander, Eichmann. Some 2281 Jews are interred beneath simple headstones, erected immediately after the Red Army's liberation of the ghetto on January 18, 1945. Beyond the cemetery looms the cuboid, domed **Heroes' Temple**, erected in 1929–31 in honour of the 10,000 Jewish soldiers who died fighting for Hungary during World War I. These days it serves as a synagogue for everyday use and may not be open to tourists unless you are on an organized tour (see p.62).

Raoul Wallenberg Memorial Garden
Upon leaving the synagogue, turn the corner on to Wesselényi utca and enter the **Raoul Wallenberg Memorial Garden**, named after the Swedish consul who saved 20,000 Jews

during World War II. Armed with diplomatic status and money for bribing officials, Wallenberg and his assistants plucked thousands from the cattle trucks and lodged them in "safe houses", manoeuvring to buy time until the Russians arrived. He was last seen alive the day before the Red Army liberated the ghetto; arrested by the Soviets on suspicion of espionage, he died in the Gulag. The park's centrepiece is a **Holocaust Memorial** by Imre Varga, shaped like a weeping willow, each leaf engraved with the names of a family killed by the Nazis. On the plinth are testimonials from their relatives living in Israel, America and Russia. Behind it, glass panels by the artist Klára Szilárd commemorate the sixtieth anniversary of the neighbouring Goldmark Hall.

Goldmark Hall

Goldmark terem, • VII, Wesselényi utca 7 • Mon–Thurs & Sun 10am–6pm, Fri 10am–4pm • 800Ft but it's cheaper to buy a combined ticket with the synagogue (2250Ft) which takes you through the memorial garden

Named after Károly Goldmark, the composer of the opera *The Queen of Sheba*, the **Goldmark Hall** houses the fascinating small Jewish Quarter exhibition. This display of objects from the **Jewish Archives** include the screenplay for a performance of *The Magic Flute* performed in the Hall in 1942, and a coffee grinder that was one family's sole possession to survive the Holocaust, as well as old films and photos of the area.

Monument to Carl Lutz

Heading north up Rumbach Sebestyén utca from the Great Synagogue you'll cross Dob utca, where you'll see a **monument to Carl Lutz**, the Swiss consul who saved many Jewish lives during the war (see p.51). His monument – a gilded angel swooping down to help a prostrate victim – is locally known as "the figure jumping out of a window".

Rumbach utca Synagogue

Rumbach utca zsinagóga • VII, Rumbach Sebestyén utca 11–13 • Mon–Thurs 10am–3.30pm, Fri 10am–2.30pm, Sun 10am–5.30pm • 500Ft

In happier times, each Jewish community within the quarter had its own place of worship, with a *yeshiva* (religious school) and other facilities within an enclosed courtyard invisible from the surrounding streets – as epitomized by the **Rumbach utca Synagogue**. Built by Otto Wagner in 1872, for the so-called "Status Quo" or middling-conservative Jews, it now belongs to the Neolog community and stands restored but empty. Decorated in violet, crimson and gold, its octagonal Moorish interior hosts occasional exhibitions and concerts. As a plaque outside notes, the building served as a detention barracks in August 1941, from where up to 1800 Slovak and Polish refugees were deported to the Nazi death camps.

Király utca

The official boundary between Terézváros and **Erzsébetváros** runs down the middle of **Király utca**, once the main street here before Andrássy út was built. In the 1870s it contained fourteen of the 58 licensed brothels in Budapest, and as late as 1934 Patrick Leigh Fermor was told that "any man could be a cavalier for five pengöes" here. After decades of shabby respectability under Communism the street is undergoing a revival, with numerous cafés, bars and restaurants popping up here, plus interior design and furniture boutiques.

Gozsdu-udvar

At Király utca 11 a grey stone portal leads into the **Gozsdu-udvar**, a 200m-long passageway built in 1904 and running through to Dob utca 16. Connecting seven courtyards, it was a hive of life and activity before the Holocaust; after many years of dereliction, it has now been sensitively redeveloped and new restaurants and shops once again populate this atmospheric space. As you walk down the Gozsdu-udvar, you cross the **Madách Walk** (Madách sétány), a hotly debated plan to modernize the district – or rip out its heart, depending on whom you listen to. The Walk, which was first mooted in the 1930s, runs parallel to Király utca, stretching from Madách tér on the Kiskörút through to the Nagykörút. A swathe is being cut through the atmospheric but decaying apartment blocks to clear the way for jazzy shops, restaurants and apartments – so far, Madách Walk has reached Kazinczy utca.

Dob and Kazinczy utcas

These two streets form the axis of the 3000-strong Orthodox community. At Dob utca 22 the *Fröhlich* patisserie is a popular haunt for locals and visitors, while further along there's a wigmaker at no. 31 and a kosher butcher at no. 35. Down to the right on Kazinczy utca are a kosher baker and pizzeria, opposite the kosher *Carmel* restaurant. The recent pedestrianizing of this section of the street makes it all the more enjoyable to wander around.

Orthodox Synagogue

VII, Kazinczy utca 29 • Sun–Thurs 10am–3.30pm, Fri 10am–12.30pm • 1000Ft

3

Looming over the middle of Kazinczy utca is the **Orthodox Synagogue**, built by Béla and Sándor Löffler in 1913 in the Art Nouveau style, with a facade melding into the curve of the street, and an interior with painted rather than moulded motifs. A smaller wood-panelled synagogue for winter use, a *yeshiva* and the *Hanna* Orthodox kosher restaurant are all contained within an L-shaped courtyard that can also be entered via an arcade on Dob utca.

The Museum of Electrotechnology

Magyar Elektrotechnikai Múzeum • Kazinczy utca 21 • Tues–Fri 10am–5pm, Sat 9am–6pm • 400Ft • ⓦ emuzeum.hu

For something quite different to the rest of the sights in the Jewish quarter visit the **Museum of Electrotechnology**, set in a former electricity substation. Its devoted curators can demonstrate the world's first dynamo (invented in 1859 by Áynos Jedlik, a Benedictine monk), tie irons and a child-proof plug from 1902 in rooms devoted to such topics as the history of light bulbs and the Hungarian section of the **Iron Curtain**, along the border with Austria. Captions are in Hungarian only, but the beauty of early domestic electrical contraptions comes across anyway.

Dohány utca

Dohány utca takes its name – Tobacco Street – from the tobacco factory that once stood on the corner of Sip utca – close to the sadly neglected Art Deco **Metro Klub** that stands there now. This narrow thoroughfare sweeps through the lower part of Erzsébetváros from the Kiskörút and out across the Nagykörút towards the Garment District.

The Hungária Baths

Halfway between the two *körúts* you pass the magnificent Art Nouveau front of the ill-fated **Hungária Baths** at no. 44 Dohány utca. When the complex opened in 1908 its main selling point – its large number of private bathtubs – was its downfall, as the building of better-equipped apartments reduced demand. The baths closed in 1929, and were used after the war as a cinema and then as a theatre until 1965. By the 1980s the inside was crumbling fast and the baths were close to complete – the little that could be saved can be seen on the facade and in the lobby of the *Zara* hotel that now stands in its place.

The New York Palace

At the junction of Dohány utca and the Nagykörút is a piece of old Budapest that for many years lay derelict. Like the Gresham Palace on Széchenyi tér (see p.47), the

New York Palace on the corner of the Nagykörút is a Budapest landmark also associated with an insurance company, in this case the New York, which commissioned the building in 1895 and included in the plans a magnificent coffee house, which became one of the great literary cafés of interwar Budapest. Under Communism the edifice housed a publishers, and its Beaux-Arts facade – with a small Statue of Liberty high up on the corner – survived being rammed by a tank in 1956. Now reopened as a luxury hotel, its gilded and frescoed restaurant-cum-coffee house is worth a look, even if you don't want to fork out to eat there.

Garment District

At the far end of Dohány utca the district changes, becoming more working class and tinged with Arab and Chinese influences as you near the "**Garment District**" around **Garay tér**. The bustling **market** on the square is a lunch spot for workers from the sweatshops in a neighbourhood where wholesalers do business in a dozen languages and travel agents offer trips to Mecca.

3

Miksa Róth Museum

Róth Miksa Múzeum • VII, Nefelejcs utca 26 • Tues–Sun 2–6pm • 800Ft • ⓦ rothmuzeum.hu

In the backstreets near Keleti Station, the **Miksa Róth Museum** showcases the work of a leading figure in the Hungarian Art Nouveau movement. Located in Róth's former home, the museum reveals the diversity of his work – both in stained glass and in mosaics – which can also be seen in the Parliament, the Gresham Palace, the Music Academy and the Jewish Museum.

The Városliget and the stadium district

Both Hősök tere (Heroes' Square) and the Városliget (City Park), at the end of Andrássy út, were created in the late nineteenth century for the nationwide celebrations of the millennium of the Magyar conquest of Hungary, but as neither was ready on time the anniversary was rescheduled for the following year. Historians revised the date of the conquest accordingly and have stuck to 896 ever since. Today, the chief attractions are the Museum of Fine Arts and the romantic Vajdahunyad Castle, followed by a wallow in the Széchenyi Baths. Budapest's zoo, circus and amusement park are also located here, along with a handful of other museums. Nearby are several indoor and outdoor stadiums, and one of Budapest's Art Nouveau masterpieces, the Geological Institute.

ARRIVAL

Városliget The best ways to reach the Városliget from the centre are on the yellow #1 metro line or bus #105, but trolleybus #74 from the Dohány utca Synagogue, #75 from the Margít híd and #72 from Arany János utca metro station are also useful.

The stadium district To reach the stadium district, catch trolleybus #75 or the red #2 metro line from the centre of town to the Puskás Ferenc Stadion stop.

Hősök tere

The enormous ceremonial plaza of **Hősök tere** is flanked by two galleries resembling Greek temples. At its centre is the **Millennary Monument** – Budapest's version of Nelson's Column in London – consisting of a 36m-high column topped by the figure of the Archangel Gabriel who, according to legend, appeared to Stephen in a dream and offered him the crown of Hungary. Around the base are figures of Prince Árpád and his chieftains, who led the seven Magyar tribes into the Carpathian Basin. They look like a wild bunch; one of the chieftains, Huba, even has stag's antlers strapped to his horse's head. As a backdrop to this, a semicircular colonnade displays statues of Hungary's most illustrious leaders, from King Stephen to Kossuth.

During the brief Republic of Councils in 1919, when the country was governed by revolutionary Soviets, the square was decked out in red banners and the column enclosed in a red obelisk bearing a relief of Marx. In 1989, it was the setting for the ceremonial reburial of Imre Nagy and other murdered leaders of the 1956 Uprising (plus an empty coffin representing the "unknown insurgent") – an event which symbolized the dawning of a new era in Hungary. Today it's more likely to be filled with rollerbladers and skateboarders – for whom the smooth surface is ideal – and tourists, or for hosting **events** such as Army Day in May or the National Gallop in September.

Műcsarnok (Exhibition Hall)

XIV, Hősök tere • Tues, Wed & Fri–Sun 10am–6pm, Thurs noon–8pm • 1400Ft, combined ticket with the Ernst Museum (p.59) 1600Ft • Ⓦ mucsarnok.hu

On the southeast side of the Hősök tere is the **Műcsarnok** (Exhibition Hall), also called the Palace of Art (not to be confused with the Palace of Arts, covered on p.85). A Grecian pile with gilded columns and a mosaic of St Stephen as patron of the arts, it was inaugurated in 1895. Its magnificent facade and foyer are in contrast to the four austere rooms used for **temporary exhibitions** (two or three at a time), often of modern art.

Museum of Fine Arts

Szépművészeti Múzeum • XIV, Hősök tere • Tues–Sun 10am–5.30pm with late opening on alternative Thurs till 10pm • 1600Ft • Free guided tours in English Tues–Fri 11am & 2pm, Sat 11am • Audio-guide 1000Ft • Temporary exhibitions 2200–3600Ft which includes entry to permanent collection • Ⓦ szepmuveszeti.hu

On the northwest side of Hősök tere, the **Museum of Fine Arts** is the pan-European equivalent of the Hungarian National Gallery, housed in an imposing Neoclassical building completed in 1906, though without the gilt of the Műcsarnok. Most exhibits are labelled in English and a free floor-plan is available, but if you want more information you should go on an English-language **tour** or rent an **audio-guide**. (The continued rearrangement of the museum's collection, the loaning of pictures and **temporary exhibitions** can alter the layout of pictures described here.) Special **events** – music and guided tours – are held on late-opening Thursdays, as advertised on the website. Art historians may be drawn to the **library** a treasure-trove of information in various languages, housed nearby at VI, Szondi utca 77 (ask at the museum information desk for more details).

Lower ground floor

In the museum's bowels, a hippopotamus-tusk wand carved with spells to protect a child presages the small but choice **Egyptian Collection**, chiefly from the Late Period and Greco-Roman eras of Egyptian civilization. The highlights of the first room are four huge painted coffins and a child-sized one from Gamhud in Middle Egypt; *shabti* figures, intended to perform menial tasks in the afterlife; and mummified crocodiles and other creatures from the Late Period, when animal cults reached their apogee. In the second room, look out for the sculpted heads of a priestess of Hathor and a bewigged youth from the New Kingdom, the painted coffin of a priestess of Amun (bearing an uncanny resemblance to Julia Roberts), and a tautly poised bronze of the cat goddess Bastet.

Across the basement lobby, the section entitled **Art around 1900** starts with **Symbolist** and **Decadent** works such as Franz von Stuck's *The Kiss of the Sphinx*, Arnold Böcklin's *Spring Evening*, and Hans Makart's *Nessus Carries off Deianeira*. The remainder musters a few works by the Hungarian **Art Nouveau** masters József Rippl-Rónai and Károly Ferenczy (better showcased in the National Gallery; see pp.96–99), an Utrillo street scene, some Bonnards and two famous images by **Oscar Kokoschka**: *Veronica's Veil* and the poster *Der Sturm*.

Ground floor

The rooms to the right of the entrance lobby are devoted to **ancient Mediterranean cultures** from Etruria to Athens, mainly represented by jugs and vases. Highlights include a pair of bronze shin-guards decorated with rams' heads, terracotta tiles portraying bestial deities, a man's torso and head from the pediment of a Campanian temple, lifelike busts of Roman worthies, and an early fifth-century BC Etruscan grave marker with reliefs of funerary games.

Across the ground-floor lobby is an excellent **bookshop**, leading to a wing used for **temporary exhibitions** (requiring a separate ticket). Before heading upstairs, visit the grand **Renaissance Hall**, used for hanging large allegorical or religious works on loan from other museums; the **Baroque Hall** (often used for televised events), and the **Prints and Drawings Room** at the far end on the right, mounting temporary displays (free) drawn from the museum's holdings of works by Raphael, Leonardo, Rembrandt, Rubens, Dürer, Picasso and Chagall.

The first floor: the Spanish Collection

The museum's forte is its hoard of **Old Masters**, based on the collection of Count Miklós Esterházy, which he sold to the state in 1871. The room numbering can make

VÁROSLIGET AND THE STADIUMS

navigation here confusing: the main rooms have Roman numerals and smaller ones down the sides have Arabic digits.

The **Spanish Collection** of seventy works is arguably the best in the world outside Spain. Located off to the right at the top of the stairs, it kicks off with vivid altarpieces by unknown Catalonians, such as the *Bishop-Saint Enthroned* (whose bewilderment belies his magnificent attire) in room II. Room V, beyond, has seven **El Grecos** – including *The Disrobing of Christ, The Agony in the Garden, The Apostle St Andrew* and *The Penitent Magdalene* – and a superb *Adoration of the Magi* by Eugenio Cajes.

Murillo's *Flight into Egypt* and *Holy Family with the Infant St John the Baptist* hang beside a tender *Holy Family* by **Zurbarán** in room IV; across the room are two depictions of St Andrew, one by Zurbarán and the gory *Martyrdom of St Andrew* by **Ribera**, together with **Velázquez**'s *Tavern Scene*. Room III next door has five **Goyas** ranging from war scenes (*2nd of May*) to portraits of the rich (*Señora Ceán Bermudez*) and humble (*The Knife-Grinder*). Murillo's *Madonna and Child with Angels Playing Music* is a highlight of room VI, and there's an annexe of Habsburg court portraits by Juan Martinez (room 1).

The Flemish Collection

Entering the adjacent **Flemish Collection** in room VII, Snyders' gigantic *Hawk in the Barnyard* and Van Valckenborch's nocturnal *Pilgrims Before a Forest* are overshadowed by room VIII, where the serenity of **Van Dyck**'s *St John the Evangelist* contrasts with the melodrama of **Rubens**' *Mucius Scaevola before Porsenna* and **Jordaens**' *The Satyr and the Peasant.*

Room IX segues into the **Dutch Collection** with an array of **Brueghels**, from Pieter the Elder's *Sermon of St John the Baptist* to Pieter the Younger's *Blind Hurdy-Gurdy Player* and Jan's *Paradise Landscape* and *Garden of Eden with the Fall of Man*. A copy of **Bosch**'s *The Bacchus Singers* (featuring a man making himself vomit) hangs in room 7. The rest of the Dutch collection is on the floor above, reached by stairs (or a lift) off room IX. There you'll find the *Parable of the Hidden Treasure* by **Rembrandt** and his pupil Gerard Dou and other works from his studio in room XVIII to the right, with portraits by **Hals** and wildlife scenes by **Melchior de Houdeleoter** in rooms XXVII and XXVI, off to the left.

The German Collection

Back on the first floor, in room X, the **German Collection** opens with **Angelika Kauffmann**'s *The Wife of Count Esterházy as Venus* – a strumpet with her jewellery box – and darkly Gothic works by **Cranach the Elder**, such as *Christ and the Adulteress* and *The Lamentation, and the Holy Virgin in Prayer by* **Dürer**. In *Salome with the Head of St John the Baptist,* Salome displays his head on a platter with the nonchalance of a hostess bringing out the roast. Every emotion from awe to jealousy appears on the faces in **Holbein**'s *Dormition of the Virgin*, at the far end of the room. Don't overlook **Dürer**'s *Young Man* with an enigmatic smile, sharing room XIV with pictures by **Altdorfer**.

From Romanticism to Postimpressionism

For a change of mood, cross the lobby and enter **From Romanticism to Postimpressionism**, where Room XII displays **Courbet**'s wild landscapes and life-sized *Wrestlers*, **Corot**'s *Remembrance of Coubrou* and **Rodin**'s sculpture *The Brazen Age*. In the small rooms alongside you'll find orchards and river-views by **Renoir** and **Monet** (room XIX), *Lady with a Fan* by **Manet**, a **Pissarro** Paris scene and **Toulouse-Lautrec**'s *These Ladies* (room XX), as well as a little-known **Gauguin**, *Black Pigs*, from his Tahitian period and more Monets (room XXII). Teutonic Romanticism rules in room XIII, with Von Lenbach's *The Triumphal Arch of Titus in Rome* and Böcklin's *Centaur at a Forge*.

English and French art

The single room (XIV) devoted to **English art** musters a dullish portrait apiece by Hogarth, Reynolds and Gainsborough, and a melodramatic theatre scene by Zoffany, while the highlight of **French art until 1800** in room XVI is *The Rest on the Flight into Egypt* by **Poussin**. However, both are totally outshone by the display of masters that follows.

Italian Collection

The superb **Italian Collection** occupies nine rooms and can be viewed in a very rough chronological order by entering from the lobby opposite the Spanish section, or in reverse from the English or French rooms; some backtracking is inevitable. A tradition of gilded altarpieces such as *The Mystic Marriage of St Catherine* (room XXIV) gave rise to **Boccacio**'s masterpiece *The Adoration of the Infant Christ*, usually displayed near **Titian**'s *Madonna and Child with St Paul* in the later rooms. **Bellini**'s pig-eyed *Queen of Cyprus* and a possible **Fra Angelico** landscape are the highlights of room XXIII.

Room XIX boasts **Raphael**'s exquisite *Esterházy Madonna* – a Virgin and Child with the infant St John – and two **Giorgione** paintings, one a self-portrait, leading to a powerful **Bronzino** portrait in room XX. The highlights of the neighbouring Room XVII are a couple of portrayals of Venetian Doges, a friendly one by **Titian** and another, more watchful character by **Tintoretto**, who is also represented by *Hercules Expelling the Faun from Omphale's Bed*; and a couple of **Veronese** paintings, including one of a disagreeable grandee in an ermine-trimmed robe.

Room XVIII hosts the biblical epic *Jael and Sara*, by **Artemisia Gentileschi**. Finally, up by the English collection, room XV has two superb **Canalettos**: one of Vienna and the other of the Pantheon, though the latter is poorly displayed high above a door. Also on show are a handful of landscapes by **Guardi** and some paintings by **Tiepolo**.

Ötvenhatosok tere

Ötvenhatosok tere, 56ers' Square, the wide avenue running off alongside the Városliget, serves as the setting for occasional **fairs** and **concerts**. In Communist times it was called Parade Square, as it was from a grandstand here that Party leaders reviewed parades. Up to 1956 they did so beneath a 25m-high statue of Stalin that was torn down during the Uprising, dragged to the Nagykörút and hammered into bits for souvenirs. After the re-imposition of Communist rule a statue of Lenin was erected in its place, which remained until it was taken away "for structural repairs" in 1989 and finally ended up in the Memento Park (see p.125).

The three monuments

Today, three monuments mark the distance that Hungary has travelled since 1989. The **Timewheel** is the world's largest hourglass, a metal canister 8m in diameter that rotates 180º on the last day of each year, symbolizing Hungary's accession to the European Union in 2004. Where the Stalin statue once stood, the **Monument to the Uprising** is a forest of oxidized columns merging into a stainless steel wedge, beside a Hungarian flag with a circle cut out, recalling the excision of the hated Soviet symbol in 1956. Beyond this, a crucifix rises over the foundations of the **Virgin Mary Church** that the Communists demolished in 1951.

The Városliget

The **Városliget** (City Park) starts just behind Hősök tere, where the fairy-tale towers of **Vajdahunyad Castle** rear above an island girdled by an artificial lake that's used for **boating** in the summer and transformed into a splendid outdoor **ice rink** in winter. (Boats and skates are rented out from the buildings by the Műcsarnok.) Like the park, the castle was created for the Millennary Anniversary celebrations of 1896, proving so popular that the temporary structures were replaced by permanent ones. Vajdahunyad is a catalogue in stone of architectural styles from the kingdom of Hungary, incorporating parts of two Transylvanian castles and a replica of the Romanesque **chapel at Ják (**May–Oct daily 10am–4pm; 100Ft), with a splendidly carved portal and a Renaissance courtyard that makes a romantic setting for evening **concerts** from July to mid-August.

Agriculture Museum

Mezőgazdasági Múzeum • XIV, Vajdahunyad Castle • Tues–Sun 10am–5pm • 1000Ft • ⓦ mezogazdasagimuzeum.hu

Vajdahunyad Castle itself is filled with the extensive displays of the **Agriculture Museum**. The most interesting section (on the ground floor to the left of the entrance lobby) relates to the early Magyars and such typically Hungarian breeds of livestock as long-horned grey cattle (favoured for their draught power rather than their milk) and woolly mangalica pigs.

To the right of the lobby are several dusty displays on forestry and hunting – the latter has not changed much in the past hundred years, judging by one old photo on display. However, the craftsmanship in antique crossbows and rifles exquisitely inlaid with leaping hares and other prey is undeniable. Upstairs, the fishing section is notable for a 270-year-old dugout boat carved from a single piece of oak, which was found at Lake Balaton, southwest of the capital.

Even if you decide to skip the museum, don't miss the hooded **statue of Anonymous** outside. This nameless chronicler to King Béla is the prime source of information about early medieval Hungary, though the existence of several monarchs of that name during the twelfth and thirteenth centuries makes it hard to date him (or his chronicles) with any accuracy. Further into the park roughly midway between the Castle and the Timewheel, a monument to **George Washington** erected in 1906 by immigrant Hungarians attests to the patriotism of the Magyar diaspora.

Petőfi Csarnok and Aviation and Space Flight Exhibition

Petőfi Csarnok XIV, Zichy Mihály utca 14 • ☏ ① 1 363 3730, ⓦ petoficsarnok.hu • **Aviation and Space Flight Exhibition** Repüléstörténeti és Űrhajózási kiállátás • May–Oct Tues–Fri 10am–5pm, Sat & Sun 10am–6pm • 500Ft, or see Transport Museum (below) for combined ticket price • Trolleybuses #70, #72 and #74 from the centre of town all go near the hall

Leaving Vajdahunyad island by the causeway at the rear, you're ten minutes' walk from the **Petőfi Csarnok** or "Pecsa" as it is often called, a 1970s "Metropolitan Youth Centre" that regularly hosts concerts (outdoors in summer), films and parties, and a fine **flea market** at weekends. At the back of the building is a stairway leading to the extensive **Aviation and Space Flight Exhibition** which, among other items, contains the spacesuit used by Hungary's first astronaut, Bertalan Farkas on the Soyuz-35 mission of 1980; an L-2 monoplane sporting an Italian Fascist symbol, which broke world speed records in the Budapest–Rome races of 1927 and 1930; and cockpits of a Tu-154 and MiG 25. One familiar name is that of **Ernő Rubik**: the father of the inventor of the cube was a big name in plane design. Alas, there seems to be nothing about Count **László Almássy**, Hungary's foremost aviator of that time, better known abroad as the hero of the book and film *The English Patient*.

Transport Museum

Közlekedési Múzeum • XIV, Városligeti körút 11 • Tues–Fri 10am–5pm, Sat & Sun 10am–6pm; Nov–March closes 1hr earlier • 800Ft, combined ticket with Aviation exhibition 1200Ft

On the edge of the City Park is the **Transport Museum**, of which the aviation exhibition is an outgrowth. Captions in English explain that the Hungarian transport network of the 1890s was among the most sophisticated in Europe; despite the country starting from a low technological base, railways, canals, trams and a metro had all been created within fifty years. Displays include vintage locomotives and carriages that you can climb into, scale models of steamboats and a wonderful collection of Hungarian Railways posters from 1900 to 1980. A model train set on the floor above the foyer attracts a crowd when it's switched on – for fifteen minutes every hour, on the hour. (There's a small one on the ground floor that runs on the half-hour.) Collectors can buy Hungarian model trains in the museum shop. Outside the building are remnants of two of the Danube bridges that were wrecked in 1945: the cast-iron Erzsébet híd (replaced by a new bridge) and a few links of the original chains from the Lánchíd, which is now supported by cables.

While you're here, check out the **Hungarian Federation of the Blind and Partially Sighted** nearby at Hermina út 47, an extraordinary pink concoction designed by Lechner.

The northern end of the Városliget

Four attractions lie on Állatkerti körút, the road that runs round the top of the Városliget. The best access is by foot from Hősök tere, by #72 trolleybus, which passes the door of all four, or by the yellow #1 metro line to the Széchenyi Fürdő stop.

The Zoo

Állatkert • XIV, Állatkerti körút 6 • Daily: Jan, Feb, Nov & Dec 9am–4pm; March & Oct 9am–5pm; April & Sept 9am–5.30pm; May–Aug 9am–6.30pm; animal houses open 1hr later and close 30min before the zoo itself • 2100Ft, family 6100Ft, with fifteen-percent reduction if you show a ticket to the Funfair • ⓦ zoobudapest.com

Tucked behind the Fine Arts Museum you'll find the delightful Elephant Gates of Budapest's **Zoo**, which opened its doors in 1866. Its superb early twentieth-century pavilions seemed the last word in zoological architecture, but it slowly stagnated until the 1990s, when the present director took long-overdue action to give the animals better habitats and make the zoo more visitor-friendly. In 2007, it proudly announced the world's first birth of a rhino conceived by artificial insemination, and in 2011 three tiger cubs, Virgil, Thrax and Manu (the mayor named them), were born. Don't miss the exotic **Elephant House**, resembling a Central Asian mosque, the **Palm House** with its magnificent **aquarium** below, or the polar bears swimming during feeding time, their size and power frankly unnerving. Look out also for children's events, evening concerts and exhibitions under the Great Rock, as advertised outside the main entrance. The children's corner is signposted "Állatóvoda", to the left from the entrance past the Palm House.

The Municipal Circus

Fővárosi Nagycirkusz • XIV, Állatkerti körút 12 • Wed & Thurs 5pm, Fri 3pm, Sat 3pm & 7pm, Sun 11am, 3pm & 7pm • 2000–3100Ft • ⓦ maciva.hu

Next door to the Zoo the **Municipal Circus** traces its origins back to 1783, when the Hetz Theatre played to spectators on what is now Deák tér. Today the building has a changing programme that ranges from traditional local circuses with clowns and animals to Columbian and Chinese acrobats. It also hosts a big international circus festival every other year in early February – check the website for details.

The Széchenyi Baths

Széchenyi Gyógyfürdő • XIV, Állatkerti körút 11 • Daily 6am–10pm • ☎ 1 363 3210, ⓦ szechenyibath.com • See p.196 for details

Across the road from the Municipal Circus the **Széchenyi Baths** could be mistaken for a palace, so grand is its facade. Outside is a statue of the geologist Zsigmondy Vilmos, who discovered the thermal spring that feeds its outdoor pool and Turkish baths. This is perhaps the best venue for mixed-sex bathing, and in one of the large outdoor pools you can enjoy the surreal spectacle of people playing **chess** while immersed up to their chests in steaming water – so hot that you shouldn't stay in for more than twenty minutes. The best players sit at tables around the pool's edge (the late former world champion **Bobby Fischer** among them in the 1980s); bring your own set if you wish to participate.

4

The Funfair

Vidám Park • XIV, Állatkerti körút 14–16 • May–Sept daily 11am–6pm, till 8pm July–Aug, and June–Sept Fri & Sat open till 1.30am; March–April & Oct Sat & Sun only 11am–6pm • 4700Ft for those over 140cm in height, 3300Ft for 90–140cm, free for children under 100cm • Ⓦ vidampark.hu

Just next door to the Municipal Circus is the **Funfair** (Vidám Park), an old-fashioned fairground known as the "English Park" before the war. This was the setting for Ferenc Molnár's play *Liliom*, which inspired the musical *Carousel*. The gilded merry-go-round to the left of the entrance and the wooden switchback at the back of the fairground both predate World War II. It has a 31m-high Ferris wheel, great dodgems and the hair-raising Flying Circus that will throw you round and round.

The stadium district

The **stadium district**, 1km south of Vajdahunyad Castle, is chiefly notable for the **Ferenc Puskás Stadium** (Puskás Ferenc Stadion), where league championship and international **football** matches, **concerts** by foreign rock stars and events such as the national dog show are held. Originally known as Népstadion ("People's Stadium") and built in the early 1950s by fifty thousand Budapestis who "volunteered" their labour, on Soviet-style "free Saturdays", it was renamed in 2002 after the legendary footballer and manager Ferenc Puskás (1927–2006), who captained the Mighty Magyars in their triumph over England at Wembley Stadium in 1953 (a team that went unbeaten for a world record of 32 consecutive games), before defecting to forge a second career at Real Madrid.

To the west of the stadium is the smaller **Kisstadion**, which is commonly used for ice sports, while to the east Stalinist statues of healthy proletarian youth line the court that leads to the indoor **Papp László Sportaréna** (or Aréna), a mushroom-shaped silver structure which also hosts concerts and sporting events – Papp was the first boxer to win three Olympic gold medals (1948, 1952 and 1956). The **Stadion bus station** completes this concrete ensemble.

Geological Institute

Földani Intézet • XIV, Stefánia út 14 • Thurs, Sat & Sun 10am–4pm • 500Ft • Trolleybus #75 from Puskás Ferenc Stadion metro station or from City Park

On Stefánia út, beyond the stadiums, you can admire the **Geological Institute**, one of the major edifices in Budapest designed by Ödön Lechner. Much of the original design has been preserved simply because the institute has never had enough money to make major changes. The exterior is as striking as his Post Office Savings Bank (see p.50) and Applied Arts Museum (see p.82), with a gingerbread facade, scrolled gables and steeply pitched Transylvanian roofs patterned in bright blue tiles, crowned by four figures supporting a globe on their backs. Lechner put numerous geological references into the design and originally planned to put dwarves holding up the globe. The institute has a small **Geological Museum**, but the helpful staff will happily show visitors round the building itself, with its gingerbread stucco and faux lapis lazuli stairways. (Ernő Rubik, the man behind the famous cube, left his mark here: he designed the museum's cataloguing system.) The little concrete turret on top of the rear of the building is said to be a 1950s machine-gun turret, though it never saw any action.

Józsefváros and Ferencváros

Separated from Erzsébetváros by Rákóczi út, which runs out to Keleti Station, Józsefváros (the VIII District) is an amalgam of high and low life. While the Hungarian National Museum, Eötvös Loránd University and the Szabó Ervin Library on Múzeum körút make for a lively student quarter, its seedier hinterland beyond the Nagykörút district – nicknamed "Chicago" between the wars – still has an association with vice and crime, despite the gentrification that is gradually taking over the old apartment blocks around the Rákóczi tér market hall. You can wander safely anywhere in Józsefváros by day, and between the Kiskörút and Nagykörút in the small hours, but elsewhere stick to main roads and avoid pedestrian underpasses after midnight – particularly around Keleti Station, where Kerepesi Cemetery and the Police History Museum are worth a visit by day.

5

Üllői út – leading to the airport – marks the boundary of the adjacent **Ferencváros** (Franz Town, the IX District), once the most solidly working class of the inner-city districts. Today, **Ráday utca** and the backstreets behind the wonderful **Great Market Hall** on Vámház körút are full of hip restaurants and bars; luxury condos rise where teenage insurgents once fought, and the district's historic far-right sympathies are challenged by a **Holocaust Memorial Centre**. Along the riverbank there is frenetic development all the way down to the **Palace of Arts** complex, which will transform the balance of the district. Football fans will want to see Fradi in action at the **FTC Stadium**, and children enjoy the **Natural History Museum**.

ARRIVAL

Transport for the two districts include the red and blue metro lines, trams #4 and #6 along the Nagykörút and tram #2, which runs down the Pest bank of the Danube to the Palace of Arts.

Józsefváros

Named after the heir to the Habsburg throne in 1777, Józsefváros has many faces. The grand but neglected apartment blocks speak of an old middle-class suburb that fell into decline. Rákóczi tér became the centre of the city's sex industry and cheap housing in the streets behind it attracted a big Roma population. Now, however, the prostitutes have been cleared away and gentrification is spreading through the district, which will no doubt gradually push out the Roma, too. In 2011 the Józsefváros mayor decided it was time to sweep the homeless off the streets, and such drastic moves will no doubt speed up the process. Some of the sights further out in the district, such as Corvin köz and the Natural History Museum, are covered under the Üllői út section of Ferencváros (see p.82).

Múzeum körút

Part of the Kiskörút, **Múzeum körút** separates the Belváros and Józsefváros. Aside from being curved rather than straight, it resembles Andrássy út in miniature, lined with trees, shops and grandiose buildings. Immediately beyond the East–West Business Centre by the Astoria junction stands the old faculty of the **Eötvös Loránd Science University** (known by its Hungarian initials as ELTE). It's named after the physicist Loránd Eötvös, whose pupils included many of the scientists who later developed the US atomic bombs at Los Alamos, including Edward Teller, "Father of the Hydrogen Bomb".

Across the street it is worth putting your head into the courtyard of no. 7. A sadly neglected building by Miklós Ybl, the neo-Renaissance **Unger House** (Unger ház) has fabulous fine old wooden tiles and a glazed first-floor colonnade.

Further down on the same side on Ferenczy utca, you can see a small crenellated section of the **medieval wall of Pest**. Originally 2km long and 8m high, the walls gradually disappeared as the city was built up on either side, but fragments remain here and there – a larger freestanding chunk lurks in the courtyard of no. 21, if you get the chance to peep inside.

Back on the outer edge of Múzeum körút, you'll find the **Múzeum** at no. 12, which was one of the earliest coffee houses in Pest (not to be confused with the 24-hour café at no. 10). Its original frescoes and Zsolnay ceramic reliefs dating from 1885 still grace what has long since become a restaurant (see p.170).

Bródy Sándor utca

From Múzeum körút you can wander down **Bródy Sándor utca**, which runs along the garden of the Hungarian National Museum. The Renaissance-style mansion at no. 8 housed the lower chamber of the Hungarian Parliament from 1867 until its present building was completed, and is now home to the **Italian Institute**. Diagonally across the street at nos. 5–7 is the **Radio Building**, from which ÁVO guards fired upon

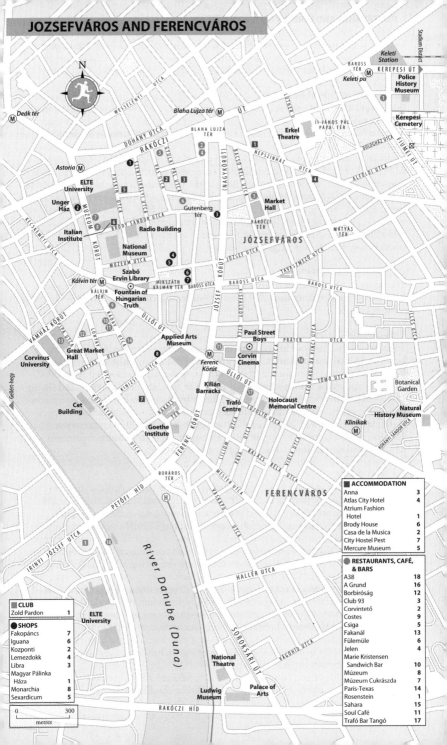

JOZSEFVÁROS AND FERENCVÁROS

N

Deák tér Ⓜ

Stadium District

Keleti Station

Keleti pu

BAROSS TÉR Ⓜ KEREPESI ÚT

Police History Museum

Kérepesi Cemetery

WESSELÉNYI UTCA

Blaha Lujza tér Ⓜ

DOHÁNY UTCA

RÁKÓCZI ÚT

BLAHA LUJZA TÉR

LÉTHER UTCA

ÚT

II. JÁNOS PÁL PÁPA TÉR

Erkel Theatre

NÉPSZÍNHÁZ UTCA

DOLOGHÁZ UTCA

FUMEI ÚT

Astoria Ⓜ

ELTE University

Unger Ház Ⓜ ②

Italian Institute

PUSKIN UTCA

SZENTKIRÁLYI UTCA

GYULAI PÁL UTCA

② ④

② ②③

⑤

NAGYKÖRÚT

BACSÓ BÉLA UTCA

ALFÖLDI UTCA

⑥

④

⑤ Market Hall

MÚZEUM KÖRÚT

BRÓDY SÁNDOR UTCA

⑥

Radio Building

⑦

⑧

Gutenberg tér ⑥ ③

RÁKÓCZI TÉR

MÁTYÁS TÉR

JÓZSEFVÁROS

National Museum

MÚZEUM UTCA

④ ⑤

JÓZSEF UTCA

JÓZSEF KÖRÚT

Szabó Ervin Library

⑥ ⑦

KÁLMÁN TÉR BAROSS UTCA

BAROSS UTCA

BAROSS UTCA

TAVASZMEZŐ UTCA

ILLÉS UTCA

Kálvin tér Ⓜ

KÁLVIN TÉR

MIKSZÁTH KÁLMÁN TÉR

Fountain of Hungarian Truth

KECSKEMÉTI UTCA

ÜLLŐI ÚT

KISFALUDY UTCA

Paul Street Boys

PRÁTER UTCA

Applied Arts Museum

RÁDAY UTCA

LÓNYAY UTCA

⑩ ⑪

⑭

⑧

Ferenc Körút Ⓜ

⑬

Corvin Cinema

FŐTŐ UTCA

LEONARDO DA VINCI UTCA

TOMÓ UTCA

⑯

Botanical Garden

VÁMHÁZ KÖRÚT

Great Market Hall

Corvinus University

MÁTYÁS UTCA

⑫

KINIZSI UTCA

TŰZOLTÓ UTCA

⑦

FERENC KÖRÚT

ÜLLŐI ÚT

Kilián Barracks

⑰

Holocaust Memorial Centre

Natural History Museum

Gellért-hegy

Cet Building

KŐBÁNYAI UTCA

BAKÁTS TÉR

Trafó Centre

Goethe Institute

LILIOM UTCA

PÁVA UTCA

BALÁZS BÉLA UTCA

VIOLA UTCA

Klinikak Ⓜ

KŐRÁNYI SÁNDOR UTCA

BORÁROS TÉR

MESTER UTCA

FERENCVÁROS

PETŐFI HÍD

Ⓗ

IRINYI JÓZSEF UTCA

VASKAPU UTCA

① ⑱

River Danube (Duna)

ELTE University

HALLÉR UTCA

SOROKSÁRI ÚT

VÁGOHÍD UTCA

National Theatre

Ludwig Museum

Palace of Arts

RÁKÓCZI HÍD

■ ACCOMMODATION	
Anna	3
Atlas City Hotel	4
Atrium Fashion Hotel	1
Brody House	6
Casa de la Musica	2
City Hostel Pest	7
Mercure Museum	5

● RESTAURANTS, CAFÉ, & BARS	
A38	18
A Grund	16
Borbiróság	12
Club 93	3
Corvintető	2
Costes	9
Csiga	5
Fakanál	13
Fülemüle	6
Jelen	4
Marie Kristensen Sandwich Bar	10
Múzeum	8
Múzeum Cukrászda	7
Paris-Texas	14
Rosenstein	1
Sahara	15
Soul Café	11
Trafó Bar Tangó	17

■ CLUB	
Zold Pardon	1

● SHOPS	
Fakopáncs	7
Iguana	6
Kozponti	2
Lemezdokk	4
Libra	3
Magyar Pálinka Háza	1
Monarchia	8
Sexardicum	5

0 — 300
metres

5

students demanding access to the airwaves, an act which turned the hitherto peaceful protests of October 23, 1956 into an uprising against the secret police and other manifestations of Stalinism.

Hungarian National Museum

Magyar Nemzeti Múzeum • VIII, Múzeum körút 14–16 • Tues–Sun 10am–6pm • 1100Ft; free on March 15, Aug 20 & Oct 23; audio-guide 750Ft • ⓦ hnm.hu

Like the National Library in the Royal Palace, the **Hungarian National Museum** was the brainchild of Count Ferenc Széchenyi (father of István), who donated thousands of prints and manuscripts to form the basis of its collection. Housed in a Grecian-style edifice by Mihály Pollack, it was only the fourth such museum in the world when it opened in 1847, and soon afterwards became the stage for a famous event in the **1848 Revolution**, when Sándor Petőfi (see p.43) first declaimed the *National Song* from its steps, with its rousing refrain "Choose! Now is the time! Shall we be slaves or shall we be free?" ("Some noisy mob had their hurly-burly outside so I left for home", complained the museum's director at the time.) Ever since, March 15 has been commemorated here with flags and speeches.

The basement and ground floor

The museum has two lower levels devoted to medieval and Roman stonework – the latter starring a second-century AD mosaic floor from a villa at Nemesvámos-Baláca in western Hungary.

The first floor

To the left of the first-floor foyer, a darkened room displays King Stephen's exquisite Byzantine silk **coronation mantle**, which was considered too fragile to be transferred to the Parliament building when the rest of the Coronation Regalia was moved there in 2000.

Equally impressive is the archeological section to the right of the foyer, called **On the East–West Frontier**, which covers the pre-Hungarian peoples of the Carpathian Basin. Besides life-size models of a Palaeolithic cave dwelling and a 6000-year-old house, its highlights include three skeletons and grave goods from a 1600 BC cemetery at Tiszafüred, gold Germanic bangles and the **Nagyszentmiklós treasure**, a gorgeous 23-piece gold dinner service belonging to an Avar chieftain.

The second floor

The main exhibition upstairs traces **Hungarian history** from the Árpád dynasty to the end of Communism, starting to the left side of the rotunda at the top of the stairs. English captions are patchier than elsewhere in the museum, so the audio-guide (available in the foyer) may be useful. Room 1 contains Béla III's crown, sceptre and sword, and in room 2, there's a gilded reliquary bust of St László and a wall fountain from the royal palace at Visegrád (see p.137). Don't miss the ivory saddles inlaid with hunting scenes in room 3, the suit of armour of the child-king Sigismund II in room 5, or the huge carved Renaissance pew in room 6. Turkish weaponry and the ornate tomb of Count György Apafi in room 7 speak of the 150 years when Hungary was divided and its destiny decided by intriguers and warlords, including the Forgáchs and Nádasdys depicted in the oldest **portraits** in Hungary, hung in room 8 – except for the infamous "Blood Countess" Erzsébet Báthori, whose picture is kept in storage. As the widow of national hero Ferenc Nádasdy, charged with torturing six hundred women to death and reputedly bathing in their blood to preserve her beauty, she was walled up in her castle and the atrocity hushed up.

From here, proceed back across the rotunda to find the Reform era and the *belle époque*, covered in rooms 11–18, followed by World War II and the Communist era in room 20. The last features newsreel footage and such items as a radio set dedicated to Stalin's 70th birthday, a scaled-down model of the Stalin statue torn down by crowds in

1956, and kitsch tributes to János Kádár, who reimposed Communist rule with a vengeance, but later liberalized it to the point that his successors felt able to abandon it entirely. Not to be missed are the **propaganda** films from the Horthy, Fascist and Stalinist eras, whose resemblance to each other makes the point.

Kálvin tér

Múzeum körút ends at **Kálvin tér**, a busy intersection with roads going to the airport, the east and westwards across the river. In 1956, street fighting was especially fierce here as insurgents battled tanks rumbling in from the Soviet base on Csepel Island. A freestanding section of the **medieval walls** of Pest can be found off Vámház körút in the courtyard of no. 16, if the door is open.

Ervin Szabó Library

Szabo Ervin Könyvtár • VIII, Szabó Ervin tér 1 • Mon–Fri 10am–8pm, Sat 10am–4pm, closed July, reduced hours in Aug • Free

It seems almost miraculous that the ornate reading rooms of the **Szabó Ervin Library**, on the corner of Baross utca, survived unscathed from the fighting in the surrounding streets in 1956. Built in 1887 by the Wenckheim family – who enjoyed a near-monopoly on Hungary's onion crop – the library has come through a thorough modernization in sparkling form. At the main entrance on Reviczky utca, you can ask at the information desk about visiting the fourth-floor reading rooms, reached by a lovely wooden staircase. Staff may ask you to register but will probably just wave you through.

Fountain of Hungarian Truth

Outside the library and facing Kálvin tér stands one of the few surviving monuments marking the hated Treaty of Trianon (see p.151): the so-called **Fountain of Hungarian Truth** (Magyar Igazság kútja). Erected in 1928, it honours the British press magnate Lord Rothermere, whose campaign against the treaty in the *Daily Mail* was so appreciated that he was offered the Hungarian crown. On June 4, the anniversary of the treaty's signing, nationalist and neo-Nazi groups gather to pay their respects.

To the Nagykörút and Keleti Station

Behind the library lies an atmospheric quarter of small squares and parochial schools; formerly shabby, it's now buzzing with cafés and bars popular with students, and is promoted by the local council as **"Budapest's Soho"**. Having given a face-lift to **Mikszáth Kálmán tér** and much of Krúdy utca, the process of gentrification is now crossing the **József körút** – one of the sleazier arcs of the Nagykörút – to embrace **Rákóczi tér**, the focus of street prostitution until it was outlawed in 1999. The square has one of Budapest's finest market halls, and the opening of the fourth metro line is likely to take the whole area gradually upmarket in the future.

The large neglected square that lies up towards Keleti Station has been given a veneer of respectability in 2011 when its name, **Köztársaság tér**, long associated with lynchings that were carried out in front of the Communist Party HQ here in 1956, was changed to **II János Pal pápa tér** (Pope John Paul II Square), much more in keeping with the new times. It remains to be seen whether Budapest's long-closed "second" opera house, the **Erkel Theatre** (named after the composer of the national anthem, Ferenc Erkel), will also get an overhaul.

The grittier side of life still prevails at **Keleti Station** on Baross tér: as the station is Budapest's "gateway to the east", it's not surprising that Chinese takeaways and Arab shops are a feature of the area.

The Police History Museum

Rendőrség-Történeti Múzeum • VIII, Mosonyi utca 7 • Tues–Sun 9am–5pm • Free • ⓦ policehistorymus.com

To check on dodgy arrivals, the **police** used to patrol Keleti Station in threes ("One can read, one can write, and the third one keeps an eye on the two intellectuals", as the old

5

joke had it). They are now trying to improve their public image in the **Police History Museum**, a couple of blocks from the station, its entrance marked by a sentry box. As you go in, ask for the English translation of the main displays to enjoy how they handle such awkward matters as the role of the police in the Communist period. To the left of the entrance is a display of uniforms and memorabilia going back to Habsburg times, while to the right is a sad display depicting a very 1960s-looking crime scene with a sign listing key points for trainee investigators, along with detailed descriptions of more crimes than you would ever want to read about, including a couple of infamous recent escapades.

Kerepesi Cemetery

Kerepesi temető • VIII, Fiumei út 16 • Cemetery Daily: April & Aug 7am–7pm; May–July 7am–8pm, Sept 7am–6pm; Oct–March 7.30am–5pm • Free • **Funerary Museum** Kegyeleti Múzeum • Mon–Fri 9am–5pm • Free

Five minutes' walk from the Police History Museum, you'll find the **Kerepesi Cemetery**, (also known as Nemzet Sírkert and Fiumei úti Sírkert). This is the Père Lachaise of Budapest, where the famous, great and not-so-good are buried. Vintage hearses and mourning regalia in the **Funerary Museum** near the main gates illuminate the Hungarian way of death and set the stage for the necropolis. In Communist times, Party members killed during the Uprising were buried in a special plot near the entrance and government ministers in honourable proximity to Kossuth, while leaders and martyrs who "lived for Communism and the People" were enshrined in a starkly ugly **Pantheon of the Working Class Movement**; some have been removed by their relatives since the demise of Communism, and all the old Communist sections are looking distinctly unkempt – in contrast to the area for 1956 insurgents. Party leader János Kádár – who ruled Hungary from 1956 to 1988 – rates a separate grave, still heaped with (mainly plastic) wreaths from admirers.

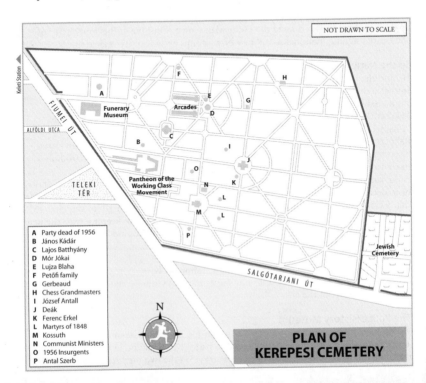

NOT DRAWN TO SCALE

Keleti Station

FIUMEI ÚT

ALFÖLDI UTCA

Funerary Museum

Arcades

TELEKI TÉR

Pantheon of the Working Class Movement

Jewish Cemetery

SALGÓTARJANI ÚT

A Party dead of 1956
B János Kádár
C Lajos Batthyány
D Mór Jókai
E Lujza Blaha
F Petőfi family
G Gerbeaud
H Chess Grandmasters
I József Antall
J Deák
K Ferenc Erkel
L Martyrs of 1848
M Kossuth
N Communist Ministers
O 1956 Insurgents
P Antal Szerb

N

PLAN OF KEREPESI CEMETERY

Further in lie the florid **nineteenth-century mausoleums** of Kossuth, Batthyány, Deák and Petőfi (whose family tomb is here, though his own body was never found). Don't miss the Art Nouveau funerary arcades between Batthyány's and the novelist Jókai's mausoleums, nor the nearby tomb of the diva Lujza Blaha, the "Nation's Nightingale", whose effigy is surrounded by statues of serenading figures. Other notables include the composer Erkel, the confectioner Gerbeaud and three chess grandmasters whose tombs are engraved with the chess moves that won them their titles. The writer Antal Szerb (see p.94) has a very humble grave on the southern edge of the cemetery. A more recent addition is József Antall, the first post-Communist prime minister of Hungary, honoured by an extraordinary allegorical monument with riders on horseback struggling out from under a sheet.

Jewish cemetery
Izraelita temető • VIII, Salgótarjáni út 6 • Mon–Fri & Sun 8am–2pm • Free

Next to Kerepesi lies an overgrown **Jewish cemetery**, with some beautiful Art Nouveau tombs of artists, politicians and industrialists, several designed by the brilliant architect Béla Lajta. That of **Manfred Weiss**, founder of the Csepel ironworks that once dominated the industrial island south of the city centre, is still maintained by Csepel's council, in gratitude and by way of apology for the fact that Weiss had to sign his factory over to the government in return for being allowed to leave Hungary with his family in 1944. The cemetery gates are on Salgótarjáni út, about ten minutes' walk from the main entrance to Kerepesi.

Ferencváros

Ferencváros was developed to house workers in the latter half of the nineteenth century, on the same lines as the more bourgeois Józsefváros. During the 1930s and 1940s, its population confounded Marxist orthodoxy by voting for the extreme right, who returned the favour by supporting the local football team **FTC** – popularly known as "**Fradi**" – which became the unofficial team of the opposition under Communism, subsequently known for its hooligan "ultras". The club's green and white colours can be seen throughout the district; its stadium is way out along Üllői út. (See p.191 for more on Fradi and the football scene in general.)

Corvinus University
Budapesti Corvinus Egyetem • VIII, Fővám tér 8 • Trams #2, #47 and #49

Standing at the Pest end of Szabadság híd, the **Corvinus University of Budapest** makes a fine sight from Buda at night, reflected in the river, and adds to the liveliness of the area by day. The building was originally Budapest's main **Customs House** (Fővámház) – hence the name of the square and the adjoining section of the Kiskörút, **Vámház körút**. The university was named after Karl Marx during Communist times and is still sometimes called the Economics University.

Great Market Hall
Nagycsarnok • VIII, Fővám tér 1–3 • Mon 6am–5pm, Tues–Fri 6am–6pm, Sat 6am–3pm

Next door to the university, the wrought-iron **Great Market Hall** is as famous for its ambience as for its produce, with tanks of live fish and stalls festooned with strings of paprika downstairs and cheap stand-up food stalls upstairs. The stalls along the right side are known to locals as the "tourist row" – so shopping there for everyday groceries will prove relatively expensive.

Ráday utca
Further inland off Kálvin tér, **Ráday utca** hums with restaurants, cafés and bars, their pavement tables packed till after midnight and occasionally frequented by raucous stag

5

partygoers. Beyond the large church on Bakáts tér, the **Goethe-Institut** at no. 58 has its own programme of events throughout the year.

Around Üllői út

Grey, polluted **Üllői út** isn't an obvious place to linger, but there's much to see within a few blocks' radius of the **Corvin negyed** metro station.

The Applied Arts Museum

Iparművészeti Múzeum • IX, Üllői út 33–37• Tues–Sun 10am–6pm • Permanent collection 1000Ft, temporary shows 600–1500Ft • Ⓦ imm.hu

The **Applied Arts Museum** is the most flamboyant creation of Ödön Lechner, who strove to create a uniquely Hungarian form of architecture emphasizing the Magyars' Ugric roots, but was also influenced by Art Nouveau. Inaugurated by Emperor Franz Josef during the 1896 Millennial celebrations, it was given a rough reception, derided by some as "the palace of the Gypsy kings". Its exterior, with its green-and-yellow-tiled dome and a portico with ceramic Turkic motifs on an egg-yolk-coloured background is crying out for restoration, especially after the yellow-tiled lantern on the top of the dome had to be taken down in 2011 for safety reasons. By contrast, the all-white interior is reminiscent of Mogul architecture: at one time it was thought that the Magyars came from India. The museum has a permanent collection on the first floor that ranges from delicately carved eleventh-century ivory to a fabulous Art Nouveau clock. Temporary shows are also held on the ground floor.

Corvin köz

On the northeast corner of the Corvin negyed junction, duck into **Corvin köz**, the grand oval passage separating the **Corvin Cinema** from the surrounding flats, from which teenage guerrillas (some as young as 12) sallied forth to battle Soviet tanks in 1956. Since the fall of Communism, they have been honoured by a statue of a young insurgent outside the cinema. Its auditoriums are named after illustrious Hungarian actors or directors such as Alexander Korda – one of many Magyars who made it in Hollywood (see p.189).

Having renovated Corvin köz, developers have upped the stakes with the **Corvin Promenade** (Corvin sétány) – a mall and luxury apartment complex stretching back between Üllői út and Práter utca. Like the Madách sétány in Erzsébetváros (p.65), the Corvin is carving a path through the old blocks. Meanwhile, you can walk around the corner to find a delightful statue of the **Paul Street Boys** – the heroes of Ferenc Molnár's eponymous 1906 novel – portraying the moment they are caught playing marbles in the yard of their enemies, the Redshirts. The most widely sold and translated Hungarian book ever, it's both a universal tale of childhood and a satire on extreme nationalism.

Kilián Barracks

If you're wondering how locals were able to fight so well in 1956, the answer lies across Üllői út from Corvin köz, where the Hungarian garrison of the **Kilián Barracks** was the first to join the insurgents, organizing youths already aware of street-fighting tactics due to an obligatory diet of films about Soviet partisans. It was in Budapest that the Molotov cocktail proved lethal to T-54s, as the "Corvin Boys" trapped columns in the backstreets by firebombing the front and rear tanks. Memorial plaques honour Colonel Pál Maleter and others who directed fighting from the Corvin Cinema.

The Holocaust Memorial Centre

Holokauszt Emlékközpont • IX, Páva utca 39 • Tues–Sun 10am–6pm • 1000Ft • Ⓦ hdke.hu

One block past the Kilián Barracks, a right turn into Páva utca brings you to the **Holocaust Memorial Centre**, more chilling than the House of Terror (see p.60); think

5

twice about bringing children here. Like Libeskind's Jewish Holocaust Museum in Berlin, the building is distorted and oppressive; darkened ramps resounding to the crunch of jackboots and the shuffle of feet lead to artefacts, newsreels and audiovisual testimonies relating the slide from "deprivation of rights to genocide". From 1920 onwards, Jews were increasingly stripped of their assets by right-wing regimes with the participation of local citizens, and Gypsies forced into work gangs. The family stories and newsreel footage of the death camps after liberation are truly harrowing, accompanied by the roar and clang of a furnace being stoked. (In 2011 one minister said the display "superfluously aroused tensions", which is a curious take on the Holocaust. The newly appointed director will no doubt want to make changes.) Visitors emerge from the bowels of hell to find themselves within a glorious and sunlit Art Deco **synagogue**, built by Leopold Baumhorn in the 1920s, which has been restored and incorporated in the memorial centre, itself designed by István Mányi.

On your way back to the main road it's worth a detour on to Liliom utca to see another striking building – an old transformer plant turned into an outstanding contemporary arts centre, **Trafó** (see p.186 for details).

The Natural History Museum

Magyar Természettudományi Múzeum • VIII, Ludovika tér 2 • Daily except Tues 10am–5pm • 1200Ft, 400Ft for dinosaur garden, 2000Ft for temporary displays • Ⓦ nhmus.hu

A kilometre further down Üllői út just past the Klinikák metro stop, a left turn up Korányi Sándor utca brings you to the revamped **Hungarian Natural History Museum**. Though slightly out on a limb, it's worth the hike, especially if you have children: the presentation is captivating, with lots of colour, wide-open spaces, interactive displays, explanations in English and, for the weary, benches made from huge tree trunks.

From the entrance hall, dominated by a whale skeleton, you walk through to a fantastic **underwater room**, which has colourful fish in sea- and freshwater aquariums – the mock seabed under the glass floor makes you feel as if you're walking on water. Upstairs are displays on animals and their Hungarian habitats, an Africa exhibition and a Noah's Ark that focuses on animals under threat and what Hungary is doing for the environment. The shop downstairs by the entrance sells an excellent range of animal-related souvenirs, from fridge magnets to games and books.

Botanical Garden

Fűvészkert • VIII, Illés utca 25 • Daily: April–Oct 9am–5pm; Nov–March 9am–4pm, greenhouses closed noon–1pm and from 4pm • 700Ft • Ⓦ fuveszkert.org

Across the road from the Natural History Museum is a small **Botanical Garden**. Delightfully jungle-like, this shady idyll in the city is emerging from a much-needed revamp. Press on past the greenhouses by the entrance and you come to a pleasantly landscaped garden with ponds and streams, and the magnificent Palm House.

The Ferencváros riverbank

Spectacularly floodlit in blue and gold on the banks of the Danube, the **National Theatre** and **Palace of Arts** look like the crowning jewel of Budapest's cultural life from a distance – being a 3km ride from Deák tér. The positioning of the city's major new cultural centre this far down the river a decade ago is bearing fruit as the empty wastelands have at last been filled. Taking the #2 tram down from the Corvinus University, you pass a striking development, locally known as **The Whale**: two old warehouses on Közraktár utca have been united by a huge waving glass roof to form a major retail and cultural centre, but a fall-out between the developer and the City Hall has delayed the project's finish.

To the south of Petőfi híd the bank is lined with hip office and flat developments, all the way down to the major arts complex near the Rákóczi híd.

The National Theatre

Nemzeti Szinház • IX, Bajor Gizi park • ⓦ nemzetiszinhaz.hu • Take tram #2 to the penultimate stop, Vágóhíd utca, or take the Csepel HÉV from Boráros tér one stop

The **National Theatre** resembles a Ceauşescu folly, its exterior and environs strewn with random architectural references and statuary. The Classical facade is a replica of the frontage of the original theatre on Blaha Lujza tér, torn down to build the metro in 1964 – a Communist plot to undermine Hungary's identity, many said – which condemned the company to a dump in the backstreets of Pest while the debate continued as to where this national institution should be housed. The fiasco of the "National Hole" on Erzsébet tér (see p.45) was followed by a scandal over the existing site, when it emerged that the minister in charge awarded the contract to the architect of his holiday home. Lacklustre performances since the theatre opened haven't helped.

Palace of Arts and Ludwig Museum

Művészetek Palotája • IX, Komor Marcell utca 1 • **Palace of Arts** ⓦ mupa.hu • **Ludwig Museum** Kortárs Művészti Múzeum • Tues–Sun 10am–6pm, with one exhibition open Thurs till 8pm • 700Ft for permanent collection, 1200–2200Ft for temporary exhibitions • ⓦ ludwigmuseum.hu

Next door is the **Palace of Arts**, a vast edifice that is the new home of the excellent Philharmonic Orchestra and National Dance Theatre. Resembling a dull office block by day, it comes alive each evening with spectacular lighting and events – from world music and dance to the likes of Philip Glass's latest composition and Cecilia Bartoli performances. No expense has been spared to make this a top venue; particularly in the concert hall, whose acoustics are so sharp that some orchestras are said to dislike it, as you can hear their mistakes.

The Palace also encompasses the **Ludwig Museum** or Museum of Contemporary Art, established in 1996 to build upon an earlier bequest by the German industrialist Peter Ludwig. The collection includes US Pop Art such as Warhol's *Single Elvis* and Lichtenstein's *Vicki*, as well as Picasso's *Musketeer with a Sword* and a *Sealed Letter* by Beuys, but most of the recent acquisitions are works by lesser-known Europeans, in such styles as Hyper-Realism and neo-Primitivism. It also hosts **temporary exhibitions** – so the permanent collection is not always on view.

The Vár and central Buda

The Vár (or Várhegy – Castle Hill) is Buda's most prominent feature. A 1500m-long plateau encrusted with bastions, mansions and a huge palace, it dominates both the Víziváros below and Pest, over the river, making this stretch of the river one of the grandest, loveliest urban waterfronts in Europe. Often referred to as the Várnegyed (Castle District), the hill is studded with interesting museums, from the National Gallery and the Budapest History Museum in the Royal Palace to the Golden Eagle Pharmacy and the Telephone Museum, but it's equally enjoyable just walking the streets and admiring such florid creations as the Mátyás Church and the Fishermen's Bastion, or exploring the World War II Hospital in the Rock and the surrounding nuclear bunkers and labyrinth of caves that lie beneath the hill.

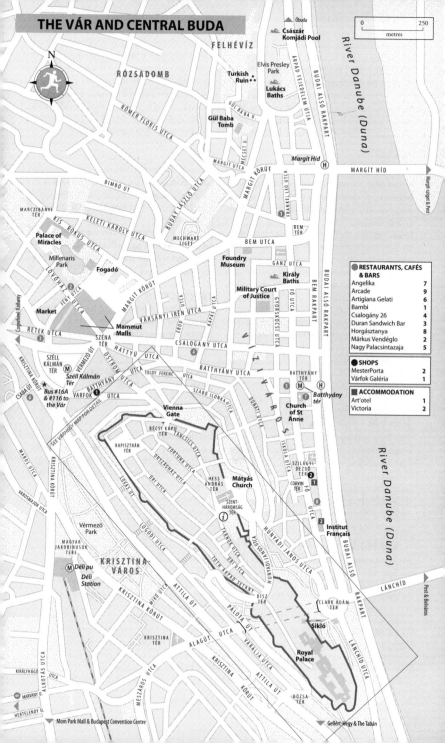

Between the castle and the river, the **Víziváros** is something of a quiet residential backwater in the heart of Buda, with a distinctive atmosphere but few specific sights other than the Lánchíd and the Sikló funicular at the southern end, the **Church of St Anne** on **Batthyány tér** in the middle, and the **Király Baths** further up.

The area to the **north of the Vár** has a variety of attractions in the backstreets off Margít körút: a lively **market** and the **Millenáris Park**, a major concert venue, exhibition centre and children's playground all in one. Further north, on the edge of the affluent Rózsadomb district, is one of Budapest's Turkish remnants, **Gül Baba's tomb**.

ARRIVAL

THE VÁR

By funicular The simplest and most novel approach to the Vár is to ride up to the palace by the Sikló, a renovated nineteenth-century funicular that runs from Clark Ádám tér by the Lánchíd.

By bus From Pest, the most direct approach is to get bus #16 from Erzsébet tér across the Lánchíd to the lower terminal of the Sikló, or straight up to the Vár. From Széll Kálmán tér (on the red metro line #2) you can take buses #16, #16A or #116 from the raised side of the square, which all run through to Dísz tér.

On foot From Széll Kálmán tér head up Várfók utca or Ostrom utca to the Vienna Gate at the northern end of the Castle District. Walking from Batthyány tér via the steep flights of steps (*lépcső*) off Fő utca involves more effort, but the dramatic stairway up to the Fishermen's Bastion is worth the sweat. There are also stairs leading up from the southern end of the Vérmező on the western side of the hill.

Lift A passenger lift by the Lion Gateway of the Royal Palace provides direct access to and from Dózsa tér, on the western foot of the hill (Mon 6am–7pm, Tues–Sat 6am–9m, Sun 9am–6.30pm; 100Ft).

CENTRAL BUDA

Víziváros The red metro line and bus #16 are the best approach. For **Rózsadomb** Trams #4 and #6 skirt the southern edge, running between Pest and Széll Kálmán tér.

INFORMATION

Tourist office The official tourist office, Budapestinfo, at Szentháromság tér 6 (round the corner from the main part of the square, opposite *The Hilton*), can supply a free map of the Vár and other information.

The Vár

The Vár's striking location and its strategic utility have long gone hand in hand: Hungarian kings built their palaces here because it was easy to defend, a fact appreciated by the Turks, Habsburgs and other occupiers. The **Royal Palace** serves as a reminder of this past, rising like a house of cards at the southern end of the hill, as proud yet insubstantial as those who ruled there while Hungary's fate was determined by mightier forces.

The hill's buildings have been almost wholly reconstructed from the rubble of 1945, when the Wehrmacht and the Red Army battled over the hill while Buda's inhabitants

STREET LIFE

The **streets of the Vár** to the north of the palace still follow their medieval courses, with Gothic arches and stone carvings half-concealed in the courtyards and passages of eighteenth-century Baroque houses, whose facades are embellished with fancy ironwork grilles. For many centuries, residence here was a privilege granted to religious or ethnic groups, each occupying a specific street. This pattern persisted through the 145-year-long Turkish occupation, when Armenians, Circassians and Sephardic Jews established themselves under the relatively tolerant Ottomans. The liberation of Buda by a multinational Christian army under Habsburg command was followed by a pogrom and ordinances restricting the right of residence to Catholics and Germans, which remained in force for nearly a century. Almost every building here displays a stone *műemlék* (listed) **plaque** giving details of its history (in Hungarian), and a surprising number are still homes rather than embassies or boutiques – there are even a couple of schools and corner shops. At dusk, when most of the tourists have left, pensioners walk their dogs and toddlers play in the long shadows of Hungarian history.

cowered underground. This was the eighty-sixth time that the Vár had been ravaged and rebuilt over seven centuries, rivalling the devastation caused by the recapture of Buda from the Turks in 1686. It was this repeated destruction that caused the melange of styles characterizing the hill. Adding to the mix, the neo-Gothic **Mátyás Church** and **Fishermen's Bastion** are romantic nineteenth-century evocations of medieval glories, interweaving past and present national fixations. The plain exterior of the Royal Palace, an uninspiring reconstruction of the prewar behemoth that stood here, fails to evoke any such glory. Here, it's what is inside that matters: two major museums, the **Hungarian National Gallery**, and the **Budapest History Museum**, as well as the **National Széchenyi Library**.

Szentháromság tér

The obvious starting point is **Szentháromság tér** (Holy Trinity Square), the historic heart of the district, named after an ornate **Trinity Column** erected in 1713 in thanksgiving for the abatement of a plague; a scene showing people dying from the Black Death appears on the plinth. To the southwest stands the former **Town Hall**, Buda having been a municipality until its unification with Pest and Óbuda in 1873; note the corner statue of Pallas Athene, bearing Buda's coat of arms on her shield.

Mátyás Church

Mátyás templom • I, Szentháromság tér • Mon–Fri 9am–5pm, Sat 9am–1pm, Sun 1–5pm • 990Ft, audio-guide 500Ft • Tickets from the office across the road by the Fishermen's Bastion • Mass is celebrated daily at 7.30am and 6pm, and on Sun at 10am (in Latin with a full choir), noon and 6pm • ⓦ matyas-templom.hu

Szentháromság tér's most prominent feature is the neo-Gothic **Mátyás Church** with its wildly asymmetrical diamond-patterned roofs and toothy spires. Officially dedicated to Our Lady but popularly named after "Good King Mátyás", the building is a late nineteenth-century recreation by architect Frigyes Schulek, grafted onto those portions of the original thirteenth-century church that survived the siege of 1686. Ravaged yet again in World War II, the church was laboriously restored by a Communist regime keen to show its patriotic credentials, and the transition to democracy in 1989–90 saw the sanctity of this "ancient shrine of the Hungarian people" reaffirmed – which means that visitors are expected to be properly dressed and respectfully behaved.

As you enter the church through its twin-spired **Mary Portal**, the richness of the interior is overwhelming. Painted leaves and geometric motifs run up columns and under vaulting, while shafts of light fall through rose windows onto gilded altars and statues with

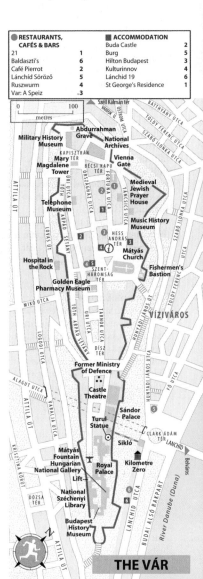

● RESTAURANTS, CAFÉS & BARS		■ ACCOMMODATION	
21	1	Buda Castle	2
Baldaszti's	6	Burg	5
Café Pierrot	2	Hilton Budapest	3
Lánchíd Söröző	5	Kulturinnov	4
Ruszwurm	4	Lánchíd 19	6
Var: A Speiz	3	St George's Residence	1

THE VÁR

stunning effect. Most of the **frescoes** were executed by Károly Lotz or Bertalan Székely, the foremost historical painters of the nineteenth century. The **coat of arms of King Mátyás** can be seen on the wall to your left, just inside; his family name, Corvinus, comes from the raven (*corvus* in Latin) that appeared on his heraldry and on every volume in his famed Corvin Library.

Loreto Chapel

Beneath the south tower is the **Loreto Chapel**, containing a Baroque Madonna, while in the bay beneath the **Béla Tower** you can see two medieval capitals, one carved with monsters fighting a dragon, the other with two bearded figures reading a book. The tower is named after Béla IV, who founded the church, rather than his predecessor in the second chapel along, who shares a **double sarcophagus** with Anne of Chatillon. The tomb, originally located in the old capital, Székesfehérvár, 60km southwest of Budapest, was moved here after its discovery in 1848. Although Hungary's medieval kings were crowned at Székesfehérvár, it was customary to make a prior appearance in Buda – hence the sobriquet, the "Coronation Church".

Treasury

The Mátyás Church has a small collection of **ecclesiastical treasures** and relics, including the right foot of St János. The **crypt**, normally reserved for prayer, contains the red-marble tombstone of a nameless Árpád prince. Otherwise, climb a spiral staircase to the **Royal Oratory** overlooking the stained-glass windows and embossed vaulting of the nave; here votive figures and vestments presage a **replica of the Coronation Regalia**, whose attached exhibition is more informative about the provenance of St Stephen's Crown than that accompanying the originals, on display in Parliament (see p.53).

    Mass is celebrated in the Mátyás Church daily, on Sundays and public holidays. The church is also a superb venue for **concerts** during the festival seasons, and evening organ recitals throughout the year. Details appear in listings magazines and on the church's own website. Tickets are available at the church or from any booking agency (see p.185).

Fishermen's Bastion

Halászbástya • 500Ft to go up to the upper level – tickets from the ticket office next door

After the Mátyás Church, the most impressive sight in the Vár is the **Fishermen's Bastion** just beyond. An undulating white rampart of cloisters and stairways intersecting at seven tent-like turrets (symbolizing the Magyar tribes that conquered the Carpathian Basin), it looks as though it was dreamt up by the illusionist artist Escher, but was actually designed by Schulek as a foil to the Mátyás Church. Although fishermen from the Víziváros reputedly defended this part of the hill during the Middle Ages, the bastion is purely decorative. The **view** of Pest across the river, framed by the bastion, is only surpassed by the vistas from the terrace of Buda Palace, and the Citadella on Gellért-hegy. However, you might baulk at paying the 500Ft fee to climb to the upper level as the free view from the ground level is just as good.

Statue of King Stephen

Between the Fishermen's Bastion and the Mátyás Church, an equestrian **statue of King Stephen** honours the founder of the Hungarian nation, whose conversion to Christianity and coronation with a crown sent by the pope presaged the Magyars' integration into European civilization (see box, p.92). The relief at the back of the plinth depicts Schulek offering a model of the church to Stephen. Like the church and the bastion, his statue is reflected in the copper-glass facade of the **Budapest Hilton**,

6

KING STEPHEN

If you commit just one figure from Hungarian history to memory, make it **King Stephen**, for it was he who welded the tribal Magyar fiefdoms into a state and won recognition from Christendom. Born Vajk, son of Grand Duke Géza, he emulated his father's policy of trying to convert the pagan Magyars and develop Hungary with the help of foreign preachers, craftsmen and merchants. By marrying Gizella of Bavaria in 996, he was able to use her father's knights to crush a pagan revolt after Géza's death, and subsequently received an apostolic cross and crown from Pope Sylvester II for his coronation on Christmas Day, 1000 AD, when he took the name Stephen (István in Hungarian).

Though noted for his enlightened views (such as the need for tolerance and the desirability of multiracial nations), he could act ruthlessly when necessary. After his only son Imre died in an accident and a pagan seemed likely to inherit, Stephen had the man blinded and poured molten lead into his ears. Naming his successor, he symbolically offered his crown to the Virgin Mary rather than the Holy Roman Emperor or the pope; ever since, she has been considered the Patroness of Hungary. Swiftly canonized after his death in 1038, **St Stephen** became a national talisman, his mummified right hand a holy relic, and his coronation regalia the symbol of statehood. Despite playing down his cult for decades, even the Communists eventually embraced it in a bid for some legitimacy, while nobody in post-Communist Hungary thinks it odd that the symbol of the republic should be the crown and cross of King Stephen.

---

incorporating chunks of a medieval Dominican church and monastery on the side facing the river, and an eighteenth-century Jesuit college on the other, which bears a copy of the **Mátyás Relief** from Bautzen in Germany that's regarded as the only true likeness of Hungary's Renaissance monarch.

Ruszwurm patisserie

Along the road from the Mátyás Church the tiny **Ruszwurm patisserie**, at Szentháromság utca 7, has been a pastry shop and café since 1827 and was a gingerbread shop in the Middle Ages. Its Empire-style decor looks much the same as it would have done under Vilmos Ruszwurm, who ran the patisserie for nearly four decades from 1884.

North along Táncsics Mihály utca

In the fifteenth century, when both Ashkenazi and Sephardic Jews lived here, **Táncsics Mihály utca** was known as Zsidó utca (Jewish Street). The Ashkenazi community was established in 1251 in the reign of Béla IV, but was completely wiped out when Buda was captured from the Ottomans in 1686. The Jews, who had fared well under Turkish rule, assisted in the defence of Buda, and those who had not fled or died in the siege were carted away as prisoners by the victorious Christian army. After several name changes, the street was renamed in 1948 after **Mihály Táncsics**, a radical Hungarian politician of the 1848 uprising who was imprisoned here. As it happens, Táncsics, though not Jewish, joined a Jewish platoon of the National Guard in protest against anti-Semitism.

Music History Museum

Zenetörténeti Múzeum • I, Táncsics Mihály utca 7 • Tues–Sun 10am–4pm • 600Ft • Ⓦ zti.hu

The **Music History Museum** occupies the Baroque Erdödy Palace where Beethoven was a guest in 1800, and where Bartók once had a workshop before he emigrated. The museum puts on temporary exhibitions that draw on its superb collection of letters, manuscripts, scores and instruments. On your way out, have a look at no. 9 next door, which was once the Joseph Barracks where the Habsburgs jailed Hungarian radicals such as Mihály Táncsics.

Medieval Jewish Prayer House

Középkori Zsidó Imaház • I, Táncsics Mihály utca 26 • May–Oct Tues–Sun 10am–5pm • 600Ft • ⓦ btm.hu

Evidence of Buda's Jewish past can be found at Táncsics Mihály utca 26, which contains a **Medieval Jewish Prayer House**. Around 1470, King Mátyás allowed the Jews to build a synagogue and appointed a Jewish council led by Jacobus Mendel; part of Mendel's house survives in the entrance to the prayer house. All that remains of its original decor are two Cabbalistic symbols painted on a wall, and though the museum does its best to flesh out the history of the community with maps and prints, all the real treasures are in the Jewish Museum in Pest (see p.63).

6

Kapisztrán tér

At the end of Táncsics Mihály utca lies **Bécsi kapu tér**, named after the **Vienna Gate** (Bécsi kapu) that was erected on the 250th anniversary of the recapture of Buda. Beside it, the forbidding-looking neo-Romanesque **National Archives** (no admission) guard the way to **Kapisztrán tér**, a larger square centred on the **Mary Magdalene Tower** (Magdolna-torony), whose accompanying church was wrecked in World War II. In medieval times this was where Hungarian residents worshipped (Germans used the Mátyás Church), so its reconstruction is occasionally mooted by nationalist politicians. Today the tower boasts a peal of ornamental bells that jingle through a medley composed by the jazz pianist György Szabados, including Hungarian folk tunes, Chopin *Études* and the theme from *Bridge over the River Kwai*.

Beyond the tower is a statue of **Friar John Capistranus**, who exhorted the Hungarians to victory at the siege of Belgrade in 1456, a triumph which the pope hailed by ordering church bells to be rung at noon throughout Europe. The statue, showing Capistranus bestriding a dead Turk, is aptly sited outside the Military History Museum.

Tóth Árpád sétány

Running along the western edge of the Vár is **Tóth Árpád sétány**, a promenade lined with cannons and chestnut trees, looking across to the Buda Hills. Just to the east of its northern end, past a giant **flagpole** striped in Hungarian colours, you'll find the symbolic **grave of Abdurrahman**, the last Turkish Pasha of Buda, who died on the walls in 1686 – a "valiant foe", according to the inscription.

The Military History Museum

Hadtörténeti Múzeum • I, Tóth Árpád sétány 40 • Tues–Sun: April–Sept 10am–6pm; Oct–March 10am–4pm • 800Ft • ⓦ militaria.hu

At the northern end of Tóth Árpád sétány stands the entrance to the **Military History Museum**. Housed in a former barracks, the museum has a good display on Hungarian military history that starts upstairs with the birth of the Honvéd (national army) during the 1848–49 War of Independence. The section covering 1918–48 has some harrowing pictures of two horrendous campaigns, the Italian front in World War I and the Russian front in World War II, and also covers the siege of Budapest at the end of the war and its aftermath – more misery for the Hungarians. The ground-floor exhibition covers the period 1948–68: the grand military parades of the Communist period look distinctly hollow now. Lovers of flags and uniforms will enjoy the display "One Thousand Years of Military Symbols". In the courtyard are post-Communist memorials to the POWs who never returned from the Gulag.

Országház utca

Running south from Kapisztrán tér towards Szentháromság tér, there's more to be seen on **Országház utca**, which was the district's main thoroughfare in the Middle Ages and was known as the "street of baths" during Turkish times. Its present name, Parliament Street, recalls the sessions of the Diet held in the 1790s in a former Poor Clares' cloister at no. 28, where the Gestapo imprisoned 350 Hungarians and foreigners in 1945. No. 17, over

6

ANTAL SZERB

"Best of all I loved the Castle District. I never tired of its ancient streets." So speaks Mihály, the anti-hero of one of Hungary's most popular novels, *Journey by Moonlight* (*Utas és Holdvilág*), by **Antal Szerb** (1901–45). As Mihály recalls his Bohemian past, this enchanting book captures very strongly the Mittel Europa feel of the Vár. Brought up a staunch Catholic in an assimilated Jewish family, Szerb was a highly respected writer in the interwar period, writing histories of Hungarian and world literature and penning a series of short stories and novels that have been brilliantly translated into English (see p.223). Yet he was classified as Jewish in 1942 by the Third Jewish Law, and was shot in Balf, western Hungary on a forced march. Szerb turned down the chance to escape because he and two friends on the march had made a pact that they would either escape or die together. His grave can be found in Kerepesi Cemetery (p.81).

Unfortunately Hungarians like their thinkers to be weighty, and the underlying seriousness of Szerb's books is all too often dismissed on account of their wit and lightness of touch.

---

the road, consists of two medieval houses joined together and has a relief of a croissant on its keystone, from the time when it was a bakery. A few doors down from the old Parliament building, Renaissance graffiti survive on the underside of the bay window of no. 22 and a Gothic trefoil-arched cornice on the house next door, while the one beyond has been rebuilt in its original fifteenth-century form.

Úri utca

Úri utca (Gentleman Street) boasts historic associations, for it was at the former Franciscan monastery at no. 51 that the five Hungarian Jacobins were held before being beheaded on the "Blood Meadow" below the hill in 1795. As you walk down the street from Kapisztrán tér, notice the statues of the four seasons in the first-floor niches at nos. 54–56, Gothic sedilia in the gateway of nos. 48–50, and three arched windows and two diamond-shaped ones from the fourteenth and fifteenth centuries at no. 31. In the wall at no. 27 is a ventilation shaft for the secret hospital below.

Telephone Museum

Telefónia Múzeum • I, Úri utca 49, entered from Országház utca 30 on weekends and holidays • Tues–Sun 10am–4pm • 7590Ft

At Úri utca 49 is a wing of the Poor Clares' cloister that served as a postwar telephone exchange, before being turned into a **Telephone Museum**. The curator strives to explain the development of telephone exchanges since their introduction to Budapest in the early 1900s, activating a noisy rotary one that's stood here since the 1930s – a quieter, more streamlined modern exchange still operates there. You're invited to dial up commentaries in English or songs in Hungarian, check out the webcam and internet facilities, and admire the personal phones of Emperor Franz Josef, Admiral Horthy and the Communist leader János Kádár.

The Hospital in the Rock

Sziklakórház • I, Lovas út 4/c – down the steps at the western end of Szentháromság utca and 50m to the right • Tues–Sun 10am–8pm • 3000Ft • ⓦ sziklakorhaz.hu

Some six to fourteen metres beneath the Vár's streets lie 10km of galleries formed by hot springs and cellars dug since medieval times. In 1941, a section was converted into a military hospital staffed from the civilian Szent János hospital, which doubled as an air-raid shelter after the Red Army broke through the Attila Line and encircled Budapest in December 1944. In the 1950s, a nuclear bunker was added to the complex and was secretly maintained in readiness until 2000, a time capsule of the Cold War. Ramped throughout for wheelchairs and trolleys, its operating theatres contain 1930s military field X-ray and anaesthetic machines (used in the film *Evita* in 1996) and gory waxworks; bed-sheets in the wards were changed every fortnight until 2000.

The ventilation system is run by generators installed in the **nuclear bunker** built in 1953, with charcoal air-filters, a laboratory for detecting toxins, atropine ampoules to be injected against nerve gas, and an airlock fitted when the bunker was enlarged between 1958 and 1962. To preserve its secrecy, fuel was delivered by trucks pretending to "water" flowerbeds on the surface, via a concealed pipeline.

The Golden Eagle Pharmacy Museum

Arany Sas Patikamúzeum • Tárnok utca 18 • Tues–Sun 10.30am–5.30pm • 500Ft

South from Szentháromság tér towards the palace, the **Golden Eagle Pharmacy** was the first pharmacy in Buda, established after the expulsion of the Turks, and moved to its present site in the eighteenth century. Its original murals and furnishings lend authenticity to dubious nostrums, including the skull of a mummy used to make Mumia powder to treat epilepsy; there's also a reconstruction of an alchemist's laboratory, complete with dried bats and crocodiles, and other obscure exhibits such as the small, long-necked Roman glass vessel for collecting widows' tears. The museum has a brief account in English, but the staff can usually explain the more interesting bits. Notice the portrait of the Dominican nun pharmacist – it was common practice for nuns and monks in the Middle Ages to double up as apothecaries. The *Tárnok* coffee house, next door but one, occupies a medieval building with a Renaissance graffiti facade of red and yellow checks and roundels and, like the street, is named after the royal treasurers who once lived there.

Dísz tér

Both Tárnok utca and Úri utca end in **Dísz tér** (Parade Square), whose cobbled expanses are guarded by a mournful Honvéd memorial to the dead of 1848–49. To the south lies the scarred hulk of the old **Ministry of Defence**, to the east of which stands the **Castle Theatre** (Várszínház), which was a Carmelite church until the order was dissolved by Josef II; its conversion was supervised by Farkas Kempelen, inventor of a chess-playing automaton. It was here that the first-ever play in Hungarian was staged in 1790, and where Beethoven performed in 1808; today it is used by the National Dance Theatre. The last building in the row is the **Sándor Palace** (Sándor Palota), formerly the prime minister's residence, where Premier Teleki shot himself in protest at Hungary joining the Nazi invasion of Yugoslavia. It is now the residence of the country's president, a figurehead who is elected by Parliament rather than the electorate.

The Turul statue

Next door to Sándor Palace, the upper terminal of the **Sikló** funicular (see p.101) is separated from the terrace of the Royal Palace by stately railings and the ferocious-looking **Turul statue**– a giant bronze eagle clasping a sword in its talons, which is visible from across the river. In Magyar mythology, the Turul sired the first dynasty of Hungarian kings by raping the grandmother of Prince Árpád, who led the tribes into the Carpathian Basin. The Turul also accompanied their raids on Europe, bearing the sword of Attila the Hun in its talons. During the nineteenth century it became a symbol of Hungarian identity in the face of Austrian culture, but wound up being co-opted by the Habsburgs, who cast Emperor Franz Josef as a latter-day Árpád for the next millennium. Today, the Turul has been adopted as an emblem by Hungary's right-wing extremists.

From here, you can go through the wrought-iron gates and down some steps to the **terrace** of the palace, commanding a sweeping **view** of Pest. Beyond the souvenir stalls prances an equestrian **statue of Prince Eugene of Savoy**, who captured Buda from the Ottomans in 1686. The smaller bronze statues nearby represent **Csongor and Tünde**, the lovers in the play of the same name, by Vörösmarty.

6

A HISTORY OF THE ROYAL PALACE

As befits a former royal residence, the lineage of the **Royal Palace** (Királyi palota) can be traced back to medieval times, the rise and fall of various palaces on the hill reflecting the changing fortunes of the Hungarian state. The first fortifications and dwellings, hastily erected by Béla IV after the Mongol invasion of 1241–42, were replaced by the grander palaces of the Angevin kings, who ruled in more prosperous and stable times. This process of rebuilding reached its zenith in the reign of Mátyás Corvinus (1458–90), whose palace was a Renaissance extravaganza to which artists and scholars from all over Europe were drawn by the blandishments of Queen Beatrice and the prospect of lavish hospitality. The rooms had hot and cold running water, and during celebrations the fountains and gargoyles flowed with wine. After the Turkish occupation and the long siege that ended it, only ruins were left – which the Habsburgs, Hungary's new rulers, levelled to build a palace of their own.

From modest beginnings under Empress Maria Theresa (when there were a mere 203 rooms, which she never saw completed), the palace expanded inexorably throughout the nineteenth century, though no monarch ever dwelt here, only the Habsburg palatine (viceroy). After the collapse of the empire following World War I, Admiral Horthy inhabited the building with all the pomp of monarchy until he was deposed by a German coup in October 1944. The palace was left unoccupied, and it wasn't long before the siege of Buda once again resulted in total devastation. Reconstruction work began in the 1950s – you can see the contrast between the fancier prewar stonework in the Lion Courtyard and the tacky postwar version on the side overlooking the river. The interior also lacks the elegance of the prewar version, being designed to accommodate cultural institutions. However, one benefit of the reconstruction was that it revealed the medieval substrata beneath the rubble, which were incorporated into the new building.

The Hungarian National Gallery

Magyar Nemzeti Galéria • Royal Palace wings A, B, C and D • **National Gallery** Tues–Sun 10am–6pm, MNG Extra: 6–10pm first Fri of month • 1000Ft for permanent displays, 2000Ft for visiting shows, 2000Ft for MNG Extra • **Habsburg crypt** Advance notice required – ask at the desk or ring ☎ 06 20 439 7331 • 600Ft • ⓦ mng.hu

The biggest attraction in the Royal Palace is the **Hungarian National Gallery**, which is devoted to Hungarian art from the Middle Ages to the present. It contains much that's superb, but the vastness of the collection and the confusing layout can be fatiguing. Though all the paintings are labelled in English, other details are scanty. Until the new English catalogue is ready it is worth taking the free guided tours in English (Thurs 2pm & Sun 11am). On the first Friday of every month the gallery stays open till 10pm for MNG Extra, which consists of talks, tours (in English too), concerts and other events.

The main entrance is on the eastern side of Wing C, overlooking the river, behind the statue of Eugene of Savoy. You'll need to give a couple of days' notice to see the separate **Habsburg crypt**, containing the tombs of several Habsburgs who ruled as palatines of Hungary up until 1849.

Ground Floor

Through the shop to the left of the ticket office, a lovely **wooden ceiling** from a sixteenth-century church and marble reliefs of knightly tombs are the highlights of a **Medieval and Renaissance Lapidarium**. Between the two, doors on the left lead to the fantastic collection of fifteenth-century **Gothic altarpieces** and panels at the rear of Wing D. Salvaged from churches great and small that escaped destruction by the Turks, some are artful and others rustic, but all are full of character and detail: notice the varied reactions expressed within the *Death of the Virgin* from Kassa (Kosice, a Slovakian centre of altar-painting) and the gloating spectators in the Jánosrét *Passion* in the second room. From the same church comes a *St Nicholas* altar as long as a limo and lurid as a comic strip, whose final scene shows cripples being cured by the saint's corpse. Also strange to modern eyes are *The Expulsion of St Adalbert*, who seems blithely oblivious to the demolition of his church, and the woodcarving of *St Anthony the Hermit*, carrying a hill upon his back. The pointed finials on the high altar from Liptószentmária (Liptovská Mara in Slovakia) anticipate the winged altarpieces of the sixteenth century on the floor above. To get there without returning to the foyer, use the small staircase outside the doors to this section and turn left, left and left again at the top.

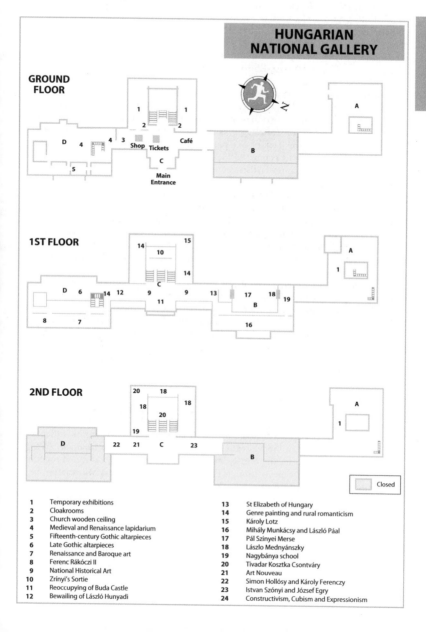

HUNGARIAN NATIONAL GALLERY

GROUND FLOOR

1ST FLOOR

2ND FLOOR

Closed

1	Temporary exhibitions	**13**	St Elizabeth of Hungary
2	Cloakrooms	**14**	Genre painting and rural romanticism
3	Church wooden ceiling	**15**	Károly Lotz
4	Medieval and Renaissance lapidarium	**16**	Mihály Munkácsy and László Páal
5	Fifteenth-century Gothic altarpieces	**17**	Pál Szinyei Merse
6	Late Gothic altarpieces	**18**	László Mednyánszky
7	Renaissance and Baroque art	**19**	Nagybánya school
8	Ferenc Rákóczi II	**20**	Tivadar Kosztka Csontváry
9	National Historical Art	**21**	Art Nouveau
10	Zrínyi's Sortie	**22**	Simon Hollósy and Károly Ferenczy
11	Reoccupying of Buda Castle	**23**	Istvan Szónyi and József Egry
12	Bewailing of László Hunyadi	**24**	Constructivism, Cubism and Expressionism

First floor

The **first floor** covers the widest range of art and is likely to engage you the longest. It picks up where the ground floor left off in the former Throne Room, where **late Gothic altarpieces** with soaring pinnacles and carved surrounds are displayed. Most of them come from churches now in Slovakia or Romania, such as the Annunciation altarpiece from Csíkmenaság (now Armaseni in Romania) or the homely St Anne altarpiece from Kisszeben (Sabinov, Slovakia), which looks like a medieval playgroup. On an altar from Berki (Rokycany, Slovakia), Mary Magdalene is raptured by angels as bishops are impaled, while another piece from Liptószentandrás (Liptovsky Ondrej, Slovakia) shows St Andrew clutching the poles for his crucifixion. Also look out for **The Visitation** by the anonymous "Master MS", in the anteroom, and the coffered **ceiling** from Gogánváralija (Gogan-Varolea, Romania), in the room behind the Kisszeben Annunciation altarpiece.

Many of the works in the adjacent section on **Baroque art** once belonged to Count Miklós Esterházy (including his portrait), or were confiscated from private owners in the 1950s. The prolific Austrian **Anton Maulbertsch**, who executed scores of altars and murals reminiscent of Caravaggio, is represented here by works such as *The Death of St Joseph*. On the back of one panel running across the room, don't miss **Ádám Mányoki**'s portrait of Ferenc Rákóczi II from 1712, a sober study of a national hero that foreshadowed a new artistic genre of **National Historical art** in the nineteenth century.

People coming up the **main stairs** from the ticket office will find, at the rear of the mid-floor landing, two vast canvases by **Peter Krafft**. *Zrínyi's Sortie* depicts the suicidal sally by the defenders of Szigetvár against a Turkish army fifty times their number; not a drop of blood spatters the melee, as Count Zrínyi leads the charge across the bridge. The other shows Franz Josef being crowned King of Hungary in equally slavish detail. Facing you in the large first-floor **atrium** is **Gyula Benczúr**'s *Reoccupying of Buda Castle*, whose portrayal of Eugene of Savoy and Karl of Lotharingia suggests a mere exchange of Turkish rulers for Habsburg ones, while *The Bewailing of László Hunyadi* by **Viktor Madarász** (hung off towards Wing D) would have been read as an allusion to the execution of Hungarian patriots after the War of Independence. At the other end, near Wing B, you'll find **Sándor Lilzen-Mayer**'s *St Elizabeth of Hungary* offering her ermine cape to a ragged mother and child, and two iconic scenes by **Bertalan Székely**: *The Battle of Mohács*, a shattering defeat for the Hungarians in 1526; and *The Women of Eger*, exalting their defiance of the Turks in 1552.

The remainder of the first floor illustrates other trends in nineteenth-century Hungarian art, namely genre painting, **rural romanticism** and Impressionism. On the Buda side of Wing C, *Thunderstorm on the Puszta* and *Horses at the Watering Place* evoke the hazy skies and manly world of the Hungarian "Wild West" – the Great Plain southeast of Budapest. Both are by **Károly Lotz**, better known for his frescoes around the city, such as in the Mátyás Church, Opera House and Parliament. Wing B devotes a section to works by **Mihály Munkácsy** and **László Paál**, exhibited together since both painted landscapes – though Paál did little else, whereas Munkácsy was internationally renowned for pictures with a social message (*The Last Day of a Condemned Man*, *Tramps of the Night*) and bravura historical works like *The Conquest* (in the Parliament building).

Impressionism was introduced to Hungary by **Pál Szinyei Merse**, whose models and subjects – such as in *A Picnic in May* – were cheerfully bourgeois. Nearby you'll find two luminous landscapes by the prolific **László Mednyánszky** – *Watering-place* and *Fishing on the Tisza* – and paintings from the **Nagybánya school**, an influential artists' colony in what is now Baia Mare in Romania. Look out for peasants discussing *The Country's Troubles*, by the school's guru, **Simon Hollósy**, who quit during a spiritual crisis; a cheerful *Drying the Laundry*, by his successor

HUNGARY'S GREAT PAINTERS

They were two of Hungary's finest painters, living in the same age, yet the lives they led could not have been more different. While **Mihály Munkácsy** (1844–1900) was fêted for his work and buried like a national hero, his funeral attended by government ministers and his body lying in state in Hősök tere, **Tivadar Kosztka Csontváry** (1853–1919) died alone and unrecognized.

Munkácsy spent much of his life in Paris, but always declared himself Hungarian. He painted large dusty landscapes and pictures of peasants and outlaws as well as grand portrayals of Christ before Pilate. His realist style sold very well, but that financial success was his downfall, and he died of syphilis at the age of 56. Time has not been kind to his work, either: many canvases have suffered from his use of bitumen in mixing paint, which has caused them to darken and crack.

Trained as a pharmacist, Csontváry was 27 when a voice told him: "You will be the world's greatest plein-air painter, greater than Raphael." When he began to study painting at the age of 41 he did not belong to any school, and his canvases, simple yet expressive, display an extraordinary use of colour and light. Most of his work was completed in just six years – he painted his last work in 1909, overwhelmed by lack of recognition and schizophrenia. When Picasso saw an exhibition of his works in the 1940s he remarked: "And I thought I was the only great painter of our century."

6

Béla Iványi Grünwald; and *Boys Throwing Pebbles*, by the school's most adept pupil, **Károly Ferenczy**.

There's more of their work on the next floor, off towards Wing D. Midway up the **stairs** hang three canvases by the visionary **Tivadar Kosztka Csontváry**, whose obsession with the Holy Land and the "path of the sun" inspired scenes such as *Pilgrimage to the Cedars in Lebanon* and the vast *Ruins of the Greek Theatre at Taormina*, with its magical twilight colours.

Second floor

The **second floor** covers **twentieth-century Hungarian art up to 1945**, starting with the vibrant **Art Nouveau** movement off to the right of the atrium. Pictures by **János Vaszary** (Golden Age) and **Aladár Körösfői Kriesch** (founder of the Gödöllő artists' colony – see p.149) are set in richly hand-carved frames, an integral part of their composition. **József Rippl-Rónai** was a pupil of Munkácsy whose portraits such as *Woman in a White-dotted Dress* went mostly unrecognized in his lifetime – they're now regarded as Art Nouveau classics. Here you'll also find Csontváry's magically lit *Coaching in Athens at the Full Moon*, and more works by Hollósy (*Rákóczi March*) and Ferenczy (*Morning Sunshine*).

Across the atrium, **István Szőnyi**'s wintry *Burial at Zebegény*, and **József Egry**'s watery *St John the Baptist* have simple lines and muddy colours in common. Both belonged to a generation of artists whose sympathies were on the left in largely right-wing times: Constructivists such as **Béla Uitz**, Cubists **János Kmetty** and **Gyula Derkovits**, the Expressionist **Vilmos Aba-Novák** and the "Hungarian Chagall", **Imre Ámos** (who died in a Nazi death camp – see.p.132) are all represented in Wing C off the stairs.

Third floor

Climbing the **stairs** to the **third floor**, **Tamás Lossonczy**'s abstract-surrealistic *Cleansing Storm*, **Béla Kondor**'s whimsical *The Genius of Mechanical Flying* and a wire sculpture by Tibor Vilt portraying the awful fate of the peasant rebel leader Dózsa presage the section on **Hungarian art since 1945**. Exhibits are rotated to showcase the museum's collection of work by modern artists such as Endre Bálint, Attila Szűcs, Sándor Altorjai and Erzsébet Schaár. On fine days, visitors can ascend to the palace's **dome** for a **view** of the city.

6

The Mátyás Fountain

An archway just before the entrance to the National Gallery leads through a square flanked on three sides by the palace overlooking Buda to the west, though the **view** is marred by the MTI (Hungarian News Agency) building on Nap-hegy. Against the wall on the left stands the flamboyant **Mátyás Fountain**, whose bronze figures recall the legend of Szép Ilonka. This beautiful peasant girl met the king while he was hunting incognito, fell in love with him, and died of a broken heart after discovering his identity and realizing the futility of her hopes. The man with a falcon is the king's Italian chronicler, who recorded the story for posterity (it is also enshrined in a poem by Vörösmarty).

The Lion Courtyard

Down to the left past the Mátyás Fountain, a gateway guarded by lions leads into the **Lion Courtyard**, totally enclosed by further wings of the palace. To the right of the gateway entrance a passage leading to the passenger lift down to Dózsa György tér is lined with photos that bear witness to the grandeur of the prewar palace.

National Széchenyi Library

Országos Széchenyi Könyvtár • Royal Palace Wing F • Tues–Sat 10am–8pm, closed mid-July to late Aug • Reading room day pass 1200Ft; passport or identity card required to apply • ⓦ oszk.hu

On the right-hand side of the Lion Courtyard is the **National Széchenyi Library** occupying the palace's nineteenth-century Ybl block, whose full size is only apparent from the far side of the hill, where it looms over Dózsa György tér like a mountain. The library was founded in 1802 on the initiative of Count Ferenc Széchenyi, the father of István (see p.101). A repository for publications in Hungarian and material relating to the country from around the world, by law it receives a copy of every book, newspaper and magazine that is published in Hungary. The library hosts regular exhibitions from its collection of books and newspapers. You can only visit the reading room on guided tours or with a reader's pass. During library hours, one can use the passenger **lift** in the adjacent building by the Lion Gateway – open to all – which provides direct access to and from Dózsa tér, at the foot of the Vár.

Budapest History Museum

Budapest Történeti Múzeum • Royal Palace Wing E • Mid-March to mid-Sept daily 10am–6pm; mid-Sept to Oct daily 10am–6pm; Nov to mid-March daily except Tues 10am–4pm • 1400Ft, audio-guide 1000Ft • ⓦ btm.hu

On the far side of the Lion Courtyard, the **Budapest History Museum** covers two millennia of history on three floors, and descends into original vaulted, flagstoned halls from the Renaissance and medieval palaces unearthed during excavations. It's worth starting with **prehistory**, to the left on the top floor, to find out about Paleolithic inhabitants of the area. The Avars, the nomadic precursors of the Magyars who overran the Pannonian Plain after the Romans left, are represented by some impressive items retrieved from their burial mounds, such as a gold bridle and stirrup fastenings in a zoomorphic style. Owing to the ravages inflicted by the Mongols and the Turks, there's little to show from the time of the Conquest on the first floor, and only a few artefacts from Hungary's medieval civilization (there is more in the medieval palace below). From the Turkish period there are some fine pots and metal-work, as well as Jewish gravestones, but most of this floor is occupied by the new display on **Budapest in Modern Times**, an exhibition giving insight into urban planning, fashions, trade and vices, from 1686 onwards. At the far end of the ground floor there is a fine display of **statues** from the late fourteenth century that were discovered in 1974.

The **remains of the medieval palace** are reached from the basement via an eighteenth-century cellar spanning two medieval yards on a lower level. A wing of the ground floor of King Sigismund's palace and the cellars beneath the Corvin Library form an intermediate stratum overlaying the cross-vaulted crypt of the **Royal Chapel** and a **Gothic Hall** where lute **concerts** are held. In another chamber are portions of red marble fireplaces and a massive portal carved with cherubs and flowers from the palace of King Mátyás. Emerging into daylight, bear left and up the stairs to reach yet another imposing hall, with a view over the castle ramparts.

The Sikló

Daily 7.30am–10pm, closed every other Mon • 840Ft one-way, 1450Ft return; Budapest Card not valid

Between the Royal Palace and the Sándor Palace stands the upper station of the **Sikló**, a nineteenth-century **funicular** that takes you down to the river and the Lánchíd. Constructed on the initiative of Ödön Széchenyi, whose father built the bridge below, it was only the second funicular in the world when it was inaugurated in 1870, and functioned without a hitch until wrecked by a shell in 1945. The wooden carriages, replicas of the originals, are now lifted by an electric winch rather than a steam engine; they're divided into three sections at different heights to give as many people as possible a view (the bottom compartment gives the most unimpeded views). Capacity is limited, however, so in summer you can expect to queue to go up. In the small park at the foot of the Sikló stands **Kilometre Zero**, a zero-shaped monument from where all distances from Budapest are measured.

The Víziváros

Inhabited by fishermen, craftsmen and their families in medieval times, the **Víziváros** ("Watertown"), between the Vár and the Danube, became depopulated during the seventeenth century, and was resettled by Habsburg mercenaries and their camp followers after the Turks were driven out. The following century saw the neighbourhood gradually gentrified, with solid apartment blocks meeting at odd angles on the hillside, reached by alleys which mostly consist of steps rising from the main street, **Fő utca**. Some of these are still lit by gas lamps and look quite Dickensian on misty evenings.

The Széchenyi Lánchíd

The majestic **Lánchíd** (Chain Bridge) has a special place in the history of Budapest and in the hearts of its citizens. As the first permanent link between Buda and Pest

---

COUNT SZÉCHENYI

Count István Széchenyi (1791–1860) was the outstanding figure of Hungary's Reform era. As a young aide-de-camp he cut a dash at the Congress of Vienna and did the rounds of stately homes across Europe. While in England, he steeplechased hell-for-leather, but still found time to examine factories and steam trains, providing Bernard Shaw with the inspiration for the "odious Zoltán Karpathy" of *Pygmalion* (and the musical *My Fair Lady*). Back in Hungary, he pondered solutions to his homeland's backwardness and offered a year's income from his estates towards the establishment of a Hungarian Academy. In 1830 he published *Hitel* (Credit), a hard-headed critique of the nation's feudal society.

Though politically conservative, Széchenyi was obsessed with **modernization**. A passionate convert to steam power after riding on the Manchester–Liverpool railway, he invited Britons to Hungary to build rail lines and the Lánchíd. He also imported steamships and dredgers, promoted horsebreeding and silk-making, and initiated the dredging of the River Tisza and the blasting of a road through the Iron Gates of the Danube. Alas, his achievements were rewarded by a melancholy end. The 1848 Revolution and the short-lived triumph of the radical party led by his *bête noire*, Kossuth, triggered a nervous breakdown, and Széchenyi eventually shot himself. Today he is often referred to as "the greatest Hungarian" – though curiously it was Kossuth who originally called him this.

(replacing seasonal pontoon bridges and ferries), it was a tremendous spur to the country's economic growth and eventual unification, linking the rural hinterland to European civilization so that Budapest became a commercial centre and transport hub. The bridge symbolized the abolition of feudal privilege, as nobles (hitherto exempt from taxes) were obliged to pay the toll to cross it. It also embodied civic endurance, having been inaugurated only weeks after Hungary lost the 1849 War of Independence, when Austrian troops tried and failed to destroy it.

However, in 1945, the Wehrmacht dynamited all of Budapest's bridges in a bid to check the Red Army. Their reconstruction was one of the first tasks of the postwar era, and the reopening of the Lánchíd on the centenary of its inauguration (Nov 21) was heralded as proof that life was returning to normal, even as Hungary was becoming a Communist dictatorship. Today, the bridge is once again adorned with the national coat of arms rather than Soviet symbols. A positive development in recent years has been its closing to traffic for up to ten weekends over the summer for popular festivities

The idea for a bridge came to **Count István Széchenyi** after he was late for his father's funeral in 1820 because bad weather had made the Danube uncrossable. Turning his idea into reality was to preoccupy him for two decades, and it became the centrepiece of a grand plan to modernize Hungary's communications. Owing to Britain's industrial pre-eminence and Széchenyi's Anglophilia, the bridge was designed by **William Tierney Clark** (who based it on his earlier plan for Hammersmith Bridge in London) and constructed under the supervision of a Scottish engineer, **Adam Clark** (no relation), from components cast in Britain. Besides the technical problems of erecting what was then the longest bridge in Europe (nearly 380m), there was also the attempt by the Austrians to blow it up – which Adam Clark personally thwarted by flooding its chain-lockers. He also dissuaded a Hungarian general from setting it alight in 1849.

Whereas Széchenyi died in an asylum, Clark settled happily in Budapest with his Hungarian wife. After his death, he was buried on the spot that now bears his name, though his remains were subsequently moved to Kerepesi Cemetery. Adam Clark also built the **tunnel** (*alagút*) under the Vár – another Széchenyi project – which Budapestis joked could be used to store the new bridge when it rained.

Szilágyi Dezső tér

If you head north past the **Institut Français** at Fő utca 17 and a former Capuchin church featuring Turkish window arches at no. 30, you come to **Szilágyi Dezső tér**, a square infamous for the events that occurred here in January 1945. When Eichmann and the SS had already fled, the Arrow Cross massacred hundreds of Budapest's Jews and dumped their bodies in the river; an inconspicuous plaque commemorates the victims. From here, you can make a brief detour left up Vám utca, just north of the square, to see the **Iron Block**, a replica of a wooden block into which itinerant apprentices once hammered nails for good luck (the original is in a museum).

Batthyány tér

The main square and social hub of the Víziváros, **Batthyány tér** is named after the nineteenth-century prime minister, Lajos Batthyány, but started out as Bomba tér (Bomb Square) after an ammunition depot sited here for the defence of the Danube. Today, it's busy with shoppers visiting the supermarket in an old market hall on the western side of the square, and commuters using the underground metro/HÉV interchange. The sunken two-storey building to the right of the market used to be the *White Cross Inn*, where Casanova reputedly once stayed. Many of the older buildings in this area are sunken in this way owing to the ground level being raised several feet in the nineteenth century to combat flooding.

Church of St Anne

The twin-towered **Church of St Anne** (Szent Anna templom), at Batthyány tér 7 on the southern corner of Fő utca, is one of the finest Baroque buildings in Budapest. Commissioned by the Jesuits in 1740, it wasn't consecrated until 1805 owing to financial problems, the abolition of the Jesuit order in 1773, and an earthquake. During Communist times there were plans to demolish the building, as it was feared that the metro would undermine its foundations, but these, fortunately, came to nothing. Figures of Faith, Hope and Charity hover above the entrance, and in the middle of the facade St Anne cherishes the child Mary, while God's eye surmounts the Buda coat of arms on its tympanum. The interior is ornate yet homely, the high altar festooned with statues of St Anne presenting Mary to the Temple in Jerusalem, accompanied by a host of cherubim and angels, while chintzy bouquets and potted trees welcome shoppers dropping in to say their prayers.

6

Military Court of Justice

Heading up Fő utca from Batthyány tér, on the left stands the hulking Fascist-style **Military Court of Justice** (Fővárosi Katonai Ügyészség) where Imre Nagy and other leaders of the 1956 Uprising were secretly tried and executed in 1958. The square next door has now been renamed after Nagy, whose body lay in an unmarked grave in the New Public Cemetery for over thirty years (see p.125).

Király Baths

Király gyógyfürdő • II, Fő utca 84 • ☎ 1 202 3688 • Daily 9am–9pm • See p.195 for more details

You can identify the **Király Baths** by the four copper cupolas, shaped like tortoise shells, poking from its eighteenth-century facade. Together with the Rudas, this is the finest of Budapest's Turkish baths; the octagonal pool, lit by star-shaped apertures in the dome, was built in 1570 for the Buda garrison. The baths' name, meaning "king", comes from that of the König family who owned them in the eighteenth century.

Bem tér

Fő utca terminates at **Bem tér**, named after the Polish general Joseph Bem, who fought for the Hungarians in the War of Independence, and was revered by his men as "Father". A **statue of Bem** with his arm in a sling recalls him leading them into battle at Piski, crying "I shall recapture the bridge or die! Forward Hungarians! If we do not have the bridge we do not have the country." Traditionally a site for demonstrations, it was here that the crowds assembled prior to marching on Parliament at the beginning of the 1956 Uprising. In the northwest corner, at the junction of Frankel Leó utca, stands a Budapest institution, the *Bambi* – one of the few unreformed café-bars that retains its 1970s furnishings and fierce waitresses.

Foundry Museum

Öntödei Múzeum • II, Bem utca 20 • Tues–Sun 9am–4pm • 400Ft

A century ago, the neighbourhood surrounding Bem tér was dominated by a foundry established by the Swiss ironworker Abrahám Ganz, which grew into the mighty Ganz Machine Works. The original ironworks only ceased operation in 1964, when it was turned into a **Foundry Museum**, 200m up the hill from Bem tér. You can still see the old wooden structure and the foundry's huge ladles and cranes *in situ*, together with a collection of cast-iron stoves, tram wheels, lamp posts and other exhibits.

Széll Kálmán tér to Rózsadomb

The area immediately north of the Vár is defined by the transport hub of **Széll Kálmán tér** (Kálmán Széll Square). A former clay quarry that was turned into tennis courts between the wars, it was named in 1929 after Széll, a former finance and prime minister who had restored stability to the economy at the turn of the century. It was renamed **Moszkva tér** in 1951, and even after 1989 kept its old name. However, the new-broom Fidesz administration, which had named its economic programme after Széll, gave it back its old name in 2011. The new mayor is also promising to give the scruffy square a long-overdue revamp. To the north, the **Mammut mall** (fronted by a statue of the woolly beast) is a magnet for shoppers, as is the lively Fény utca **market** and the **Millenáris Park**.

The park provides a cultural focal point, augmenting the long-standing tourist attraction of Gül Baba's tomb, on the lower slopes of Rózsadomb. Otherwise, Széll Kálmán tér is the place to catch buses to the Cogwheel Railway (see p.120) or the Farkasréti Cemetery (see p.123), as well as tram #4 or #6 to Pest.

Millenáris Park

Millenáris • II, Fény utca 20–22 • Daily 6am–11pm • Free • Information centre daily 10am–6pm • ☎ 1 336 4000, ⓦ millenaris.hu

The main attraction of the area is the **Millenáris Park**, the site of the former Ganz Machine Works behind the Mammut malls. The converted factory buildings and the park between them host indoor and outdoor concerts and theatre, as well as an interactive playhouse. The park includes water features, vineyards and plots of corn to represent different regions of Hungary, and kids can be let loose on the **playground** themed around a Hungarian folk tale. You can get details from the information centre, the Fogadó, in Building G.

Palace of Miracles

Csodák palotája • Mid-June to late Aug daily 10am–6pm; rest of the year Mon–Fri 9am–5pm, Sat & Sun 10am–6pm • 1350Ft, family 3800Ft • ⓦ csodapalota.hu

A big draw for those with kids or an interest in science is the **Palace of Miracles** (in Building D). This interactive playhouse is the brainchild of two Hungarian physicists and aims to explain scientific principles to 6- to 12-year-olds, using devices such as optical illusions, a bed of nails, a simulated low-gravity "moonwalk" and a "miracle bicycle" on a tightrope.

Gül Baba's tomb

Gül Baba Türbe • II, Mecset utca 14 • Daily 10am–6pm • 500Ft (free until the park is restored)

The smoggy arc of **Margít körút** underlines the gulf between the polluted inner city and the breeze-freshened heights of Budapest's most affluent neighbourhood, **Rózsadomb** (Rose Hill). The hill is named after the flowers that were reputedly introduced to Hungary by a revered Sufi dervish, Gül Baba, the "Father of the Roses", who participated in the Turkish capture of Buda but died during the thanksgiving service afterwards. **Gül Baba's Tomb** is located up the steps at the end of Mecset utca (Mosque Street), five-minutes' walk uphill from Margít körút via Margít utca. Its octagonal shrine is adorned with Arabic calligraphy and Turkish carpets, and is surrounded by a colonnaded parapet with fine views and a park with rose bushes and marble fountains decorated with tiles.

Rózsadomb

The **Rózsadomb** itself is as much a social category as a neighbourhood: a list of residents would read like a Hungarian *Who's Who*. During the Communist era this included the top Party *funcionárusok*, whose homes featured secret exits that enabled ÁVO chiefs to escape lynching during the Uprising. Nowadays, wealthy film directors and entrepreneurs predominate, and the sloping streets are lined with spacious villas and flashy cars.

The baths

Lukács Baths Lukács Fürdő • II, Frankl Leó út 25–29 • ☎ 1 326 1695 • Daily 6am–8pm • **Császár Komjádi Pool** Császár Komjádi
Uszoda • II, Árpád fejedelem útja 8 • Daily 6am–7pm • ☎ 1 212 2750 • See p.195 for more details

Two noteworthy baths dominate the Buda bank of the Danube, north of the Margít
híd. The Neoclassical **Lukács Baths**, harbours a thermal pool, a small swimming pool
and whirlpools – the entry is on the Frankl Leó side; the ruined Turkish bath further
up on the other side of the road testifies to the long history of baths here. Next to
the Lukács, with an entrance on the riverside, is the modern **Császár Komjádi Pool**. The
first European swimming and water polo championships were held here in 1926 and it
is still a training pool for Hungary's water polo players.

6

Elvis Presley Park

The strip of park between the Lukács Baths and the river is the surprisingly named
Elvis Presley Park. Elvis earned this tribute with his call on the radio for donations for
the Hungarian people after the defeat of the 1956 revolution – and Mayor Tarlós is
also a great Elvis fan. The park itself is pretty nondescript, with no special features, and
if you ask for directions you'll find that few locals know where it is.

Gellért-hegy and the Tabán

Gellért-hegy, a craggy dolomite hill rearing 130m above the embankment, is one area you'd be foolish to miss: it offers a fabulous view of the city and is as much a feature of Budapest's waterfront panorama as the Vár and the Parliament building. At its foot are three baths, the best known being the Gellért, with its Art Nouveau thermal baths and summer terrace, attached to the stately old hotel. North of Gellért-hegy is the Rudas, one of Budapest's most historic and magical Turkish baths, while the nearby Rác is being incorporated into a luxury hotel. These two baths lie in the Tabán, Buda's former artisan quarter, though now with more roads than buildings; on its northern edge you'll find the interesting Semmelweis Medical Museum, as well as the Várkert Kioszc and Bazár.

ARRIVAL

Transport to the district is plentiful: bus #7 and trams #47 and #49 go from Pest to Gellért tér and Móricz Zsigmond körtér, while tram #18 from Széll Kálmán tér and tram #19 from Batthyány tér via the Tabán serve the same points.

Gellért-hegy

Surmounted by the Liberation Monument and the Citadella, **Gellért-hegy** makes a distinctive contribution to Budapest's skyline. The hill is named after the Italian missionary Ghirardus (Gellért in Hungarian), who converted pagan Magyars to Christianity at the behest of King Stephen. After his royal protector's demise, vengeful heathens strapped Gellért to a barrow and toppled him off the cliff, where a larger-than-life **statue of St Gellért** now stands astride an artificial waterfall facing the Erzsébet híd, his crucifix raised as if in admonition to motorists.

The Gellért Hotel and Baths

Gellért Gyógyfürdő XI, Kelenhegyi út 4 • Daily 6am–8pm • ☎ 1 466 6166, Ⓦ gellertbath.com • For more details, see p.195

At the foot of the hill, the graceful wrought-iron **Szabadság híd** (Liberty Bridge) links the inner boulevard of Pest to Szent Gellért tér on the Buda side, dominated by the Art Nouveau **Gellért Hotel**. Opened in 1918, it was commandeered as a staff headquarters by the Reds, the Romanian army, and finally by Admiral Horthy, following his triumphal entry into "sinful Budapest" in 1920 – in his eyes it was a decadent, Communist and, above all, a Jewish city. During the 1930s and 1940s, the hotel's balls were the highlight of Budapest's social calendar, when debutantes danced on a glass floor laid over its pool. The ostentatious domed **drinking fountain** in front of the hotel has been the source of some controversy: symbolizing the eight springs of Budapest, it was erected without planning permission, and the city authorities toyed with the idea of pulling it down before relenting.

The attached **Gellért Baths** (entered from Kelenhegyi út to the right of the main entrance, though hotel guests can go down in the lift in their bathrobes) are magnificently appointed with majolica tiles and mosaics, and a columned, Roman-style **thermal pool**, with lion-headed spouts. In the summer visitors can also use the **outdoor pools**, including one with a wave machine, on the terraces behind the main baths.

The Cave Church (Pauline Welcome Centre)

Sziklatemplom (Pálos Fogadóközpont) • I, Szent Gellért rakpart 1 • Mon–Sat 10am–7.30pm but closed during 5pm service • 500Ft • Service daily 8.30am, 5pm & 8pm and also Sun 11am

On the hillside opposite the *Gellért Hotel* you'll find the **Cave Church**, where masses are conducted by white-robed monks of the Pauline order, the only religious order indigenous to Hungary. Founded in 1256, its monks served as confessors to the Hungarian kings until Josef II dissolved the order in 1773, though it was re-established 150 years later. The church itself was created in the 1930s to mark the return of the monks to Hungary, and functioned until the whole community was arrested by the ÁVO at midnight mass on Easter Monday, 1951, whereupon the chapel was sealed up until 1989. Flickering candles and mournful organ music create an eerie atmosphere during services. Outside the entrance stands a **statue of St Stephen** with his horse.

The hillside behind, which still bears fig trees planted by the Turks, was covered in vineyards until a phylloxera epidemic struck in the nineteenth century; kids will enjoy the long tubular **slides** on the hotel-facing slopes.

The Liberation Monument and Citadella

Felszabadulási emlékmű • Bus #27 from Móricz Zsigmond körtér to the Busuló Juhász stop, followed by a 10min walk, or 25min walk up from the *Gellért Hotel* up past the Cave Church

Whether you walk up or get there by bus, the **summit** of Gellért-hegy affords a stunning **panoramic view**, drawing one's eye slowly along the curving river, past bridges and monumental landmarks, and then on to the Buda Hills and Pest's suburbs, merging hazily with the distant plain.

On the summit, in front of the Citadella, stands the **Liberation Monument**, a female figure brandishing the palm of victory over 30m aloft. There is a famous tale that the monument was originally commissioned by Admiral Horthy in memory of his son István (who was killed in a plane crash on the Eastern Front in 1942), and that, by

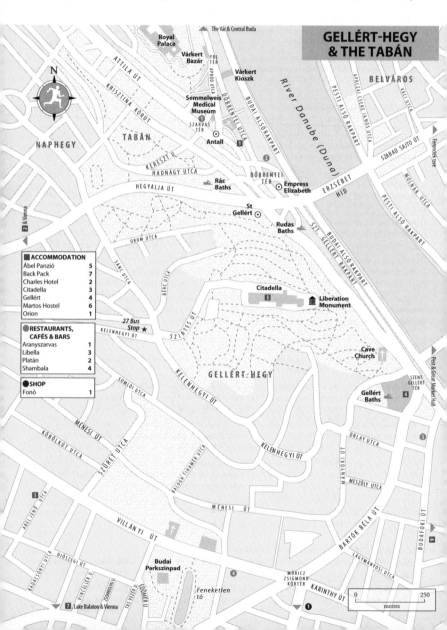

GELLÉRT-HEGY & THE TABÁN

ACCOMMODATION
Ábel Panzió	5
Back Pack	7
Charles Hotel	2
Citadella	3
Gellért	4
Martos Hostel	6
Orion	1

RESTAURANTS, CAFÉS & BARS
Aranyszarvas	1
Libella	3
Platán	2
Shambala	4

SHOP
| Fonó | 1 |

substituting a palm branch for the propeller it was meant to hold and placing a statue of a Red Army soldier at the base, the monument was deftly recycled to commemorate the Soviet soldiers who died liberating Budapest from the Nazis. While the story may not be true, the monument's sculptor, **Zsigmond Kisfaludi-Strobl**, certainly succeeded in winning approval as a "Proletarian Artist", despite having previously specialized in busts of the aristocracy – and was henceforth known by his compatriots as "Kisfaludi-Strébel" (*strébel* meaning "to climb" or "step from side to side"). The monument survived calls for its removal following the end of Communism, but its inscription was rewritten to honour those who died for "Hungary's prosperity", and the Soviet soldier was banished to the Memento Park on the outskirts of Budapest (p.125).

The Citadella

The **Citadella** behind the monument was built by the Habsburgs to dominate the city in the aftermath of the 1848–49 Revolution; ironically, both its architects were Hungarians. When the historic Compromise was reached in 1867, citizens breached the walls to affirm that it no longer posed a threat to them – though in fact an SS regiment did later hole up in the citadel during World War II. Today it has been usurped by a private company, which charges visitors 1200Ft to set foot inside the walls (daily 9am–7pm) and view an outdoor exhibition on the hill's history since the Celtic Eravisci lived here two thousand years ago; the recreation of a **Nazi bunker** in a concrete cellar is pretty dull – more interesting is the photo display on wartime Budapest. The *Citadella Hotel* (see p.159) is reached by a separate entrance.

The Tabán

The **Tabán** district, bordering the northern end of Gellért-hegy, chiefly consists of arterial roads built in Communist times on land left vacant by the prewar demolition of a quarter renowned for its drinking dens and open sewers. Traditionally this was inhabited by Serbs (Rác in Hungarian), who settled here en masse after the Turks were expelled, though in a typically Balkan paradox, some were present earlier, working in the Ottoman gunpowder factories which may have been the origin of the name Tabán (from *tabahane*, the Turkish for "armoury"). Thankfully, the slum-clearance and motorway building spared Tabán's historic Turkish baths, and its traditions of lusty nightlife are kept alive by summertime concerts in the park.

The Rudas Baths

Rudas Gyógyfürdő • I, Döbrentei tér 9 • Daily 6am–8pm, plus Fri & Sat night swimming 10pm–4am • ☎ 1 356 1322 • See p.196 for more details

The relaxing and curative effects of Buda's **mineral springs** have been appreciated for two thousand years (see p.194 for a full account), though it was the Turks who consolidated the habit of bathing and built proper bathhouses which function to this day. The **Rudas Baths**, in the shadow of Gellért-hegy, harbour a fantastic octagonal pool constructed in 1556 on the orders of Pasha Sokoli Mustapha. Bathers wallow amid shafts of light pouring in from the star-shaped apertures in the domed ceiling, surrounded by stone pillars with iron tie-beams and a nest of smaller pools for parboiling oneself or cooling down.

Rudas Drinking Hall

Rudas Ivócsarnok • Mon, Wed & Fri 11am–6pm, Tues & Thurs 7am–2pm

Walking north from the Rudas Baths, you'll pass the **Drinking Hall,** nestling beneath the road leading on to the bridge, which sells inexpensive mineral water from three nearby springs by the tumbler. Regular imbibers bring bottles or jerrycans to fill.

Statue of Empress Elizabeth

In the island of grass amid the swirl of roads leading to the Buda end of the bridge is a seated **statue of Empress Elizabeth** (1837–98), after whom the Erzsébet híd (Elizabeth Bridge) is named. The Austrian empress – she was also the Queen of Hungary – endeared herself to Hungarians by learning their language and refusing to be stifled by her crusty husband, Franz Josef. For more on the empress, see box, p.149.

The Rác Baths

Retaining an octagonal stone pool from Turkish times, the **Rác Baths** (Rác Gyógyfürdő) are tucked away beneath Hegyalja út, which leads uphill away from the bridgehead of the Erzsébet híd. At the time of writing, the baths were being turned into a luxury spa hotel complex, but the redevelopment has been snagged by problems.

A cuboid **memorial stone** outside commemorates the 51st Esperanto Congress held in Budapest in 1966 – an event that would have been inconceivable in Stalin's day, when Esperanto was forbidden for conflicting with his thesis that the time for an international language had yet to come.

The Semmelweis Medical Museum

Semmelweis Orvostörténeti Múzeum • I, Apród utca 1–3 • Tues–Sun: mid-March to Oct 10.30am–6pm; Nov to mid-March 10.30am–4pm • 700Ft • ⓦ semmelweis.museum.hu

Often overlooked by tourists, the **Semmelweis Medical Museum** contains a fascinating collection of artefacts relating to the history of medicine, with mummified limbs from ancient Egypt, and a shrunken head used by Borneo witchdoctors giving an international dimension to the display. Other exhibits – including a medieval chastity belt, trepanning drills, a life-size wax model of a dissected female cadaver, and a sewing machine with what looks like a bicycle chain attached, for closing stomach incisions – all give an idea of the centuries of misconceptions and the slow progress of medicine through fatal errors. The museum is named after nineteenth-century doctor **Ignác Semmelweis** (see box, below), who lived in this house until he was 5 and is buried in the garden.

The museum also contains the 1876 **Holy Ghost Pharmacy**, transplanted here from Király utca, and a collection of portraits, including one of Vilma Hugonai, Hungary's first woman doctor, and one of Kossuth's sister, Zsuzsanna, who founded the army medical corps during the War of Independence.

Szarvas tér

Just around the corner from the Semmelweis Medical Museum is **Szarvas tér** (Stag Square), named after the eighteenth-century *Stag House* inn at no. 1, which functions as a restaurant to this day. In between the museum and the restaurant stands a bust of **Dr József Antall** (1931–93), the first democratically elected prime minister of Hungary after the fall of Communism. For many years, while working as the director of the

---

DR IGNÁC SEMMELWEIS

Dr Ignác Semmelweis (1818–65) discovered the cause of puerperal fever – a form of blood poisoning contracted in childbirth, which was usually fatal. While serving in Vienna's public hospitals in the 1840s, he noticed that deaths were ten times lower on the wards where only midwives worked than on the ones attended by doctors and students, who went from dissecting corpses to delivering babies with only a perfunctory wash. His solution was to sterilize hands, clothes and instruments between operations – an idea dismissed as preposterous by the hospital, which fired him. Embittered, he wrote open letters to obstetricians, accusing them of being murderers, and was sent to an asylum where he died within a couple of weeks. Only after Pasteur's germ theory was accepted was Semmelweis hailed as the "saviour of mothers".

Semmelweis Museum, he had been dreaming of the chance to emerge from the political shadows, and as prime minister he skilfully ran his centre-right coalition to give Hungary a stable start, though his social conservatism was loathed by his opponents. He died in office and is buried in the Kerepesi Cemetery (see p.81).

Ybl Miklós tér

Past the museum and by the riverbank on **Ybl Miklós tér** are two buildings designed in 1876 by Miklós Ybl, the man behind the Opera House and other major works. To the left of the road, the grand facade and terraces of the **Várkert Bazár** stand in deep decay, awaiting a saviour. Designed as the grand entrance to the Várkert, the park running up to the palace, with shops either side of the steps, the Bazár was never in the right location to attract business and by 1920 was occupied by artists' studios. After suffering damage in the war, it reopened in1961 as a "youth park" and was one of the few places offering entertainment for the younger generation. Its outdoor pop concerts became legendary, but the crumbling building was forced to close in the 1980s, and numerous plans for redevelopment came to nothing. In its mission to show it can succeed where all others have failed, the Fidesz government appointed a commissioner in 2011 to restore the area – yet another big project awaiting money.

Some insignificant-looking stones in the gardens behind (accessible from Szarvas tér) are actually Turkish gravestones. By the river across the road is the **Várkert Kioszk**, a former pumping station with an ornate interior and Ybl's statue standing in front.

7

BAROQUE BUILDINGS ON FŐ TER, ÓBUDA

Óbuda and Margít-sziget

Óbuda is the oldest part of Budapest, though that's hardly the impression given by the industrial sites and high-rises that dominate the district today, hiding such ancient ruins as remain. Nonetheless, it was here that the Romans built a legionary camp and a civilian town, later taken over by the Huns. Under the Hungarian Árpád dynasty this developed into an important town, but in the fifteenth century it was eclipsed by the Vár. The original settlement became known as Óbuda (Old Buda) and was incorporated into the newly formed Budapest in 1873. The tiny old town centre is as pretty as the Castle District, with several museums worth seeing, but to find the best-preserved Roman ruins you'll have to go to the Rómaifürdő district, further out.

To the west, there is a pair of striking caves near the valley of Szépvölgy, a visit to which can be combined with the Kiscelli Museum, with its interesting collection of furniture and interior furnishings in a former monastery.

In the middle of the Danube, leafy **Margít-sziget** is a haven from the noise and pollution of the city. One of Budapest's favourite parks and summer pleasure-grounds, the island is part of its grand waterfront panorama – unlike shabby **Óbudai-sziget** just north which, like Cinderella, gets but one chance to have fun, by hosting Hungary's equivalent of Glastonbury, the **Sziget festival**, each August (see p.185).

ARRIVAL

Public transport The HÉV from Batthyány tér (see p.24) provides easy access to riverside Óbuda, while a variety of trams and buses serve Margít-sziget. You can also reach Margít-sziget on one of the ferries that zigzag up the river from Boráros tér; see p.24 for details.

Óbuda

After its incorporation within the city, **Óbuda** became a popular place to eat, drink and make merry, with garden restaurants and taverns serving fish and wine from the locality. Some of the most famous establishments still exist around **Fő tér**, the heart of eighteenth-century Óbuda, with its ornate Trinity Column. While there's no denying the charm of their Baroque facades and wrought-iron lamps, many are simply trading on past glories; see p.171 for our pick of Óbuda's eating places.

8

Vasarely Museum

Vasarely Múzeum • III, Szentlélek tér 6 • Tues–Sun 10am–5.30pm • 800Ft • ⓦ vasarely.tvn.hu • Szentlélek tér/Árpád híd stop on Szentendre HÉV or #1 tram from northern Pest

The **Vasarely Museum** displays eyeball-throbbing Op Art works by Viktor Vasarely (1906–99), the founder of the genre, who was born in Pécs in southern Hungary, emigrated to Paris in 1930 and spent the rest of his life in France. You can also get a sense of his artistic development from earlier works such as a more conventional self-portrait.

Óbuda Museum

Óbudai Múzeum • III, Szentlélek tér 1 • Tues–Sun 10am–6pm • Entry 800Ft, information booklet 800Ft • ⓦ obudaimuzeum.hu

Round the corner from the Vasarely Museum the **Óbuda Museum** is an excellent local history collection with Roman and medieval finds, reconstructed shops and a kitchen – including a pre-electric fridge – from the early twentieth century, as well as a living room from the 1950s. The only information in English is an 800Ft booklet on the displays available at the ticket desk.

Kassák Museum

Kassák Múzeum • III, Fő tér 1 • Wed–Sun 10am–5pm • 500Ft

On Fő tér itself the run-down Baroque Zichy mansion contains the small but fascinating **Kassák Museum**. Located upstairs on the far side of the courtyard, the collection is dedicated to the Hungarian Constructivist **Lajos Kassák** (1887–1967) and features his paintings, magazine designs, publications and possessions. A self-taught artist and publisher who devoted much of his younger life to the Socialist cause (publishing work by Cocteau and Le Corbusier), Kassák's avant-garde style fell foul of regimes on both the left and right. In a selective form of censorship typical of the post-1956 Communist years, he was recognized as a writer but was pretty much banned from exhibiting his art from 1948.

Varga Museum

Varga Imre Múzeum • III, Laktanya utca 7 • Tues–Sun 10am–6pm • 800Ft

Whatever the weather, you'll see several figures sheltering beneath umbrellas just off Fő tér, life-sized sculptures by Imre Varga, Hungary's best-known living artist, whose

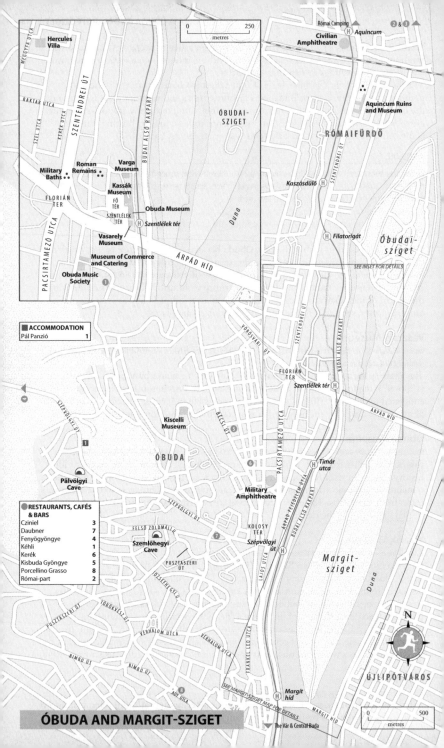

ÓBUDA AND MARGIT-SZIGET

Hercules Villa

Military Baths
Roman Remains
Varga Museum
Kassák Museum
FŐ TÉR
Obuda Museum
SZENTLÉLEK TÉR
Szentlélek tér
Vasarely Museum
Museum of Commerce and Catering
Obuda Music Society

FLORIÁN TÉR

MEGGYFA UTCA
RAKTÁR UTCA
SZÉL UTCA
KEREK UTCA
SZENTENDREI ÚT
BUDA ALSÓ RAKPART
PACSIRTAMEZŐ UTCA

ÓBUDAI-SZIGET

Duna

ÁRPÁD HÍD

Római Camping
Civilian Amphitheatre
Aquincum

Aquincum Ruins and Museum

RÓMAIFÜRDŐ

Kaszásdűlő

SZENTENDREI ÚT

Filatorigát

Óbudai-sziget

SEE INSET FOR DETAILS

ACCOMMODATION
Pál Panzió   1

VÖRÖSVÁRI ÚT
SZENTENDREI ÚT
BUDA ALSÓ RAKPART

FLORIÁN TÉR
Szentlélek tér

ÁRPÁD HÍD

Kiscelli Museum

BÉCSI ÚT

ÓBUDA

SZÉPVÖLGYI ÚT

Pálvölgyi Cave

Tímár utca

Military Amphitheatre

KOLOSY TÉR
Szépvölgyi út

RESTAURANTS, CAFÉS & BARS
Cziniel   3
Daubner   7
Fenyögyöngye   4
Kéhli   1
Kerék   6
Kisbuda Gyöngye   5
Porcellino Grasso   8
Római-part   2

FELSŐ ZÖLDMÁLI

Szemlőhegyi Cave

PUSZTASZERI ÚT

JÓZSEFHEGYI U.

PUSZTASZERI ÚT

TÖRÖKVÉSZI ÚT

VERHALOM UTCA

VERHALOM UTCA

BIMBÓ ÚT

BIMBÓ ÚT

ADY UTCA

FRANKEL LEÓ UTCA

LAJOS UTCA

ÁRPÁD FEJEDELEM ÚTJA

BUDA ALSÓ RAKPART

Margit-sziget

Duna

ÚJLIPÓTVÁROS

N

Margit híd

MARGIT HÍD

SEE MARGIT-SZIGET MAP FOR DETAILS

The Vár & Central Buda

0   250
metres

0   500
metres

oeuvre is the subject of the nearby **Varga Museum** at Laktanya utca 7. Pathos and humour pervades his sheet-metal, iron and bronze effigies of famous personages, including Pope John Paul II and Bartók. Varga's career has spanned the eras of "goulash Socialism" and democracy – evinced by state-commissioned monuments to Béla Kun (in the Memento Park, see p.125) and Imre Nagy (near Parliament; p.52) – but nobody accuses him of being a hack like Kisfaludi-Strobl (see p.107).

Museum of Commerce and Catering

Kereskedelmi és Vendéglátóipari Múzeum • III, Dugovics Titusz tér 13–17 • Tues–Sun 10am–6pm • 1000Ft • ⓦ mkvm.hu

South of the bridgehead of the Árpád híd is another remnant of the old town that is even more isolated than Fő tér among the modern blocks. The cluster of a church, restaurant and cultural centre was augmented in 2011 by the **Museum of Commerce and Catering.** This was the world's first such museum when it opened in 1966, but has suffered from the lack of a permanent home, moving twice in the past five years. Initially confined to temporary displays, the museum hopes to display its fantastic collection of shopfronts, merchandise and adverts, including a model dog that raps on the shop window with its paws to draw in passers-by. It also has a reconstructed prewar bedroom from the *Gellért Hotel* and specialized items of cutlery from the same period, such as asparagus clippers and a 25-bladed pocket knife, both made by a Hungarian firm.

Ruins of Aquincum

Aquincumi Múzeum • III, Szentendrei út 139 • Tues–Sun: May–Sept 9am–6pm; late April & Oct 9am–5pm; Nov 10am–4pm; museum opens at 10am • 1300Ft • ⓦ aquincum.hu.

North of Óbuda, the riverside factory belt merges into the **Rómaifürdő** (Roman Bath) district, harbouring a campsite, a lido and the ruins of **Aquincum**. Originally a settlement of camp followers spawned by the legionary garrison, Aquincum eventually became a *municipium* and then a *colonia*, the provincial capital of Pannonia Inferior. The **ruins** are visible from the Aquincum HÉV stop, from where a brief walk south under the main-line rail bridge brings you to the site itself. Enough of the foundation walls and underground piping survives to give a fair idea of the town's layout, with its forum and law courts, its sanctuaries of the goddesses Epona and Fortuna Augusta, and the *collegia* and bathhouses where fraternal societies met. Its bare bones are given substance by an excellent **museum** and smaller exhibitions around the site. Its star exhibit is the superb **mosaic** from the third century AD of Nessus abducting Deianeira, whom Hercules had to rescue as one of his twelve labours. This originally consisted of sixty thousand stones, selected and arranged in Alexandria before shipment to Europe. Other highlights include a mummy

8

> ### ROMAN REMAINS
>
> Roman soldiers had been in the region since the first century AD, but the larger settlement only came a century later, lasting until the fourth century. While Aquincum was the main civilian centre, the Romans' **military garrison** was to the south, and today its remains lurk in the concrete jungle of Óbuda's centre. On Flórián tér, 500m west of Fő tér, weathered columns rise next to a shopping plaza, while the old **military baths** (*thermae maiores*) are exposed in the pedestrian underpass beneath the Szentendrei út flyover. You'll also find the odd Roman wall protruding between the apartment blocks near Fő tér. The largest ruin is a **military amphitheatre** (*amfiteátrum*) which once seated up to 13,000 spectators, at the junction of Pacsirtamező utca and Nagyszombat utca, 800m further south – accessible by bus #86 or by walking 400m from Kolosy tér, near the Szépvölgyi út HÉV stop. (The remains of a **civilian amphitheatre** are by the Aquincum HÉV stop.)
>
> A more elusive relic is the **Hercules Villa**, Meggyfa utca 19–21, north of Florian tér, which contained the **mosaic floor** of the centaur Nessus abducting Deianeira that can now be seen in the Aquincum Museum. A fragment of another mosaic remains *in situ*, featuring a delightfully rendered tiger and Hercules about to vomit at a wine festival.

preserved in natron, a cult-relief of the god Mithras and a reconstructed water-organ. The **Floralia Festival** (May 17–18) sees theatrical performances, craft-making displays, mock gladiator battles and other events staged here.

The caves

Bus #86 from Flórián tér or Batthyány tér, or bus #6 from Nyugati tér in Pest, from where you catch bus #65 five stops to the Pálvölgyi Cave, or bus #29 four stops to the Szemlőhegyi Cave

The hills rising to the west of Óbuda feature a network of caves that are unique for having been formed by thermal waters rising up from below, rather than by rainwater. Two of the sites have been accessible to the public since the 1980s, with guided tours only (some English spoken). In both cases the starting point is **Kolosy tér** in Óbuda. As the two caves are ten minutes' walk apart, it's possible to see them both within two and a half hours if you start with the Szemlőhegyi Cave.

Pálvölgyi Stalactite Cave

Pálvölgyi cseppkőbarlang • III, Szépvölgyi út 162 • 60min tours hourly at quarter past the hour, Tues–Sun 10am–4.15pm • 1150Ft • ⓦ palvolgyi.atw.hu

The **Pálvölgyi Stalactite Cave** is the more spectacular of the two labyrinths; part of the longest of the cave systems in the Buda Hills, it is still being explored by speleologists. It was discovered in 1904 by a quarryman searching for a sheep that disappeared when the floor of the quarry fell in. Tours, on which you negotiate hundreds of steps and dank constricted passages, last about half an hour. You start on the lowest level, which boasts rock formations such as the "Organ Pipes" and "Beehive". From "John's Lookout" in the largest chamber, you ascend a crevice onto the upper level, there to enter "Fairyland" and finally "Paradise", overlooking the hellish "Radium Hall" 50m below.

Szemlőhegyi Cave

Szemlőhegyi barlang • III, Pusztaszeri út 35 • 40min tours hourly on the hour daily except Tues 10am–4pm • 950Ft • ⓦ szemlohegyi.atw.hu

Quite different to the Pálvölgyi Stalactite Cave is the **Szemlőhegyi Cave**, with less convoluted and claustrophobic passages and no stalactites. Instead, the walls are encrusted with cauliflower- or popcorn-textured precipitates. Discovered in 1930, the cave has exceptionally clean air, and its lowest level is used as a respiratory sanatorium. After the tour you can view a museum of cave finds and plans from all over Hungary.

For refreshment after the caves you should schedule in a stop at the *Daubner* patisserie at Szépvölgyi út 29 (near Kolosy tér at the bottom of the hill), which does some of the most delicious cakes in the city and attracts huge queues at weekends. Alternatively, you can combine a visit to the Szemlőhegyi Cave with the Bartók Memorial House (see p.122) or the Kiscelli Museum (see below).

The Kiscelli Museum

Kiscelli Múzeum • III, Kiscelli utca 108 • Tues–Sun: April–Oct 10am–6pm; Nov–March 10am–4pm • 900Ft • ⓦ btmfk.iif.hu; for events, ⓦ kiscell.org • Bus #165 from Kolosy tér or bus #160 from Batthyány tér

On a hillside above Óbuda, fifteen minutes' walk north of the Szemlőhegyi Cave, the **Kiscelli Museum** occupies a former Trinitarian monastery in a beautiful wooded setting. The museum's collection includes antique printing presses and the 1830 Biedermeier furnishings of the Golden Lion pharmacy, which used to stand on Kálvin tér. The blackened shell of the monastery's Gothic church makes a dramatic backdrop for exhibitions of contemporary art, classical **concerts**, animated film shows and other events.

Margít-sziget

Trams #4 and #6 stop at the southern entrance on the Margít híd, and bus #26 runs down the middle of the island to and from the Árpád híd station on the blue metro line #3; Motorists can only approach from the north of the island, via the Árpád híd, at which point they must leave their vehicles at a paying car park. Near both entrances you can rent bikes, pedaloes and electric cars.

There's a saying that "love begins and ends on **Margít-sziget**", for this verdant island has been a favourite meeting place for lovers since the nineteenth century (though before 1945 a stiff admission charge deterred the poor). A royal game reserve under the Árpáds and a monastic colony until the Turkish conquest, today Margít-sziget has two public baths fed by thermal springs, an outdoor theatre and other amenities.

The island was named at the end of the nineteenth century after Princess **Margít** (Margaret), the daughter of Béla IV. Legend has it that he vowed to bring her up as a nun if Hungary survived the Mongol invasion, and duly confined the 9-year-old in a convent when it did. She apparently made the best of it, acquiring a reputation for curing lepers and other saintly deeds, as well as for never washing above her ankles. Beatification came after her death in 1271, and a belated canonization in 1943, by which time her name had already been bestowed on the **Margít híd**, built by a French company in the 1870s.

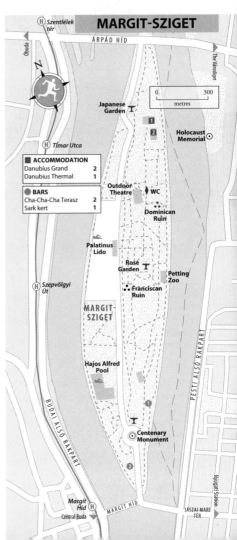

Linking Margít-sziget to Buda and Pest, it's an unusual bridge in the form of a splayed-out V, with a short arm joined to the southern tip of the island. In November 1944 it was blown up by the Nazis, killing hundreds of people including the German sappers who had detonated the explosives by mistake.

The pools

Walking down from the tram stop on Margít híd, you are greeted by a Millennial Monument and a **fountain** that emits bursts of grand music. Further on, behind trees to the left, is the **Hajós Alfréd Pool** (known as the "Sport"; see p.195), named after the winner of the 100m and 1200m swimming races at the 1896 Olympics. Hajós was also an architect and designed the indoor pool, but the main attractions here are the all-season outdoor 50m pool, where the national swimming team trains. Another swimming venue, the **Palatinus Strand** (see p.195), lies nearly a kilometre further north. With a monumental entrance from the 1930s, this lido can hold as many as ten thousand people at a time in numerous open-air thermal pools, complete with a water chute, wave machine and segregated terraces for nude sunbathing.

Ruins and gardens

Turning right off the road that runs northwards up the island before you get to the Palatinus, you'll come to the ruins of a **Franciscan church** from the late thirteenth century and, beyond that, the renovated **petting zoo**. Walking north up the middle of the island takes you through the **Rose Garden** and on up to the ruined **Dominican church and convent**. The nearby **Outdoor Theatre** (Szabadtéri Színpad) hosts plays, operas, fashion shows and concerts during summer. The café here makes a convenient stop for a beer and a snack and **also has public toilets** – it is easily located by the **water tower** that rises above the complex.

A short way northeast of the tower is a **Premonstratensian Chapel**, whose Romanesque tower dates back to the twelfth century, when the order first established a monastery on the island. The tower's fifteenth-century bell is one of the oldest in Hungary. Beside the *Thermal* hotel, the less appealing of the two luxury hotels to the north, is a **Japanese Garden** with warm springs that sustain tropical fish and giant water lilies.

8

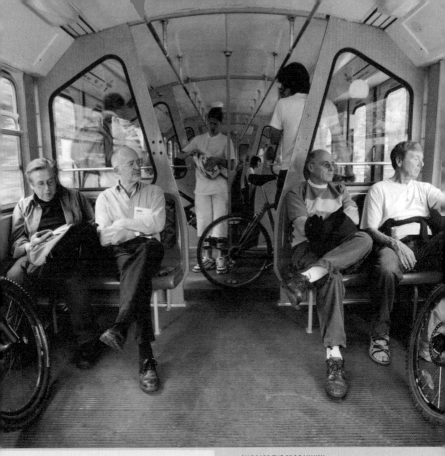

ON BOARD THE COG RAILWAY

The Buda Hills

A densely wooded arc around a sixth of Budapest's circumference, the Buda Hills are as close to nature as you can get within the city limits. The hills are a favourite place for walking in all seasons, with trails marked with the distance or the duration ("ó" stands for hours; "p" for minutes). While some parts can be crowded with walkers and mountain-bikers at the weekend, it's possible to ramble for hours during the week and see hardly a soul. The most rewarding destinations for those with limited time are the "railway circuit", using the Cogwheel and Children's railways and the chairlift, and the Bartók Memorial House. Further south is the Farkasréti Cemetery, noted for its architecture as well as the celebrated personages buried here.

9

ARRIVAL AND GETTING AROUND

By public transport Széll Kálmán tér (formerly Moszkva tér) is the easiest starting point for all the destinations in the hills, including all points along the railway circuit. The Cogwheel Railway is two stops away on tram #59 or #61 or bus #155 or #156; alight opposite the cylindrical *Budapest Hotel*; bus #155 goes on to the bottom of the Chairlift while tram #61 goes on to Hüvösvölgy (although it may be renamed #56). Bus #21 and #21A go up to Normafa, the #21 goes on to Csillebérc.

By bike Exploring the Buda Hills by trail-bike is a more ambitious option, if you've got a day to spare and the stamina. Velo-Touring (XI, Előpatak utca 1 ☎ 1 319 0571, ⓦ velo-touring.hu) rents 21-gear bikes (from €14/day; €100 deposit) and can advise on routes; its office is about 1km from Farkasréti Cemetery. Bikes can be carried on the Cogwheel (validate an extra ticket) and Children's railways (200Ft fee).

The railway circuit

This is an easy and enjoyable way to visit the hills that will especially appeal to kids. The whole trip can take under two hours if connections click, or a half-day if you prefer to take your time.

The Cogwheel Railway

Fogaskerekűvasút, also designated tram #60 · Daily 5am–11pm · BKV fares and passes apply

The circuit begins at the lower terminal of the **Cogwheel Railway**. This was the third such railway in the world when it was inaugurated in 1874, and was steam-powered until its electrification in 1929. Running every ten minutes or so, its cogs fitting into a notched track, the train climbs 300m over 3km through the villa-suburb of **Svábhegy**; for the best view on the way up, take a window seat on the right-hand side, facing backwards.

The Children's Railway

Gyermekvasút · Tues–Sun June–Aug also Mon, trains go every 45–60min 9am–5pm · 500Ft to any mid-station, 700Ft from terminus to terminus · ⓦ gyermekvasut.hu

From the upper terminal on **Széchenyi-hegy**, it's a minute's walk to the **Children's Railway**. A narrow-gauge line built by Communist youth brigades in 1948, it's almost entirely run by 13- to 17-year-old members of the Scouts and Guides movement, enabling them to get hands-on experience if they fancy a career with MÁV, the Hungarian Railways company. Watching them wave flags, collect tickets and salute departures with great solemnity, you can see why it appealed to the Communists. The forty-minute ride along the full 11km length of the line is a delightful run through the wooded hills. In summer, they sometimes run heritage trains, pulled by a steam engine or vintage diesel loco, for which a 200Ft supplement is charged

Normafa

The first stop along the Children's Railway route, **Normafa**, is a popular excursion centre with a modest **ski-run** and sledging slopes. Its name comes from a performance of the famous aria from Bellini's *Norma* given here by the actress Rozália Klein in 1840. A popular destination at the top of the slope is the *Rétes Büfé*, a wooden shack that sells a range of delicious *rétes*.

Csillebérc adventure playground

April–Oct daily 10am–6pm; Nov–March Sat & Sun 10am–5pm · 2900–3900Ft · ⓦ kalandpalya.com

Right by the next stop, **Csillebérc**, there's an **adventure playground**, with tree-top walkways and wire-slides for anyone over 100cm in height – a smaller version of the tree-top canopy at Visegrád (see p.138). On a hot day the trees offer a refreshing shelter from the sun.

János-hegy

Alighting at **János-hegy**, two stops on from **Csillebérc**, you can either strike out down through woods to the town of **Budakeszi**, from where bus #22 takes you back to Széll

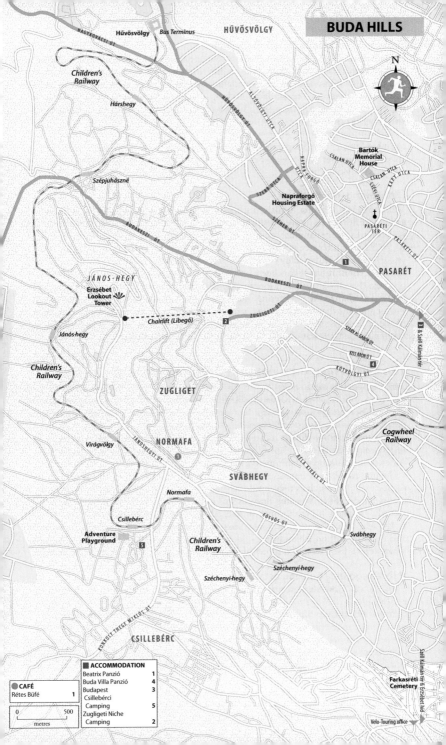

BUDA HILLS

N

NAGYKOVÁCSI ÚT
Hűvösvölgy
Bus Terminus
HŰVÖSVÖLGY

Children's Railway

Hárshegy

HŰVÖSVÖLGYI ÚT
ALSÓ LIGETI UTCA

NAPPÁ FORGÓ UTCA
SZERB UTCA

CSALÁN UTCA
CSALÁN UTCA
ESPY UTCA

Bartók Memorial House

CSÉVI UTCA

Szépjuhászné

BUDAKESZI ÚT

Napraforgó Housing Estate

SZÉHER ÚT

PASARÉTI TÉR

PASARÉTI ÚT

1

BUDAKESZI ÚT

PASARÉT

JÁNOS-HEGY

Erzsébet Lookout Tower

Chairlift (Libegő)

János-hegy

ZUGLIGETI ÚT

2

SZALÓNAK GÁBOR ÚT

KISS ÁRON ÚT

4

KÚTVÖLGYI ÚT

& Széll Kálmán tér

Children's Railway

ZUGLIGET

Cogwheel Railway

Virágvölgy

JÁNOSHEGYI ÚT

NORMAFA

1

BÉLA KIRÁLY ÚT

SVÁBHEGY

Normafa

Csillebérc

EÖTVÖS ÚT

Svábhegy

Adventure Playground

5

Children's Railway

Széchenyi-hegy

Széchenyi-hegy

Svábhegy

PÜRKÖLT-THEGE MIKLÓS ÚT

CSILLEBÉRC

Széll Kálmán tér & Erzsébet híd

Farkasréti Cemetery

● **CAFÉ**
Rétes Büfé   1

■ **ACCOMMODATION**
Beatrix Panzió   1
Buda Villa Panzió   4
Budapest   3
 Csillebérci
 Camping   5
Zugligeti Niche
 Camping   2

0   500
metres

Velo-Touring office

9

Kálmán tér, or make the steep twenty-minute climb from the station to the top of **János-hegy** (527m), the highest point in Budapest. The Romanesque-style **Erzsébet lookout tower** (daily 8am–8pm; free) on the summit offers a panoramic view of the city and the Buda Hills. The tower was designed by Frigyes Schulek, who also designed the Fishermen's Bastion – the similarity is clear. It takes its name from Empress Elizabeth, the Queen of Hungary (see p.149), who visited this spot in 1882 and came back on two other occasions.

By the buffet below the summit is the upper terminal of the **chairlift** or **Libegő**, meaning "floater" in Hungarian, which wafts you down over trees and gardens to the suburb of **Zugliget** (daily: May–Sept 10am–5pm; Oct–April 9.30am–4pm; closed every other Mon; 750Ft)

Hárshegy and Hűvösvölgy

Wild boar, which prefer to roam during the evening and sleep by day, are occasionally sighted in the forests above **Hárshegy**, one stop before the terminus at **Hűvösvölgy**. This is also a great place for **mushrooms** – most big markets, such as the Fény utca market by Széll Kálmán tér (see p.201) have stalls where you can get your mushrooms checked (*gombavizsgáló*). **Hűvösvölgy** (Cool Valley) is a vast suburb spreading into the hills and valleys beyond. It has always been a popular destination for Budapestis, trundling out on the old tram #56. Wicked tongues say that after the riots of 2006 the Socialist Party decided to change the numbering of the tram (with its connotations of 1956) to #61 – which means that the new populist administration may well make a big song and dance of restoring the #56. The **Arts and Crafts bus terminus**, with its covered stairways leading to the train station, has been restored to its original elegance.

The Bartók Memorial House and Napraforgó utca

Bartók Béla Emlékház • II, Csalán utca 29 • Tues–Sat 10am–5pm, closed for three weeks in Aug • 1200Ft • ⓦ bartokmuseum.hu • Chamber music concerts 2000Ft (includes entry to museum) are held here from Sept until June (☎ 1 394 2100 for information) • Bus #29 from the Szemlőhegyi Cave to the Nagybányai út stop, or bus #5 from Ferenciek tere in Pest or Széll Kálmán tér to the Pasaréti tér terminus, and then a 10min walk uphill along Csévi utca (follow it round to the left at the first corner)

The **Bartók Memorial House**, located in a leafy suburb below Láto-hegy, was the residence of Béla Bartók, his wife and two sons from 1932 until their emigration to America in 1940, by which time Bartók despaired of Hungary's right-wing regime.

The museum has an extensive range of Bartók memorabilia: the three rooms on the second floor are much as they would have looked when Bartók lived here, with his piano, cupboards and writing desk, as well as the phonograph he used to make field recordings during his ethno-musical research trips to Transylvania with Zoltán Kodály. In the new attic display you can also see folk handicrafts Bartók collected on his travels and the shirt cuff on which he wiped his pen-nibs when composing scores. (The shop, which sells CDs, books and scores of Bartók's music, does not accept credit cards.)

Napraforgó utca housing estate

II, Napraforgó utca • Signposted from Pasaréti tér, the terminus of bus #5: follow Pasaréti út until you reach a playing field and cross the bridge on the left

Before you return to Széll Kálmán tér from the Bartók Memorial House, it's worth a brief detour to see the delightful **Napraforgó utca housing estate**, built in 1931. Its 22 houses – designed by as many architects – embody different trends in Modernist architecture, from severe Bauhaus to folksy Arts and Crafts style. The houses are all occupied – you can't go in – but they have pretty much preserved their original look. For refreshment afterwards, head for the café in the listed 1930s **bus shelter** on Pasaréti tér. The shelter's curving horizontal form contrasts with the slender vertical lines of the Franciscan Church of St Antal across the road – both were designed by the architect Géza Rimanóczy as a single project for the square.

Farkasréti Cemetery

Farkasréti temető • XII, Némétvölgyi út 99 • Daily 7.30am–5pm • Free • Tram #59 from Széll Kálmán tér or bus #8 from Astoria in Pest

Two kilometres west of Gellért-hegy in the hilly XII district is the **Farkasréti Cemetery**, where a mass of flower stalls and funerary masons indicate that you've arrived. Among the 10,000 graves in the "Wolf's Meadow Cemetery" are those of **Béla Bartók** (whose remains were ceremonially reburied in 1988 following their return from America, where he died in exile in 1945); his fellow composer **Zoltán Kodály**; and the conductor **Georg Solti**, who left Hungary in 1939 to meet Toscanini and thus escaped the fate of his Jewish parents.

Less well known abroad are the actress Gizi Bajor, Olympic-medal-winning boxer László Papp and some infamous figures from the Communist era: Hungary's Stalinist dictator **Mátyás Rákosi** (as a precaution against vandalism, only the initials on his grave are visible), his secret police chief Gábor Péter (see box, p.61), and András Hegedüs, the Politburo member who asked the Soviets to crush the Uprising. Also look out for the many wooden grave markers inscribed in the ancient runic Székely alphabet.

However, the real attraction is the amazing **mortuary chapel** by architect Imre Makovecz – one of his finest designs, dating from 1975, which was used for his own funeral in 2011. Its wood-ribbed vault resembles the inside of a human ribcage, with a casket for corpses where the heart would be. Be discreet, as the chapel is in constant use by mourners. Visitors keen to see more of Makovecz's work could pay a visit to Visegrád (p.139), an hour's journey north of the capital.

The city limits

While the centre of Budapest is hardly short of attractions, it would be a shame to overlook some others out towards or just beyond the city limits. In Pest, the Railway History Park – where visitors can drive steam trains – is popular with Hungarian tourists, while the New Public Cemetery completes the roll call of illustrious Hungarian dead begun at Kerepesi. In Buda, the Memento Park, with its exiled Communist memorials, is the prime destination for foreigners, and children will also enjoy the Tropicarium, with its rainforest creatures and sharks – leaving the Nagytétényi Castle Museum to devotees of stately homes. You can reach any of these places from the city centre within an hour.

Railway History Park

Magyar Vasúttörténeti Park • XIV, Tatai út 95 • Tues–Sun: April–Oct 10am–6pm; late March & Nov 10am–3pm • 1100Ft • Trains to Esztergom from Nyugati Station at 10.20am, 11.20am and 1.20pm stop at the museum's own station; a slower route is by bus #30 from Keleti Station or Hősök tere to the Rokolya utca stop, a short walk from the gates • ⓦ mavnosztalgia.hu • See map p.5

The engagingly hands-on **Hungarian Railway History Park**, or Hungarian Railway Museum, lurks in the freight yards of the XIV district. Its roundhouse and sidings house over seventy locomotives and carriages from 1870 onwards, including the Árpád railcar that set the 1934 speed record from Budapest to Vienna in just under three hours, and a 1912 teak dining carriage from the *Orient Express*. Many of the museum's staff are ex-employees of MÁV (Hungarian State Railways), proud of a tradition inherited from the Royal Hungarian Railways. Between April and October (10am–4pm), you can **drive** a steam train (1000Ft), luggage cart (500Ft) or engine simulator (800Ft), ride a horse-drawn tram (400Ft) or a turntable used for turning locomotives around (free), and operate a model railway (300Ft) – wear old clothes. The MÁV Nosztalgia office next to platform 10 at Nyugati Station can also give information.

10

New Public Cemetery

Új köztemető • X, Kozma utca 8–10 • Daily 8am–dusk • Free • Tram #28 or #37 from Népszínház utca, by Blaha Lujza tér • See map p.5

The **New Public Cemetery** is located in the X district of Pest beyond the breweries of Kőbánya, near the end of one of the longest tram rides in town. This is Budapest's largest cemetery – reflecting the city's growth in the latter half of the nineteenth century – and it was in a remote corner that **Imre Nagy** and 260 others, executed for their part in the 1956 Uprising, were secretly buried in unmarked graves in 1958. Any flowers left at **Plot 301** were removed by the police until 1989, when the deceased received a state funeral on Hősök tere. The plot is 2km from the main gates on Kozma utca – but note that the minibuses that shuttle back and forth every twenty minutes only run between 9am and 3pm Tuesday to Friday. Near the graves, an ornate wooden gateway and headposts mark a mass grave now designated as a **National Pantheon** – as opposed to the Communist pantheon in Kerepesi (see p.80).

Jewish cemetery

Izraelita temető • X, Kozma utca 6 • Mon–Fri & Sun 8am–2pm • Free • Last stop on tram #28 or #37 • See map p.5

The **Jewish cemetery**, 700m up the road from the New Public Cemetery, is the burial place of Ernő Szép (author of *The Smell of Humans*, a searing Holocaust memoir), as well as many rabbis and industrialists. Beside the wall on Kozma utca stand the grand crypts of the Goldberger and Kornfeld manufacturing dynasties, and the dazzling blue-and-gold-tiled Art Nouveau tomb of shopkeeper **Sándor Schmidl**, designed by Ödön Lechner and Béla Lajta (who later became supervisor of Budapest's Jewish cemeteries).

Memento Park (Statue Park)

Szoborpark • XXII, Balatoni út • Daily 10am–dusk • 1500Ft; guided tours 1200Ft • ⓦ mementopark.hu • Memento Park bus goes from Deák tér bus stop with the Park logo by the old bus station at 11am (also 3pm in July & Aug) for 4500Ft (including entry and a guided tour; tickets are purchased on the bus); alternatively, you can take tram #47 or #49 from Deák tér to Etele tér, and then a Volán bus (not covered by BKV passes) from stand 7 or 8 towards Diósd–Érd, which takes 10min to reach the park • See map p.5

Easily the most popular site on the city's outskirts, the **Memento Park** or Statue Park brings together 42 of the monuments that glorified Communism in Budapest, to celebrate its demise. The park is way out beside Balatoni út in the XXII District, 15km southwest of the city centre.

Built in stages (1994–2004) as an "unfinished project" by architect Ákos Eleőd, the complex is an anti-temple to a bankrupt ideology. Visitors are greeted by a replica of the **Stalin grandstand**, from which Party leaders reviewed parades; the giant boots recall the

8m-high Stalin statue toppled in 1956. Beyond lies Witness Square, representing all those squares in Eastern Europe where people defied Communism; it's flanked by buildings with Socialist Realist facades. Of these, the **Barrack Hall** is used to screen *Life of an Agent*, a montage of ÁVO training films on how to bug or search premises and recruit informers. Across the way, the **Red Star Store** sells Lenin and Stalin candles, model Trabant cars and selections of revolutionary songs, which can be heard playing from a 1950s' radio set.

10 The park proper lies behind a bogus Classical facade framing giant statues of **Lenin**, **Marx** and **Engels**. Lenin's once stood beside the Városliget, while Marx's and Engels' are carved from granite quarried at Mauthausen, a Nazi concentration camp in Austria, later used by the Soviets. Inside the grounds, you'll encounter the **Red Army soldier** that guarded the foot of the Liberation Monument on Gellért-hegy, and dozens of other statues and memorials, large and small. Here are prewar Hungarian Communists such as Béla Kun (secretly shot in Moscow on Stalin's orders) and Jenő Landler (afforded a place in the Kremlin Wall); Georgi Dimitrov, hero of the Comintern; and the Lenin statue from outside the Csepel ironworks. Artistically, the best works are the **Republic of Councils Monument** – a giant charging sailor based on a 1919 revolutionary poster – and Imre Varga's **Béla Kun Memorial**, with Kun on a tribune surrounded by a surging crowd of workers and soldiers (plus a bystander with an umbrella).

Budapestis fondly remember the statue of **Captain Ostapenko**, which once stood on the highway to Lake Balaton, where hitchhikers would arrange to meet their friends (a locality still known as "Ostapenko"), while the decision to move to the park the monument commemorating the Hungarian contingent of the International Brigade in the Spanish Civil War (three robotic figures with fists clenched to their heads) provoked a heartfelt debate that few of the others engendered. The lack of information in English makes the guided tour useful.

Tropicarium

Campona Shopping Centre • XXII, Nagytétényi út 37–43 • Daily 10am–8pm • 2300Ft, children 1600Ft • Ⓦ tropicarium.hu • Bus #33 from Móricz Zsigmond körtér, or #114 and #214 from Kosztolányi Desző tér, or quicker is the main-line train from Deli Station to Budatétény • See map p.5

A must-see for kids, Budapest's **Tropicarium** is the largest aquarium-terrarium in Central Europe, covering three thousand square metres. Its saltwater section has an 11m-long glass tunnel for intimate views of sand, tiger and brown **sharks**, clownfish, triggerfish and wrasses; you can even feed stingrays. The freshwater part has piranhas, mouth-breeding cichlids from Africa's Great Lakes, and an outdoor pool to show fish lying dormant when it freezes over. Even better is the **mini-rainforest**, complete with macaws, marmoset monkeys, iguanas and alligators, kept steamy by a downpour with thunder and lightning effects every fifteen minutes. The Tropicarium is in the Campona Shopping Centre, which is named after a Roman fort that guarded the riverside, where excavations yielded a cult-statue of Mithras, now in the Aquincum Museum (see p.115).

Nagytétényi Castle Museum

Nagytétényi Kastélymúzeum • XXII, Kastélypark utca 9 • Tues–Sun 10am–6pm • 600Ft, 800Ft for temporary exhibitions • Ⓦ nagytetenyi .hu • In July and Aug, historical dances and concerts are held in the grounds (☎ 1 207 0005 for details) • Bus #33 from Móricz Zsigmond körtér (30–45min) or the Tropicarium (15min) to the Petőfi utca stop; cross the road and follow Hugonnay utca down past the children's playground to the kastély; or take a main-line train from Déli Station to Nagytétény (20min) and then it's a 15min walk • See map p.5

Further out in the XXII district, the **Nagytétényi Castle Museum** is strictly for lovers of antique furniture. Though rendered as "castle" in English, "*kastély*" generally signifies a manor house or chateau without fortifications, which Hungarian nobles began building after the Turks had been expelled – in this case by converting an older, ruined castle into a Baroque residence. Nowadays, its 28 rooms display furniture from the Gothic to the Biedermeier epochs, owned by the Applied Arts Museum; the most outstanding exhibit is a walnut-veneered refectory table from Trencsen Monastery.

ROYAL PALACE, GÖDÖLLŐ

Excursions from Budapest

The attractions in this chapter are all within an hour or so of the city. Foremost are three sites on the picturesque Danube Bend to the north of Budapest. Szentendre is a historic Serbian settlement and artists' colony with a superb open-air ethnographic museum. Further north, Visegrád boasts medieval ruins, splendid scenery, "organic" buildings and a tree-top zip-slide, while across the Danube from Slovakia, the cathedral town of Esztergom is steeped in history. While each site merits a full day (though don't go on a Monday, when most attractions are closed), you could cram two into one long day. On the other side of the Danube, Vác has a magnificent Baroque centre and some fascinating museums, or there's the former Habsburg palace at Gödöllő, where classical concerts are held all year round. Further afield, Székesfehérvár, the former royal seat, has a good collection of museums.

Szentendre

Szentendre (St Andrew), 20km north of Budapest, is both the most popular tourist destination in the vicinity of the capital and the easiest to reach. Despite a rash of souvenir shops, the centre remains a delightful maze of houses in autumnal colours, with secretive gardens and lanes winding up to hilltop churches, and plenty of museums and craft stalls; you should also allow at least a couple of hours for the open-air village museum outside town (see p.134). Szentendre's location on the lower slopes of the Pilis Hills is not only beautiful, but ensures that it is one of the sunniest places in Hungary, making it a perfect spot for an artists' colony – it has more artists per square metre than anywhere in Europe, it is said, though most of them seem to be turning out tourist tat.

Kossuth utca and Dumtsa Jenő utca

The road into the centre from the HÉV and bus stations – Kossuth utca, which turns into Dumtsa Jenő utca after you cross the Bükkos Stream – serves as an introduction to the two key features of the town: the Serbian and the artistic

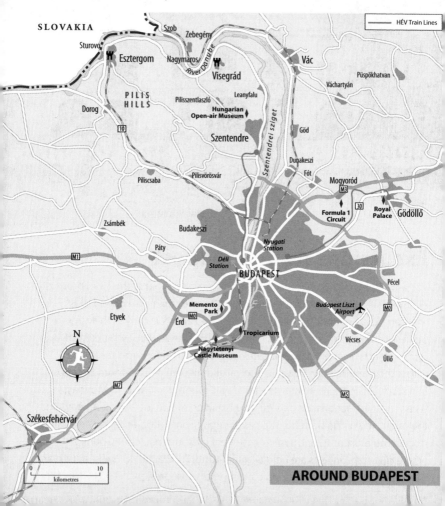

THE SERBIAN CONNECTION

Before artists moved in during the first decades of the twentieth century, Szentendre's character had been forged by waves of refugees from **Serbia**. The first followed the catastrophic Serb defeat at Kosovo in 1389; the second, the Turkish recapture of Belgrade in 1690, causing 30,000 Serbs and Bosnians to flee. Six thousand settled in Szentendre, which became the seat of the Serbian Church in exile. Prospering through trade, they replaced their wooden churches with stone ones and built handsome townhouses, but as Habsburg toleration waned and phylloxera (vine-blight) and floods ruined the local economy they trickled back to Serbia, so that by 1890 less than a quarter of the population was Serb. Between ten or twenty families of Serbian descent remain today – depending whom you ask.

---

heritages. Dumtsa Jenő utca heralds the onset of the tourist-zone – another defining feature of Szentendre.

Požarevačka Church

Kossuth utca 1 • Daily noon–4pm, but opening times not reliable • 300Ft

Heading up Kossuth utca, you'll encounter the first evidence of a Serbian presence just before the bridge over the Bükkos Stream in the form of an Orthodox church. Like many others in Szentendre, the slender **Požarevačka Church** was built from stone in the late eighteenth century to replace an older wooden structure in a grove of trees.

Marzipan Museum

Marcipán Múzeum • Dumtsa Jenő utca 12, entry from Batthyány utca • Daily 9am–7pm • 450Ft

Beyond the Bükkos Stream and the Tourinform office lies the chintzy *Múzeum Cukrászda* (see p.136), behind which lies the **Marzipan Museum** showcasing confections by the family firm Szabo, including portraits of Princess Diana, busts of Emperor Franz Josef and Sisi, and a model of the Hungarian Parliament.

Barcsay Collection

Barcsay Gyűjtemény • Dumtsa Jenő utca 10 • Wed–Sun 10am–5pm • 600Ft

Next door to the Marzipan Museum, the **Barcsay Collection** strikes a sterner note, with dark Cézanne-ish canvases and Quattrocento anatomical studies by Jenő Barcsay (1900–88), a long-standing resident and teacher at Szentendre's artists' colony.

Peter-Paul Church

A bit further along from the Barcsay Exhibition, Dumtsa Jenő utca is crossed by Péter-Pál utca, where a left turn brings you to the **Peter-Paul Church**, a yellow and white Baroque edifice built in 1708, whose original furnishings were taken back to Serbia after World War I. Since then, it has served as a Catholic church, noted for its organ recitals (ask Tourinform for details).

Fő tér and around

Beyond the Peter-Paul Church, triangular **Fő tér** swarms with horse-drawn carriages and sightseers milling around an ornate **Plague Cross**, erected by the merchants' guild after Szentendre escaped infection in 1763.

Szentendre Gallery

Szentendrei Képtár • Fő tér 2–5 • Wed–Sun: May–Sept 10am–6pm, Oct–April 2–6pm

The square and surrounding streets are teeming with galleries of varying quality – the **Szentendre Gallery** (Szentendrei Képtár) on the east side of the square at nos. 2–5 mainly holds temporary contemporary art exhibitions, but sometimes features names such as István Szőnyi, the twentieth-century Hungarian painter much loved for his Danube Bend landscapes.

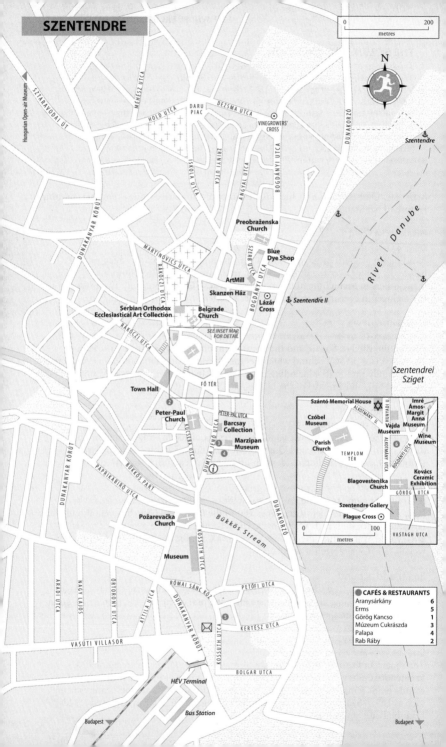

SZENTENDRE

0   200
metres

Hungarian Open-air Museum

STARAVODAI ÚT

MÉHÉSZ UTCA

HOLD UTCA

DARU PIAC

DEZSMA UTCA

ISKOLA UTCA

ZRÍNYI UTCA

ANGYAL UTCA

BOGDÁNYI UTCA

VINEGROWERS' CROSS

DUNAKORZÓ

Szentendre

River Danube

Preobraženska Church

SZER UTCA

Blue Dye Shop

MARTINOVICS UTCA

RÁKÓCZI UTCA

ArtMill

Skanzen Ház

BOGDÁNYI UTCA

Lázár Cross

Szentendre II

Serbian Orthodox Ecclesiastical Art Collection

Belgrade Church

DUNAKANYAR KÖRÚT

RÁKÓCZI UTCA

SEE INSET MAP FOR DETAIL

FŐ TÉR

❶

Town Hall

❷

Peter-Paul Church

PÉTER-PÁL UTCA

Barcsay Collection

KUCSERA UTCA

DUMTSA JENŐ UTCA

Szentendrei Sziget

Marzipan Museum

❸

❹

ⓘ

BÜKKÖS PART

DUNAKORZÓ

PAPRIKABÍRÓ UTCA

Požarevačka Church

KOSSUTH UTCA

Bükkös Stream

Inset map

Szántó Memorial House

Czóbel Museum

ALKOTMÁNY U.

Ú IDVARNOK U.

Imré Ámos-Margit Anna Museum

Vajda Museum

ALKOTMÁNY UTCA

BOGDÁNYI UTCA

❻

Wine Museum

Parish Church

TEMPLOM TÉR

Blagovesteňska Church

Kovács Ceramic Exhibition

GÖRÖG UTCA

Szentendre Gallery

Plague Cross ⊙

VASTAGH UTCA

0   100
metres

Museum

ARADI UTCA

NAGY LAJOS

ÖRTORONY UTCA

ATTILA UTCA

RÓMAI SÁNC KÖZ

DUNAKANYAR KÖRÚT

PETŐFI UTCA

❺

KERTÉSZ UTCA

VASÚTI VILLASOR

KOSSUTH UTCA

BOLGÁR UTCA

HÉV Terminal

Bus Station

Budapest ▽

Budapest ▽

CAFÉS & RESTAURANTS

Aranysárkány	6
Erms	5
Görög Kancso	1
Múzeum Cukrászda	3
Palapa	4
Rab Ráby	2

Kovács Ceramic Exhibition

Kovács Margit Kerámia Kiállítás • Past the Blagovestenska Church at Vastagh György utca 1 • Daily 10am–6pm • 1000Ft

Unjustly overlooked in the National Gallery, the sculptor and ceramicist Margit Kovács (1902–77) left a legacy that's by far the most popular of Szentendre's art collections. The **Kovács Ceramic Exhibition** never fails to delight, the themes of legends, dreams, religion, love and motherhood giving her graceful sculptures and reliefs universal appeal. Her expressive, big-eyed statues are not particularly well known abroad, but in Hungary Kovács is honoured as one of the country's finest ceramicists.

Blagovestenska Church

Fő tér 4 • Tues–Sun 10am–5pm • 250Ft

Looming over the north side of Fő tér, the **Blagovestenska Church** or Church of the Annunciation, is the most accessible of the town's Orthodox churches. Painted by Mihailo Zivkovia of Buda in the early eighteenth century, its icons evoke all the richness and tragedy of Serbian history. Look out for the tomb of a Greek merchant of Macedonian origin to the left of the entrance, and the Rococo windows and gate facing Görög utca (Greek Street).

Next door to the church, a portal carved with emblems of science and learning provides the entrance to a former Serbian church school, which for many years housed the **Ferenczy Museum**. The building has been restored to the church, while some of the Ferenczy paintings are in the Vajda Museum (see below).

Templom tér and beyond

Off the opposite side of Fő tér to the **Blagovestenska Church,** an alley of steps ascends to **Templom tér**, a walled hilltop with a great view of Szentendre's rooftops and gardens.

Parish Church and Czóbel Museum

Szent János templom • Mon & Thurs–Sun 10am–6pm, but opening times not reliable • Museum Czóbel Béla Múzeum • Wed–Sun 10am–6pm • 600Ft

Craft fairs are regularly held outside the Catholic **Parish Church**. Of medieval origin with Romanesque and Gothic features, it was rebuilt in the Baroque style after falling derelict in Turkish times. The frescoes in its sanctuary were collectively painted by members of the town's artists' colony – among them Béla Czóbel (1883–1976), whose Bonnard-like portraits hang in the **Czóbel Museum** at no. 12, behind the church.

Belgrade Church and Serbian Orthodox Ecclesiastical Art Collection

Belgrád templom • Pátriáka utca 5 • April–Oct Tues–Sun 10am–6pm, but ask at the museum if the doors are locked • 600Ft • Ecclesiastical Collection Szerb Ortodox Egyháztörténeti Gyüjtemény • Mid-March to Oct Wed–Sun 10am–4pm; Nov to mid-March Fri–Sun 10am–4pm • 800Ft

North of Templom tér, the rust-red spire of the Orthodox cathedral or **Belgrade Church** rises above a walled garden on Alkotmány utca. Built during the late eighteenth century, it has a lavishly ornamented interior with icons depicting scenes from the New Testament and saints of the Orthodox Church. The old tombstones with Cyrillic inscriptions in the churchyard bear witness to a tale of demographic decline, echoed by the **Serbian Orthodox Ecclesiastical Art Collection** in the Episcopal palace, whose hoard of icons, vestments and crosses comes from churches in Hungary that fell empty after the Serbs returned to the Balkans and the last remaining parishioners died out. (The collection is to be moved to the former school on Fő tér, but the staff say that is a long way off.)

Vajda Museum

Vajda Lajos Múzeum • Hunyadi utca 1 • Wed–Sun 10am–6pm • 600Ft

From the Belgrade Church you can follow Alkotmány utca back down towards Fő tér, passing another artist's legacy on Hunyadi utca. The upper floor of the **Vajda Museum** pays homage to Lajos Vajda (1908–41), whose playful fusion of Serbian, Jewish and Swabian traditions with Cubism and Surrealism gave way to anguished charcoal drawings in the years before his death in a Nazi labour camp. Downstairs is a selection of works by the Ferenczy twins Nóemi and Béni. Their father Károly was one of the big Hungarian Impressionists, and his children branched out into Expressionism, textiles and bronzeware. There is much talk about a new Ferenczy Museum being set up at Kossuth utca 5 near the station, but locals despair of this ever happening.

Szántó Memorial House and Synagogue

Szanto Emlékház és Imaház• Hunyadi utca 2 • Tues–Sun 10am–5pm • Donations accepted

At the far end of Hunyadi utca the **Szántó Memorial House** was set up by the grandson of a Jewish couple who were among a 250-strong Jewish community in the town that was almost completely wiped out in the Holocaust. While Budapest has the second largest synagogue in the world, this one is reputed to be the smallest; the documents and relics inside are few but they make a moving display

Bogdányi utca

Sloping gently downhill north from Fő tér, **Bogdányi utca** is packed with craft stalls and folk-costumed vendors – it's souvenir heaven if you like that kind of thing, though there are also some more interesting sights along the street's length.

Wine Museum

Bor Múzeum • Bogdányi utca 10 • Daily 10am–10pm • 100Ft; wine-tasting 1500Ft for five different types, 2400Ft for eight • ⓦ bor-kor.hu

The **Wine Museum** is really just a clever way of attracting people into the *Labirintus* restaurant above, but it does offer a handy introduction to Hungary's wine-making regions via maps, wine-bottle labels and other artefacts, with an English-speaking sommelier on hand for **wine tasting**. Its cool cellars also provide welcome relief on a hot day.

Imre Ámos-Margít Anna Museum

Bogdányi utca 12 • Thurs–Sun 10am–10pm •. 600Ft

Next door to the Wine Museum, the **Imre Ámos-Margít Anna Museum** commemorates the work of a painterly couple. Imre Ámos (1907–44) was a distinguished artist who was repeatedly called up on Jewish labour service from 1940 – painful excerpts from his diary are on display – where he died in 1944, and the museum presents some of his later works, including the disturbing Apocalypse series painted in the year of his death. Downstairs, his wife's works go from mellow prewar pictures to the uncomfortably bright and sometimes grotesque works she painted after the war.

Lázár Cross

Past the Ámos-Anna Museum, Bogdányi utca opens onto a square where the small iron **Lázár Cross** – easy to miss behind parked cars – honours the Serb king Lázár, whom the Turks beheaded after the Battle of Kosovo to avenge the death of Sultan Murad. Lázár's body was brought here by the Serbs and buried in a now long-gone wooden church, before being taken back to Serbia in 1774. Between March and October, horse-drawn carriages can be rented on Bogdányi utca for rides round town (from 1000Ft per person for 30min); bargain hard.

ArtMill

Művészeti-Malom •Bogdanyi utca 32 • Daily 10am–6pm • 1000Ft

Continuing along Bogdányi utca, the *Skanzen ház* at no. 28 is a bakery selling delicious produce made in the Open-Air Museum (see p.134) – it also has information about access and special events at the museum. A short walk further on, the **ArtMill** is a

converted watermill hosting installations and performance art events. A couple of doors up, admire the deep blue hues of clothes, tablecloths and bedspreads at the Kovács **Blue Dye Shop** (no. 36; ⓦkekfestokovacs.hu), showcasing a traditional style of folk dyeing once popular with ethnic Germans, and now with Hungarians.

Preobraženska Church

At the end of Bogdányi utca the **Preobraženska Church**, on Vujicsics Tihamér tér, was erected by the tanners' guild in 1741–76, and its stoutness enhanced by a Louis XVI gate the following century. During the Serbian festival on August 19 it hosts the Blessing of the Grapes ceremony, recalling Szentendre's past as a wine-producing centre, as does the **Vinegrowers' Cross** at the end of Bogdányi utca.

The Hungarian Open-Air Museum

Szabadtéri Néprajzi Múzeum • April–Oct Tues–Sun 9am–5pm; Nov to mid-Dec Sat & Sun 10am–4pm • 1400Ft or 1600Ft for festivals; tickets for train inside museum 600Ft • ⓦskanzen.hu • Buses leave from stand 7 at the Szentendre bus station; a direct bus from Budapest runs from outside the chemist on Madách tér, near to Deák tér, at 10am, 11am and noon, stopping at Batthyány tér 20min later (900Ft adult fare).

Set in rolling countryside 4km north of town, the amazing **Hungarian Open-Air Museum** should not be missed. This museum is Hungary's largest outdoor museum of peasant architecture (termed a *skanzen*, after the first such museum, founded in a Stockholm suburb in 1891).

It takes at least two hours to tour the naturalistic village ensembles transported here from eight ethnographic regions of Hungary, representing rural life from the nineteenth century up until the 1920s and complete with dwellings, demonstrations of cottage industries and traditional breeds of livestock in barns. Each building has a custodian who can explain everything in detail, though usually only in Hungarian.

The various areas are connected by a mini-railway (the longest of its kind in Europe), which makes it easier to cover the large site.

Demonstrations of **crafts** such as pottery, weaving and boot-making occur in each section at weekends and during **festivals**, along with folk music and rituals, grape-pressing, children's games and other activities.

Upper Tisza

Downhill to the right from the entrance, a village from the isolated **Upper Tisza** region in the northeast corner of the country reveals that the homes of the poorest squires were barely superior to those of their tenants, yet rural carpenters produced highly skilled work, such as the circular "dry mill", the wooden bell tower, and the Greek Catholic church (on a hilltop beyond). Walking up past the Calvinist graveyard with its boat-shaped grave-markers, signs point you to the scant remains of a Roman village and on to the next region.

Northern Hungary

The following region takes you to the region northwest of Budapest: **Northern Hungary** includes an original stone house furnished in nineteenth-century style and recreates cave dwellings typical of the poorer parts of the region. You can also taste or get recipes for "Palóc" delicacies – the Palóc people being an ethnic Hungarian group retaining its own traditions, with a distinctive dialect to match.

The Uplands

Next comes the **Uplands** region, which on the map of Hungary is sandwiched between the two previous sections. This region includes the wine-growing area of Tokaj, where vineyards brought considerable privileges – and wealth, evident in the proud stone buildings from these market towns, with their stoves, well-stocked kitchens and, of course, wine cellars.

Bakony and Balaton Uplands

A short walk from the Uplands region brings you to a water-powered mill and grape-press, a washhouse and a fire station comprise the "centre" of a village from the **Bakony and Balaton Uplands**, where stone and hornbeam were used for building.

Western Transdanubia

Across the stream and to the right, **Western Transdanubia** – on the Austrian border – was a poor region of clay soil and heavy rainfall, where houses were linked by covered verandas. Here, a schoolroom is equipped with benches, slates for writing on, a towel and basin for washing, and homespun schoolbags.

Southern Transdanubia

Large adobe dwellings were typical of the wealthier, predominantly Protestant German and Hungarian villages in **Southern Transdanubia**, in the southwest of the country – their carved gateways big enough for haywains – but there are also wooden-framed thatched buildings typical of the more isolated areas. The region has a strong tradition of wine-making – it includes the areas of Szekszárd, which made the first Bull's Blood, and Villány – and you can see evidence of that here.

11

The Small Plain

The section representing the ethnic German communities of the **Small Plain**, in northern Transdanubia, seems far more regimented: neatly aligned whitewashed houses filled with knick-knacks and embroidered samplers bearing homilies like "When the Hausfrau is capable, the clocks keep good time". The village layout here is designed to show the diversity of the region: on one side of the street are stately brick buildings, while on the other are more humble dwellings with earth walls and thatched roofs.

The Great Plain

Large adobe dwellings were also typical of the market towns on the **Great Plain**. A Baroque cottage from Sükösd has its visitors' room or "clean room" laid out for Christmas celebrations with a nativity crib and a church-shaped box. Beyond the houses are stables and pastures for long-horned cattle and Rácka sheep, and a windmill built in 1888, its sails still operating.

ARRIVAL

SZENTENDRE

By train Szentendre is easily accessible by HÉV train from Batthyány tér metro station (every 20min 6.30am–10pm; 40min). BKV tickets are valid as far as the city limits; punch extra tickets to cover the remaining cost, or show a BKV pass when buying a ticket at the station. The station is a 10min walk south of the town centre: cross Dunakanyar körút by subway and continue along Kossuth utca.

By bus Buses run from Budapest's Újpest-Városkapu bus station to Szentendre's bus station (30min), next to the HÉV station.

By boat Excursion boats (1hr 30min; 1590Ft) sail from Vigadó tér at 10.30am and Batthyány tér at 10.40am (May–Sept Tues–Sun; April & Oct Sat & Sun) and dock at the Szentendre II landing near the heart of town. ⓦ mahartpassnave.hu

INFORMATION

Tourist office Walking into the centre from the HÉV station, you can drop into Tourinform at Dumsta Jenő utca 22 (June–Aug Mon–Fri 9.30am–7pm, Sat & Sun 9am–4pm; Sept–May Mon–Sat 9.30am–4.30pm, Sun 10am–2pm; ☎ 26 317 965, ⓦ szentendre.hu) to obtain a map of town and information on concerts and festivals.

EATING AND DRINKING

Restaurants in Szentendre – particularly the ones on Fő tér used by coach parties – are relatively pricey by Hungarian standards. You'll do better in the backstreets or on Dunakorzó (though it's no less crowded in summer), or in **cafés** on the periphery of the centre. Look out for traditional local dishes such as Serbian *pljeskavica* and *cevapi* (lamb and beef burgers or meatballs served in thick, soft pittas), Dalmatian *prsut* (wafer-thin wind-cured ham), Greek moussaka and tzatziki, and Croatian fish recipes.

FESTIVALS

There is a plethora of folk events at Szentendre. One new event is the **Szentendre Open Night and Day** (Éjjel-Nappal Nyitva) in late August, when the town's shops, museums, cafés and restaurants all stay open late into the evening.

At the Hungarian Open-Air Museum, the highlights of the events calendar are Easter, the **Pentecostal Games** (May 27–28), a culinary **Feast of the Soil** (Aug 11) and two **wine festivals** (Sept & Nov) – these and more are listed on the museum's website. Additionally, plays are staged at the outdoor Amphitheatre during the **Theatre Evenings** of June and July, as advertised on the spot.

Aranysárkány Alkotmány utca 1a ☎ 26 311 0670, ⓦ aranysarkany.hu. The award-winning "Golden Dragon" serves Hungarian nouvelle cuisine from an open kitchen, and is a/c. Try the goose-liver pâté with rose-petal jam (2200Ft) or the honeyed goose steak with red cabbage and mashed potatoes (3100Ft). Three-course menu 3800Ft. Booking advisable. Daily noon–10pm.

Erm's Kossuth utca 22. One of the best places in town, run by Robert Erm and his wife and situated close to the station. The ingredients are fresh and the cooking is inspired. Its slogan is "Knuckle & Jazz": roasted pork knuckle from 1960Ft and jazz events, mainly in the winter months. Has a good children's play area. Mon–Wed & Fri–Sat 11am–11pm, Sun 11am–10pm.

Görög Kancsó Dunakorzó 9 ☎ 26 303 178. A lively, affordable taverna by the river on the corner of Görög utca below Fő tér with tables outside, serving seafood such as

prawn kebabs (2590Ft) and Greek specialities including stuffed vine leaves (1090Ft). Daily noon–midnight.

Múzeum Cukrászda Dumsta Jenő utca 14. For afters or mid-morning refreshment, head to this place where cakes and ices have been served in the beautifully tiled salon since 1889. There's an upstairs terrace. Daily 9am–7pm.

Palapa Dumsta Jenő utca 14a (entrance on Batthyány utca) ☎ 26 302 418. A brilliant Mexican bar-restaurant with high-quality food including fajitas (2490Ft) and enchiladas (2190Ft), great service, fine cocktails and regular live music in the yard. Book ahead or arrive early to bag a table. Mon–Fri 5pm–midnight, Sat & Sun noon–midnight.

Rab Ráby Kucsera utca 1a. This vintage restaurant, decorated with suits of armour, is more traditionally Hungarian in style than the *Aranysárkány* and a touch cheaper, with a meat- and fish-heavy menu. Daily noon–11pm.

Visegrád

Approaching **Visegrád** from Szentendre, the hillsides start to plunge and the river twists shortly before you catch first sight of the citadel and ramparts of the ancient fortified site whose Slavic name means "High Castle". The view hasn't changed much since 1488, when János Thuroczy described its "upper walls stretching to the clouds floating in the sky, and the lower bastions reaching down as far as the river". At that time, courtly life in Visegrád was nearing its apogee and the palace of King Mátyás and Queen Beatrice was famed throughout Europe. The papal legate Cardinal Castelli described it as a "paradiso terrestri", seemingly unperturbed by the presence of Vlad the Impaler, who resided here under duress between 1462 and 1475. Today, Visegrád is a mere village, where the ferry docks and a few bars and restaurants round the church are the hub of local life. Tourists tend to focus on the **historic sites** north of the centre: the Royal Palace and Solomon's Tower near the river, and the hilltop citadel. All the river sites are in easy walking distance of each other but you might prefer taking a bus up to the citadel, thus saving your energy for gung-ho **activities** in the **Visegrád Hills**.

The layout of the **ruins** dates back to the thirteenth century, when Béla IV began fortifying the north against a recurrence of the Mongol invasion, while the construction of a royal palace below the hilltop citadel was a sign of greater security during the reign of the Angevins. However, its magnificence was effaced by the Turkish conquest, and later mud washing down from the hillside gradually buried the palace entirely. Subsequent generations doubted its existence until archeologist János Schulek had a lucky break after searching in vain for years. At a New Year's Eve party in 1934, the wine ran out and Schulek was sent to get some more from the neighbours. An old woman told him to go down to the wine cellar, and there he found clues in the stones that convinced him the palace was there, beneath the surface.

Royal Palace

Királyi Palota • Fő utca 23 • Tues–Sun 9am–5pm • 1100Ft • ⓦ visegradmuzeum.hu

Now excavated and tastefully reconstructed, Visegrád's **Royal Palace** spreads over four terraces. Founded in 1323 by the Angevin king Charles Robert, it was the setting for the Visegrád Congress of 1335, attended by the monarchs of Central Europe and the Grandmaster of the Teutonic Knights. Although nothing remains of this palace, the **Court of Honour** constructed for his successor Louis, which provided the basis for additions by kings Sigismund and Mátyás, is still to be seen on the second terrace.

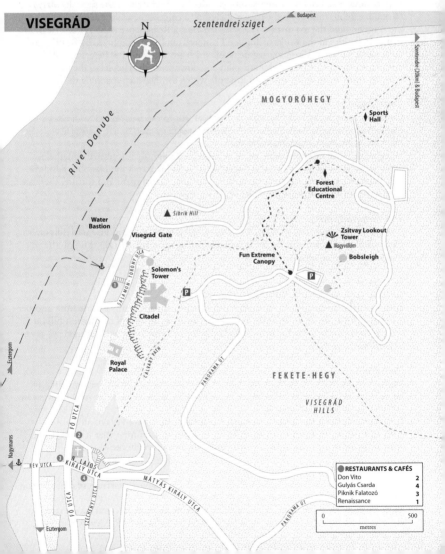

VISEGRÁD

RESTAURANTS & CAFÉS	
Don Vito	2
Gulyás Csarda	4
Piknik Falatozó	3
Renaissance	1

A pilastered **Renaissance loggia** surrounds a replica of the famous **Hercules Fountain**, which cools the tiled, gilded uppermost storey, overlooking the court. On the third terrace, where Mátyás and Beatrice resided, stands a copy of the **Lion Fountain**, bearing his raven crest and standing on leg-rests in the form of sleepy-looking lions and dogs. A bathhouse with underfloor heating, the huge tiled stoves in the dining rooms and a reconstruction of the palace herb gardens all contribute to the impression of courtly life.

Solomon's Tower and Mátyás Museum

Salamon-torony • Salamon torony utca • May–Sept daily 9am–5pm • 700Ft

Leaving the Royal Palace, turn right along Fő utca and then follow Salamon-torony utca up through a fortified gate to reach **Solomon's Tower**. Named after an eleventh-century Hungarian king once thought to have been imprisoned there after being deposed, this mighty hexagonal keep is buttressed on two sides by unsightly concrete slabs. Its **Mátyás Museum** exhibits finds from the palace, including a copy of the white Anjou Fountain of the Angevins and the red marble *Visegrád Madonna*, a Renaissance masterpiece that shows many similarities to the works of Tomaso Fiamberti, an Italian employed by Beatrice to carve other statues at Visegrád, fragments of which are also displayed here. From the top of the tower you can see ramparts plunging down from the Citadel to the riverside **Water Bastion**, a squat, long-derelict structure with a fortified arch spanning the highway.

The Citadel

Fellegvár • Mid-March to April & Oct daily 9.30am–5pm; May–Sept daily 9.30am–6pm; Nov to mid-March 9.30am–4pm but Jan–Feb usually open only weekends; closed when it snows • 1700Ft • You can come from the rear gate of Solomon's Tower (40min), or an easier climb (20min) via the Calvary footpath behind Visegrád's church

Visegrád's hilltop **Citadel** is only partly restored but mightily impressive nonetheless, commanding a superb view of the Börzsöny Mountains across the Danube. Besides two **museums** devoted to medieval hunting, fishing, punishment and torture, there are outdoor displays of **archery** and **falconry** in the summer.

The Visegrád Hills

A popular rambling spot with fantastic views, the densely wooded **Visegrád Hills** offer great walks and views, and for thrill-seekers there is the chance to zip through the tree tops or go bobsleighing.

Zsitvay lookout tower

Zsitvay-kilátó • 10am–6pm: May–Oct daily; Nov–April Sat & Sun • 400Ft

Four hundred metres up the road from the Citadel car park, paths radiate from another car park. One leads up to the **Zsitvay lookout tower** on the top of the highest hill on the Danube Bend, Nagy-Villám (Great Lightning; 377m), with wonderful views as far as Slovakia.

Bobsleigh

Bobpálya • March Mon–Fri 11am–4pm, Sat & Sun 10am–5pm; April Mon–Fri 10am–5pm, Sat & Sun 9am–7pm; May–Aug Mon–Fri 9am–6pm, Sat & Sun 9am–7pm; Sept–Oct Mon–Fri 10am–5pm, Sat & Sun 10am–6pm; Nov–Feb daily 11am–4pm; closed on rainy days • 400Ft for one go • ☎ 26 397 397, ⓦ bobozas.hu

Just downhill from the higher car park is a **bobsleigh**, where kids of all ages (and adults) can whizz down a 1km-long track and chute; note that it's closed on rainy days, when the sleds' brakes are ineffective – call to check.

Fun Extreme Canopy

Canopy pálya • March–Nov Tues–Sun 10am–6pm • 3900Ft • Trips require a minimum of four people, max twenty; individuals who turn up can be put with a group, but it's wiser to book ahead • ☎ 30 246 3381, ⓦ canopy.hu

More thrilling than the Bobsleigh is the **Fun Extreme Canopy**, inspired by the tree-top walkways in Costa Rica's Monteverde Cloud Forest National Park. Eleven platforms,

14m high, are linked by wires to form an amazing zip-ride through the forest, which takes about fifty minutes to complete, sliding at speeds of up to 50km an hour. Guides, safety harnesses and helmets are provided; nerve rather than strength is needed. Under-12s are excluded. The zip-wire's upper terminus is by the *Hunter's Inn*, on the far side of the car park from the bobsleigh run. Riders end up on a lower hill, Mogyoróhegy, from which they can return by minibus or walk up through the woods to Nagy-Villám.

The Imre Makovecz buildings

Two hundred metres along from the lower terminus of the Fun Extreme Canopy stand a trio of wooden buildings by **Imre Makovecz** (1935–2011), the Hungarian guru of "organic architecture". After creating the breathtaking crypt at Farkasréti Cemetery (p.123), he was branded a troublemaker for his outspoken nationalism and "exiled" to Visegrád's forestry department, where he acquired a following by teaching summer schools on how to construct buildings using low-tech methods and materials such as branches and twigs. In the 1980s he built here a campsite **restaurant** with a roof like a nun's wimple, the yurt-like, turf-roofed **Forest Education Centre**, and a **Sports Hall** resembling a Viking church, before being allowed to work elsewhere and given the honour of designing the Hungarian Pavilion at the 1992 Seville Expo. Though Makovecz's work was by this point widely acclaimed, his lavish use of wood vexed some environmentalists, and his dabbling in right-wing politics made his call for a return to a "real" Hungarian style of building somewhat suspect.

11

ARRIVAL AND INFORMATION

VISEGRÁD

By bus Bus #880 leaves from stand 7 at Budapest's Újpest Városkapu terminal (every hour; 1hr 25min) and stops at Szentendre's bus station, Visegrád's landing stage and by the local ferry stop before running on to Esztergom.

By boat Given the majestic scenery of the Danube Bend, arriving by river is far more scenic. The boat leaves Budapest's Vigadó tér at 9am (April Sat; May–Aug Tues–Sun; Sept Fri–Sun) and takes three and a half hours to make the journey upriver (1hr less back down to Budapest) – the pier is at the end of Rév utca; a one-way trip costs 1790Ft. ⓦ mahartpassnave.hu

By hydrofoil The hydrofoil leaves Vigadó tér at 9.30am (May–Sept Fri–Sun) and takes only an hour, but costs 2690Ft. The landing stage in Visegrád is by the highway, just below Solomon's Tower. ⓦ mahartpassnave.hu

Information Visegrád has no tourist office as such, but staff at the Royal Palace and the Fun Extreme Canopy are all sources of information, and you can also get directions at the Visegrád Tours desk in the *Visegrád Hotel*, Rév utca 15, near where the boat comes in.

EATING AND DRINKING

Don Vito Fő utca 83 ☏ 26 397 230. An enjoyable, inexpensive pizzeria themed on *The Godfather*; Luca Brasi or Don Corleone would approve of the dishes cooked in their name, in a wood-fired oven – such as Pizza Michael Corleone (1850Ft). Daily noon–midnight.

Gulyás Csárda Nagy Lajos király utca 4. This 1980s-style inn right in the centre of Visegrád does hearty, traditional Hungarian and German dishes at very affordable prices, and has a beer garden. Daily noon–11pm.

FESTIVALS

Each year (usually on the second weekend in July), Visegrád hosts the **International Palace Games**, an orgy of medieval pageantry, jousting and archery tournaments, craft workshops and plenty of eating and drinking, held in the grounds of the Royal Palace, Solomon's Tower and the Citadel; the Royal Palace website (see p.137) or Tourinform in Szentendre (see p.135) have more information.

During the second half of June, the **Danube Bend Summer Games** see sports, musical and cultural events in all the villages between Szentendre and Visegrád; for details, visit ⓦ dunakanyar.org.

Piknik Falatozó Fő utca 42 – entrance on Rév utca. A self-service snack bar at the main crossroads in the middle of Visegrád, with tables outside, where locals hang out drinking beer. Very handy for a quick – and very cheap – bite. Daily 9am–6pm.

Renaissance Fő utca 9 ☎ 26 398 081. A medieval-themed restaurant mainly frequented by coach parties, where diners can feast on suckling pig while wearing a cardboard crown and being serenaded by a lute-player. Daily noon–10pm.

Esztergom

Beautifully situated in a crook of the Danube facing Slovakia, **Esztergom** is dominated by its basilica, whose dome is visible for miles around – a richly symbolic sight, as it was here that Prince Géza and his son Vajk (the future king and saint Stephen) brought Hungary into the fold of Christendom. Even after the court moved to Buda following the Mongol invasion, Esztergom remained the centre of Catholicism until the Turkish conquest, and resumed this role in the 1820s – as the poet Mihály Babits (who lived there) remarked, "this is the Hungarian Rome". Persecuted in the Rákóczi

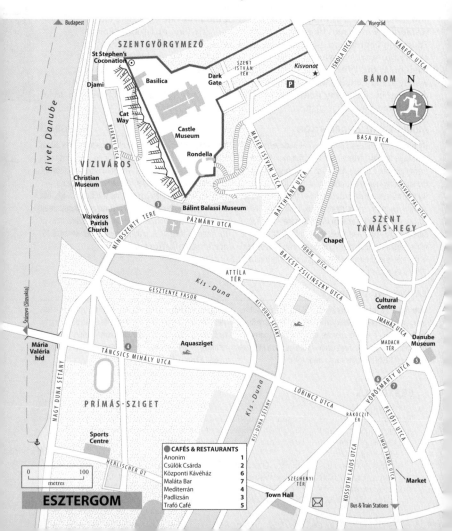

CAFÉS & RESTAURANTS

Anonim	1
Csülök Csárda	2
Központi Kávéház	6
Maláta Bar	7
Mediterrán	4
Padlizsán	3
Trafó Café	5

ESZTERGOM

THE BATTLE OF ESZTERGOM

In 2010, Esztergom was crippled by an extraordinary political stalemate when the Fidesz mayor was roundly defeated by an independent candidate but would not admit defeat. He finally vacated his office, but the Fidesz-controlled town council refused to cooperate with the new mayor in any way. It then emerged that the town was massively in debt, but Fidesz did not help the new mayor take any steps. Even the Prime Minister, who had spoken about the symbolic importance of the town, has refused to admit Fidesz's mistakes, while the local people despaired at the crisis that by the end of 2011 had decimated local services and left the centre of town looking very neglected. At the time of writing, the stalemate continued.

era but increasingly tolerated by the regime from the 1960s onwards, the Church regained much of its former property and influence under Christian governments in the post-Communist era, making Esztergom an obligatory stop for politicians in election year.

For tourists, Esztergom makes an ideal day-trip, combining historic monuments and small-town charm in just the right doses, with the bonus of being within strolling distance of the Slovak town of Štúrovo (Párkány in Hungarian). However, recent political problems and an ongoing debt crisis have tarnished the town centre of late, and could jeopardize the events and festivals mentioned below (see box, p.144).

Esztergom consists of an upper town beside the basilica, the waterfront Víziváros below it with its magnificent Turkish remains, and a sprawling lower town separated from the island of Prímás-sziget by a tributary of the Danube. Basic **orientation** is simple, but if pushed for time you might be tempted by a sightseeing **tour** on the **Kisvonat,** a road train with open carriages that runs every hour from the basilica, down to Rákóczi tér, around Prímás-sziget and back to the terminus, a forty-minute run (April–Sept; 600Ft).

The basilica

Cathedral • Daily 8am–6pm • Free • **Crypt** • Daily 9am–5pm (Nov–Feb closes at 3pm) • 200Ft • **Cupola** • May–Oct daily 9am–5pm (closed in bad weather in winter) • 500Ft • **Treasury** • March–Oct daily 9am–4.30pm; Nov–Feb Tues–Sun 11am–2.30pm • 800Ft

Built upon the site of the first cathedral in Hungary, where Vajk was crowned as King Stephen by a papal envoy on Christmas Day 1000 AD, Esztergom's **basilica** is the largest in the country, measuring 118m in length and 40m in width, and capped by a dome 100m high. Liszt's *Gran Mass* (Gran being the German name for Esztergom) was composed for its completion in 1869. Admission to the cathedral (enter by an entrance under the arch on the south side) is free, but tickets are required for the spooky **crypt** (*krypta*), where Cardinal Mindszenty (see box, p.142) is buried; the **cupola**, reached by three hundred steps and offering a superb view of Esztergom; and the collection of bejewelled crosiers and kitsch papal souvenirs in the **treasury** (*kincstár*). The last is at the back of the nave, whose main altarpiece was painted by the Venetian Michelangelo Grigoletti, based on Titian's *Assumption* in the Frari Church in Venice. Don't miss the red and white marble **Bakócz Chapel** (below the relief of Christ on a donkey), whose Florentine altar was salvaged from the original basilica that was destroyed by the Mongols.

The Castle Museum

Vármúzeum • Tues–Sun 10am–6pm • 900Ft

On higher ground 30m south of the basilica are the red-roofed, reconstructed remains of the palace founded by Prince Géza, now presented as the **Castle Museum**. A royal seat for almost three hundred years, it was here that Béla III entertained Philip of France and Frederick Barbarossa on their way to the Third Crusade, while the Renaissance prelate János Vitéz made it a centre of humanist culture, where Queen Beatrice spent her widowhood. Despite being sacked by the Turks and twice

11

CARDINAL MINDSZENTY

When the much-travelled body of **Cardinal József Mindszenty** was finally laid to rest with state honours in 1991, it was a vindication of his uncompromising heroism – and the Vatican realpolitik that he despised. As a conservative and monarchist, Mindszenty had stubbornly opposed the postwar Communist takeover, warning that "cruel hands are reaching out to seize hold of our children, claws belonging to people who have nothing but evil to teach them". Arrested in 1948, tortured for 39 days and nights, and sentenced to life imprisonment for treason, Mindszenty was freed during the Uprising and took refuge in the US Embassy, where he remained for the next fifteen years – an exile in the heart of Budapest.

When the Vatican struck a deal with the Kádár regime in 1971, Mindszenty had to be pushed into resigning his position and going to Austria, where he died in 1975. Although his will stated that his body should not return home until "the red star of Moscow had fallen from Hungarian skies", his reburial occurred some weeks before the last Soviet soldier left, in preparation for Pope John Paul II's visit. Nowadays the Vatican proclaims his greatness, without any hint of apology for its past actions.

besieged before they were evicted in 1683, enough survived to be excavated in the 1930s.

The main entrance is round to the left on the courtyard: past archeological finds and visualizations of the palace in various epochs, you reach the best part of the museum, the royal suite. Traces of the frescoes that once covered every wall can be seen in the vaulted living hall from Béla III's reign, from which stairs ascend to the study of Archbishop Vitéz – known as the **Hall of Virtues** after its allegorical murals. Beyond lies the **royal chapel**, whose Gothic rose window and Romanesque arches were executed by craftsmen brought over by Béla's French wives, while the reconstructed tower offers a panoramic view of Esztergom and the river.

Returning to the courtyard, there is a lapidarium and a further section of the museum, where you can see archeological finds and a less enthralling collection of weapons.

From the basilica, you can walk down the slope that descends to the Kisvonat terminus, or take the steps at the side down to the former primate's wine cellars – now the *Prímás Pince* restaurant – and the monumental **Dark Gate**. This imposing tunnel was built in the 1820s as a short cut between church buildings on either side of the hill.

The Víziváros

At the northern end of the parapet overlooking the Danube is the striking **white statue** of the crowning of St Stephen. Nearby, the stairs of the precipitous **Cat Way** (or Cat Stairs – Macskaút or Macskalépcső) offer a dramatic way down from the heights, and provide a splendid view of the river and Štúrovo. At the bottom lies the **Víziváros**, a Baroque enclave of churches and seminaries – and the most magnificent Turkish relic.

Oziceli Hacci Ibrahim Djami

Ozicseli Hadzsi Ibrahim Dzsami • Berényi utca 18 • Tues–Sun 10am–5pm

To the right at the bottom of the Cat Way, at the northern end of Berényi utca, lies the fascinating **Oziceli Hacci Ibrahim Djami** – a seventeenth-century mosque. Built on what was then the northern edge of the Ottoman Empire, this is a rare example of a two-storey *djami* – the only other ones are in Bosnia. The mosque was later turned into a granary, and many of its original features have been very well preserved, including a partly restored minaret. The lower floor is even more remarkable: squeezed between the city wall and the castle hill, the *djami* was built over the medieval road that led to the gate in the city walls. You can walk down the excavated road and out of the gate, on the outside of which stands a tablet commemorating the victory of Suleiman I: when the Turks besieged Esztergom in 1543 they broke through this gate and discovered that the well inside supplied water for the castle. With their water cut off, the Hungarians surrendered.

Christian Museum

Keresztény Múzeum • Mindszenty tér 2 • March–Nov Wed–Sun 10am–5pm • 900Ft • ⓦ christianmuseum.hu

Walking back from the mosque past the Cat Way, you come to the wedge-shaped plaza named after Cardinal Mindszenty. Next to the Italianate Baroque **Víziváros Parish Church** stands the old Primate's Palace, which now houses the **Christian Museum**. This is Hungary's richest hoard of religious art, featuring the largest collection of Italian prints outside Italy; Renaissance paintings and woodcarvings by German, Austrian and Hungarian masters; and a wheeled, gilded catafalque once used in Easter Week processions.

Bálint Balassi Museum

Balassi Bálint Múzeum • Péter Pázmány utca 13 • Tues–Sun 9am–5pm • 600Ft

Following the road from Mindszenty tér – after the square it becomes Péter Pázmány utca – on around the foot of the hill, you come to the **Bálint Balassi Museum**, which has an interesting collection of medieval remains – carvings, seals and fragments – from around the town, as well as the oldest bell in the country, dating from the early eleventh century. Thankfully it does not dwell on the poet **Bálint Balassi** (1554–94), who died trying to recapture Esztergom from the Turks: a half-crazed philanderer, he was famous for sexually assaulting women and then dedicating verses to them.

Prímás-sziget

From Mindszenty tér, you can cross a bridge to **Prímás-sziget** (Primate's Island), a popular recreation spot separated from the mainland by the narrow Kis-Duna (Little Danube). Lined with chestnut trees and weeping willows, Gesztenye fasor and Kis-Duna sétány form a lovely shady promenade frequented by lovers and anglers, where outdoor **art exhibitions** are held during the week-long Arts Promenade festival in mid-August.

Aquasziget

Mon–Fri 10am–8pm, Sat 9am–8pm, Sun 9am–8pm • 1800Ft, children 1100Ft • ⓦ aquasziget.hu

Elsewhere, the main attraction on Prímás-sziget is **Aquasziget**, a superbly equipped water park and wellness centre offering all kinds of treatments from collagen refreshment to honey massages. However, in 2011 the political stalemate forced it to close its doors, hopefully temporarily.

Mária Valéria híd

Further west along Táncsics Mihály utca, the reconstructed **Mária Valéria híd** links Esztergom with Slovak Štúrovo (also signposted as Párkány, its Hungarian name), five minutes' stroll across the river. Blown up by retreating Germans at the end of World War II, the bridge was left in ruins until an agreement to rebuild it was finally signed in 1999 after years of bilateral negotiations, with the European Union footing the bill. It seems only fair that EU citizens can **walk into Slovakia** with barely a flourish of their passports – other nationalities may need visas. Bring your passport anyway.

The lower town

From Prímás-sziget, it's an easy walk into the lower town, whose civic focus is **Széchenyi tér**, framed by an imposing **Town Hall** with Rococo windows that once belonged to Prince Rákóczi's general, János Bottyán. With its elaborate fountains and flowerbeds, the plaza is the setting for concerts each August, but otherwise it's quieter than nearby Rákóczi tér, the hub of everyday life with its supermarkets, banks and outdoor **market** running off along Simor János utca. Stop for cake and coffee at the Art Nouveau *Központi Kávéház* (see p.145) on the corner of Vörösmarty utca before exploring the backstreets beyond.

Danube Museum

Duna Múzeum • Kölcsey utca 2 • Daily except Tues: May–Oct 9am–5pm; Nov–April 10am–4pm; closed Jan • Free • Ⓦ dunamuzeum.hu

The **Danube Museum** mounts a visitor-friendly exhibition on the history and hydrology of Hungary's great rivers, the Danube and the Tisza. Interactive models, videos and a children's section explain the principles of fluid hydraulics, regulating rivers and disaster relief during floods, the most recent of which occurred in 2002.

Szent Tamás-hegy

To get a final overview of the lower town, walk up Imaház utca past a flamboyant, Moorish-style edifice that was once Esztergom's synagogue and is now a **Cultural Centre** (Művelődési Ház) with a variety of programmes. Shortly afterwards you'll find a flight of steps leading to **Szent Tamás-hegy** (St Thomas's Hill), a rocky outcrop named after the English martyr Thomas à Becket. A **chapel** was built here in his honour by Margaret Capet, whose English father-in-law, Henry II, prompted Thomas's assassination by raging "Who will rid me of this turbulent priest?" Even after her husband died and Margaret married Béla III of Hungary, her conscience would not let her forget the saint. The existing chapel (postdating the Turkish occupation) is fronted by a trio of life-size statues representing Golgotha.

ARRIVAL AND INFORMATION   ESZTERGOM

By train The train station, 1km further south, is linked to the centre by bus #1 and #5, or it's a 15min walk.

By bus Unless you can afford to travel by hydrofoil, Esztergom is best reached by road. Buses run from Budapest's Újpest Városkapu terminal via Visegrád (#880 hourly from stand 7; 2hr) or from the Árpád híd terminal via Dorog, west of the Pilis Hills (#800 every 30min from stand 6; 1hr 20min), a less scenic but faster route. Arriving from Visegrád, get off near Basilica Hill rather than riding on to the bus station in the south of town.

By boat The 9am ferry (April Sat; May–Aug Tues–Sun; Sept Fri–Sun; 1990Ft) takes 5hr; it returns at 4.45pm and takes 3hr 30min to get back downriver. Ⓦ mahartpassnave.hu

By hydrofoil The 9.30am hydrofoil (May–Sept Fri–Sun; 3990ft; 1hr 30min either way) from Budapest ties up at Prímás-sziget, a 15min walk from the centre. Ⓦ mahartpassnave.hu

Information At the time of writing there is no tourist office in the town, a victim of the local squabbles, but you can try Cathedrális Tours at Bajcsy-Zsilinszky utca 26 at the foot of Basilica Hill.

EATING AND DRINKING

Anonim Berényi utca 4 ☎33 411 880. Opposite the Cat Way in the Víziváros, this romantic restaurant specializes in game dishes. Try the *cserhat* (saddle of lamb braised with sauerkraut) or *racponty* (fried carp fillet layered with paprika and sour cream). Mon–Sat noon–midnight.

Csülök Csárda Batthyány utca 11–13 ☎33 412 420. Popular with tourists and locals alike, the reasonably priced "Knuckle Inn" serves hearty Hungarian, Czech and German dishes, including pig's knuckle (2390Ft). Daily noon–midnight.

FESTIVALS

Esztergom is big on summer festivals. **Fesztergom** (Ⓦ fesztergom.hu) is a three-day rock festival held in the Sports Centre on Prímás-sziget towards the end of June, while August kicks off with a **folk and children's festival**, followed by a two-day **wine festival**, outdoor art exhibitions and jazz concerts – dates are posted (in Hungarian) on Ⓦ esztergomprogram.hu. **Art exhibitions** are held in **Prímás-sziget** during the week-long **Arts Promenade festival** in mid-August.

Központi Kávéház Vörösmarty utca 2 ⓦ kozpontikavehaz.hu. A stylishly revamped Art Nouveau coffee house in the centre of town with a chocolate museum upstairs. Mon–Fri noon–10pm, Sat & Sun noon–midnight.

Maláta Bar Vörösmarty utca 3. A late-night hangout for ageing rockers and smooching teenagers, with dance music on its jukebox and an overhead tangle of varnished branches. Mon–Thurs 1pm–1am, Fri 1pm–3am, Sat 3pm–2am, Sun 3pm–midnight.

Mediterráneo Prímás-sziget, Helischer út 2 ☏ 33 311 411. A new venture attached to the hotel of the same name, with an excellent reputation, with good salads and

reasonable prices – the roast duck with rosemary is 1850Ft. Large terrace. Daily noon–10pm.

Padlizsán Pázmány Péter utca 21 ☏ 33 311 212. Another excellent new restaurant in the Vizíváros with modern cooking and a pleasant courtyard and an atmospheric interior. Pike perch with roast potatoes is 3250Ft. Mon–Thurs noon–10pm, Fri–Sun noon–11pm.

Trafó Vörösmarty utca. Small bar in an old electrical substation across the road from the Danube Museum: it's a popular place, with a terrace under the trees, and serves good wines, *palinkas* and coffee as well as Hungarian dishes. Mon–Sat 7am–2am, Sun 8am–midnight.

Vác

11

The town of **VÁC**, 40km north of Budapest, has a worldlier past than its sleepy atmosphere suggests, allowing you to enjoy its architectural heritage in relative peace. Its bishops traditionally showed a flair for self-promotion, like the cardinals of Esztergom, endowing monuments and colleges. Under Turkish occupation (1544–1686), Vác assumed an oriental character, with seven mosques and a public *hammam*, while during the Reform Era it was linked to Budapest by Hungary's first rail line (the second continued to Bratislava). In 1849 two battles were fought at Vác, the first a victory for the town over the

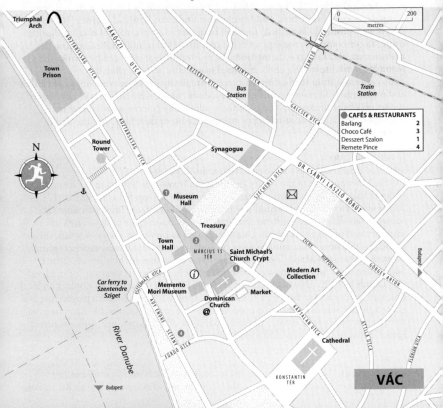

Austrian army, followed a few months later by a defeat in July 1849 when the town was captured; the battles are commemorated by a bright green **obelisk** by the main road from Budapest, shortly before you enter the town. More recently Vác became notorious for its prison, which has one of the toughest regimes in the country and was used to incarcerate leftists under Admiral Horthy and "counter-revolutionaries" under Communism.

Március 15 tér

One of the most eye-catching squares in the entire country, **Március 15 tér** is a perfect triangular wedge framed by a handsome melange of sunny, pastel-coloured Baroque and Rococo buildings. Here you'll find the tourist office, ruins, museums – and the chimes ringing out from the set of bells in the corner of the square.

St Michael's Church crypt

Szent Mihály Altemplom • Március 15 tér • April–Oct Thurs & Fri 10am–2pm, Sat & Sun 10am–6pm • 300Ft

At the heart of the square are the recently excavated ruins of **St Michael's Church**, developed piecemeal since its thirteenth-century origins. What you see now – foundation walls, sections of nave and parts of a crypt – dates mainly from the eighteenth century; the crypt itself can be visited in summer.

Memento Mori (Ignác Tragor Museum)

Memento Mori (Tragor Ignác Múzeum) • Március 15 tér 19 • Tues–Sun 10am–6pm • 1000Ft

The Baroque style evolved into a fine art in Vác, as evinced by the gorgeous decor of the **Dominican church** – also known as the White Friars' Church (Fehérek temploma) – on the south side of the square. During renovation work in 1994, the church crypt was rediscovered, unearthing some remarkable finds, not least 262 corpses (166 of which were positively identified) that had been preserved in a state of mummification owing to the crypt's microclimatic conditions. Three of the mummified corpses (a male, female and infant) – dating from the eighteenth century – can be seen in the **Memento Mori** display in a chilly medieval wine cellar near the church.

Also retrieved from the bodies were an immaculately preserved assortment of clothes and other burial accessories (including crucifixes, which were traditionally placed in the hands of the deceased), alongside their colourfully painted wooden coffins – typically, the adult coffin would be painted brown or dark blue, and the child's coffin green and white.

Diocesan Treasury

Székesegyházi kincstár • Március 15 tér 4 • May–Oct Wed–Fri 2–6pm, Sat & Sun 10am–6pm • 500Ft

On the northeast side of the square the **Diocesan Treasury** is housed in the former Bishop's Palace (Nagypréposti palota). It was built for Bishop Kristóf Migazzi (1714–1803) who erected Vác's cathedral (see p.147) and the Baroque **Town Hall** across the square, its gable adorned with two prostrate females bearing the coats of arms of Hungary and of Migazzi himself. During his years as Bishop of Vác (1762–86), this ambitious prelate was the moving force behind the town's eighteenth-century revival, impressing Empress Maria Theresa sufficiently to make him Archbishop of Vienna. Meanwhile his former palace was converted into Hungary's first Institute for the Deaf and Dumb in 1802. Downstairs is a collection of church treasures and displays on local diocesan history and architecture (no English captions). But it is worth persevering and going upstairs, where recent restoration work has uncovered fabulous Rococo frescoes from two periods of the eighteenth century in four of the rooms, one with a winter garden scene, another decorated with fruit and flowers.

Museum Hall

Értéktár • Köztársaság út 19 • May–Oct Thurs & Fri 10am–2pm, Sat & Sun 10am–6pm • 400Ft, joint ticket with the crypt 500Ft

Two doors along from the Treasury – the main square turns seamlessly into Köztársaság út – is the **Museum Hall**, which has a delightful display of works by the popular Hungarian children's illustrator Gyula Hincz (1904–86).

The museum is also covered by a combined ticket that includes the St Michael's crypt (See p.146) and the Modern Art Collection (see below).

The cathedral

Székesegyház • Konstantin tér • April–Nov Mon–Sat 10am–noon & 1.30–6pm, Sun 7.30am–7pm

A short walk further down Káptalan utca, the **Modern Art Collection** at no. 16 has little to recommend it – you would be better off going to the lively **market** (Mon–Sat 8am–2pm) selling flowers, fruit and vegetables across the road. Pressing on along the road you come to the back of Vác's **cathedral**. Chiefly impressive for its gigantic Corinthian columns, Migazzi's church is a temple to self-esteem more than anything else. Its Neoclassical design by Isidore Canevale was considered revolutionary in the 1770s, the style not becoming generally accepted in Hungary until the following century. Migazzi himself took umbrage at one of the frescoes by Franz Anton Maulbertsch, and ordered *The Meeting of Mary and Elizabeth*, above the altar, to be bricked over. His motives for this are unknown, but one theory is that it was because Mary was depicted as being pregnant. The fresco was only discovered during restoration work in 1944. From the cathedral you can head along Múzeum utca to Géza király tér, the centre of Vác in medieval times, where there's a Baroque **Franciscan church** with a magnificent organ, pulpits and altars.

11

Along the waterfront

From the Franciscan church you can follow the road down to the **riverside promenade**, József Attila sétány, where the townsfolk of Vác walk on summer weekends and evenings. The northern stretch of the promenade, named after Liszt, runs past the **Round Tower**, the only remnant of Vác's medieval fortifications.

The prison

Beyond the dock for ferries to Budapest and Esztergom rises the forbidding hulk of the town's **prison** (*fegyház*). Ironically, the building was originally an academy for noble youths, founded by Maria Theresa. Turned into a barracks in 1784 – you can still see part of the older building peering awkwardly above the blank white walls of the prison – it began its penal career a century later, achieving infamy during the Horthy era, when two Communists died here after being beaten for going on hunger strike to protest against maltreatment. In October 1956 a mass escape occurred. Thrown into panic by reports from Budapest where their colleagues were being "hunted down like animals, hung on trees, or just beaten to death by passers-by", the ÁVO guards mounted guns on the rooftop, fomenting rumours of the Uprising among prisoners whose hopes had been raised by snatches of patriotic songs overheard from the streets. A glimpse of national flags with the Soviet emblem cut from the centre provided the spark: a guard was overpowered, locks were shot off, and the prisoners burst free.

Triumphal Arch

The **Triumphal Arch** (Kőkapu or Diadalív) flanking the prison was another venture by Migazzi and his architect Canevale, occasioned by Maria Theresa's visit in 1764. Migazzi initially planned theatrical facades to hide the town's dismal housing (perhaps inspired by Potemkin's fake villages in Russia, created around the same time), but settled for the Neoclassical arch, from which Habsburg heads grimace a stony welcome.

ARRIVAL AND DEPARTURE VÁC

By train There are regular services from Nyugati Station to Vác – the *zónázó* trains are the faster ones. From the train station, at the northern end of Széchenyi utca, it's a 10min walk down to Március 15 tér.

By bus Buses go from Ujpest Városkapu bus station in Budapest every half-hour and take 55min. They arrive at Szent István tér, a few minutes closer to the main square than the train station.

11

VÁCI VILÁGI VIGALOM FESTIVAL

Vác's major annual **festival** is the three-day **Váci Világi Vigalom** (literally, the Vác Secular Entertainment, though why secular no one seems able to say) at the end of July, which includes folk, rock and pop music and exhibitions, and takes place on Március 15 tér, down by the river and in churches and the synagogue.

By ferry The boat leaves Budapest's Vigadó tér at 9am (April Sat; May–Aug Tues–Sun; Sept Fri–Sun) and takes two hours to make the journey upriver (1hr back down to Budapest); a one-way trip costs 1490Ft. Disembarking at the landing stage for ferries from Budapest, you can see the prison and triumphal arch to the north; head south along the promenade and the town centre is on the left. ⓦmahartpassnave.hu

INFORMATION

Tourist office The helpful Tourinform, at Március 15 tér 17 (Mon–Fri 9am–5pm, Sat & Sun 10am–noon; ☎27 316 160, ⓦtourinformvac.hu), has all the information you need.

EATING AND DRINKING

Whereas the medieval traveller Nicolaus Kleeman found Vác's innkeepers "the quintessence of innkeeperish incivility", modern visitors should find things have improved.

Barlang Marcius 15 tér ☎27 315 584. Down some steps in the very centre of the square, the *Barlang* is a neon-lit but friendly cellar with red leather seating, serving pizza. In summer it has a large outdoor terrace in the square. Daily 11am–10pm.

Choco Café Marcius 15 tér 20. You can mull over a long menu of chocolate drinks in every conceivable flavour, such as almond, cinnamon, and orange and nutmeg. Mon–Thurs & Sun 9am–9pm, Fri–Sat 9am–10pm.

Desszert Szalon Köztársaság út 21. Also known as *Mihályi László Cukrászda* – László is the award-winning confectioner who produces a toothsome selection of the most perfectly formed cakes in this tiny, salon-like place. Outdoor terrace in summer. Daily 9am–8pm.

Remete Pince Fürdő lépcső 3 ☎27 302 199. The town's best restaurant is by the town's lido: an elegant but not too pricey brick-vaulted cellar with candle-topped tables and wrought-iron chairs, while the flower-bedecked terrace is lovely in warmer weather. Daily noon–10pm.

Gödöllő

The small town of **Gödöllő** boasts a former Habsburg summer palace and a famous artists' colony, but being 30km northeast of Budapest rather than on the Danube Bend, it gets far fewer tourists than Szentendre, despite a reliable HÉV service from Örs Vezér tere (the terminus of the red metro line #2) that means you can enjoy an evening concert and return easily to the capital afterwards. The town received a big boost in 2011 when Hungary took its six-month turn in the EU presidency. All the grand ceremonial occasions were held in the riding hall of the palace.

The Royal Palace

Királyi Kastély • Daily: April–Oct 10am–6pm; Nov–March 10am–5pm • 1800Ft; last tickets sold 40min before closing; guidebook 1500Ft, audio-guide 500Ft • ⓦkiralyikastely.hu

The **Royal Palace** was commissioned by a confidante of Empress Maria Theresa's, Count Antal Grassalkovich, and designed by András Mayerhoffer, who introduced the Baroque style of mansion to Hungary in the 1740s. The palace suffered as a result of both world wars, being commandeered as a headquarters first by the Reds and then by the Whites in 1919–20, and pillaged by both the Nazis and the Red Army in 1944. One wing was later turned into an old people's home, while the rest was left to rot until 1985, when the restoration of the palace finally began. The work gathered pace after the palace was chosen as the venue for Hungary's EU presidency in 2011.

Pick up a plan of the palace's 26 rooms in the ticket office. The formal **state rooms**, reached by a grand staircase, precede the private apartments used by Emperor Franz Josef

SISI, THE FRIEND OF HUNGARY

One of the most popular historical figures in Hungary today is **Empress Elizabeth** (1837–98), the beautiful wife of the Austrian Emperor Franz Josef. She might seem a strange choice, given that her husband crushed the Hungarians in 1848, but that may be the clue to the bond that developed between the empress and Hungary. She loathed life in the Viennese court and was none too attached to the emperor either, and Budapest came to represent a refuge for her. She also avoided staying in the empty Royal Palace in Budapest, preferring to spend her time in the palace in Gödöllő and a villa in the Buda Hills near the Jánoshegy (p.122). The Hungarians called her Sisi (pronounced see-see) and she pleaded their cause in Vienna. There were even rumours of affairs with the Hungarian statesman Count Gyula Andrássy.

Sisi's later years were blighted by tragedy – the death of her siblings and the suicide of her son Rudolf at Mayerling – before she herself was stabbed to death by an anarchist in 1898 in Switzerland. Mourned throughout Hungary, she became the focus of a cult that outlasted all attempts to stifle it under Communism.

11

and his wife Elizabeth – his decorated in grey and gold, hers draped in her favourite colour, violet. Sisi, as she was known, stayed two thousand nights in the palace at Gödöllő, preferring it to Vienna. While her possessions are reverentially displayed – right down to a horseshoe from her stallion – there's no sign to identify the secret staircase that she had installed as a means of getting some privacy in a relentlessly public life.

Temporary exhibitions are held in the Rudolf and Gizella wings, while the **Riding Hall** (Lovárda), which hosted the EU presidency, is used for exhibitions and concerts. The **Baroque Theatre** (Barokk színház) that Count Grassalkovich established in a side-wing (used for only two weeks each year when he was in residence), the **Royal Hill Pavilion** (Királydombi pavilion) and **Baths** (Fürdő) in the large park that stretches behind the Palace are occasionally open to individual visitors. The baths were last enjoyed by Admiral Horthy, who used Gödöllő as a holiday home from 1920 till 1944, installing a swimming pool and an air-raid shelter (it is rumoured that the latter will be opened to the public soon – ask at the palace ticket desk). Musical and cultural programmes are staged within the palace throughout the year.

Gödöllő Town Museum

Gödöllői Városi Múzeum • Szabadság tér 5 • Tues–Sun 10am–6pm • 600Ft

Back across the main road and the HÉV tracks and down to the right, the delightful **Gödöllő Town Museum** focuses on the **Gödöllő Artists' Colony**. Founded in 1901, the colony was inspired by the English Pre-Raphaelites and the Arts and Crafts movement of William Morris and John Ruskin, whose communal, rural ethos it took a stage further. Members included Aladár Körösfői-Kriesch, who wrote a book about Ruskin and Morris, and Sándor Nagy, whose home and workshop may eventually become a separate museum. There was a strong tradition of weaving in the artists' colony – here at least the lack of English captions is no obstacle to enjoyment. The museum's other displays include good exhibitions of regional history, including mock-up rooms illustrating the life of the Gödöllő estate; the displays on hunting and the Gödöllő scout troop should not detain you too long.

ARRIVAL AND DEPARTURE   GÖDÖLLŐ

By train HÉV trains from Örs Vezér tere (every 30min) take about 50min to reach Gödöllő; get off at the Szabadság tér stop, bang opposite the palace. BKV tickets are valid as far as the city limits: punch extra tickets to cover the remaining cost, or show a BKV pass or ticket when buying a ticket at the station or on the train.

INFORMATION

Tourist booth There's a Tourinform booth inside the palace (Tues–Sun: Nov–March 10am–4pm; April–Oct 10am–5pm; ☎ 28 415 402, ⓦ gkrte.hu).

EATING AND DRINKING

Solier Café Dózsa György utca 13. Some 300m north of the HÉV station are the best meals and cakes in town. Set in a modern block on the corner of Kossuth Lajos utca, *Solier* serves up local specialities such as Gödöllő chicken leg (2390Ft). Daily 9am–9pm.

Sulyán Cukrászda Szabadság tér. In the big square behind the Gödöllő Town Museum, this is a popular place for cakes, ices and coffee. Outside tables in summer. Daily 9am–7pm.

Székesfehérvár and around

Reputedly the site where Árpád pitched camp and founded his dynasty, **Székesfehérvár**, 60km southwest of Budapest, was probably the first Hungarian town. Its name (pronounced "**saik**-esh-fehair-var") comes from the white castle (*fehérvár*) founded by Prince Géza, whose son Stephen made it his royal seat (*szék*). As the centre of his efforts to civilize the Magyars, it was named in Latin "Alba Civitas" or "Alba Regia". Since this medieval town was utterly destroyed by the Turks, Székesfehérvár today owes its Belváros to the Habsburgs, and its high-rise suburbs to the final German counterattack in 1945, which levelled almost everywhere else. The town's narrow winding streets, its diverse museums and galleries, and the wonderful suburban folly known as **Bory's Castle**, make it fully deserving of a visit. Football fans might want to catch the local team, Videoton. They were the Hungarian league champions in 2011, much to the delight of the football-loving Prime Minister, Viktor Orbán, who hails from here – another major fillip for the town.

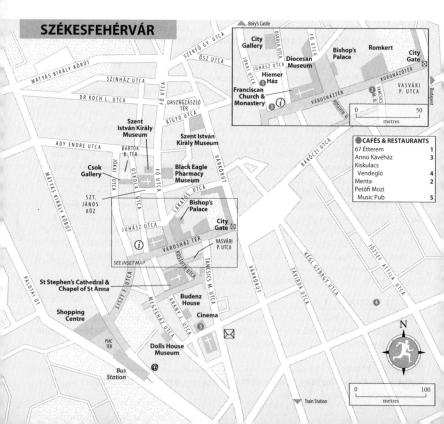

Városház tér

Városház tér, the gorgeous, elongated main square, recalls Székesfehérvár's revival under Maria Theresa, with its Baroque town hall, Franciscan church and Zopf-style **Bishop's Palace** (Puspöki palota), built with stones from the ruined cathedral by Bishop Milassin, whose coat of arms appears on the gable.

Diocesan museum

Egyházmegyei Múzeum • Városház tér 4 • Tues–Sat 10am–6pm • 980Ft

Opposite the Bishop's Palace stands the eighteenth-century **Franciscan church and monastery**, on the corner of which is Ferenc Megyessy's fine relief of warring Turks and Hungarians. Up on the first floor the monastery houses the **Diocesan museum**, featuring a glittering array of reliquaries, cups and ciboria, sculptures and altarpieces, and several rooms dedicated to **Ottokár Prohászka**, the town's bishop from 1905 until his death in 1927. Extolled as a theological modernist, Prohászka was no less renowned for his frequent anti-Semitic tirades; that is clearly no obstacle to the cult that has grown around him.

Hiemer House

At the western end of **Városház tér** stands the **Hiemer House** (Hiemer ház), the "Sleeping Beauty" of the town. After mouldering as a wreck for fifteen years, it is now emerging from a glorious restoration that is revealing the best of its medieval foundations and eighteenth-century frescoes and stucco decoration. The Dolls' House Museum (see p.152) is moving here from its present location in 2012 and other rooms may also be opened to the public – ask at the Tourinform, which is conveniently located in the Városház tér facade of the house.

Romkert

Középkori Romkert • Koronázó tér • April–Oct Tues–Sun 9am–5pm • 600Ft

A short walk east of Városház tér, along pedestrianized Koronázó tér, brings you to the **Romkert**, or "Garden of Ruins", which holds the excavated **foundations of the cathedral** where King Stephen was buried. Designed for him by Italian architects in an attempt to rival St Mark's in Venice, it hosted the coronations of 38 Hungarian kings. After the town fell to the Turks in 1543, the cathedral was plundered of its gold and jewels, and then blown up. In the mausoleum next to the entrance is a richly carved Roman sarcophagus found in 1803 and believed to hold the remains of King Stephen, minus his right hand which resides in St Stephen's Basilica in Budapest (see p.49). Around the walls are displays on St Stephen and the town, but unless you want to see the sarcophagus, you may as well save the entrance fee by viewing most of the ruins from Koronázó tér.

Fő utca and around

Running off to the north of Városház tér, **Fő utca** is so perfectly preserved that you expect to see crinoline-clad ladies emerging from one of the museums that line its streets.

Black Eagle Pharmacy Museum

Fekete Sas Patika Múzeum • Fő utca 5 • Tues–Sun 10am–6pm • 500Ft

The eighteenth-century **Black Eagle Pharmacy Museum** was an operating pharmacy right up until 1971. There remains much to see, not least the original Baroque wood-carved fixtures and fittings – made in the local Jesuit workshop in 1758 – and displays on traditional remedies. The showpiece items are a splendid horseshoe-shaped Empire-style table complete with glass cabinets, and a medicine press.

King Stephen Museum

Szent István Király Múzeum • Fő utca 6 • Wed–Fri 10am–4pm, Sat & Sun noon–6pm • 700Ft • **Ethnographic collection** Országzászló tér 3 • Daily 10am–6pm • 900Ft • ⓦ szikm.hu

Across the street from the Pharmacy Museum, next to the Baroque church of St John (founded by the busy Jesuits) the **King Stephen Museum** has a lively exhibition on local history (again on the first floor). It features a superb collection of archeological finds and domestic treasures from the Neolithic period through to the time of Turkish rule. Especially notable is the hoard of Celtic goods, including pottery, urns and jewellery, and a stone dedication block featuring a relief of Mithras, the sun god, ritually slaying the bull.

The King Stephen Museum continues a few blocks away at the top of Fő utca, where you can see its ethnographic collection. The highlights of a display that includes pots, linens, furniture and photos are the carved shepherds' crooks. The museum also puts on temporary shows of contemporary Hungarian art here.

City Gallery

Városi Képtár • Oskola utca 10 • Tues–Sun: April–Oct 10am–6pm; Nov–March 9am–5pm • 600Ft

On the other side of Fő utca around the back of St John's Church is the **City Gallery**, which has a brilliant display of nineteenth- and twentieth-century Hungarian art. The Deák Collection, which was bequeathed to the city by Dénes Deák, a local collector, is housed in three interconnecting medieval houses, with a labyrinth of small rooms exhibiting works by top Hungarian artists, such as Victor Vasarely, Rippl-Rónai, Jenő Barcsay and József Egry, whose typically warm Balaton scenes, *Greeting* and *Lake Balaton Region with a House*, are the highlights here. In the same block is a collection of sculptures by Erzsébet Schaár: it has been closed for a while pending restoration – ask the people at the main desk if it has reopened. The gallery also holds joint exhibitions with the István Csók Gallery (Csók István Képtár) a few doors up on the corner of Bartók Béla tér.

South of Városház tér

There is more of interest clustered in the winding streets to the south of the main square.

St Stephen's Cathedral and Chapel of St Anna

Walking south down Arany János utca from Városház tér, you'll pass the hulking **St Stephen's Cathedral** (Szent István székesegyház), a much rebuilt Baroque edifice that dates back to the thirteenth century – crane your neck to view the impressive, oversized stone statues of Stephen, László and Imre. Standing in the cathedral's shadow is the **Chapel of St Anna** (Szent Anna kápolna) the only remnant of medieval Székesfehérvár spared by the Turks, who put it to use as a mosque – notice the Koranic inscriptions and arabesque murals.

Budenz House

Budenz ház • Arany János utca 12 • April–Oct Tues–Sun 10am–4pm • 500Ft • Booking required five days ahead on ☎ 061 22 313 027, but worth ringing in case

Continuing south along Arany János utca from the cathedral you'll come to the fanciful Zopf-style **Budenz House** at no. 12, with a collection of beautiful old furniture and Hungarian art belonging to the Ybl family. The renowned architect **Miklós Ybl** (1814–91) was born here, and in one of the rooms downstairs you can see his drawing cabinet and photos of buildings he designed, including the Budapest Opera House (see p.57). The house itself is over two hundred years old and named after its former owner Budenz József, a researcher of Finno-Ugrian languages and founder of Hungarian comparative linguistics. Further down the street, a left turn takes you into **Petőfi utca**; a **plaque** on the wall of the cinema marks the house where the ubiquitous Sándor Petőfi lived for a couple of months at the end of 1842 as a travelling actor – it's now a popular jazz music club (see p.153).

Dolls' House Museum

Fehérvári Babaház • Megyeház utca 17 • March–Oct Tues–Sun 9am–5pm • 700Ft

Close by the Budenz House, the **Dolls' House Museum** features an exquisite collection of eighteenth- and nineteenth-century dolls' house furniture and porcelain dolls, as well as a small assemblage of model toys. The collection is due to move to the Hiemer House (see p.151) sometime in 2012.

Bory's Castle

Bory Vár • Máriavölgy utca 54 • March–Nov daily 9am–5pm; rooms only open Sat & Sun 10am–noon & 3–5pm • 800Ft • Buses #26 and #26A from the bus station, and #32 from the train station, run regularly to the castle.

The town's most popular, and curious, sight is **Bory's Castle**, situated out in the eastern suburbs. An extraordinary and wildly eclectic structure combining features of Scottish, Romanesque and Gothic architecture, it was built between 1923 and 1959 in an ordinary suburban street by a group of students directed by the architect and sculptor **Jenő Bory** (1879–1959). Originally just a small cottage with a vineyard, Bory gradually enlarged the premises so as to include a gallery, loggia and a large courtyard spotted with numerous columns and towers. The castle's rooms are stuffed with paintings of Ilona Komocsin, Bory's wife, while the colourful gardens are filled with statues of Hungarian kings and other eminent characters. Although the overall effect of Ilona's multiple images is slightly morbid, the castle is a marvellous place to wander around and explore.

11

ARRIVAL AND DEPARTURE

SZÉKESFEHÉRVÁR

By train Trains leave Déli Station in Budapest for Székesfehérvár regularly: the train station is 1km south of the centre; catch bus #33 or #35 up Prohászka Ottakár út, which subsequently becomes Várkörút, and get off at the city gates leading to the Romkert. You can buy local bus tickets (270Ft) from the driver on board.

By bus The well-run bus station is more conveniently located on Piac tér, just a few minutes' walk from the Belváros.

INFORMATION

Tourist office The helpful Tourinform, inside the Hiemer House on Városház tér (mid-May to mid-Sept Mon–Fri 9am–6pm, Sat 9am–4pm, Sun 9am–2pm; mid-Sept to mid-May Mon–Fri 9am–5pm; ☎22 537 261, ⊚szekesfehervar .hu), has lots of useful information to hand.

Festivals A particularly good time to be here is for the Royal Days International Folk Dance Festival, a week-long jamboree of music and dance taking place in mid-August.

EATING, DRINKING AND NIGHTLIFE

The town is not exactly blessed with an abundance of places to eat, though there are a couple of **restaurants** worth investigating and several **cafés** around Varoshaz tér, with two good **music venues** nearby as well.

67 Jókai utca 1–3 ☎20 970 4997. You'll find the finest food in town at the side of the Hiemer House, where the elegant *67* (the owner was born in 1967) serves up delicacies such as breaded fried pork (2900Ft) – some reckon these are the best breadcrumb crusts in the country. Its wines are top quality and it scores high on presentation too. Mon–Sat 11.30am–11.30pm.

Anno Kávézó Hiemer House, Városház tér. A cosy café handily placed next to Tourinform in the Baroque masterpiece. Lounge at the outdoor tables while sipping your coffee or beer. Daily 8am–10pm.

Kiskulacs Vendéglő Budai út 26 ☎22 502 920. The refined *Kiskulacs*, with its elegant interior and rather more prosaic outdoor dining area, offers moderate to expensive Hungarian food plus an accomplished wine list. It also does a very reasonable lunch menu for 920Ft. Daily 11am–11pm.

Menta Café and Lounge Koronázó tér 3. A well-placed bar right in the centre of town with a terrific terrace overlooking the Romkert. Local DJs run the show on Saturday nights. Mon–Thurs & Sun 8am–10pm, Fri & Sat 9am–1am.

Petőfi Mozi Music Pub Arany János utca 22. Groovy venue in an old cinema where you can expect to hear live jazz, blues and folk at least two or three nights a week; gigs start at 8pm. Wed–Sat 6pm–2am.

GELLÉRT HOTEL

Accommodation

In recent years, Budapest's accommodation has improved markedly, both in terms of availability and quality. That said, prices are significantly higher than elsewhere in Hungary, and in many cases on a par with most Western Europe capitals. The city is flush with high-end hotels, typically around the Belváros and up in the Vár (Castle District), which includes the burgeoning trend for ultra-chic design, or fashion, hotels. That said, there's still a decent spread of affordable three-star hotels out beyond the main downtown areas. Pensions are an even cheaper alternative, often with much the same facilities as small hotels, while the city is bursting with hostels. If you're on a tight budget, your safest bet is a private room, though these are getting harder to find – the trend nowadays is for self-contained studio flats or apartments rented through internet-based companies.

All hotels are **star-rated**, though this is not always an accurate guide to the standard or ambience of a place. Some of the newer, smaller hotels have facilities that belie their star rating, while some of the more luxurious establishments can be disappointingly bland with an impersonal feel. Budapest is awash with well-run and well-equipped youth hostels, many of which now offer smart en-suite private rooms to go alongside the traditional large dorm. You'll see them all over the place, though you're best off avoiding any that advertise themselves just as "hostel" and stick to those listed in this guide. Some represent the cheapest form of accommodation in the city, while others are more expensive than private rooms. While it's unlikely that you'll come to Budapest to **camp**, there are a few year-round possibilities over on the Buda side.

ESSENTIALS

Reservations It's advisable to book a room during high season (roughly May–Sept). Otherwise, rooms are most in demand at Christmas, New Year, and during the Spring and Autumn Festivals in March/October respectively, when many hotels ramp up the rates; unless you're here for the Grand Prix in early August, you may wish to avoid the city then, as most hotels double their prices. Also during August, many hostels get booked up months in advance for the Sziget Festival –here, too, most up their rates. Even so, it should always be possible to find somewhere that's reasonably priced, if not well situated.

Booking a room Aside from booking a room directly (either by phone or online), there are several online accommodation sites. ⓦ hotelinfo.hu lists the city's hotels and pensions and has information about Hungary Card discounts, but doesn't allow you to make bookings. To book online, try the following: ⓦ budapesthotelreservation.hu, ⓦ destinationbudapest.hu or ⓦ hotels.hu. Agencies in Budapest that can arrange accommodation include: Ibusz V, Attila József utca 20, ☎1 501 4910, ⓦibusz.hu. (Mon–Fri 8.30am–5pm, Sat 8.30am–12.30pm), Vista Visitor Center VI, Paulay Ede utca 7–9 ☎1 429 9999, ⓦ vistahungary.com (Mon–Fri 9.30am–6pm, Sat 10am–2.30pm), and Best Hotel Service, in the courtyard next to Tourinform at II, Sütő utca 2 ☎1 318 5776, ⓦ besthotelservice.hu (daily 8am–8pm).

Prices Accommodation rates are usually quoted in euros; where prices are given in forints, we have followed suit, but note that you can always pay in forints. Rates given in our reviews reflect the typical cost of a double or twin room in high season. That said, rates fluctuate wildly according to both season and demand, and you can find some terrific deals, particularly in some of the top-end hotels – indeed, book early enough and out of season, and you'll often find prices much lower than the ones given here. The cheapest rooms in a three-star hotel or pension go for between €50–70, while you'll typically pay upwards of €100–120 applicable for a room in a four-star or design hotel. Beyond this, in many of the five-star establishments, you're often entering the realms of the stratospheric. Hostel dorm beds vary between €10 and €15, with a double room (with shared facilities) going for around €35–40, while a private double room costs about €45. Note that some hotels do not include twenty percent VAT (*Áfa*) and three percent tourist tax in quoted prices, so check before you commit yourself.

Internet Nearly all the hotels listed here have internet access, and the majority of these have wi-fi – if not in the room, then certainly in the lobby area. Access is usually free, although a handful of places still charge (either an hourly or day rate), but we have indicated where this is the case. In any case, it's always best to check first.

HOTELS AND PENSIONS

The greatest choice of accommodation, particularly hotels and hostels, is in **Pest**, which is where you'll also find the greatest concentration of restaurants and bars – though you will have to contend with more traffic noise. The grand hotels that lined the riverbank were all destroyed during World War II, and while their replacements – such as the *Marriott* and *InterContinental* – offer fantastic views, they don't have quite the same elegance. Going in the other direction, there are plenty of hotels along and beyond the Nagykörút (the larger ring road) and up towards City Park. Across the water, **Buda** offers more restful possibilities, especially within the Castle District where there are several first-rate hotels, with more along the riverfront. It's on this side of the river, too, that you'll find Budapest's most appealing pensions, notably up in the **Buda Hills**, which is within easy reach of Széll Kálmán tér. In this city of baths, it's no surprise that several of the big hotels offer **spa packages**: the *Gellért* and the *Danubius* (on Margít-sziget) hotels were built next to springs, while several other five-star hotels in the centre have luxury spa complexes.

THE BELVÁROS

Astoria V, Kossuth utca 19–21 ☎1 889 6000, ⓦdanubiushotels.com/astoria; map p.38. Four-star vintage hotel which has given its name to the major junction in central Pest on which it's located, though fortunately all the windows are fully soundproofed. The two categories of room available (standard and classic) differ little by way of facilities, but the latter are larger and

TOP 5 COOL HOTELS

Brody House p.158
Buda Castle p.158
Gerlóczy below
La Prima Fashion below
Soho p.157

markedly more pleasing on the eye. Wi-fi costs extra. The hotel's *Mirror* coffee house (see p.173) and bar is a popular meeting point. €140

Best Western Hotel Art V, Királyi Pál utca 12 ☎1 266 2166, ⓦbwhotelart.hu; map p.38. Occupying the city's first telephone call centre (check out the lobby), this small, welcoming hotel resides in a central but very quiet backstreet. The rust-brown-coloured rooms, including triples, are airy and cool, if a little too tightly packed together, and there's a sauna, fitness room and laundry service. €120

Cosmo Fashion V, Váci utca 77 ☎1 799 0077, ⓦcosmohotelbudapest.com; map p.38. Despite its location smack-bang in the heart of tourist central, the tall, slender *Cosmo* is well insulated against the passing traffic. The deep purple, black and pink furnished rooms might be a bit much for some tastes, but there's no disputing the level of comfort on offer. Breakfast is taken in the adjoining Italian restaurant. €120

★ **Gerlóczy** V, Gerlóczy utca 1 ☎1 501 4000, ⓦgerloczy.hu; map p.38. Above the café of the same name, the fifteen elegant *Gerlóczy* rooms all lead off a beautiful wrought-iron spiral staircase. The rooms are colour themed according to floor (grey, green and red from the bottom upwards), though all have similar fixtures and fittings – high doors and ceilings, parquet flooring and, best of all, gorgeous, brass-fitted bathrooms, some with clawfoot tubs. One of the best value-for-money places in the city. €90, breakfast €12

Kempinski Corvinus V, Erzsébet tér 7–8 ☎1 429 3777, ⓦkempinski-budapest.com; map p.38. Flashy five-star establishment on the edge of the Belváros holding more than three hundred rooms. Luxurious to a fault, the rooms are fitted with handsome beige and black Art Deco furnishings, and a host of mod cons to boot. The hotel's comprehensive leisure facilities include a spa, indoor pool and a gym, and there's also the fabulous *Nobu* restaurant (see p.165). Rooms from €350.

La Prima Fashion V, Pesti Barnabás utca 6 ☎1 799 0088, ⓦlaprimahotelbudapest.com; map p.38. A stone's throw from the Elizabeth Bridge, this sparkling fashion hotel oozes sophistication, from the smart lobby to the plush rooms decorated in fetching turquoise and chocolate brown colours. The cool factor extends to the oversized wall mirrors embedded with a TV, and designer bathrooms with walk-in showers. €140

Le Méridien V, Erzsébet tér 9–10 ☎1 429 5500, ⓦlemeridien-budapest.com; map p.38. Originally built for the Adria insurance company at the turn of the twentieth century, this building housed the police headquarters in the Communist years until it was totally gutted and reopened as a luxury hotel. It's magnificently furnished throughout, with a pronounced French influence manifest in grand sofas, big chests and wall-length mirrors, and beautifully tiled marble bathrooms. Wi-fi costs extra. Rooms from €400

Peregrinus V, Szerb utca 3 ☎1 266 4911, ⓦperegrinushotel.hu; map p.38. Low-key, university-owned place on a quiet backstreet in central Pest, whose 25 rooms (including six singles and two apartments) are spacious, light-filled and come with TV, radio and writing tables – the last provided to meet the needs of visiting academics. €90

Zara Boutique V, Só utca 6 ☎1 577 0700, ⓦzarahotels.com; map p.38. Four-star boutique hotel off the bottom of Váci utca, close to the Main Market Hall. Although by no means large, the rooms are impressive, with smart, dark furniture set against hardwood flooring and light, design-papered walls. Double and twin-bedded rooms in equal measure, and all with showers. €190

LIPÓTVÁROS AND ÚJLIPÓTVÁROS

★ **Four Seasons** V, Széchengi tér 5–6 ☎1 268 6000, ⓦfourseasons.com/budapest; map p.48. A magnificent restoration of this Budapest landmark has produced an unprecedented level of luxury in the city; the rooms have Art Nouveau-style fittings (even down to the beautiful radiators) and are excellently equipped; those overlooking the Danube naturally have the best aspect. Both the restaurants are excellent – the *Kávéház* is slightly cheaper than the *Páva* but still a very good option – and the service throughout the hotel is superlative. Standard rooms from €310

Starlight Suiten V, Mérleg utca 6 ☎1 484 3700, ⓦstarlighthotels.com; map p.48. Amazingly good value given its location near the Lánchíd (right behind the *Four Seasons*), with 54 immaculate and incredibly roomy suites. Each has a kitchenette with a microwave, two televisions (one in each room), a sofa and a writing desk. Facilities include a sauna, steam bath and fitness rooms. Wi-fi costs extra. Suites from €189

TERÉZVÁROS AND ERZSÉBETVÁROS

Benczúr VI, Benczúr utca 35 ☎1 479 5650, ⓦhotelbenczur.hu; map p.58. Large, modern and functional hotel on a leafy street off Andrássy út offering up two categories of room; boxy, no-frills standard rooms, and bigger, brighter superior rooms which come with showers, a/c and cable internet – several also have a balcony. There are also some apartments for families. Standard €64, superior €86

Continental Hotel Zara V, Dohány utca 42–44 ☎1 815 1000, ⓦcontinentalhotelzara.com; map p.58. Occupying the old Hungaria bathhouse, this towering Secessionst edifice has been superbly restored. From the shiny lobby with its magnificent glass-panelled ceiling, to the sumptuous Art Deco rooms, the place oozes class. The spa centre, meanwhile, is as swish as any in Budapest, though its real selling point is the rooftop garden with a sparkling little pool offering views across the city. €150

Corinthia Grand Royal VII, Erzsébet körút 43–49 ☎1 479 4000, ⓦcorinthiahotels.com; map p.58. One of Budapest's grand prewar hotels, this imposing building was used as offices for some forty years, while the ballroom acted as the very opulent Red Star cinema. The rebuilding – only the facade is original – has been beautifully executed, and the four hundred or so rooms now provide unbridled luxury. Many of these look out onto the main boulevard, though a good number face inwards, overlooking the splendid, marble-tiled atrium. The centrepiece of the hotel's Royal Spa complex is a stunning pool. Doubles from €125

easyHotel VI, Eötvös utca 25/a ☎1 411 1982, ⓦeasyhotel.com; map p.58. Decent location near Oktogon with the same approach as easyJet, where cheapness and simplicity rule. The a/c rooms have one bright orange wall and come in two sizes: small (7–9 square metres, enough room for a bed and your bag, as long as it's not too big); and standard, which has slightly more space and even a couple of hooks. The en-suite shower/toilets have the feel of an airplane cubicle, and, in true Easy style, you pay for everything else, such as TV and internet – if you really fancy it, the Grab'n'Go breakfast is available for €5. There are two larger rooms with disabled access on the ground floor. Bookable online only, rooms start at around €19 according to demand, but are usually €60–70

K&K Opera VI, Révay utca 24 ☎1 269 0222, ⓦkkhotels.com; map p.58. Opulent, and very expensive, four-star hotel that really trades on its location right by the Opera House. Most of its two-hundred-plus rooms are of average size, but they are supremely comfortable; around half have baths, the others showers, some walk-in. €265

★ **Mamaison Hotel Andrássy** VI, Andrássy út 111 ☎1 462 2100, ⓦmamaison.com; map p.58. Housed in a fine Bauhaus building up near the Városliget (but with easy access to the Belváros), Mamaison offers five-star accommodation without the corporate feel. The rooms, some of which have a balcony, are beautifully appointed in silvery-grey tones offset with splashes of red, while bathrooms feature turquoise and cream

patterned tiles. Try and bag one of the rooms away from busy Andrássy út. The tree-shaded terrace is a lovely spot to take in the first meal of the day. Doubles from €105, breakfast €20

Medosz VI, Jókai tér 9 ☎1 374 3001, ⓦmedoszhotel .hu; map p.58. Overlooking a leafy square near Oktogon, this friendly hotel was a trade union hostel until 1989. Not much has changed – it's still an unappealing modern block from the outside, and the small rooms have the simple bathrooms and basic institutional furniture that resonates with Communist Hungary nostalgia – but the location, good prices and the helpful staff make it a popular choice. €69

Pest VI, Paulay Ede utca 31 ☎1 343 1198, ⓦhotelpest .hu; map p.58. Pleasant hotel housed in an old Pest apartment block – the bared walls in the bar area and foyer reveal its eighteenth-century origins. Most of the generously sized, gracefully furnished rooms face inwards over a balconied courtyard crawling with greenery, which is also where breakfast is served. €95

Radio Inn VI, Benczúr utca 19 ☎1 342 8347, ⓦradioinn.hu; map p.58. Situated in a leafy street next to the Chinese embassy, and with a pleasant garden, the Radio Inn offers spacious, simply furnished one- and two- bedroom apartments complete with a living room, TV, big twin beds and a small kitchen with two electric rings; no a/c, however. A good-value option. €50–80

Radisson Blu Béke VI, Teréz körút 43 ☎1 889 3900, ⓦradissonblu.com/hotel-budapest; map p.58. Large, vintage hotel in a handy location on the Nagykörút near Nyugati station. The rooms are smooth without being spectacular, though other facilities include a pool, sauna and gym, underground garage and an agreeable café on the ground floor. If you're passing, take a look at the corner facade, which is distinguished by a nineteenth-century mosaic of St George and the Dragon. €100

★ **Soho** V, Dohány utca 64 ☎1 872 8292, ⓦsohohotel.hu; map p.58. The visual assault begins in the Pop Art-inspired lobby, and continues through to the modestly sized but snappily designed rooms, decked out in cool reds, greys and blacks, and sporting Swedish hardwood flooring, bamboo-covered walls and glass-partitioned bathrooms. A filling American-style buffet breakfast rounds things off. €135

Star Inn VI, Dessewffy utca 36 ☎1 472 2020, ⓦstarinnhotels.com; map p.58. This rather non-descript glass and brick building does little to inspire, but the rooms concealed within are fresh and contemporary; deep-red walls, white armchairs and low-slung beds. The location and price makes this a very respectable option. €50

12

JÓZSEFVÁROS AND FERENCVÁROS

Anna VIII, Gyulai Pál utca 14 ☎1 327 2000, ⓦannahotel.hu; map p.77. Located in a quiet road and with off-street parking, the fairly basic rooms in this small three-star hotel won't set the pulse racing, but they're a good size and very cheaply priced for such a central location. Some rooms have a/c, and there are also apartments with double beds and baths. **€45**

Atlas City Hotel VIII, Népszinház utca 39–41 ☎1 299 0256, ⓦatlashotelbudapest.com; map p.77. There are few frills about this solid three-star hotel, located in a slightly down-at-heel neighbourhood ten minutes' walk from Blaha Lujza tér. However, the rooms are perfectly adequate, it's fairly priced, and you'll get a friendly welcome. Triples and quads available too. **€60**

★ **Atrium Fashion Hotel** VIII, Csokonai utca 14 ☎1 299 0777, ⓦhotelatrium.hu; map p.77. This otherwise glum-looking street has been given a welcome dollop of colour, thanks to this cleverly conceived hotel. The focal point of the building is a gloriously sunny atrium, encircled by state-of-the-art rooms with floor-to-ceiling windows, built-in flat-screen TVs, and bits of artwork; some rooms have tubs, others have showers. **€60**

★ **Brody House** VIII, Bródy Sándor utca 10 ☎70 931 1402, ⓦbrodyhouse.com; map p.77. This fine eighteenth-century building is where the Hungarian Prime Minister used to live when Parliament was located next door in what is now the Italian Cultural Centre. The Brody House is now a fabulously hip retreat, accommodating eight individually styled rooms, each one named after the eponymous artist whose studio it used to be. **€60–90**

Mercure Museum VIII, Trefort utca 2 ☎1 485 1080, ⓦmercure.com; map p.77. Having established itself in an imaginatively transformed Pest apartment block on a quiet street behind the National Museum, the *Mercure* has expanded into the next-door block. The newer half is sleek and modern in design, but the older, Italian-flavoured part has more appeal, set around a glass-roofed courtyard. There's a small Wellness centre in the basement and the hotel also holds its own permanent art gallery. **€130**

THE VÁR AND THE VÍZIVÁROS

Art'otel I, Bem rakpart 16–19 ☎1 487 9487, ⓦartotels.com; map p.87. Boutique hotel that combines eighteenth-century buildings – comprising beautiful, spacious rooms with original doors and high ceilings – with a modern wing overlooking the river, offering marvellous views; here, too, the rooms are well equipped and come with funkily designed bathrooms, most with shower. **€115**

★ **Buda Castle** I, Uri utca 39 ☎1 224 7900, ⓦbudacastlehotelbudapest.com; map p.89. Located midway along one of the quieter streets in the Vár, this

fifteenth-century merchant's house has been superbly converted into a handsome design hotel. The rooms – which are essentially mini suites – are of the highest order, constructed around a small grassy courtyard, which is where guests can also take breakfast. The place is impeccably staffed too. **€200**

Burg I, Szentháromság tér 7–8 ☎1 212 0269, ⓦburghotelbudapest.com; map p.89. Anonymous white-brick building right in the heart of the Castle District, opposite the Mátyás Church. The 26 rooms are nothing out of the ordinary, but most of them do overlook the bustling main square and church. **€115**

Hilton Budapest I, Hess András tér 1–3 ☎1 889 6600, ⓦ1.hilton.com; map p.89. By the Mátyás Church in the Vár, with superb views across the river, this top hotel incorporates the remains of a medieval monastery, where summertime concerts are held in the former church. Luxurious to a fault, the rooms veer between classic and modern, and it's worth paying the extra for a room with river view. **€170**

Kulturinnov I, Szentháromság tér 6 ☎1 224 8102, ⓦmka.hu; map p.89. Well positioned for sightseeing in a large neo-Gothic building right by Mátyás Church, and on the first floor of the Hungarian Cultural Foundation, which hosts cultural events, concerts and exhibitions. The fifteen rooms (some with a/c and TV) are pretty basic and a little rough around the edges, but if you want to stay in the Castle District on the cheap, then this place does the job. **€50**

Lánchíd 19 I, Lánchíd utca 19 ☎1 419 1900, ⓦlanchid19hotel.hu; map p.89. Located by the Chain Bridge, as its name suggests, this is award-winning design hotel includes such features as an exterior facade of moving panels and suspended glass walkways leading to artfully conceived rooms, each of which has been individually themed – for example on a wedding, a film or the like. **€190**, breakfast **€12**

★ **St George's Residence** I, Fortuna utca 4 ☎1 393 5700, ⓦstgeorgehotelbudapest.hu; map p.89. Variously a medieval inn, art school and law court, this fabulous building has been tastefully restored to become one of the city's most characterful hotels; the 26 sumptuously decorated suites, all furnished in Grand Empire style, are priced according to size but all essentially comprise a bedroom, bathroom (some with jacuzzi), and living room with a study corner and kitchenette. A fine location and cheerful, obliging staff make this a first-class stopover. Suites from **€150**

★ **Victoria** I, Bem rakpart 11 ☎1 457 8080, ⓦvictoria.hu; map p.87. Small, super-friendly hotel on the embankment directly below the Mátyás Church. The neat, a/c rooms are handsomely furnished and there are big windows through which you can soak up the excellent views of the Lánchíd and the river. **€99**

12

GELLÉRT-HEGY AND THE TABÁN

★ **Ábel Panzió** XI, Ábel Jenő utca 9 📞 1 209 2537, ⓦ abelpanzio.hu; map p.108. There are few more enjoyable pensions in Budapest than this graceful, early- 1900s villa situated in a quiet, leafy street 20min walk from the Belváros. It boasts ten rooms of charming simplicity (none has TV), a drawing room where you can watch TV or listen to music, and a delightful garden and terrace for further relaxation. A popular place so advance booking is essential. €60

Charles Hotel XI, Hegyalja út 23 📞 1 212 9169, ⓦ charleshotel.hu; map p.108. On the hill up from the Erzsébet híd on the main road to Vienna, this friendly apartment hotel was one of the first of its kind in the city. It has a wide range of studios and apartments (with double or twin beds, bath or shower) all of which come with a decently equipped kitchen; those facing the inner yard are better, as the road is very busy. Bikes available for rent. Apartments from €65

Citadella I, Citadella sétány 📞 1 466 5794, ⓦ citadella .hu; map p.108. Breathtaking views of the city from this hotel inside the hulk of the old citadel, with a dozen double rooms and one dorm sleeping fourteen. The entrance gate is beside the restaurant outside the walls – press the buzzer. Be warned that at weekends the neighbouring disco can be a bit noisy. To get here, take bus #27 from Móricz Zsigmond körtér, then it's a 10min walk from the Busuló Juhász stop. Double rooms with shared facilities €40, dorm bed €10

Gellért XI, Szent Gellért tér 1 📞 1 889 5500, ⓦ danubiushotels.com/gellert; map p.108. There's no escaping the magnificence of this Art Nouveau building, which also incorporates one of the city's largest, most popular bath complexes. Once inside, there's a rather stiff atmosphere about the place, though the rooms are impressive enough, if overpriced; try and bag one facing the river, some of which also have a balcony. Hotel guests receive free entry to the pools. Otherwise, the beer hall (*söröző*) serves good food, and the coffee shop is excellent. Wi-fi costs extra. Rooms start at €160

Orion I, Döbrentei utca 13 📞 1 356 8583, ⓦ bestwestern-ce.com/orion; map p.108. Small modern block in the Tabán district, just south of the Vár. The simple rooms have little in the way of furnishings, and the bathrooms are pretty cramped, but it's reasonably priced

and in a useful location for the baths. Guests can also make use of a sauna. €79

ÓBUDA AND MARGIT-SZIGET

Danubius Grand and Danubius Health Spa Resort XIII, Margit-sziget 📞 1 889 4752, ⓦ danubiushotels.com; map p.117. Both hotels are at the northern end of the island and provide a very wide range of spa facilities from mud spas to massages, as well as medical and cosmetic services from pedicures to plastic surgery. Rates include access to the thermal baths, pool, sauna, gym and other facilities. The *Grand* is the island's original, *fin-de-siècle* spa hotel; rooms here have period furniture, balconies and high ceilings. The *Health Spa Resort* is the big modern one, with balconies offering views over the island. Rooms in both €200

Pál Panzió III, Pálvölgyi köz 15 📞 1 388 7099; map p.114. Four double rooms in this small, welcoming pension, situated in the hills near the Pálvölgy Stalactite Cave. Doubles from €60

THE BUDA HILLS

★ **Beatrix Panzió** II, Szehér út 3 📞 1 275 0550, ⓦ beatrixhotel.hu; tram #56; map p.121. Friendly pension in the villa district northwest of Széll Kálmán tér, keeping 22 good-sized rooms with modern amenities. There's a bar on the ground floor, while you're quite likely to find yourself attending one of the grill and goulash parties held in the landscaped garden. €60

Budapest II, Szilágyi Erzsébet fasor 47 📞 1 889 4200, ⓦ danubiushotels.com; map p.121. Cylindrical tower facing the Buda Hills, opposite the lower terminal of the Cogwheel Railway, 500m from Széll Kálmán tér. The three hundred a/c rooms are functional as opposed to fancy, but there's lots of window space and the views over the city from the upper floors are excellent. There's a sauna, fitness room and business centre too. €90

★ **Buda Villa Panzió** XII, Kiss Áron utca 6 📞 1 275 0091, ⓦ budapansio.hu; bus #156 (note that the last bus leaves about 10.45pm); map p.121. Up in the hills above Széll Kálmán tér, this comfortable and friendly pension has ten personable rooms, a bar in the lounge on the first floor, and a small garden that's perfect for relaxing in after a day's sightseeing. €58

12

HOSTELS

Most hostels offer a combination of same- and mixed-sex dorms, in addition to private rooms (singles or doubles) at much the same price as hotel or pension accommodation. Student dormitories – many of them located in the university area south of Gellért-hegy – are open during July and August only. As well as the year-round *Marco Polo Hostel*, the Mellow Mood group (📞 1 413 2062, ⓦ hostels.hu) runs a couple of excellent summer hostels and also handles some of the university accommodation open during the summer. Staff at the office in Keleti Station (see p.22) can make bookings and organize transport to their hostels from the station. You can't be sure of getting a bed in the hostel of your choice in summer without **booking** in advance. Note that many of Pest's hostels are in residential blocks – exceptions being *Marco Polo* and *City Hostel Pest* – therefore rowdy guests are generally frowned upon. All the hostels below offer free internet access as well as laundry facilities, for which there's usually a charge of around €5

TOP 5 HOSTELS

Home-Made below
Case de la Musica below
Red Bus below
Marco Polo below
Back Pack below

PEST

Astoria City VII, Rákóczi út 4.III.27 ☎ 1 266 1327, ⓦ astoriacityhostel.com; map p.58. On the third floor (with a lift), this is a pleasant, well-run hostel in the heart of the city, with two eight-bed dorms, one six-bed, as well as quads, triples and doubles, some en suite. The six-bed overlooks a quiet inner courtyard, the others to the noisy main road. They also have apartments in the same block, and rooms a few doors along. Price includes breakfast. Dorm beds €14, double rooms €40

★ **Casa de la Musica** VIII, Vas utca 16 ☎ 70 373 7330, ⓦ casadelamusicahostel.com; map p.77. Colour is the watchword at the sparky *Casa*, located in a super spot and within easy walking distance of the Belváros. Brightly painted stripes adorn the exterior walls, a theme echoed in the retro-styled dorms, which sleep four to twelve people, and double rooms. The complex is arranged in a U-shape looking down onto a smart wood-decked terrace, where you'll find a bar and an inflatable swimming pool. Dorm beds €10, double rooms €26, breakfast €3

Caterina VI, Teréz körút 30.III.28 ☎ 1 269 5990, ⓦ caterinahostel.hu; map p.58. Long-established hostel located above the Művész cinema near the Oktogon, and although it's on the third floor with no lift, the small setup gives it a friendly feel. There are rooms of five, six, eight and ten beds, as well as doubles and singles. The eight-bed room is the quietest, looking onto the courtyard – the others overlook the noisy boulevard. Price includes breakfast. Dorm beds €10, double rooms €28

City Hostel Pest IX, Ráday utca 43–45 ☎ 20 443 2883, ⓦ cityhostels.hu; map p.77. Large summer-only hostel on this buzzing street has rooms of one to four beds with and without shower facilities. Open July & Aug. Single rooms from €25, twin rooms from €37, breakfast €4

Green Bridge V, Molnár utca 22 ☎ 1 266 6922, ⓦ greenbridgehostel.com; map p.38. Small hostel in a quiet street near the Danube in the Belváros. Accessed via a wonderful stuccoed corridor, it's on the ground floor of a handsome apartment building, and has rooms of four to eight beds (no bunks), plus two double rooms and

apartments for groups. Breakfast is not included but there is a sweet little kitchen where you can prepare your own food. Dorm beds €13, double rooms €50

★ **Home-Made Hostel** VI, Teréz körút 22 ☎ 1 302 2103, ⓦ homemadehostel.com; map p.58. As homely as its name suggests, this is a gem of a hostel, and its location, near Oktogon, isn't bad either. The brilliantly conceived, rustically styled dorms (a four-, six- and eight-bed) feature household accoutrements (radios, typewriters, sewing machines) stuck to the walls, alongside patchwork rugs, paper lamps and random scattered suitcases. There are also two cosy double rooms, one with a loft space, the other with a bathroom, and a cute little kitchen which guests are free to use. Dorm beds €13, double rooms €42

Marco Polo VII, Nyár utca 6 ☎ 1 413 2555, ⓦ marcopolohostel.com; map p.58. Very large, busy and popular hostel close to Blaha Lujza tér, with simply furnished four- and twelve-bed dorms with bunks, as well as a triple, twin and single rooms; all rooms except dorms are en suite and have a TV. Internet wi-fi on the ground floor and in the courtyard. Dorm beds €13, double rooms €60, breakfast €3

Red Bus V, Semmelweis utca 14 ☎ 1 266 0136, ⓦ redbusbudapest.hu; map p.38. Another hostel set within an attractive apartment block, this friendly and relaxed place close to Deák tér has well-appointed, brightly painted rooms sleeping two to six. Breakfast is not included but there is a self-catering kitchen. Dorm beds €14, double rooms €38

BUDA

Back Pack XI, Takács Menyhért utca 33 ☎ 1 385 8946, ⓦ backpackbudapest.hu; tram #49 or bus #7 to Tétényi út stop; map p.108. Charming fifty-bed hostel about 20min from the centre, with perky rooms holding four to eleven beds, as well as doubles. The cool vibe continues in the common-room area and garden, where guests can chill out in one of the hammocks or under the gazebo. The staff also provide lots of information on the city, and organize cave trips. Dorm beds €14, double rooms €40

Martos XI, Stoczek utca 5–7 ☎ 1 209 4883, ⓦ erik-apartments.hu; tram #47 or #49 from Deák tér to Bertalan út stop; map p.108. Close to the Gellért Baths, with basic one-, two- and three-bed rooms, and shared bathrooms down the corridor. There's also internet access and a basic kitchen for guests' use. Open July & Aug only. A bed in a three- or two-bed room is €12; a single room is €16

CAMPING

Budapest's **campsites** are generally well equipped and pleasant, with trees, grass and sometimes even a pool. They can get crowded between June and September, when smaller places might run out of space. It is illegal to camp anywhere else, and the parks are patrolled to enforce this. The campsites listed here are all in Buda, since the Pest ones are not very inviting. Expect to pay around €20 per night for two people and a tent and around €25 for a basic two-bed bungalow.

12

PRIVATE ROOMS AND APARTMENTS

The budget option is a **private room**, bookable through any of the agencies listed on p.155. You'll find people touting rooms outside the metro station on Deák tér and the nearby Tourinform office, and less commonly at the train stations. However, while getting a room this way may be cheaper, the chances are that you'll be located further out from the centre; in any case, check first.

Depending on location and amenities, **prices** for a double room start at around 6000Ft a night, 7500Ft with a bathroom, while a one-bedroom apartment costs around 8000–10000Ft. For stays of less than four nights, there's usually a thirty-percent surcharge, though this is sometimes only applicable on the first night. The *Budapest Atlasz* is invaluable for checking the location of sites and access by public transport. For atmosphere, you can't beat the nineteenth-century blocks where spacious, high-ceilinged apartments surround a courtyard with wrought-iron balconies. For these, the best areas to choose are Pest's V, VI and VII districts – you're best keeping inside or near the Nagykörút – and the parts of Buda nearest the Vár. Avoid the run-down VIII and IX districts unless you can get a place inside the Nagykörút. Elsewhere – particularly in Újpest (IV), Csepel (XXI) or Óbuda (III) – you're likely to end up in a box on the twelfth floor of a *lakótelep* (housing estate). Some knowledge of Hungarian facilitates **settling in** to private rooms; guests normally receive an explanation of the boiler system and multiple door keys (*kulcs*), and may have use of the washing machine (*mosógép*), which might itself require a demonstration.

Self-contained **studio** flats or **apartments** are available to rent through agencies such as Ibusz or To-Ma at V, Október 6 utca 22 (Mon–Fri 9am–noon, Sat & Sun 9am–5pm; ☎1/353 0819, ⓦtomatour.hu), and internet-based companies such as Budapest Lets (ⓦbudapestlets .com), a UK-Hungarian venture managing about forty well-equipped properties, from one-room studio flats on Ráday utca to luxury apartments in the Vár.

12

Csillebérci Camping XII, Konkoly Thege Miklós út 21 ☎1 395 6537, ⓦcsilleberciszabadido.hu; bus #90 from Széll Kálmán tér to the Csillebérc stop or bus #90A to Normafa, then a short walk; map p.121. Large, well-equipped site up in the Buda Hills, with space for over a thousand campers and a range of bungalows. Open all year.

Római Camping III, Szentendrei út 189 ☎1 388 7167, ⓦromaicamping.hu; map p.115. Huge site beside the road to Szentendre in Rómaifürdő (25min by HÉV from Batthyány tér), with space for 2500 campers. They also have wooden bungalows, and the price includes use of the neighbouring Rómaifürdő lido. Open all year.

Zugligeti Niche Camping XII, Zugligeti út 101 ☎1 200 8346, ⓦcampingniche.hu; map p.121. At the end of the #158 bus route from Széll Kálmán tér, opposite the chairlift up to János-hegy, this is a small, terraced ravine site in the woods with space for 260 campers and good facilities, including a pleasant little restaurant occupying the former tram station at the far end. Open all year.

GUNDEL RESTAURANT

Restaurants

There has been a dramatic transformation of the Budapest dining scene in recent years, both in terms of the range of cuisines represented, and in the standard of the top restaurants, which have changed beyond recognition. Spearheading the charge is the Michelin-starred *Costes*, closely followed by any number of establishments keen to apply refreshingly creative gourmet touches to Hungarian classics. Despite the occasional tourist trap in the Vár, Buda offers some terrific eating possibilities, with a handful of restaurants that can comfortably hold their own alongside any in the city; *21*, *Arcade* and *Csalogány 26* to name but three. Inevitably, Pest has a much wider range of places, with the largest concentration to be found within the Nagykörút, and the likes of *Babel*, *Bock* and *Café Kör* leading the way.

One of the effects of this transformation has been the increased **cost** of eating out. There are now plenty of wealthy businessmen, Hungarian and foreign, eager to indulge, and it's true to say that some new restaurants still think that pretentious décor, a few gimmicks and some nouvelle cuisine are a recipe for ridiculous prices. That said, many do now offer terrific value for money, and Budapest rates well when compared to dining out in capital cities elsewhere in Western Europe. Moreover, the renaissance in Hungarian **wine** is now being reflected in Budapest's restaurants, and you'll find superb wine cards in many of the classier places – indeed, some restaurants deem the quality of the wine to be as important as the food.

Despite many places now being out of the reach of the locals, there has been a revival in cheap outlets and self-service restaurants offering generous portions of cheap food. Look out for a *önkiszolgáló étterem* (self-service restaurant), a *főzelék* establishment (dishes of creamed vegetables, *főzelék*, which taste much better than they sound) or another Hungarian peculiarity, the *étkezde* – a small lunchtime diner where customers sit at shared tables and eat hearty home-cooked food. Otherwise, many of the market halls are good places to grab a bite, while the Chinese stand-up joints and Turkish kebab outlets all over town are cheap, though you may wonder what goes into some of the food.

ESSENTIALS

Prices and payment While Budapest is not the bargain gastronomic destination it once was, you can still eat out handsomely here without breaking the bank. Generally speaking, a two-course meal in most half-decent restaurants

HUNGARIAN CUISINE

For foreigners, the archetypal Magyar dish is still goulash – historically the basis of much **Hungarian cooking**. The ancient Magyars relished cauldrons of this *gulyás* (pronounced "gou-yash"), a soup made of potatoes and whatever meat was available, which was later flavoured with paprika and beefed up into a variety of stews, modified over the centuries by the various foreign influences which helped diversify the country's cuisine. Hungary's Slav visitors probably introduced native cooks to yogurt and sour cream – vital ingredients in many dishes – while the influence of the Turks, Austrians and Germans is apparent in a variety of sticky pastries and strudels, as well as in recipes featuring sauerkraut or dumplings. There's a lot of fish, too – fish soup (*halászlé*) is one of the national dishes, a marvellously spicy bouillabaisse in the right hands – but it's worth remembering that landlocked Hungary's fish, such as the very bony carp and the more palatable catfish, all come from lakes and rivers – anything else will be imported. For a glossary of **food and drink terms** see p.227.

Traditionally, Hungarians take their main meal at **lunchtime**. While some restaurants offer a bargain set menu (*napi menü*) – some places call them business lunches – the majority of places are strictly à la carte. The menu (*étlap*) usually kicks off with **cold and hot starters** (*hideg* and *meleg előételek*), **soups** (*levesek*) and then the **main courses** (*főételek*) – sometimes divided into meat (*hús*) and fish (*hal*). These are followed by vegetables (*zöldségek*), salads (*saláták*) and sometimes pasta (*tészták*). Finally, there are the desserts (*édességek* or *desszertek*). Bread is provided automatically, on the grounds that "a meal without bread is no meal". **Drinks** are under the heading **italok** – or may be on a separate drinks or wine menu (*itallap* or *borlap*). If you don't want a full meal, you might just order a filling soup, such as a fish or bean soup like *Jókai bableves*, along with a salad.

Compared to yesteryear, **vegetarians** are much better catered for, with the rapid emergence of *vegetáriánus* restaurants in Budapest, and a growing understanding of the concept. That said, in all but the very finest restaurants, you'll still find yourself existing on a diet of vegetables and cheese fried in breadcrumbs known as *rántott gomba* (with mushrooms), *rántott karfiol* (cauliflower), or *rántott sajt* (cheese). *Gomba paprikás* (mushroom paprika stew) is also fine, though check if it has been cooked in oil rather than in lard. Alternatively there are eggs – fried (*tükörtojás*), soft-boiled (*lágy tojás*), scrambled (*tojásrántotta*), or in mayonnaise (*kaszinótojás*) – or salads, though Hungary is surprisingly weak in the latter, given the excellent produce you can see in the shops.

13

will set you back anywhere between 3000Ft and 4000Ft (€10–14) a head, while dining at the very top end will cost somewhere in the region of 5000–6000Ft (€18–22). A number of the smarter restaurants also offer tasting menus, which, if you have the time and inclination, are a great way to sample a range of varied dishes; however, they usually start around 8000Ft (€30). Credit and debit cards are now widely accepted, though not necessarily in cheaper places, so check in advance if this is how you wish to pay.

Reservations While few restaurants in Budapest require you to make a reservation, it's best to do so at the more fashionable end of the market, especially if you're really determined to eat somewhere in particular.

Opening hours Restaurants are generally open 11am or noon to 10 or 11pm, though those that serve breakfast – of which there are an increasing number -- will open around 8am. Most restaurants are open daily, though quite a few do close on Sundays; some of the top-end establishments, such as *Babel*, *Costes* and *Csalogány 26*, also close on Mondays. Restaurants along Váci utca invariably keep longer hours, and many stay open until midnight and beyond in the summer.

Menus It's unusual now to find any establishment that doesn't have a menu in English, although dishes chalked up on a blackboard may not have a translation. Look out for menus that offer smaller portions (of a main course dish), usually for around seventy percent of the full price. Menus should clearly state whether there is a service charge (typically ten or twelve percent) or not, but if you're not sure, ask before ordering. If you're with children it's always worth asking whether there's a kids' menu, or whether they're able to knock up a small portion (*kisadag*).

Smoking The smoking ban finally came into being in 2012, though how strictly this is enforced remains to be seen.

A warning The days of waiters in Budapest overcharging or making "mistakes" with your bill are largely gone. However, you should still be on your guard; avoid any establishment that doesn't display its prices (either food or drink), and don't be at all shy about querying the total amount if you think it looks suspect. One particularly annoying practice is waiters touting for business, which is a highly conspicuous activity along Váci utca.

THE BELVÁROS

FAST-FOOD DINERS, SNACK AND SANDWICH BARS

Fresh Factory V, Petőfi Sandor utca 7; map p.38. Sunny central joint doling out freshly squeezed juices, fruit smoothies and shakes, and crisp, colourful salads. Sit down or takeaway. Mon–Fri 7.30am–7pm, Sat & Sun 11am–11pm.

Princess V, Deák tér and outlets at the exits of metro stations all over the city. Sweet and savoury puff pastries to go – try a mushroom or cheese-filled *bürek*. Mon--Fri from 6am, Sat from 9am.

★ **Vapiano** V, Bécsi utca 5; map p.38. Fast food Italian-style, and what style it is; excellent pizzas, pastas and salads made with fresh ingredients before your eyes.

Collect a card as you enter, place your order at the counter, and the meal will appear in minutes; your purchases are recorded on the card which is then handed over as you leave. Pasta and pizzas 1290–2290Ft, salads 800–1800Ft. Mon–Thurs & Sun 11am–11pm, Fri & Sat till midnight.

RESTAURANTS

★ **Babel** V, Szarka utca 1 ☎1 338 2143, ⓦbabeldelicate.hu; map p.38. *Babel* comfortably ranks among the very best gastronomic experiences that Budapest has to offer, thanks to a breathtakingly creative menu that leaves many of its rivals in the shade – how about pigeon and sour cream consommé (2400Ft), salmon and langoustine with tomato water jelly (4700Ft), or lamb

---

BREAKFAST AND BRUNCH

A nation of early risers, Hungarians traditionally have a calorific **breakfast** (*reggeli*). Commonly, this includes cheese, eggs or salami together with bread and jam, washed down with coffee; in rural areas it's often accompanied by a shot of *pálinka* (brandy) to "clear the palate" or "aid digestion". While we're not suggesting that you should start the day with a brandy, quite a few city-centre restaurants now offer breakfast menus, from the standard coffee-and-croissant option to French toast with ham and cheese, or Viennese sausages with mustard. Breakfast favourites include *Café Kör*, *Gerlóczy* and *Ket Szerescen*, while a number of cafés also do a decent breakfast, such as *Bambi*.

Sunday brunch is a popular development in the restaurant scene, usually an all-you-can-eat buffet for a fixed price. Brunch at *Gundel* is a great way to taste its cuisine without the usual formality, though it will still set you back 6400Ft; most of the top hotels also lay on a spread. Prices can be slightly higher there, but most of the hotels have children's play areas. Brunch usually starts around 11am and lasts till about 3pm; booking is advisable.

13

silverside with polenta and savoy cabbage (5800Ft)? The restaurant itself looks fantastic, though it is slated to move to a new location within the Belváros, so do check beforehand. Booking advised. Tues–Sat 6pm–midnight.

Cucina V, Váci utca 20 ☎1 266 4144; map p.38. If you deign to eat at any of the restaurants along Váci utca – which is otherwise lined with dull, one-dimensional places – then make it *Cucina*. This self-styled "Italian Kitchen" stands out from the crowd for its crisply presented food, a decent-sized terrace and an overall lack of pretension. Daily 11.30am–midnight.

Gerlóczy V, Gerlóczy utca 1 ☎1 235 0953, ⓦgerloczy .hu; map p.38. This atmospheric corner café on quiet Károly Kammermayer tér gets packed at lunchtime with office staff popping in for a quick bite – the two-course (1400Ft) and three-course (1800Ft) set lunch menus are good value – but it's equally enjoyable for breakfast or a steaming cappuccino. Daily 8am–11pm.

Nobu V, Erzsébet tér 7–8 ☎1 429 4242, ⓦnoburestaurants.com/budapest; map p.38. Located inside the *Kempinski Corvinus Hotel*, this was the first Central-Eastern European branch of the celebrated Japanese chain to open, in 2010, and it's been a big hit since. All the usual exotic suspects are here, such as Yellowtail sashimi with jalapeno, and Alaskan Black Cod, though local ingredients have been cleverly incorporated into the menu too, for example crispy Mangalica pork belly with spicy miso. It doesn't come cheap though, with mains hovering around 5000Ft. Daily noon–11.45pm.

Rézkakas V, Veres Pálné utca 3 ☎1 318 0038, ⓦrezkakasrestaurant.com; map p.38. The smart "Golden Cockerel" is one of the better places to dine in traditional Hungarian style, particularly if you enjoy a little musical accompaniment with your meal. Many of the classic Hungarian favourites are represented on the menu, from Baja fish soup to pressed goose liver with Tokaj wine jelly. Mains 3500Ft–6000Ft. Daily noon–midnight.

Trattoria Toscana V, Belgrád rakpart 13 ☎1 327 0045, ⓦtoscana.hu; map p.38. On the Danube riverfront near Szabadság Bridge, this is a favourite spot for authentic Italian cuisine at reasonable prices, and with appealing faux-Tuscan surroundings. The atmosphere is relaxed despite the smart business clientele. Mains 2500–3500Ft. Daily noon–midnight.

LIPÓTVÁROS AND ÚJLIPÓTVÁROS

FAST-FOOD DINERS, SNACK AND SANDWICH BARS

Briós V, Pozsonyi út 16 ☎1 789 6110; map p.48. Early birds should pay a visit to this sweet little neighbourhood café for its cracking breakfast menu (700–1000Ft) – American pancakes, French toast with ham and cheese, and a fruit skewer with honey are just some of the tempters. If visiting later in the day, try a duck confit baguette or a smoked goose breast wrap (900Ft). Those with children will love this place as there's a dedicated kiddies' menu and a small play area upstairs, leaving you to drink your coffee in peace. Daily 7.30am–8pm.

Duran Sandwich Bar VI, Bajcsy Zsilinszky út 7, V, Október 6 utca 15, & XII, Retek utca 18; map p.48. Filling a surprising gap in the sandwich market, this small chain ticks all the right boxes. Its artistic open sandwiches (150–300Ft) of caviar, pureed paprika, smoked beef, pickled herring and such like really zap the tastebuds. Mon–Fri 8am–7pm, Sat 8am–3pm, Sun 8am–noon.

RESTAURANTS

★ **Borkonyha** V, Sas utca 3 ☎1 266 0835, ⓦborkonyha.hu; map p.48. This sublime restaurant is fronted by a beautiful, gleaming bar stacked high with bottles of Hungarian wine, which gives some indication as to how seriously they take their plonk here. The food is no less exciting – expect suckling pig carpaccio, rabbit roasted in bacon, and milk rice with dill sorbet, though it's not nearly as expensive as similar restaurants in its class. Mains 3000–4000Ft. Mon–Sat noon–midnight.

★ **Café Kör** V, Sas utca 17 ☎1 311 0053, ⓦcafekor .com; map p.48. Top-drawer restaurant a few paces down from *Borkonyha*, with a very relaxed feel, despite a boxy interior that seems overrun at times. Its grilled meats (predominantly chicken but also turkey and duck) are excellent, as are the salads and specials of the day – the roasted pike-perch in garlic is always a favourite – and the wine list is second to none. Moreover, this place has retained its traditionally high standards of service. Mains 2000–4300Ft. Booking advised. Cash payment only. Mon–Sat 10am–10pm; breakfast served between 10am and noon.

13

Csarnok V, Hold utca 11 ☎ 1 269 4906; map p.48. Good, down-to-earth Hungarian restaurant that used to serve the workers at the market a few doors along; despite a slightly more upmarket clientele these days, its unpretentious feel is still very much in evidence, with faded wood-panelled walls and red-and-white-check tablecloths. The food, too, is honest-to-goodness fare, such as veal paprika stew and pickled shank of smoked pork (1600Ft). Daily 10am–10pm.

Firkász XIII, Tátra utca 18 ☎ 1 450 1118; map p.48. Done up like a journalists' haunt from the turn of the last century – witness the walls covered in newspaper cuttings and the rows of empty wine and *pálinka* bottles – Firkász serves decent traditional Hungarian dishes along the lines of crispy roast pork and goose leg with cabbage. The resident pianist tinkles his way into action nightly at 7pm. Mains 2000–4000Ft. Daily noon–3.30pm & 6–10pm.

Govinda V, Vigyázó Ferenc utca 4 & Papnövelde utca 1 ☎ 1 267 7631; (map p.48). Two branches of this Hare Krishna vegetarian restaurant, serving individual portions (pakora, samosa, bulgar and so on for 200Ft), as well as inexpensive set meals (990–1800Ft), and an all-you-can-eat menu after 4pm (2490Ft), all accompanied by the whiff of soporific incense. Mon–Sat noon–9pm.

★ **Momotaro** V, Széchenyi utca 16 (entrance on Nádor utca) ☎ 1 269 3802; map p.48. There's nothing obviously eye-catching about this Chinese restaurant, but it's one of the few ethnic eateries in the city that really holds its own. Sup a complimentary cup of tea while perusing a long menu comprising the likes of pan-fried pork buns, braised meatballs and steamed sea bass in soya sauce; each dish goes for around 1000–1500Ft a pop, making this a cheap-and-cheerful evening out. Daily 11am–10pm.

Okay Italia XIII, Szent István körút 20 ☎ 1 349 2991; map p.48. It's not the best location in the world, but that doesn't seem to deter the locals and expats who flock to this lively restaurant not far from Nyugati station. Its lengthy menu is a refreshingly original take on Italian standards, for example, green noodle pasta with mussels, and garganelli pasta with octopus, garlic and chilli pepper. Mains 2000–4000Ft. Daily 11am–midnight.

Pomo D'Oro V, Arany János utca 9 ☎ 1 302 6473, ⓦ pomodorobudapest.com; map p.48. An established fixture on the Budapest dining scene, this refined, split-level trattoria also rates highly among the city's Italian community. The wood-burning oven turns out excellent pizzas from 1600Ft, and the pastas and risottos (2200–3000Ft) are also exceptional, although if you're only here once, seek out the charcoal grill (3000–4000Ft). A surprisingly varied selection of wines rounds things off beautifully. Daily noon–midnight.

TERÉZVÁROS AND ERZSÉBETVÁROS

FAST FOOD DINERS, SNACK AND SANDWICH BARS

Bahn mi Bistro VI, Hajós utca 26/a; map p.58. The name suggests otherwise, but this Vietnamese venture is little more than a shop with a snack counter. The menu, such as it is, consists of a handful of both meat and vegetarian dishes, the pick of which is a delicious *bahn bao*, a steamed dumpling stuffed with egg, pork and noodles – all dishes come in at under 1000Ft. Mon–Sat 11am–11pm.

Bombay Express VI, Andrássy út 44; map p.58. Pop into this self-service Indian place a few paces down from the Oktogon for vegetable samosa, dahl, chicken tikka masala, lamb Hyderabad or spicy kebabs, to eat in or take away. A typical menu costs around 1500Ft, but between 11am and 4pm, you can get stuck into the Express Menu for just 1000Ft. Daily 11am–11pm.

★ **Falafel** VI, Paulay Ede utca 53; map p.58. Budapest's most popular falafel joint for years, which is perhaps why it's never changed its formula; you just pay your money and stuff your pitta breads as full as you can. Seating upstairs. Mon–Fri 10am–8pm, Sat 10am–6pm.

RESTAURANT GYPSY BANDS

A traditional accompaniment to a Hungarian meal is the **Gypsy band**, dressed in blue and red waistcoats and displaying astonishing skill – one favourite piece of music imitates the sound of the lark (*pacsirta*). This music arouses strong passions – and not just among the diners who stand up and sing with the band: tell a Hungarian that these schmaltzy tunes are Hungarian folk and you'll be informed, in no uncertain terms, that this is Gypsy music. The rural Vlach Roma will say exactly the opposite: that the songs are a Hungarian entity, quite different to what the Roma play for themselves (see p.217). In fact, the tunes you'll hear in the restaurants are popularized versions of the old folk songs – **magyar nóta** – composed in the nineteenth century (and played today) by Romungro Gypsy dynasties. To get the full charm of this entertainment try the *Rézkakas* in the Belváros, or the *Kéhli* in Óbuda – the latter has a big local following and the atmosphere is great on Friday nights. If you ask for a tune when the *primás* (the lead violinist in the all-blue waistcoat) comes round the tables, bear in mind that you'll be expected to pay for the privilege.

Ganga VI, Bajcsy-Zsilinszky út 25 ☎1 705 7732; map p.58. One of the growing band of vegetarian restaurants, *Ganga* has just a handful of tables both inside and out and knocks up uncomplicated but tasty dishes such as spiced potatoes and lasagne. It's worth popping by after 5pm for the all-you-can-eat menu costing just 990Ft. Mon–Fri 8am–10pm, Sat noon–10pm.

Hummus Point VI, Dohány utca 1/b; map p.58. Busy, lime-green coloured veggie hangout serving up fresh plates of salad (450Ft) and falafel (1000Ft), in addition to the odd leftfield dish like hot cherry paprika. A convenient pitstop after inspecting the synagogue opposite. Mon–Fri & Sun 10am–10pm.

Kádár Étkezde VII, Klauzál tér 10; map p.58. Diner with delicious home cooking; traditional Budapest Jewish food (non-kosher) on Friday. Mon–Sat 11.30am–3.30pm; closed mid-July to mid-Aug.

★ **Montenegrói Gurman** VII, Rákóczi út 54; map p.58. Fans of the traditional Balkan grill should make this place their first port of call. Gut-busting portions of succulent Čevapčiči (spiced mincemeat rissoles) and *pljeskavica* (hamburger style patty) served with spicy paprika and *lepinja* (doughy bread), and all washed down with a bottle of Slovenian Laško beer. It's open around the clock, so just the job for post-drink munchies. Daily 24hr.

RESTAURANTS

★ **Bock Bisztró** VII, Erzsébet körút 43–49 ☎1 321 0340, ⓦbockbisztro.hu; map p.58. Located within the *Grand Corinthia Hotel*, *Bock* takes its name from one of Hungary's top vintners, József Bock, and its stock includes many labels that you won't find elsewhere in the city. It's a great place to eat, both classy (check out the cork-filled glass tables) and relaxed, with friendly staff and beautifully crafted food; if you don't fancy a full-blown meal, try something from the tapas menu, such as duck tongue salad or oven-roasted beetroot. Tapas 1400Ft, mains 3000–4400Ft. Booking advised. Mon–Sat noon–midnight.

★ **Café Bouchon** VI, Zichy Jenő utca 33 ☎1 353 4094, ⓦcafébouchon.hu; map p.58. A real neighbourhod stalwart, and popular with the nearby opera-going crowd, *Café Bouchon* is a cracking place. The Art Deco furnishings look fab, the Hungarian/French-fused cuisine (Tokaj grape salad with walnuts and Camembert, Hungarian sausage with goose-liver pâté) is first class, and the place is serviced by friendly, knowledgeable staff. The wine card is up there with the best in the city, too, stocked with the likes of Légli from Balaton and Oremus and Degenfeld from Tokaj. Mains 2600–4000Ft. Mon–Sat 9am–11pm.

Carmel VII, Kazinczy utca 31 ☎1 322 1834, ⓦcarmel .hu; map p.58. Long-established Jewish restaurant that turned *glatt* kosher in 2008. The atmosphere is occasionally rather staid, though the larger downstairs seating area generates more spark, particularly in August and

TOP 5 CHEAP EATS

Bahn mi Bistro p.166
Falafel p.166
Montenegrói Gurman p.167
Sahara p.169
Vapiano p.164

13

September when klezmer-style concerts are held here. The menu is surprisingly diverse, from goulash stew with egg barley, to veal in honey with braised apple. Alternatively, there's a choice of "tourist menus" between noon and 6pm each day. Mains 3000–5000Ft. Mon–Fri & Sun noon–11pm, Sat noon–2pm & 6–11pm.

Frici Papa VI, Király utca 55 ☎1 351 0197; map p.58. The plastic-covered tables give a fair indication of what to expect, and this no-nonsense place (which includes the waiters) certainly won't win any awards for class, but if it's cheap, no-frills grub you're after, look no further. A menu of grilled or fried chicken with chips, beef and mushroom goulash, and not much else, all for under 1000Ft. Daily 11am–10pm.

Il Terzo Cerchio VII, Dohány utca 40 ☎1 354 0788; map p.58. The Third Circle of Dante's hell was full of gluttons, and this handsome Florentine-run pizzeria has its share. Pizzas aside (from 2000Ft), there's superb risotto (red wine and sirloin; 2750Ft) and pasta, where seafood is a speciality – try the linguine with octopus (2900Ft) or gnocchi with salmon and orange sauce (2850Ft). Be warned, though: the combination of open kitchen and lack of a/c means that you'll need a handkerchief to wipe away the sweat. It's popular with Italian visitors, which must be a good sign. Daily noon–11.30pm.

Két Szerecsen VI, Nagymező utca 14 ☎1 343 1984, ⓦketszerecsen.com; map p.58. Buzzy place nicely secreted away just off Andrássy út, that's good for coffee and breakfast (8–11am) or full-blown supper. The most appealing aspect, though, is the tapas menu (veg, meat and seafood), which can be taken individually or as an assortment. A varied mains menu includes salmon steamed in white wine, and a Thai green curry. There's an offer of a starter and main course, plus half a bottle of wine, for 7500Ft. Mains 1900–3000Ft. Mon–Fri 8am–midnight, Sat & Sun 9am–midnight.

★ **Klassz** VI, Andrássy út 41 ☎1 413 1545; map p.58. *Klassz* means "super", which describes this strikingly decorated restaurant-cum-wine bar to a tee. The food is of a definite international bent – typical staples include duck breast with creamy polenta and lamb shank confit with couscous and sage – while its links with the Budapest Wine Society ensure a choice of top Hungarian vintages, most of which are available by the glass; the staff can advise on what goes well with what. It's small, extremely popular and does not take reservations, so arrive early to be sure of

13

a table. Mains 2000–3000Ft. Mon–Sat 11.30am–11pm, Sun 11.30am–6pm.

Kőleves VII, Dob utca 26 ☎1 322 1011, ⓦkoleves .com; map p.58. Brightly striped walls, upturned umbrellas and kooky lighting lend this easy-going place on the corner of Kazinczy utca a certain art-house vibe. Mains include veal and chicken dishes (with olive or goat's cheese stuffings, for example) and smoked turkey leg with *sólet* (Jewish baked beans). Mains 2200–2800Ft and a menu of the day for 1000Ft. Mon–Sat 11am–midnight, Sun till 11pm.

★ **Krizia** VI, Mozsár utca 12 ☎1 331 8711, ⓦristorantekrizia.com; map p.58. All the pasta at this refined Italian restaurant is made here on the premises, as is the delicious prosciutto, resulting in a long list of well-thought-out creations like pappardelle noodle with porcini mushrooms and scallops and stracchi noodles with spinach and chicken. There's also a daily "From the Market" menu,

sourcing local ingredients, and a dedicated truffle menu, which, not surprisingly, comes at a price. Mains 2500–3000Ft. Mon–Sat noon–3pm & 6.30pm–midnight.

M VII, Kertész utca 48 ☎1 322 3108; map p.58. Easily missed, this small boho-style French-Hungarian bistro is just the spot for a low-key evening dalliance. Although half a dozen starters and a similar number of mains doesn't constitute a huge menu, it is fairly bold; duck liver mousse with cantaloupe salad, and stewed trout with smoked cod are regulars. Mains 2000–3500Ft. Mon–Fri 6pm–midnight, Sat & Sun noon–midnight.

Marquis de Salade VI, Hajós utca 43 ☎1 302 4086; map p.58. One of the city's few worthwhile ethnic restaurants, the *Marquis* specializes in Azerbaijani cuisine. The starters are particularly tasty, though not a match for the outstanding lamb main dishes – the steamed lamb with chestnut and prunes is divine. If you can, try and bag a table down in the basement cellar room, decorated with

---

HUNGARIAN WINE

Hungary's **wines** are a delight, thus far under-appreciated in the global market. In general, the country's climate favours whites, especially crisp and floral varieties, but its reds are also delicious and offer more complexity and variation, including light and spicy vintages that are often chilled before drinking, as well an emerging number of fine rosés.

In the Communist era **wine production** emphasized quantity over quality, throwing any number of different grapes together and shipping as much as possible to an undemanding Soviet market. Since 1989, however, there has been a huge investment in wine production, especially by foreign concerns in the internationally recognized Tokaj region, but also by native vintners in other regions. These smaller producers have turned their quality around extremely quickly, reviving older grape varieties and introducing new treatments, such as barrique (ageing the wine in small oak barrels).

Although Hungary has twenty official wine regions, the best producers are concentrated in a few areas. For **reds** seek out Eger in the north (Vilmos Thummerer is a name to look out for), Szekszárd to the south (Ferenc Vesztergombi, Takler, Tamás Dúzsi and others) and Villány near the Croatian border (the long list of producers here includes József Bock, Attila Gere and Tiffán and Vylyan). The last two regions also produce excellent **rosés** – those of Bock and Dúzsi are particularly recommended. For **whites**, the best regions are located around Lake Balaton to the southwest of Budapest (Huba Szeremley, Jásdi and Otto Légli), and of course Tokaj, the wine region famed for its incredibly sweet Aszú wines.

Many of the grape varieties used in Hungarian wines will be familiar, even if their Hungarian names are less so, but there are also some indigenous grapes that are worth trying. Among red wines, alongside the well-known Cabernet Franc and Cabernet Sauvignon and others, the **Kadarka** yields a light, spicy, cherry-coloured wine that has undergone a revival in the past decade. It is a common ingredient in Bull's Blood, the famous blend made in Eger and Szekszárd. Many producers turn out cuvées – special blends that, like the barrique wines, tend to be more expensive than varietal wines.

Alongside the familiar whites of Sauvignon Blanc and Olaszrizling (Italian Riesling) are Irsai Olivér, which produces a floral, aromatic wine, and Cserszegi Fűszeres which has a slightly smoother, spicier flavour. Among **Tokaj** wines Aszú is the best known, but the drier Furmint and the honeyed Hárslevelű (lime or linden leaf), less cloying than the Aszú, are both worth looking for.

For a sophisticated white, try the Taposó-kút 2006 from the Szent Ilona Borház, a blend that captures the characteristics of the Furmint and Hárslevelű with Olaszrizling grapes. Taposó-kút hails from Somló, a hill west of Balaton whose volcanic soil produces fascinating results, just as it does around Tokaj; this is a crisp yet rich wine with a minerally character.

13

beautiful Persian carpets. Mains 3500Ft. Daily 11am–midnight.

Menza VI, Liszt Ferenc tér 2 ✆1 413 1482, ⓦmenzaetterem.hu; map p.58. Few places on this lively square merit too much consideration – at least where food is concerned – but *Menza* is one of them. The stylish retro decor, and very affordable retro-influenced Hungarian dishes, such as *hagymás rostélyos* (braised steak piled high with onions) and *kolozsvári töltött káposzta* (stuffed cabbage) seem to evoke nostalgic memories among the locals. The two-course lunch menu is terrific value at 990Ft. Mains 2000–3000Ft. Daily 10am–midnight.

Osteria VII, Dohány utca 5 ✆1 269 6806, ⓦosteria .hu; map p.58. This excellent and elegant Italian restaurant was originally opened by master chef Fausto DiVora. Even though he has moved to his more upmarket

Fausto's, off Andrássy út, the service and cooking here remain outstanding, and you'll have a tough time choosing between the likes of home-made codfish ravioli, duck breast with grape sauce and honey vegetables, and king prawns with green pea cream and spring rice. Mains 2500–4500Ft. Mon–Sat noon–11pm.

Trofea VI, Király utca 30–32 ✆1 878 0522, ⓦtrofeagrill.eu; map p.58. The concept is simple: for a fixed price, eat as much as you want. The self-service buffet includes goose-liver pâté, catfish paprika and venison ragout, as well as meat and fish prepared to order. You also get an unlimited consumption of drink, including beer, wine and champagne (there's no catch). Although it looks like a significant spend, the food is very accomplished and the restaurant itself is extremely well run. Mon–Fri lunch (till 5pm) 3499Ft, Mon–Thurs evenings 4999Ft, Fri–Sun all day 5499Ft. Daily noon–midnight.

THE VÁROSLIGET

RESTAURANTS

Bagolyvár XIV, Állatkerti körút 2 ✆1 468 3110, ⓦbagolyvar.com; map p.69. Sister to the *Gundel*, the "Owl's Castle" offers traditional Hungarian family-style cooking at far lower prices. Housed in an intriguing Károly Kós-style building, it aims to recreate the atmosphere of the interwar middle-class home, both in its menu and its service (all the staff are women – reflecting the quaint idea that in those days all women stayed at home). There's music nightly at 7pm courtesy of the resident cimbalom player. Mains 2000–3300Ft. Daily noon–11pm.

Gundel XIV, Állatkerti körút 2 ✆1 321 3550, ⓦgundel .hu; map p.69. Budapest's most famous restaurant – opened in 1910 – may have lost some of its lustre in the face of the city's gastronomic revolution, but it remains something of an institution. The menu is, predictably enough, very expensive, but the range and quality of food, alongside the ornate surroundings and impeccable service,

will ensure a unique experience. Formal dress is not compulsory, but smart attire (trousers/shirt) is preferred. Mains 5600Ft. The all-you-can-eat Sunday brunch (11.30am–3pm; 6400Ft) remains hugely popular. Booking advised. Daily noon–4pm & 6.30pm–midnight.

★ **Olimpia** VII, Alpar utca 5 ✆1 321 2805; map p.69. Small place by the Garay tér market hall with nothing Greek about it except the decor: the management here have concentrated purely on the food, which they serve up in a quirky, personable manner. There is no menu, just a choice of three- to six-course meals for up to just 6000Ft, and the rest you leave to them. The dishes are small but the combinations are fascinating and delicious, while wines are spectacular, though not cheap. The service is very laidback – a six-course meal may end up stretching to eight, and can take four hours or more, though lunches are quicker. Booking required. Mon–Fri noon–3pm & 7–10pm, Sat 7–10pm.

JÓZSEFVÁROS AND FERENCVÁROS

FAST-FOOD DINERS, SNACK AND SANDWICH BARS

Fakanál IX, Great Market Hall; map p.77. A perfect spot to refuel after slogging your way around the market below. Grab a tray, help yourself to some veal stew or stuffed paprika, then plonk yourself down at one of the check-clothed tables. Mon–Fri 6am–6pm, Sat 6am–3pm.

Marie Kristensen Sandwich Bar IX, Ráday utca 7; map p.77. The main concession to any Danish roots is the upturned boat hanging from the ceiling. The sandwiches, meanwhile, run the full gamut, from smoked cheese to tuna spread with fried bacon and Camembert – and there's plenty of choice for veggies too. Mon–Fri 8.30am–8.30pm, Sat 10am–6pm.

Sahara VIII, József körút 82; map p.77. Sparky little Turkish/Middle Eastern dive close to the Corvin cinema at Ferenc körút metro station; try a spiced lamb or chicken kebab with fettush followed by a slice of baklava. Sit down at shared tables or take away. A good place to wind up at after a night of bar-hopping. Daily 11am–1am.

RESTAURANTS

★ **Borbíróság** IX, Csarnok tér 5 ✆1 219 0902, ⓦborbirosag.com; map p.77. The marvellous "Wine Court" offers one of the most affordable and enjoyable introductions to modern Hungarian cuisine anywhere in the city. The menu is by no means exhaustive, but that doesn't detract from what is an exceptional medley of dishes; try the Hortobagy pancake for starter, followed by grilled duck liver with

13

caramelized fruits, and if there's still space, get stuck into a portion of cottage cheese dumplings. The wine list, on the other hand, will leave you completely spoilt for choice, with some of Hungary's finest vintners represented. Mains 2000–2500Ft. Mon–Sat noon–11.30pm.

★ **Costes** IX, Ráday utca 4 ☎ 1 219 0696, ⓦcostes .hu; map p.77. Hungary's first Michelin-starred restaurant and Budapest dining at its most serious. The silky-smooth interior and commanding service can almost make this place seem too slick, but the food speaks for itself; roasted quails with *pomme* puree and pan-seared duck liver, wood pigeon with sage and pancetta, paprika-buttered poached John Dory. You'll pay through the nose to eat here, but it'll almost certainly be worth it. Mains 6000–8000Ft. Booking advised. Wed–Sun noon–3.30pm & 6.30pm–midnight.

Fülemüle VIII, Kőfaragó utca 5 ☎ 1 266 7947, ⓦfulemule.hu; map p.77. Popular and relaxed family-run restaurant a few minutes' walk from Rákóczi út, serving typical dishes of middle-class secular Jewish Budapest: *sólet* (beans), goose soup with matzo dumplings, and duck leg with cabbage and "broken" potato. Moreover, there are some scrummy *cholent* plates, made with home-made hickory meat. Mains 2500–4000Ft. Mon–Thurs & Sun noon–10pm, Fri & Sat noon–11pm.

Múzeum VIII, Múzeum körút 12 ☎ 1 267 0375, ⓦmuzeumkavehaz.hu; map p.77. This grand nineteenth-century restaurant, adorned with Lotz ceiling frescoes and Zsolnay tiles, is another old-school venture working hard to retain standards in the face of stiff competition. For the most part, it succeeds, with a line-up of core Hungarian classics like breaded Mangalica pork chops with mashed potato, and grilled goose liver with Tokaji Aszú cream. Part of the restaurant has been turned back into a coffee house, serving lighter fare and sandwiches. Mains 2900–6000Ft. Saturday lunch menu 3300Ft. Mon–Sat 6pm–midnight, coffee house section open from 9am.

★ **Rosenstein** VIII, Mosonyi utca 3 ☎ 1 333 3492, ⓦrosenstein.hu; map p.77. Ignore the dingy location, in an anonymous side street near Keleti Station, and savour one of the city's finest dining experiences. Family-run, thus inviting a slightly more personal touch than most places, the setting is sophisticated but not showy. Give yourself plenty of time to digest the menu, where you'll discover dishes as diverse as wild boar ragout with forest mushrooms, leg of wild hare, and breaded calf's foot with tartar and chips. Booking advised. Mains 3000–4500Ft. Mon–Sat noon–11pm.

Soul Café IX, Ráday utca 11–13 ☎ 1 217 6986, ⓦsoulcafe.hu; map p.77. One of the few truly decent places to eat on Ráday, offering a fusion of Hungarian and French cooking – and a *soupçon* of North African to reflect the interior surrounds. Expect the likes of beef steak with red wine and mushroom ragout, and pork fillet with dijon sauce and asparagus, in addition to a good selection of Hungarian wines (try the Tüske Pince rosé). Day menu 980Ft, business menu 1980Ft. Mains 2000–4000Ft. Daily noon–midnight.

THE VÁR, CENTRAL BUDA AND THE TABÁN

FAST FOOD DINERS, SNACK AND SANDWICH BARS

Bambi I, Frankel Leó utca 2–4; map p.87. This excellent old bar with its stern waitresses and red plastic-covered seats, is also a good breakfast venue for sandwiches, omelettes and a good strong coffee. Mon–Fri 7am–9pm, Sat & Sun 9am–8pm.

Nagyi Palacsintazója I, Batthyány tér; map p.87. Popular outlet rammed day and night with punters seeking a quick pancake fix; the prolific menu offers dozens of both sweet (apple and walnut, banana and honey) and savoury (ham and mushroom, sour cream and cheese) crepes. Daily 24hr.

RESTAURANTS

★ **21** I, Fortuna utca 21 ☎ 1 202 2113, ⓦ21restaurant .hu; map p.89. Perhaps the pick of the restaurants in the Vár, and there's some stiff competition hereabouts. A thoroughly modern enterprise, the restaurant looks great (and there's a terrific patio terrace), while the food is fresh, contemporary Hungarian fare superbly cooked and beautifully presented. Mains 3000–5000Ft. Booking advised. Daily 11am–midnight.

Aranyszarvas I, Szarvas ter 1 ☎ 1 375 6451, ⓦaranyszarvas.hu; map p.87. Not in the most promising of locations, at the junction of several busy roads, the "Golden Deer" is, nevertheless, a fine restaurant, rustling up superb flavours like duck breast with orange carrot and pak choi. As well as an enviable choice of wines, the restaurant boasts some highly distinctive *pálinkas*; carrot, asparagus and dogberry to name but three of the offbeat flavours. Mains 3000–5000Ft. Booking advised. Daily noon–11pm.

Arcade XII, Kiss János altábornagy utca 38 ☎ 1 225 1969, ⓦarcadebistro.hu; map p.87. It's a bit of a trek to get to, and it's right at the upper end of the price scale, but this upmarket restaurant is worth every effort. A modest but flawless menu brings together a pronounced French/Asian influence, as dishes such as rooster fillet with tarragon and sesame potato, and sushi tuna with raspberry vinegar, testify. As you'd expect in a place of this class, the wine card is first rate, and features some exceptional *furmints* from Tokaj. Mains 4000–5000Ft. Booking advised. Mon–Sat noon–3.30pm & 6.30–11pm, Sun noon–4pm.

Baldaszti's I, Lánchíd utca 7–9 ☎ 30 422 5981; map p.89. A new stylish venture by the inspired chef Viktor Segal near the Lánchíd. The eclectic menu has something for everyone, with tantalizing combinations of flavours. It has taster plates of Hungarian hams and salamis (1900Ft) and veal with chilled creamed marrow (2700Ft). The wine list is superb and even its range of soft drinks is interesting. Mon 11.30am–11pm, Tues–Sat 9am–11pm, Sun 9am–5pm.

Café Pierrot I, Fortuna utca 14 ☎1 375 6971, ⓦpierrot.hu; map p.89. A rare elegant hangout in the late Communist era, *Pierrot* remains an important fixture some thirty years after opening. The interior has an almost retro feel – with one eye on the 1980s perhaps – the walls adorned with images of actors and musicians like De Niro and Depeche Mode. Alternatively take a seat out in the handsome vaulted corridor, which leads through to a pretty garden terrace. Mains 3500Ft. Booking advised. Daily 11am–midnight.

★ **Csalogány 26** I, Csalogány utca 26 ☎1 210 7892, ⓦcsalogany26.hu; map p.87. Notwithstanding the very ordinary location and occasionally muted atmosphere, this is undoubtedly one of Budapest's finest restaurants. It's neither showy nor prohibitively expensive, and the menu, which changes regularly according to the whim of the chef, contains some wonderfully executed dishes; expect creations like glazed rabbit leg with veg ragout, scallop with corn risotto and rice pudding with red-fruit ice cream. Mains 2800–5000Ft, and if you can face it, there's a four-course menu for 8000Ft and an eight-course one for 12000Ft. Booking advised. Tues–Sat noon–3pm & 7pm–midnight.

Horgásztanya I, Fő utca 27 ☎1 212 3780, ⓦhorgasztanyavendeglo.hu; map p.87. Nets and other maritime paraphernalia strung along the walls rather give the game away in this enjoyable fish restaurant that has remained unchanged for many years. Some of the best fish soups in the city are served in generous (mug or kettle) portions, while the wet stuff mainly takes the form of stewed or roasted river fish; pike-perch, carp, catfish and trout. Mains 2500Ft. Daily noon–midnight.

Márkus Vendéglő II, Lövőház utca 17 ☎1 212 3153; map p.87. Close to Széll Kálmán tér, this is a great no-frills option after a long walk in the Buda Hills. Large portions of traditional Hungarian dishes, including an excellent *Jókai bableves* (a filling, smoky bean soup) and various stuffed turkey dishes. Daily noon–midnight.

Var: A Speiz I, Hess András tér 6 ☎ 1 488 741, ⓦvaraspeiz.hu; map p.89. The distinguished "pantry" is currently teasing out some of the most exquisite dishes in the city, not least some outstanding breadcrumbed meats. At the opposite end of the restaurant proper is the fabulous Ham and Wine Bar, where some half-dozen huge hams (from Spain, Italy and Hungary) dangle temptingly. Mains 3000–4500Ft. Daily noon–midnight.

ÓBUDA

RESTAURANTS

Kéhli III, Mókus utca 22 ☎1 368 0613, ⓦkehli.hu; map p.114. One hundred years ago this was the favourite haunt of one of Hungary's great gourmands, the turn-of-the-century writer Gyula Krúdy, and today the *Kéhli* still serves the dishes he loved, such as beef soup with bone marrow on garlic toast. Set in one of the few old buildings in Óbuda to survive the 1960s planning blitz, it's a big place and does attract large groups, but there are plenty of local regulars, too; eat your fill to the accompaniment of a lively Hungarian Gypsy band (from 8pm). Mains 2500–4500Ft. Daily noon–midnight.

Kerék III, Bécsi út 103 ☎1 250 4261, ⓦkerek.hu; map p.114. There is an unchanging feel to the "Wheel", a small place just near the amphitheatre in southern Óbuda. It serves traditional Hungarian food, such as *bableves füstölt csülökkel* (bean soup with smoked pork knuckle) and *vasi pecsenye* (pork marinated in garlic and milk) at very reasonable prices. No haute cuisine here, just locals out for a meal. *Srámli* (accordion) music is provided by a couple of old musicians (Mon–Sat from 6pm), and there's outside seating in summer. Mains 1300–2500Ft. Daily noon–11pm.

Kisbuda Gyöngye III, Kenyeres utca 34 ☎1 368 6402, ⓦremiz.hu; map p.114. Excellent Hungarian food in the elegant surroundings of the "Pearl of Little Buda", which is filled with furniture from a *fin-de-siècle* well-to-do Budapest home, including a sprinkling of Herend porcelain. The menu isn't massive but there are some intriguing food combinations at work; paprika chicken with curd cheese pasta, and breaded veal with jasmine rice and mayonnaise. Gentle piano music and a small courtyard at the back. Booking advised. Mains 2300–4000Ft. Tues–Sat noon–11pm.

Porcellino Grasso II, Ady Endre utca 19 ☎1 886 7880; map p.114.. A welcoming Italian restaurant, with a large terrace, in a rather unpromising setting on the ground floor of a Rozsadomb office block. Pizzas start at 1490Ft; the duck breast with walnut tagliatelle in an orange sauce (3690Ft) is delicious. Excellent wine list, and children's play areas both inside and out. Daily noon–midnight.

CÉNTRÁL KÁVÉHÁZ

Coffee houses and patisseries

Daily life in Budapest is still punctuated by the consumption of black coffee drunk from little glasses, though cappuccinos and white coffee are generally the drink of choice among younger people. These quintessentially Central European coffee breaks are less prolonged these days than before the war, when the coffee house (*kávéház*) was the social club, home and haven for its clientele. Free newspapers were available to the regulars – writers, journalists and lawyers (for whom the cafés were effectively "offices") or posing revolutionaries – with sympathy drinks or credit to those down on their luck. Today's coffee houses and patisseries (*cukrászda*) are less romantic but still full of character, whether fabulously opulent, with silver service, or homely and idiosyncratic. Tea-lovers won't be short-changed either, with several fine tea houses around the city.

Despite the all-too predictable invasion of chain coffee shops – both international and domestic – old stalwarts like the *Centrál Kávéház* and *Gerbeaud* remain popular stomping grounds, their grand surrounds and sumptuous menus a hit with tourists and locals alike. That said, the tendency in some places (such as *Lukács* and *New York*) to charge high prices has driven away some of the older regulars and cut off these institutions from their roots. Most coffee houses offer a full complement of coffees and other beverages, as well as counters stocked with scrumptious, beautifully crafted **cakes and pastries** like *dobos torta*, *somlói*, *rétes* and *flódni*. Hungarians love their **ice cream**, too, and there are several excellent parlours dotted around the city.

14

THE BELVÁROS

Astoria Kávéház V, Kossuth utca 19 ☎ 1 889 6000; map p.38. Dating from the turn of the last century the *Astoria* hotel's *Mirror* coffee house-bar has retained much of its old charm, even if some of the old glitz has faded; oversized chandeliers, dusty pink tablecloths and red velvet seating combine to make this a still popular meeting place. Daily 7am–11pm.

★ **Azték** V, in the Röser-bazár, a courtyard running between Károly körút 22 and Semmelweis utca 19 ☎ 1 266 7113; map p.38. The diminutive *Azték* is the best place in the city for chocolate gourmands, selling home-made chocolate as well as imported products (all made with a minimum of sugar) and fabulous hot chocolate – ask for the extra-thick variety which will warm you up on a cold day. The coffee's not bad either. In summer, take a seat outside in the wonderfully cool courtyard. Mon–Fri 7am–7pm, Sat 9am–2pm.

★ **Centrál Kávéház** V, Károlyi Mihály utca 9 ☎ 1 266 2110; map p.38. In its heyday, the decades around World War I, this large coffee house was a popular venue in Budapest's literary scene. After many years as a dowdy university club, it was restored to its former grandeur and today stands as the city's most sophisticated café. Superb coffee (500–650Ft) and an immaculate selection of cakes (600–700Ft), which, surprisingly, are cheaper than at many other places in the Belváros. The only thing missing is a terrace. Daily 8am–midnight or 1am.

Gerbeaud V, Vörösmarty tér 7 ☎ 1 429 9000; map p.38. Another Budapest institution, *Gerbeaud* has been a fixture on this square since 1858. The gilded salon is magnificent, though most people park themselves outside on the massive terrace, one of the best in the city. But be warned, this is very much tourist-central, with prices that reflect this; coffee will set you back 800–1000Ft. Daily 9am–9pm.

LIPÓTVÁROS

Bedő Ház V, Honvéd utca 3 ☎ 1 269 4622; map p.48. Housed in a gem of a building just north of Szabadság tér, the café shares the same space as the Museum of Hungarian Art Nouveau, though it's hard to tell where one begins and the other ends, such is its pleasantly cluttered nature. A quiet place, and with a fairly modest range of drinks and pastries, it is, nevertheless, a delightful spot for a coffee break if you're in the neighbourhood. Mon–Fri 8am–7pm, Sat 10am–5pm.

Europa V, Szent István körút 7 ☎ 1 312 2362; map p.48. Large and perennially busy coffee house a short stroll from the Margit híd, with lots of seating, including

a segregated, salon-style room, plus pavement terrace (the latter to be avoided if you prefer your beverage without fumes). Both the coffee and cake is first rate, though nothing tops the delicious, and very generously sliced, *rétes* or *flódni*. Daily 9am–10pm, May–Oct till 11pm.

Szalai V, Balassi Bálint utca 4 ☎ 1 269 3210; map p.48. One of the few remaining old-style cake shops in Budapest, serving pastries baked on the premises. Beneath its large gilt-framed mirrors are a few tables where the regulars watch the world pass by. Daily except Tues 9am–7pm, Nov–April closed Mon.

TERÉZVÁROS AND ERZSÉBETVAROS

Eco Café VI, Andrássy út 68; map p.58. Welcoming little organic café with sweet little countrified tables and cushioned seating, serving up a small selection of very reasonably priced sandwiches, salads and cakes; it also does a nice line in freshly baked breads. Mon–Fri 7am–8pm, Sat & Sun 8am–8pm.

★ **Fröhlich** VII, Dob utca 22 ☎ 1 266 1733; map p.58. Excellent kosher patisserie 5min walk from the Dohány utca synagogue, with sweet wrought-iron garden-bench-like

seating and red and orange painted walls. Specialities include the best *flódni* (apple, walnut and poppyseed cake) in the city. Mon–Fri 9am–4pm, Sun 10am–6pm; closed Sat & Jewish holidays.

Godot VII, Madách út 8 ☎ 1 322 5274; map p.58. Lively street-corner venue attracting a loyal band of regulars that also plays host to regular evenings of comedy on a stage at one end of the café. Mon–Fri 9am–midnight, Sat noon–midnight.

14

TOP 5 COFFEE HOUSES
Centrál Kávéház p.173
Cziniel p.175
Gerbeaud p.173
Mai Manó below
Ruszwurm below

Király VII, Király utca 19 ☎1 351 9532; map p.58. Long-standing local patisserie sporting Empire-style furnishings and serving excellent pastries, cakes and ice cream. Mon–Fri 9am–8pm, Sat–Sun 10am–8pm.

Lukács VI, Andrássy út 70 ☎1 302 8747; map p.58. Beautifully restored by the bank with which it now shares the building (the lobby is a bit of a giveaway), this is another of the city's old-style coffee houses, and is also good for breakfasts. However, as sumptuous as the coffees and the supremely prepared choc-and-cream-filled cakes are, steep prices have sadly ended its status as a popular locals' haunt. Mon–Fri 8.30am–8pm, Sat & Sun 9am–8pm.

⭐ **Mai Manó** VI, Nagymező utca 20 ☎1 269 5642; map p.58. One of the more agreeable spots in the theatre quarter, this small café underneath the Mai Manó Photography Museum retains a cutesy interior with patterned tables and images splayed across the walls, as well as a convivial outdoor terrace. Daily 10am–1am.

Művész VI, Andrássy út 29 ☎1 352 1337; map p.58. There's an air of faded grandeur in this coffee house that's as notable for its decor – deep leather seating, chandeliers and gilt – as it is for its coffee and cakes. Still, the presence of elderly ladies in fur hats bears witness to the venue's success in retaining a loyal clientele over the years. Mon–Sat 9am–10pm, Sun 10am–10pm.

Podma Café VI, Podmaniczky utca 14 ☎1 302 2696; map p.58. Tea has really yet to catch on in Budapest, but this unassuming, two-floored café is a good place to start. Row upon row of teas from around the world are lined up in old-fashioned tins on the lovely mahogany shelves, and while you're here, you may as well grab a home-made cookie too. Mon–Sat 8am–11pm.

New York Café VII, Erzsébet körút 9 ☎1 886 6111; map p.58. This opulent coffee house was a popular haunt of writers in the early 1900s. Restored as part of the *Boscolo* hotel, it has lost none of its magnificence, and the service is first class, but exorbitant prices mean it has struggled to win back its place among today's impoverished intelligentsia. Daily 10am–midnight.

Sugar VI, Paulay Ede utca 48 ☎1 321 6672; map p.58. This eye-wateringly colourful patisserie/confectioners does exactly what its name suggests; chocolate bars, pick'n'mix, metre-high tubes of jelly beans, cakes, tarts and ice creams. Kid's'll love it and so will the parents. Mon noon–10pm, Tues–Sun 10am–10pm.

JÓZSEFVÁROS AND FERENCVÁROS

Múzeum Cukrászda VIII, Múzeum körút 10 ☎1 338 4415; map p.77. Friendly hangout which makes for a good spot to rest up at after digesting the nearby National Museum. Decent breakfasts with fresh pastries arriving in the very early hours. Open daily 24hr.

THE VÁR AND CENTRAL BUDA

Angelika I, Batthyány tér 7 ☎1 225 1653; map p.87. Atmospheric old coffee house in a former convent whose modern refit has meant a shift in the type of clientele visiting in recent years – you are less likely to get old ladies meeting for their regular coffees these days, rather bright young things enjoying the lively, sprawling terrace with views across to Parliament. Daily 9am–midnight.

⭐ **Artigiana Gelati** XII, Csaba utca 8 ☎1 212 2439; map p.87. A couple of minutes up the road from Széll Kálmán tér, this Italian-run parlour has been concocting the city's finest ice cream for the best part of twenty years. A magical assortment of wondrous flavours, such as beetroot, cherry and chilli, and lavender and rosemary, served up in cones or cups. Tues–Fri 10.30am–8pm, Sat & Sun till 8.30pm.

Ruszwurm I, Szentháromság utca 7 ☎1 375 5284; map p.89. Near the Mátyás Church in the Vár, this diminutive Baroque coffee house can be so packed that it's almost impossible to get a seat in summer. Still, it's definitely worth seeking out for its respectably priced coffee (600Ft) and cakes, the pick of which is its mouth-watering *rétes* (400Ft). Daily 10am–7pm.

GELLÉRT-HEGY

⭐ **Shambala** I, Villányi út 12 ☎1 279 1133; map p.108. Charming, just below street level teahouse with lots of jaunty seating areas either side of the main lounge, whose main feature is a miniature goldfish pond. Although tea is very much the speciality here – over eighty types kept fresh in bright red tins – there are lots of other beverages to mull over. Mon–Fri 11am–11pm, Sat & Sun 3–11pm.

ÓBUDA

Cziniel III, Nánási út 55 ☎1 240 1188; map p.114. Large, popular café just north of the Roman ruins at Aquincum, with excellent ice creams and chestnut *puree*. A good place to bring children too, as it has its own play area, and handy if you've been on the riverbank enjoying the bars and restaurants on the Római-part or want to head further out from Aquincum. Daily May–Sept 9am–10pm, Oct–April 9am–7.30pm.

Daubner III, Szépvölgyi út 50 ☎1 335 2253; map p.114. It is a trek to get to this patisserie in Óbuda, and it has no tables, but the place is always crowded, especially at weekends, when people will patiently

> ### TOP 5 PLACES FOR CAKES
> **Centrál Kávéház** see p.173
> **Daubner** see p.175
> **Fröhlich** see p.173
> **Rétes Bufé** see p.175
> **Szalai** see p.173

14

queue up for its delicious cakes, such as the plum slipper (*szilvás papucs*) or pumpkin-seed scone (*tökmagos pogácsa*). Mon–Sat 9am–7pm.

THE BUDA HILLS

Rétes Büfé XII, Normafa; map p.121. This hut at the top of the Buda Hills by the old tree where Bellini's aria was sung (see p.120) is a place of pilgrimage for families, walkers and (in winter) skiers who flock to the hills. You can expect to queue for the excellent *rétes* on fine days. The *Rétes Kert* across the road is run by the same crowd. Daily 10am–5pm.

SZIMPLAKERT, EZSÉBETVÁROS

Bars and clubs

Trendy, traditional or bohemian – whatever you're after in Budapest, you're likely to find it. The city's nightlife continues to evolve, and in some ways it mirrors the recent gastronomic revolution. Rather than being focused on one central zone, the scene is fairly diffuse, albeit heavily skewed towards Pest and contained within several distinct areas on that side of the river: posey Liszt Ferenc tér, semi-pedestrianized Ráday utca, running down from Kalvin tér, and, most excitingly, a concentration of bars in the VII and VIII districts, more distinctively known as ruin pubs, or *kert* bars (garden bars). Set up in condemned buildings, or the courtyards of ruined blocks, these free-spirited haunts have become an integral, and iconoclastic, constituent of Budapest's nocturnal landscape. In addition, the outdoor bars on Margit-sziget and at various spots along the Danube do a roaring trade in the summer.

The place to see and be seen is Liszt Ferenc tér, the large, leafy square near Oktogon, though you should expect to pay a premium for the privilege of drinking here. Ráday utca is perhaps even more generic, its innumerable cafés and terraces running the entire length often indistinguishable from one another – that said, "Budapest's Soho", as it optimistically likes to call itself, is great for bar-crawling, and there's no denying the buzz created along here on a warm summer's evening. Best of all, though, are the *kert* bars (or "garden bars"); these artfully contrived, ramshackle venues – such as *Szimplakert* and *Instant* – maintain a cheerful bohemian disposition and offer a wide range of activities and entertainment, from live music and DJs, to themed parties, film screenings and table football (*csocsó*). Of the outdoor summer bars, you'll find several at the southern end of Margit-sziget, while the biggie, *Zöld Pardon*, is down near Petőfi híd – many of them have dancefloors, and charge a small entry fee.

The traditional Hungarian **wine bars** (*borozó*) are nothing like their counterparts in the West, being mainly working men's watering holes offering such humble snacks as *zsíros kenyér* (bread and pork dripping with onion and paprika). However, the recent upsurge of interest in Hungarian wine has led to the emergence of far more modern and sophisticated equivalents, *Dobló* being a fine example. For a step up in class, splash out on a fancy cocktail or two at any one of the increasingly glamorous hotel bars.

The **club** scene is especially varied in the summer, when it expands into several large outdoor venues, and there are also one-off events held in the old Turkish baths or sites further out of town (advertised via promotional posters). DJs to look out for include Sterbinszky and Kühl, the more alternative Naga and Mango, and anything with the Tilos Rádió stamp on it.

15

ESSENTIALS

Opening hours Most places open around lunchtime and stay open until well after midnight, unless otherwise stated, though bars in residential areas have to close their terraces at 10pm.

Costs Note that the warnings about rip-offs in restaurants (see p.164) apply equally to bars. Most bars do not take credit cards. Expect to pay 500–1000Ft upwards to get into a club.

Transport There is a good network of night buses (see p.25) that can help you make your way home, taxis are easy to flag down, and the streets are generally safe.

THE BELVÁROS

Mélypont V, Magyar utca 23; map p.38. A retro basement bar with a strong flavour of 1970s Hungary, "Rock Bottom" is full of memorabilia that won't mean much to the average non-Hungarian. Popular with a youngish crowd, and has table football. Mon–Fri 4pm–1am, Sat 6pm–1am, Sun 6pm–midnight.

Spoon V, on the river by the Inter-Continental hotel ☎ 1 411 0933, ⓦ spooncafe.hu; map p.38. Set in a boat on the Danube, the swanky *Spoon* offers a great setting above all, with killer views across to the Lánchíd and the Buda Palace, while the men's toilets have grandstand views of the Royal Palace. Although the restaurant is the dominant aspect, the venue also counts five bars, and features regular live piano music among its happenings. Daily noon–midnight.

DRINKING ETIQUETTE

Hungarian has a variety of tongue-twisting ways to **toast** fellow drinkers. *Egészségedre!* ("Your health") is the most common, but it's usually said to one person whom you know well. To a group, you might use *Egészségetekre!*; if your acquaintance is more formal, it would be *Egészségére!* To friends, a simple *Szia!* is fine.

Clinking glasses of **beer** used to be frowned upon, as it was said that this was how the Austrians celebrated the execution of the Hungarian generals in 1849; the "right" Hungarian way was to bang your glass on the table before raising it to your lips. These days, though, people say that there was a 150-year time limit on that taboo, and clinking beer-glasses is back.

LIPÓTVÁROS

Tokaji Borozó V, Falk Miksa utca 32 ☎ 1 269 3143; map p.48. Lively, smoky old-style cellar wine bar serving wines from the Tokaj region in northeast Hungary – though at 110Ft for a small glass this is not top-end stuff – as well as snacks such as *lepcsánka* (potato pancakes) and *zsíros*

kenyér. Popular with the after-work crowd. Mon–Fri noon–9pm.

Trocadero Café V, Szent István körút 15; map p.48. Excellent Latin music and dancing at this club just up from Nyugati Station. Entry fee varies. Daily 9pm–5am.

TERÉZVÁROS AND ERZSÉBETVÁROS

Amigo Bar VII, Hársfa utca 1 ☎ 1 352 1424; map p.58. A fun time guaranteed at this cracking rockabilly haunt, with three floors crawling with 1950s nostalgia, right down to the bartenders with their pompadour quiffs. Live music (Sept–May) takes place down in the cellar bar, which otherwise has a fabulous jukebox and three immaculate red-clothed pool tables. Mon–Fri 3pm–3am, Sat 6pm–4am, Sun 6pm–3am.

★ **Cafe Bobek** VII, Kazinczy utca 53 ☎ 1 322 0279; map p.58. Named after a Communist rabbit, this is one of the district's more discreet *kerts*, the sort of place you could happily linger for hours. The venue is divided between a cosy covered terrace, with cushioned benches, leather sofas, and pink-and-white lanterns, and an adjoining garden spilling over with trees and plants. There also a very creditable food menu to hand if you decide to stay just that little bit longer. Mon–Thurs 10am–midnight, Fri & Sat 11am–2am.

Castro Bistro VII, Madách Imre tér 3 ☎ 1 215 0184; map p.58. Located on a rather dull square, this casual, cheery bar with a misleadingly Cuban name nevertheless draws a mixed crowd of Hungarians and foreigners. It's nothing particularly fancy, but the boho-style decor, good beer, and Serbian-style meats, keep people coming back. Mon–Thurs 11am–midnight, Fri & Sat 11am–1am, Sun 2pm–midnight.

Dobló VII, Dob utca 20 ☎ 1 20 398 8863, ⓦ budapestwine.com; map p.58. *Dobló* is a classy, though far from pretentious, wine bar, which looks all the better for its exposed nineteenth-century brickwork. Some two hundred varieties of Hungarian wine are available by the glass, each one costing between 850–1400Ft, which makes them neither the cheapest nor the most expensive going. Wine-tasting sessions as well as winery visits are also possible. Mon–Fri 8am–1am, Sat 5pm–3am.

Elláto VII, Klauzál tér 2; map p.58. A relative old hand on the pub scene, the dilapidated look of bare bricks and old

paintwork gives this eternally popular spot in the Jewish quarter a relaxed feel. The kitchen serves up decent retro dishes from various cuisines, though there's a strong Serbian flavour. Mon–Thurs noon–1am, Fri noon–4am, Sat 5pm–4am, Sun 5pm–1am.

Garzon VII, Wesselényi utca 24; map p.58. Another thoughtfully contrived bar, *Garzon* takes its cue from the 1970s. The whole space is fitted out to resemble an apartment from that era; gaudy wallpaper, household appliances plastered to the walls, and a corner kitchen complete with checked tablecloth and red-and-white enamel tiles. The beer and the music's pretty decent too. Daily 10am–midnight.

Instant VI, Nagymező utca 38 ☎ 1 311 0704, ⓦ instant .co.hu; map p.58. Big-hitting ruin pub whose self-proclaimed moniker, "The Enchanted Forest", suits it well; surveying the vast central courtyard are herds of rabbits suspended in mid-air, a cat-woman-sphinx figure and other fantastical creatures. Meanwhile, some twenty rooms (many bizarrely themed), half a dozen bars and three dancefloors lend the place a rollicking party vibe. Daily 4pm–6am.

★ **Kiadó** VI, Jókai tér 3 ☎ 1 331 1955; map p.58. The polar opposite of the type of bar to be found across Andrássy út on Liszt Ferenc tér, *Kiado* has few pretensions. Both the ground floor and the adjoining cellar bar (the latter open from 6pm) are divided into smaller intimate sections, with tightly packed ranks of tables and chairs squeezed into dimly lit corners and secret alcoves. Full bar menu available too. Mon–Fri 10am–1am, Sat & Sun noon–1am.

Kuplung VI, Király utca 46; map p.58. This one-time motorcycle repair shop (the name means "clutch") is accessed via a graffiti-splattered corridor leading into a concrete courtyard masked with weirdly painted murals. A lime-green-coloured bar runs the length of one side, while the remaining space is taken up with simple wooden bench seating, table football (*csocsó*) and ping-pong. Daily till 4am.

Morrison's VI, Révay utca 25 ☎ 1 269 4060, ⓦ morrisons.hu; map p.58. A long-established dance bar that's very popular with students who clearly enjoy its heaving, sweaty atmosphere; house parties, concerts and karaoke among the nightly capers. The opening of an offshoot, *Morrison's II*, at V, Szent István Korut 11, has partially helped to alleviate the crush, though both

---

TOP 5 RUIN PUBS

venues still get rammed. Entry 500Ft after 9pm. Both Mon–Sat 7pm–4am.

Most VI, Zichy Jenő utca 17; map p.58. Another of the major *kert* pubs, though a little more clean-cut, this massive complex centres around a bistro-like lounge, to the side of which is a small bar and stage, and an enormous gravel-bedded garden. *Most* is also one of the better *kerts* for food, and is especially popular for its breakfasts and brunches (1690Ft). Mon–Thurs 11am–2am, Fri–Sat 5pm–2.30am.

Old Man's Music Pub VII, Akácfa utca 13 ☎ 1 322 7645, ⓦ oldmansmusicpub.com; map p.58. It's been around for a while, but this likeably grungy joint near Blaha Lujza tér has managed to retain a loyal, fun-loving band of folllowers; live local bands every evening (9–11pm), before or after which you can get a decent bite to eat. Better still, entry is free. Daily 3pm–4am.

Piaf VI, Nagymező utca 25 ☎ 1 312 3823, ⓦ piafklub .hu; map p.58. This old favourite is basically a small ground-floor bar and cellar frequented by the odd Hungarian film star and lots of wannabes, with occasional jazz or rock live sets. Once in, you're quite easily set until the wee small hours. Entry 800Ft. Daily 7pm–6am.

★ **Pótkulcs** VI, Csengery utca 65b ☎ 1 269 1050, ⓦ potkulcs.hu; map p.58. There's not much by way of a sign on the tatty metal door, but go through and you'll find yourself in a verdant yard, with the bar straight ahead, and a room with sofas and table football off to the left. The "Spare Key" is a laidback kind of place with a reputation built largely on the strength of its live music programme, ranging from klezmer and Roma bands to underground,

folk and jazz. Mon–Wed & Sun 5pm–1.30am, Thurs–Sat 5pm–2.30am.

★ **Sark** VII, Klauzál tér 14; map p.58. Small, heaving bar, decorated with massive murals. DJs and good live music (world/klezmer/Roma) downstairs from Sept–May. From June–Sept much of the action moves to the *Sark kert* at the southern tip of Margit-sziget. Daily noon–3am.

Sirály VI, Király utca 50 ⓦ siraly.co.hu; map p.58. The "Seagull" bar is located in one of those unoccupied buildings that could at any time be closed down, part of an arty cultural centre which seems to rev up the bohemian, lefty feel. Regular jazz and theatre downstairs. Daily 10am–midnight.

Szimplakert VII, Kazinczy utca 14 ☎ 1 352 4198, ⓦ szimpla.hu; map p.58. Occupying a former stove factory, this is the grandaddy of *kert* bars. The darkened corridor feeds a warren of graffiti-strewn, junk-filled rooms, beyond which is the main, partially canopied, courtyard with bars on three sides and bangers for seating. There's free live music (jazz, rock, retro, funk) most nights of the week. Although there's a fair old din here at night, it makes a delightful refuge by day. Daily noon–2am.

Szóda VII, Wesselényi utca 18 ☎ 1 461 0007; map p.58. As enjoyable in winter as it is in summer, this hip bar behind the main synagogue sports super-cool retro stylings in the form of red leather seating, odd bits of furnishings, and cartoon strips for wallpaper. Between Wednesday and Sunday, enthusiastic groovers move downstairs to catch the latest DJ tunes. Mon–Fri 9am–midnight, Sat & Sun 2pm–midnight or later.

JOSZEFVÁROS AND FERENCVÁROS

A Grund VIII, Nagy Templom utca 32; map p.77. Occupying the courtyard of an unused house, a short trek from the centre, *A Grund* is a fabulous party place where you can count on something happening most nights of the week. The focal point of the complex is a slick, bare-brick bar with side rooms and sofas, outside of which lies a neatly landscaped terrace with grass and gravel walkways. Mon–Fri 11am–4am, Sat 4pm–4am.

Corvintető VIII, Blaha Lujza tér 1–2, entrance on Somogyi Béla utca, ⓦ corvinteto.hu; map p.77. For the best night-time views of Budapest, head on up to the inspired rooftop bar atop the old Communist-era Corvin department store. A 30m-long bar keeps happy folk going until the very early hours, while the floor below hosts discos and the occasional band. You take a lift on the left-hand side of the building – on the way up the lift attendant offers shots of Unicum, the medicinal national drink. Daily 6pm–5am.

★ **Csiga** VIII, Vásár utca 2 ☎ 1 210 0885; map p.77. An artsy, mellow atmosphere prevails at the appealing *Csiga* corner café, which remains the drinking venue of choice in

the increasingly hip area around Rákóczi tér. Stripped wood flooring, mezzanine seating and big windows set the scene for a daytime or evening chillout. The food is well worth sampling too. Mon–Sat 10am–midnight, Sun noon–midnight.

Jelen VIII, Blaha Lujza tér 1–2; map p.77. In the far right-hand corner of the same former department store as *Corvintető*, the owners of *Most* bring a similarly bright feel to this high-ceilinged bar, decked out with mismatched chairs and tables. A long wooden bar despatches crisp draught beer while a separate counter does a neat sideline in Hungarian wines. Kick back with a glass of either and enjoy some of the live music offered up during the summer months. Mon–Fri 9am–2am, Sat & Sun 10am–2am.

Paris-Texas IX, Ráday utca 22; map p.77. A welcome standout among the otherwise mostly humdrum bars along this street, the *Paris* terrace is one of the more enjoyable spots to sup a beer. During cooler months, the action moves inside, where black-and-white portraits smother every spare inch of wall space, and everyone decamps to the smart cellar lounge. Daily 1.30pm–3am.

15

THE VÁR AND CENTRAL BUDA

Bambi I, Frankel Leó utca 2–4 ☎ 1 212 3171; map p.87. One of the few surviving Socialist-Realist bars, with stern waitresses, and old men chatting and playing dominoes on red plastic-covered tables. It's quite simple; they serve breakfast, omelettes, snack lunches, cakes and alcohol all day long. Mon–Fri 7am–10pm, Sat & Sun 9am–10pm.

★ **Lánchíd Söröző** I, Fő utca 4 ☎ 1 214 3144; map p.89. Handily placed at the Buda end of the Lánchíd, this chilled little bar is a quiet place in daytime, frequented by tourists and the odd regular, but by sundown the mood is more animated. The owner is a serious music fan, as the randomly scattered instruments, gig posters, and photos of him with Robert Plant, BB King and others on the walls testify. Daily 11am–1am.

GELLÉRT-HEGY AND THE TABÁN

Libella XI, Budafóki út 7 ☎ 1 209 4761; map p.108. Friendly, agreeably down-at-heel spot near the *Gellért Hotel*, which is popular above all with the student crowd from the nearby Technical University. Bar snacks, chess and draughts seems to keep those that pop by satisfied. Mon–Fri 8am–1am, Sat–Sun noon–1am.

Platán I, Döbrentei tér; map p.108. It's nothing special to look at, but this amicable bar's location under the plane trees near the river, and with outdoor tables, guarantees a steady stream of visitors. Daily 11am–midnight.

Zöld Pardon XI, Goldmann György tér ☎ 1 279 1880, ⓦ zp.hu; map p.108. A summer of partying hard is the general idea here at this large, heaving outdoor club near the Petőfi bridgehead. Nightly concerts – ranging from some rather questionable local outfits to more established international names – alongside DJs spinning drum 'n' bass, deep house and jungle. May–Sept daily 9am–6am.

ÓBUDA AND MARGIT-SZIGET

Cha-Cha-Cha Terasz XIII, Athletics Club, Margit-sziget; map p.117. The best of the Margit-sziget outdoor bars, at the southern end of the island: turning off Margit híd it is the second bar along on the left. This buzzy place is the summer venue of an established bar on Bajcsy-Zsilinszky út, and plays 1970s and 1980s music (Hungarian and Western) for dancing and Sgt Pepper-style videos (or sports TV) on the big screen. Though it opens mid-May, it doesn't really come alive till mid-June. Late May to Sept, daily 6pm–2am.

Római-part III, Rómaifürdő; map p.114. This is not one bar, but a whole string of open-air bars and cheap snack bars lining the riverbank north of Óbuda; the food is mainly of the deep-fried meat and fish with chips variety. Take the HÉV train from Batthyány tér to Rómaifürdő and it's a 10min walk down to the river. Daily noon–10pm.

Sark kert XIII, Margit-sziget; map p.117. Another summer island bar: walking up from Margit híd it's on the right after *Cha-Cha-Cha*. Can feel like an unfinished campsite at a Red Sea resort: fairly basic in its seating and facilities, but it's a lively place once the crowds arrive. Has occasional live music. Late May to Sept, daily 6pm–2am.

15

Gay Budapest

Of all the cities in the former eastern bloc, Budapest perhaps has the most active gay scene, albeit still very underground compared to its Western counterparts. Things have really taken wing in recent years, with new overtly gay clubs replacing the old covert meeting places, and the appearance of a trilingual monthly listings magazine, *Mások* ("Outsiders"). Moreover, the city's annual Pride event is now one of the most established and well attended in the region. This greater prominence is also reflected in law – the age of consent is 14 for homosexuals and heterosexuals alike, while, in 2009, Parliament passed a new bill allowing registered partnerships for same-sex couples. These changes are gradual rather than radical, though; while Budapest is a cosmopolitan city, Hungarian society at large is socially conservative. Gays must still tread warily and lesbians even more so.

The Budapest gay scene is very male-dominated. Perhaps the best spot for lesbians is the *Eklektika* bar, though there is also a women-only lesbian group, Ösztrosokk, that arranges parties at various venues around town, usually on the second Saturday of every month (10pm–4am; entry around 1200Ft; ⓦosztrosokk.hu).

The major event in the gay calendar is **Budapest Pride**, a well-established week-long festival taking place in mid-June. The core of Pride is the film festival, though it also incorporates a varied programme of workshops, public discussion forums and gay parties, before culminating in the colourful Pride March at the weekend, which wends its way along Andrássy út up to the Városliget. The march has been disrupted by right-wing extremists in recent years, and this may well happen again, so if you're planning to be there, watch out for any signs of trouble.

ESSENTIALS

Information The largest gay and lesbian organization in town is Háttér, which runs a helpline (daily 6–11pm; ☎1 329 3380, ⓦhatter.hu) offering advice and information on events – although some of the operators only speak Hungarian.

Listings and websites You can find listings for places and events in English in the gay freebie monthly *Na Végre*, found at most gay venues, or in the monthly *Time Out Budapest*. The Magnum Szauna website (ⓦmagnumszauna.hu) has a very useful and up-to-date section on the city's best gay restaurants, bars, clubs and so on. The website ⓦgayguide.net has the latest on gay accommodation, bars, clubs, restaurants, baths and events in the city.

BARS AND RESTAURANTS

16

Most of the bars listed here levy an **entry fee** or set a minimum consumption level – being gay in Budapest is an expensive privilege. Some venues give you a card when you enter, on which all your drinks are written down; you pay for your drinks and the entry fee as you leave. Be warned that if you lose the card, you'll have to cough up a hefty penalty. Otherwise, be on the lookout for overcharging.

THE BELVÁROS

Action V, Magyar utca 42 ☎1 266 9148, ⓦaction.gay .hu; map p.38. The most hardcore of the gay bars, full of young men looking for one-night stands. Dark room, video room and live shows on Friday (1000Ft entry). Minimum consumption 1000Ft. The entrance is hard to find – it's 15m along from the big "A" sign on the door. Daily 9pm–5am.

Amstel River Café V, Párizsi utca 6 ☎1 266 4334; map p.38. Not on the river but in the middle of the Belváros, this friendly Dutch-style pub-restaurant attracts a large foreign clientele but is equally popular with gays. Daily noon–midnight.

Capella V, Belgrád rakpart 23 ⓦcapellacafe.hu; map p.38. Popular with both straights and gays, *Capella* has become a well-frequented haunt, despite the highish prices. Drag queens and lots of kitsch, with decor as outrageous as the acts; drag shows start at midnight and 1am. Wed & Thurs 10pm–4am, one mandatory drink; Fri & Sat 10pm–6am, minimum consumption 1000Ft.

ELSEWHERE IN THE CITY

Club 93 V, Vas utca 2; map p.77. Simple, cheap pizzeria just off Rákóczi út that's popular with gays and lesbians. The gallery and window seating make it a good place to people-watch. Daily 11am–midnight.

CoXx V, Dohány utca 38 ☎1 344 4884, ⓦcoxx.hu; map p.58. The most cultured of the gay bars, this men-only venue is a friendly place to meet. The ground floor is a gallery and internet café; downstairs holds a dancefloor, video rooms and numerous other spaces. Regular themed party nights. Minimum consumption 1000Ft. Mon–Thurs 9pm–4am, Fri & Sat till 5am.

★ **Eklektika** VI, Nagymező utca 30 ☎1 266 1226, ⓦeklektika.hu; map p.58. Laidback lesbian-run café-restaurant that sits in a great location near the theatres. It serves decent food all day and at very reasonable prices, and there's a sporadic programme of live music, DJ evenings and exhibitions. Free entry. Mon–Fri 10am–midnight, Sat–Sun noon–midnight.

Fenyögyöngye II, Szépvölgyi út 155 ☎1 325 9783; map p.114. This restaurant is gay-owned, not that many who go there know that. It's at the last stop of the #65 bus from Kolosy tér in Óbuda. Good Hungarian food, polite service. Daily noon–11pm.

Le Café M V, Nagysándor József utca 3 ☎1 312 1436, ⓦmysterybar.hu; map p.48. Otherwise known as the *Mystery Bar*, this is a small, friendly place near the Arany János utca metro, that's more suited to chatting rather than dancing (there's no disco). It's a good place to start or end the evening. Internet café too, with wi-fi. Free entry. Mon–Fri 4pm–4am, Sat & Sun 6pm–4am.

BATHS

In years gone by, gay activity in some of the public steam baths, like the Király and the Rác, was widespread, but this is no longer the case. That said, the sun terrace at the Palatinus strand and the roof terrace at the Széchenyi remain popular gay meeting places. Now, private saunas are slowly springing up, offering dedicated facilities to gay visitors.

Magnum Szauna VIII, Csepreghy utca 2 ☎1 267 2532, ⓦmagnumszauna.hu; near the Corvinnegyed metro stop. Budapest's first private gay bath, Magnum offers a steam room and dry sauna, gym, lounge, dark rooms and cabins. Dark and Naked parties take place on Fridays at 9pm and drag shows on Saturdays at 8pm, as well as other regular events. 2290Ft for under-30s, 2990Ft for over-30s, Wed 1490Ft for all. Mon–Thurs 1pm–midnight, Fri 1pm–4am, and open continuously Sat 1pm–Mon 1am.

Szauna 69 IX, Angyal utca 2 ☎1 210 1751, ⓦgaysauna.hu. Finnish sauna, jacuzzi and private rooms, as well as a bar. 1690Ft for under-30s, 1890Ft for over-30s. Mon & Tues 1–8pm 1400Ft for all. Mon–Thurs & Sun 1pm–1am, Fri 1pm–2am, Sat 1pm–6am.

16

HUNGARIAN GYPSY BAND

Entertainment

Hungary's cultural pedigree is strong, and this is reflected in both the diversity of performers and quality of productions available on any given night in Budapest. Hungary's formidable traditions in classical music ensure that standards are high, while opera has long been an important cultural staple. If you are undeterred by the language barrier, an evening at the theatre can be a rewarding experience, though dance in all its many forms also offers some intriguing possibilities, not least the "dance house", or *tánchaz*, movement. Live music is another Hungarian forte, and there's a huge depth of talent, particularly in folk, jazz and world music. The city also boasts some stunning cinemas worth visiting for their architecture alone. The Spring and Autumn Festivals – in March and October respectively – showcase some of the finest in both Hungarian and international cultural talent.

ESSENTIALS

Tickets and reservations Tickets for most music and theatre events are available from several outlets in the city: Ticket Express, VI, Dalszinház utca 10 ☎ 30 303 0999, ⓦ tex .hu; Broadway Ticket Office XIII, Hollán Ernő utca 10 ☎ 1 340 4040 ⓦ broadwayjegyiroda.hu; Jegymester VI, Bajcsy-Zsilinszky út 31 ⓦ jegymester.hu; Cultur-Comfort VI, Paulay Ede utca 31 ☎ 1 322 0000, ⓦ cultur-comfort.hu; Rózsavolgyi record shop V, Szervita ter 5 ☎ 1 318 3500. Note that there's often a small handling fee slapped onto ticket prices for major international shows. If you can't get tickets for a performance from one of the ticket offices, it is always worth persevering with the staff at the venue's own box office or door, as there is often some way in.

Prices Attending any kind of musical or theatrical event in Budapest needn't cost an arm and a leg. A decent seat at the opera or for a classical music concert will set you back anywhere between 2000–4000Ft, although you can bank on paying at least double that for the most expensive seats. Theatre and dance performances are slightly cheaper, and you should expect to pay around 1500–3000Ft at most venues. Ticket prices for a rock or pop concert range from 1000Ft for local bands, up to as much as 20,000Ft for stadium gigs by international superstars; expect to pay anywhere between 800–1500Ft for a gig at the Budapest Jazz Club, though considerably more for big-name acts. Cinema-going is cheap, with tickets typically costing 1200–1500Ft.

Listings The best place to find out about what's going on are listings magazines such as *Funzine*, *Where Budapest*, and *Time Out Budapest*. A comprehensive listing, in English, of classical music events can be found at ⓦ muzsikalendarium.hu and in the free monthly *Koncert Kalendárium*, available from ticket offices or in listings magazines. Many gigs and concerts by both local and international bands are publicized on posters around town – particularly around Deák tér, Ferenciek tere and the Astoria underpass. The most comprehensive cinema listings appear in the *mozi* section of the free Hungarian weekly *Pesti Est*. Note that the times of shows are cryptically abbreviated: *n8* or *1/4 8* – short for *negyed 8* – means 7.15pm; *f8* or *1/2 8* (*fél 8*) means 7.30pm; and *h8* or *3/4 8* (*háromnegyed 8*) means 7.45pm. "*Mb.*" indicates the film is dubbed – as many are – and *fel.* or *feliratos* means that it has Hungarian subtitles.

ARTS CENTRES AND MULTI-PURPOSE VENUES

The venues listed below are used for a variety of concerts and other entertainment events. Bear in mind that many arts centres close for the summer.

★**A38** XI, Pázmány Péter sétány ☎ 1 464 3940, ⓦ a38.hu. Housed on a boat that was reputedly given to Hungary in return for writing off the Ukrainian debt and is moored on the Buda side of the river, just below Petőfi híd. A brilliant venue, it has a separate admission charge for each of its three decks, where top international and Hungarian performers play rock, jazz, folk and world music.
Millenáris Park II, Kis Rókus utca 16–20 ☎ 1 336 4000, ⓦ millenaris.hu. Enormous complex comprising several buildings, though the most important are the Teátrum and Fogadó concert halls, which host an original mix of music, theatre and dance, including some international acts. In summer, concerts are held on the park's outdoor stages.

Palace of Arts (Művészetek palotája) IX, Komor Marcell utca 1 ☎ 1 555 3000, ⓦ mupa.hu. This substantial complex on the riverbank in southern Pest has a top-of-the-range concert hall, theatre and museum, and as the shop-window for the capital's culture scene, it sees a superb range of concerts, attracting the top international classical, jazz and world music orchestras and acts. Box office Mon–Fri 1–6pm, Sat & Sun 10am–6pm.
Petőfi Csarnok XIV, Zichy Mihály út 14 ☎ 1 363 3730, ⓦ petoficsarnok.hu. On the edge of the Városliget, this big hall is often used by local and international rock and jazz groups, as well as hosting weekend flea markets and occasional craft fairs.

MUSIC FESTIVALS

Budapest stages several terrific music festivals throughout the year. The big one is the week-long **Sziget festival** (ⓦ sziget.hu/fesztival), held on Óbudai (or Hajógyári) sziget north of Margit-sziget, in mid-August. Now established as one of Europe's largest and most vibrant music festivals, it draws the very biggest names in rock, pop and world music. It's great value, too, with day tickets costing around €45, and weekly tickets €140 (if bought in advance). Going by foot, you take the HÉV from Batthyány tér to the Filorigát stop and follow the crowds across the bridge to the island. Slightly less crowded is the bus from Deák tér and the boats from Batthyány tér or Jászai Mari tér, at the Pest end of the Margít híd. Another terrific festival is **Athe Sam** in the second week of June, which celebrates Roma music, film and literature; most of the concerts take place at the *Gödör Klub*, and better still, they're free.

17

★ **Trafó** IX, Liliom utca 41 ☎ 1 215 1600, ⊕ trafo.hu. A dynamic contemporary arts centre in a former transformer station, it pulls in full houses with its strong roster of dance, theatre and music, by Hungarian and foreign artistes. Excellent contemporary gallery and a good bar too. Box office daily 4–8pm. Closed July & Aug.

CLASSICAL MUSIC, OPERA AND BALLET

The city offers a wide variety of performances, with several concerts most nights, especially during the excellent Budapest Spring and Autumn festivals, when you can bank on a roll call of world-class artists pitching up. Most opera productions are in Hungarian, a custom introduced by Gustav Mahler when he was director of the Opera House, which remains Budapest's principal venue. One genre that has long appealed to the Hungarian spirit is **operetta**, with Hungarians making a major contribution to the turn-of-the-century Viennese tradition through composers such as Ferenc Lehár and Imre Kálmán. Lehár's *The Merry Widow* and Kálmán's *The Csárdás Princess* still draw the crowds with their combination of grand tunes, extravagant staging and romantic comedy in the suitably over-the-top Operetta Theatre.

VENUES

★ **Bartók Memorial House** (Bartók Emlékház) II, Csalán utca 29 ☎ 1 394 2100, ⊕ bartokmuseum.hu. Concerts – not just of the music of Bartók – are held in the villa where the composer used to live, most on Fri at 6pm but also on other days. Tickets are either included in the entry fee or are up to a modest 2500Ft.

Bartók National Concert Hall (Bartók Béla Nemzeti Hangversenyterem) in the Palace of Arts. The home of the Hungarian National Philharmonic Orchestra has superb acoustics and attracts world-class performers, not just in the classical arena.

Budapest Operetta Theatre (Budapesti Operettszínház) VI, Nagymező utca 17 ☎ 1 312 4866, ⊕ operett.hu. The magnificently refurbished home of Hungarian operetta, where you can enjoy works by Lehár and Kálmán, as well as modern musicals. Box office Mon–Fri 10am–7pm, Sat & Sun 1–7pm.

Madách Theatre (Madách Színház) VII, Erzsébet körút 29–33 ☎ 1 478 2041, ⊕ madachszinhaz.hu. Large auditorium ideal for the regular programme of showpiece musicals such as *Phantom* and *Joseph*. Box office daily 10am–12.30pm & 1–6.30pm.

★ **Music Academy** (Zeneakadémia) VI, Liszt Ferenc tér 8 ☎ 1 342 0179, ⊕ lfze.hu. Founded by Ferenc Liszt in 1875, it hosts nightly concerts and recitals in the magnificent gold-covered Nagyterem (Great Hall) or the smaller Kisterem. The music is excellent and the place has a real buzz.

Óbuda Music Society (Óbudai Társaskör) III, Kiskorona utca 7 ☎ 1 250 0288, ⊕ obudaitarsaskor .hu. Small concert hall on the edge of the housing estates south of the Árpád híd in Óbuda. The quality of performance is excellent, and big local ensembles such as the Liszt Chamber Orchestra, Budapest Strings and Auer String Quartet are based here. Also stages some jazz concerts.

Old Music Academy (Régi Zeneakadémia) VI, Vörösmarty utca 35 ☎ 1 322 9804. Performances by young musicians every Saturday morning, in the concert hall of the Liszt Memorial Museum.

Opera House (Magyar Állami Operaház) VI, Andrássy út 22 ☎ 1 332 7914, ⊕ opera.hu. Home to both the Hungarian State Opera and Hungarian National Ballet companies, this is Budapest's grandest venue, with gilded frescoes and three-tonne chandeliers. Dress tends towards smart, and you can still get cheap seats – tickets start at around 600Ft, though they go up to 16,000Ft for the best seats at the best shows. The box office is inside the main doors or, if they are closed, round on the left-hand side of the building in Dalszínház utca; Mon–Sat 11am–5pm, Sun 4–7pm.

Thália Theatre (Thália Színház) VI, Nagymező 22 ☎ 1 331 0500, ⊕ thalia.hu. On Budapest's "Broadway", the

CHURCH AND OPEN-AIR CONCERTS

Quite a few places of worship in Budapest regularly host concerts, among them the church on **Kálvin tér** (see p.79); the **Lutheran Church** on Deák tér (see p.44; the programme includes free performances of Bach before Easter, details of which are posted by the church entrance); and the **Dohány utca synagogue** (see p.62). The **Mátyás Church** on Várhegy (see p.89) stages choral or organ recitals on Fri and Sat between June and Sept (from 8pm), and less frequently the rest of the year.

While the opera, theatre and concert halls take a **summer break** at the end of May (reopening in mid-Sept) there is a summer season of concerts at open-air venues, including the outdoor stage on Margit-sziget (see p.118), the **Dominican Yard** of the *Hilton* hotel (see p.158) in the Castle District, and the **Vajdahunyad Castle** in the Városliget (see p.71), though the music most of these venues offer is fairly mainstream.

Thália hosts operas and musicals, as well as theatre and dance. Box office Mon–Thurs 10am–6pm, Fri 10am–5pm. **Vigadó** V, Vigadó tér 1. Another fabulously decorated hall, though the acoustics are inferior. Dating from 1865, it

is the oldest of the major concert venues and several Liszt premiers were performed here. Closed for restoration at the time of writing.

POP, ROCK AND JAZZ

Budapest is one of the main stops in Central/Eastern Europe for touring international bands, while every Hungarian **band** worth its amplifiers will play the capital. The city does, though, suffer from a lack of small to medium-sized venues, though this is somewhat compensated for by the number of *kert* bars hosting live music, such as *Instant, Jelen, Pótkulcs* and *Simplakert*. Apart from the venues listed below, performances are also held at some of the places listed on p.185.

VENUES

Budapest Jazz Club VIII, Múzeum utca 7 ☎1 267 2610, ⊛bjc.hu. Both the smallish venue and the high quality of acts ensure a terrific atmosphere at Budapest's premier jazz club. There are regular themed jazz evenings and weekly late-night jam sessions on Friday and Saturday.

Columbus Pub V, Vigadó tér ☎1 266 9013, ⊛majazz .hu. Ostensibly a jazz venue on a boat moored in central Pest, with nightly piano sessions, though you're just as likely to hear salsa.

Gödör Klub V, Erzsébet tér ☎20 201 3868, ⊛godorklub.hu. So named after the big hole (*gödör* means hole in Hungarian) left here following the decision not to construct the new National Theatre on the site, the underground *Gödör Klub* is the city's most adventurous venue. It's a pretty ugly space, with concrete pillars and a

mucky glass ceiling, but it plays host to a superb range of music – jazz, folk, alternative Hungarian pop and Roma acts. There's also plenty going on out front during the summer months, when people spill out onto the stepped terraces outside.

IF Kávézó IX, Ráday utca 19 ☎1 299 0694, ⊛ifkavezo .hu. Now one of the most established music venues in the city, IF offers a particularly exciting programme of jazz, though you can count on something happening most nights of the week.

Papp László Sportarena XIV, Stefánia út 12 ☎1 422 2600, ⊛budapestarena.hu; Stadionok metro station. Major sporting events aside, this vast indoor arena is where the big guns come to play when touring Budapest.

Sirály VI, Király utca 50 ⊛siraly.co.hu. Regular jazz and theatre downstairs in this bohemian place, a very deluxe squat.

FOLK MUSIC AND DANCE

Hungarian **folk music** and **dancing** underwent a revival in the 1970s, drawing inspiration from Hungarian communities in Transylvania, regarded as pure wellsprings of Magyar culture. The movement still exists today, and has been extended to other cultures – you'll also see adverts for Greek (*görög*), Roma and other dance houses. Visitors are welcome to attend the gatherings and learn the steps; see ⊛tanchaz.hu for more. Apart from the places detailed below, performances take place at the venues listed pp.185–186 and in some of the *kert* bars.

VENUES

★ **Aranytíz Cultural Centre** V, Arany János utca 10 ☎1 354 3400, ⊛aranytiz.hu. The Kalamajka ensemble plays here to a packed dancefloor on Saturday nights from late September through to early June, with dance teaching from 7pm; the children's session begins at 5pm (see p.199). As the evening rolls on a jamming session often develops with other bands joining in. The cultural

centre's programme includes Hungarian and international theatre performances and jazz concerts, too.

Fonó Music Hall (Fonó Budai Zeneház) XI, Sztregova utca 3 ☎1 206 5300, ⊛fono.hu. Lively international folk and world music venue, 2km south of Móricz Zsigmond körtér – four stops from there on tram #18 or #47. Every Wednesday evening there's a dance house led by Téka, Méta or Tükrös.

BUDAPEST JAZZ

When it comes to **jazz** (or *dzsessz*, as it is sometimes becomes in Hungarian), don't be fooled by the small number of regular venues in Budapest. The country boasts some brilliant jazz musicians, such as György Vukán, Béla Szakcsi Lakatos and the award-winning pianist Kálmán Oláh. Now there is a new phenomenon, **Roma jazz**, spawning a fresh generation of brilliant players. One jazz ensemble to look out for is the **Harmonia Jazz Workshop** (**Harmonia Jazz Műhely**), who hold regular sessions at the **Budapest Jazz Club** and elsewhere. There are also occasional jazz concerts in theatres such as the MU Színház as well as some of the *kert* bars.

17

FOLK MUSIC AND DANCE GROUPS

Concerts of Hungarian folk music by the likes of Muzsikás, Téka, Tükrös, Ökrös, Csík and Kalamajka take place regularly, while there are also performances by groups such as Vujicsics, inspired by South Slav music from Serbia, Croatia and Bulgaria. Two singers to look out for on the circuit are **Beáta Pálya**, whose repertoire draws on her Hungarian and Roma roots as well as other cultures, and **Ági Szalóki**, who captures the traditional female folk sound – she accompanies bands such as the Ökrös Ensemble as well as performing solo. There has been a huge growth in **Roma** groups, while the old Jewish musical traditions are continued by klezmer performers such as Di Naye Kapelye, who are far closer to the original spirit than the ubiquitous easy-listening Budapest Klezmer Band. An entertaining blend of the two styles is offered by the Fellegini Klezmer Gipsy band, led by Balázs Fellegi.

CINEMA

Hollywood blockbusters dominate Budapest's mainstream **cinemas**, though the city has a small chain of art-house cinemas that specialize in the latest releases and obscure European films – *angol* indicates a British film, *lengyel* Polish, *német* German, *olasz* Italian, and *orosz* Russian. In the summer some of the outdoor bars, such as *Holdudvar* on Margit-sziget, have weekly open-air film screenings, while there are also summer outdoor and drive-in cinemas on the edge of town.

CINEMAS

Cirko-gejzir V, Balassi Bálint utca 15–17 ☎ 1 269 1915, ⓦ cirkofilm.hu. One of the best alternative cinemas, with a regular selection of movies from around the globe – in any given week they might be showing films by Almodóvar, Tarkovsky, Jarmusch, Wenders and Rohmer.

Corvin Budapest Film Palace (Corvin Filmpalota) VIII, Corvin köz 1 ⓦ corvin.hu. This glitzy multiplex, near the Ferenc körút metro, is a good place to catch the latest foreign releases, and it also hosts the Hungarian Film Festival. Cheaper tickets on Wednesday (900Ft).

Muvész VI, Teréz körút 30 ☎ 1 459 5050, ⓦ artmozi.hu. Art-house cinema near the Oktogon, with one large and several smaller rooms named after big film personalities.

Puskin V, Kossuth Lajos 18 ☎ 1 459 5050, ⓦ artmozi .hu. Complex of three cinemas in the centre of town, with a large café attached. The coffered ceiling of the turn-of-the-century main screen is magnificent. Cheaper tickets on Tuesday (800Ft).

★ **Toldi** V, Bajcsy-Zsilinszky út 36–38 ☎ 1 459 5050, ⓦ artmozi.hu. Next door to Arany János utca metro station, the two-screen Toldi is one of the more dynamic alternative cinemas in town, and it's also the principal venue for the annual Titanic film festival. Decent bar too.

Uránia National Film Theatre (Uránia Nemzeti Filmszínház) VIII, Rákóczi út 21 ⓦ urania-nf.hu. With its magnificent Venetian-Moorish decorations, this might seem a strange choice of location for Budapest's main showcase of Hungarian films. But it was in this cinema, built in the 1890s as a dance hall, that the first Hungarian feature film was shot in 1901. While it places special emphasis on local films, its programme is international.

THEATRE AND CONTEMPORARY DANCE

Hungarians usually show great sophistication when it comes to building theatres: take the splendid mass of the **Vígszínház** up the road from Nyugati Station, or the **New Theatre** opposite the Opera House. By way of contrast, the **National Theatre** – opened in 2000 – took some criticism for its cold, rather unimaginative design. While theatre in the capital might be inferior compared to anything offered up in the fields of opera or classical music, do look out for performances by the provincial theatre company from the town of **Kaposvár**, in southwest Hungary, or by Hungarian companies from outside the borders, such as from Cluj, Romania.

Alternative theatre tends to be more interesting – and since music and dance play a greater part here, language can be less of a barrier. One Hungarian group that has received considerable critical acclaim abroad are **Krétakör**, while other names to look out for are **László Hudi**, **Frenák Pál** and **Péter Halász**, who have all spent time with foreign ensembles, bringing fresh new ideas back to Hungary. Two exciting names in dance are **Réka Szabó**, who runs the Tünet (Symptom) group, and **Krisztián Gergye**. And finally, Hungary has a strong puppet tradition and the shows in the two **puppet theatres** will appeal to adults and children alike.

VENUES

★ **Budapest Bábszínház** VI, Andrássy út 69 ☎ 1 342 2702, ⓦ budapest-babszinhaz.hu. Budapest Puppet Theatre has a lot of shows for adults – masked grotesqueries or renditions of Bartók's *The Wooden Prince* and *The Miraculous Mandarin* and Mozart's *Magic Flute*. Open all year.

Kolibri Pince VI, Andrássy út 77 ☎ 1 311 0870, ⓦ kolibriszinhaz.hu. Puppet shows and live performances

HUNGARY ON FILM

17

Hungarians have an impressive record in film, and many of the Hollywood greats were **Hungarian émigrés** – Michael Curtiz, Sir Alex Korda, George Cukor, and actors Béla Lugosi, Tony Curtis and Leslie Howard to name but a few. In the Communist years Hungarian film continued to make waves, with Miklós Jancsó, Károly Makk, István Szabó, Márta Mészáros and others directing films that managed to say much about the oppressive regime in spite of its restrictions. Now the main constraint on film makers is chronic underfunding, but what the Hungarian film industry lacks in money it makes up for in ideas.

Established directors to look out for are Péter Gothár, with his absurd humour and love of the fantastic (*Time Stands Still*, *Let Me Hang Vaska*), Ildikó Enyedi (*My Twentieth Century* and *Simon the Magician*), Béla Tarr (*Werckmeister Harmonies* and the epic eight-hour *Satan Tango*) and János Szász, whose film *The Witman Boys* won the best international film at Cannes in 1997. Other younger stars are Kornél Mundruczó, Szabolcs Hajdú, Ferenc Török and Nimród Antal, whose first film, the black comedy *Kontroll*, was a big hit abroad; as well as György Pálfi, whose *Hukkle* similarly won international acclaim. Two new names making feature films are Szabolcs Tolnai, whose film *Sand Glass* about the writer Danilo Kis won widespread praise; and Péter Fazakas, whose first feature film, *Para*, was released in 2008.

Budapest has been a popular **location** for films, both for its looks and its cheapness – though the EU has now blocked the Hungarian tax loophole that made it so appealing – serving as Buenos Aires in *Evita* and as Paris in the *Maigret* TV series; in the latter, the view towards the Basilica down Lázár utca behind the Opera House acts as the view of the Sacré-Coeur, and Paris developed a hill rising on one bank of the Seine rather like that in Budapest. But it also serves as itself: the American documentary *Divan* by Pearl Gluck captures some of the characters and atmosphere of the old Jewish quarter in its interviews.

DVDs, most of them subtitled, have made Hungarian films much more accessible, making it possible to enjoy classics such as Géza Radványi's *Valahol Európában* (1947) and Zoltán Fábri's *Körhinta* (1955).

---

for adults as well as children at three venues (see p.199 for the other two); this is the best one for grown-up performances. Closed early June–Aug.

Merlin Theatre V, Gerlóczy utca 4 ☎1 317 9338, Ⓦmerlinszinhaz.hu. In the centre of Pest, this well-regarded theatre has perhaps the strongest line-up of visiting British theatre companies.

MU Színház XI, Körösy József utca 17 ☎1 209 4014, Ⓦmu.hu. Alternative theatre venue that is particularly strong on dance, and it also hosts the odd jazz concert.

★ **National Dance Theatre** (Nemzeti Táncszínház) I, Színház utca 1–3 ☎1 201 4407, Ⓦnemzetitancszinhaz.hu. Housed in the old Castle Theatre in Buda, this is the city's premier dance venue, staging everything from classical ballet to contemporary dance. Box office Mon–Thurs 10am–6pm, Fri 10am–5pm.

National Theatre (Nemzeti Színház) IX, Bajor Gizi park 1 ☎1 476 6868, Ⓦnemzetiszinhaz.hu. The proud flagship of Hungarian theatre. Some shows are in English,

put on by local troupes. Box office Mon–Fri 10am–6pm, Sat & Sun 2–6pm.

New Theatre (Új Színház) VI, Paulay Ede utca 35 ☎1 351 1406, Ⓦujszinhaz.hu. This stunning Art Deco building across the road from the Opera House was one of the better mainstream theatres, though recent appointments (see p.59) may change this. Box office Mon–Thurs 10am–5pm, Fri 10am–4pm.

Szkéné Színház XI, Műegyetem rakpart 3 ☎1 463 2451, Ⓦszkene.hu. A small theatre housed in the main building of the Technical University near the *Gellért Hotel*, this has been an alternative venue for many years, dating back to the bad old days of Communism.

Vígszínház XIII, Szent István körút 14 ☎1 329 2340, Ⓦvigszinhaz.hu. Great for people-watching, as the locals dress up in their finest to attend performances, which are very much in the mainstream Hungarian style. Visiting companies also perform here. Box office daily 11am–7pm.

ICE-SKATING IN THE VÁROSLIGET

Sports

Hungarians are passionate about sport and the country possesses a far greater sporting pedigree than most people appreciate. The Olympics, above all, have been a source of outstanding triumph, which is all the more surprising given the country's size and resources; the men's waterpolo team, in particular, has achieved extraordinary success, taking gold at each of the last three Games. Budapest's major annual sporting event, bar none, is the Formula 1 Grand Prix, with the other main spectator sports being football and, to a lesser degree, horse racing – though years of underfunding and mismanagement have brought the last two nearly to their knees. Sports facilities have suffered similarly from a lack of funding, but you can find a reasonable range of sports and activities to choose from around the capital.

FOOTBALL

Hungary's great footballing days are long past – the golden team of the 1950s that beat England 6–3 with stars such as Ferenc Puskás and József Bozsik is a world away from today's national squad, which hasn't qualified for a major tournament since 1986. As throughout Eastern Europe, the domestic leagues are also in deep crisis, with clubs struggling along with little or no money, and their best players continuously sold off to clubs in other countries.

While **international matches** are held at the 76,000-capacity Puskás Ferenc Stadium – which is slated for a complete redevelopment – club football in Budapest revolves around the turf of three teams, listed below; if you can't find the fixtures online, the daily *Nemzeti Sport* has details. The **season** runs from late July to late Nov and late Feb to mid-June. Most matches are played on Saturday afternoons, with tickets costing 600–1800Ft.

18

TEAMS

Ferencváros (aka FTC or Fradi) IX, Üllői út 129 ☎1 215 6025, ⍟ftc.hu; Népliget metro. Fradi is the biggest club in the country and almost a national institution, though success has been harder to come by in recent times. Its supporters, dressed in the club's colours of green and white, are the loudest presence at international matches too. The club has long had right-wing ties: this was the fascists' team before the war, and in recent years it has attracted a strong skinhead – and anti-Semitic – element. Fradi's recent history has been one of tragi-comedy, having been first taken over by a second-rate demagogic politician, then by a Jewish businessman. After a three-year spell in the second division, the club (currently owned by the former Sheffield United chairman, Kevin McCabe) returned to the top division in 2009. It plays at the 18,000-capacity Stadion Albert Flórián.

MTK VIII, Salgótarján utca 12–14 ☎1 333 8368, ⍟mtkhungaria.hu; tram #37 from Blaha Lujza tér.

Fradi's big local rival, "Em-tay-kah" – as it is popularly known – has traditionally had strong support among the Jewish community. These days, however, and unlike its neighbour, it is no longer a contender in the top division, having been relegated in 2011 – only the third time in its history that this has happened. MTK's Hidegkuti Nándor stadium (capacity 12,700) was the setting for scenes in the film *Escape to Victory*.

Újpest IV, Megyeri út 13 ☎1/231 0088, ⍟ujpestfc.hu; four stops on bus #30 from Újpest Központ metro station. Formed in 1885, Újpest have traditionally been one of the powerhouses of Hungarian football, enjoying particularly golden periods in the 1930s – when it supplied half of the Hungarian national team that were runners-up in the 1938 World Cup – and the 1970s, when they reached the semi-finals of the European Cup in 1974. Known as the Lilák (Purples) – after the club colours – Újpest play at the 13,000 all-seater Szusza Ferenc Stadium north of the city.

HORSE RACING

Horse racing was introduced from England by Count Széchenyi in 1827 and flourished until 1949, when flat racing (*galopp*) was banned by the Communists. For many years punters could only enjoy trotting races, but in the mid-1980s flat racing resumed. **Betting** operates on a tote system, where your returns are affected by how the odds stood at the close of betting. The different types of bet comprise *tét*, placing money on the winner; *hely*, on a horse coming in the first three; and the popular *befutó*, a bet on two horses to come in either first and second or first and third. Winnings are paid out about fifteen minutes after the end of the race.

Kincsem Park X, Albertirsai út 2–6; Pillangó utca on the red metro, and then either walk or catch #100 bus. Flat racing takes place here on Sundays from spring to autumn; trotting – *ügető*, where the horse is harnessed to a light carriage – is all year round, mostly on Sat. Races are

advertised in *Fortuna* magazine. Both types have a devoted and excitable following, which makes attending the races entertaining; the atmosphere at the tracks is informal, but photographing the racegoers is frowned upon, since many attend unbeknownst to their spouses or employers.

GRAND PRIX RACING

The Hungarian Grand Prix usually takes place at the end of July or beginning of August at the purpose-built Formula One racing track, the Hungaroring, at Mogyoród, 20km northeast of Budapest. First held in 1986, it has managed to retain its place on the lucrative F1 calendar ever since, and has been guaranteed the event until 2016.

Tickets are available from the official online ticket agency ⍟hungarorinfo.com, or from Ostermann Forma-1, V, Apáczai Csere János utca 11, third floor (☎1 266 2040). Prices vary dramatically according to which days you go, where you are positioned on the circuit, and whether you buy in advance or not – typically, however, a day pass costs around €80, with a weekend pass costing anything between €150 and €450. You can reach the track by special buses from the Árpád híd bus station; trains from Keleti Station to Fót, and then a bus from there; or by HÉV train from Örs vezér tere to the Szilasliget stop, which is 1800m northeast of Gate C.

PARTICIPATORY SPORTS AND ACTIVITIES

Canoeing Taking a canoe or kayak out on the Danube can be exhilarating – you just have to remember to head upstream first. The Béke Boathouse is a 10min walk from the Rómaifürdő HÉV station (or take bus #34 to the door from the Árpád híd station) at III, Római-part 51–53 ☎ 1 388 9303. Open April to mid-Oct.

Caving Óbuda offers the opportunity to explore a couple of fascinating cave systems (see p.116). You can walk round them without any special equipment, or you can go on more adventurous visits with Caving under Budapest (☎ 20 928 4969, ⓦ barlangaszat.hu). The group leads two- to three-hour tours – you don't need caving experience, but you do need to be fit and fairly agile, as you'll be climbing on walls and squeezing through passageways. You are given helmets, headlights and overalls. English-speaking tours (4500Ft) are on Mon, Wed and Fri afternoons and start at the Pálvölgyi Stalactite Cave. The Hungarian Association of Speleologists, at the Szemlőhegyi Cave (☎ 1 346 0495, ⓦ barlang.hu) can put you in touch with groups exploring caves in the Buda Hills and elsewhere in Hungary.

Fitness centres and gyms Most of the larger hotels and some of the shopping malls have them – they are properly regulated, unlike some of the backstreet ones, and are open to non-residents.

Ice-skating During winter, there's skating at the City Park ice rink by Hősök tere in the Városliget (mid-Nov to Feb Mon–Fri 9am–1pm & 4–8pm, Sat & Sun 10am–2pm & 4–8pm); entry costs around 1000Ft, and skates can be rented.

Skiing If it's a snowy winter, you can ski at Normafa in the Buda Hills, best reached on bus #90 or #90A from Széll Kálmán tér. Equipment can be rented from Suli Sí by the entrance of the Császár Komjádi pool at II, Árpád Fejedelem utca 8 (☎ 1 212 0330, ⓦ sulisi.hu), or Bikebase at VI, Podmaniczky utca 19 (daily 9am–7pm; ☎ 1 269 5983, ⓦ bikebase.hu), where the friendly staff can advise you on other places to ski.

Squash Try City Squash Club, II, Marczibányi tér 13 (☎ 1 336 0408, ⓦ squashtech.hu; court rental 2200Ft/hr), 5min walk from Széll Kálmán tér; or Top Squash Club, on the fourth floor of the nearby Mammut Mall I (☎ 1 345 8193, ⓦ top-squash.hu; court rental 2500Ft/hr).

Tank-driving If you've got a day and lots of cash to spare, why not try tank-driving at Baj, near Tata, where 55 acres of muddy terrain and obstacles can be negotiated in a range of ex-Soviet armoured vehicles. Popular with stag parties – they also do paintballing. See ⓦ tank.hu for details.

Tennis Courts can be booked all year round at the Városmajor Tennis Academy in Városmajor Park, near Széll Kálmán tér (☎ 1 202 5337) and at the *Thermal Hotel Helia* in Angyalföld, XIII, Kárpát utca 62 (☎ 1 889 5800). Racquets are available for rent.

> ## TOP 5 HUNGARIAN SPORTS STARS
>
> **Ferenc Puskás** (football)
> **Aladár Gerevich** (fencing)
> **Nándor Hidegkuti** (football)
> **Natasa Janics** (kayaking)
> **Krisztina Egerszegi** (swimming)

GELLÉRT BATHS

Baths and pools

With more than a hundred springs offering an endless supply of hot water at temperatures of up to 76°C, Budapest is deservedly known as a spa city, and visiting one of the many baths is an unmissable experience. Housed in some of Budapest's finest buildings, the baths are impressive in their own right, while the thermal waters are reputed to cure myriad ailments – and of course there's the swimming itself. The baths are an important social hub too, where people come to sit and chat as they follow the rituals. As you admire the light filtering through the dome in the Rudas, watch chess players ponder strategies in the outdoor pool of the Széchenyi or peer through the mists in the steam rooms of the Gellért, there's a real sense of being part of a tradition that has lasted centuries.

There are three types of bath: *gyógyfürdő*, a **thermal bath** in its original Turkish form, as at the Rudas and Király, or the magnificent nineteenth-century settings of the Gellért and Széchenyi; *uszoda*, a proper swimming pool such as the Sport; and *strand*, a lido in a verdant setting, such as the Palatinus. Most baths are divided into a **swimming** area and a separate section for **steam baths** (*gőzfürdő* or the *gőz*, as they are popularly known). The smaller Rudas and Király baths are first and foremost steam baths, with saunas and pools fed by thermal springs. In the larger baths, such as the Gellért and Széchenyi, you can alternate between brisk dips in the swimming pool and leisurely soaks in the steam section.

The Budapest bathing experience can be a little daunting, as little is written in English once you are inside and attendants are unlikely to speak more than Hungarian and a smattering of German. However, the basic system of attendants and cabins is the same in most steam baths and swimming pools, and once you get the hang of the rituals, a visit to the baths becomes most rewarding. The websites Ⓦbudapestgyogyfurdoi.hu and Ⓦspasbudapest.com have general information on all the main baths.

19

BATHING ESSENTIALS

Tickets A standard ticket purchased from the ticket office (*pénztár*) gets you into the pools as well as the sauna and steam rooms; you'll often have the choice between changing in a communal room and using a locker (*szekrény*), or a slightly more expensive cubicle (*kabin*) – the latter gives you more privacy and, in the mixed-sex baths, this allows couples to change together.

Prices and rental Entrance prices (which are usually valid all day) are around 2500–3500Ft on weekdays, though expect to pay 200–300Ft more at weekends; cabins cost around 200Ft more; individual prices are given under each bath listing. Everything you need can be rented at all baths – costs are typically: swimsuit (1000Ft), bathrobe (1000Ft), towel (600Ft) and sheet (300Ft). In all baths bring flip-flops if you have them, as well as your own soap

BATHHOUSE HISTORY

Even though the sulphurous content of Budapest's waters mean that they don't always smell very pleasant, their therapeutic qualities have long been exploited. The earliest remains of baths here date back to the Bronze Age, and a succession of invaders have since capitalized on the benefits of the healthy waters. The **Romans**, who appreciated a good bath, set up camp along the banks of the Danube – you can see the ruins of their bathhouses in Óbuda. After their arrival from the east, the **Hungarian tribes** also recognized the value of the thermal springs, as testified by the remnants of a hospital bathhouse from 1178 found near the Lukács.

During their occupation, the **Ottomans** played a vital role in the development of Budapest's baths – the precept, under Islamic law, for washing five times a day before prayers is thought to have engendered a popular bathing culture here. The oldest baths that survive today are the Turkish baths on the Buda side of the river: built in the late sixteenth century, the Király and the Rudas baths have preserved their original layout, with a central bathing pool surrounded by smaller pools that lie below the old Turkish cupolas.

The next **golden age of bathing** occurred in the late nineteenth and early twentieth centuries, as a fashion for spas swept across Europe. Budapest's existing baths were dressed up in a new magnificence, and splendid buildings such as the neo-Baroque Széchenyi Baths in the Városliget and the Art Nouveau Gellért Baths were erected. During the **Communist era**, the baths were as popular as ever – a place to meet and gossip in the murky mists – but they suffered prolonged neglect. In recent years, however, major investments have seen the buildings restored and their facilities upgraded by way of new features such as whirlpools – Budapest's baths are now far more salubrious places to visit. And it's not just people who have benefited from the thermal waters. The success of the hippopotamus-breeding programme at Budapest Zoo is thought to be partly due to the constant supply of hot water from the Széchenyi Baths across the road – the hippos clearly benefit from wallowing in lovely thermal pools. The hot springs also saved them during the bitter winter siege of the city in 1944–45, when most of the zoo's other animals died in the freezing temperatures.

and shampoo; in the steam baths, you don't need a towel as you're given a sheet to dry yourself with. In many pools, bathing caps (*uszósapka*) are compulsory: in the Széchenyi, they're only required in the middle of the three outdoor pools (the one reserved for swimming proper); go in without a cap and you'll be whistled at by the attendant and told to get out. It's usual to tip the attendant a couple of hundred forints. Supplementary tickets will buy you a massage (*masszázs*), a soak in a private tub (*kádfürdő*) or a mud bath (*iszapfürdő*) – a list by the office will detail the available services.

Procedure As you go into the baths, you're given a counter to feed into the turnstile at the entrance – there is usually a member of staff standing around to show you what to do. Once inside the changing room (*öltöző*), an attendant will direct you to a cabin or locker. In the steam baths, the attendant will give you a *kötény* – a small loincloth for men or an apron for women – which offers a vestige of cover. Once you've changed, you need to find the attendant again; they will lock your locker or cabin

door and give you a tag (or another key with which to double lock your door for security). You tie the tag or key to your swimming costume or the strings of your *kötény*, making a note of your cabin number and taking with you any supplementary tickets.

In the baths The best way to enjoy the steam baths is to go from room to room, moving on whenever the heat gets too much. A popular sequence is: sauna (dry steam – often divided into three rooms, the furthest being the hottest), cool pool, steam room, cold plunge (if you can bear it), hot plunge (this makes your skin tingle wonderfully, but don't stay in for long), followed by a wallow in the larger, warmer pools that are usually at the centre of the baths. Most people then repeat the whole thing again, but the sequence you choose is entirely up to you. When you're completely finished, take a sheet from the pile to dry yourself. Relax in the rest room if you feel exhausted – certainly don't plan on anything too strenuous afterwards – and then find the attendant to unlock your cabin or locker.

THE BATHS

Császár Komjádi Uszoda II, Árpád fejedelem útja 8 ☎ 1 212 2750. Hungary's national swimming stadium is a large, modern pool complex just north of Margit híd on the Buda side – the entrance faces the river. The large outdoor swimming pool (bathing caps compulsory) is covered over in winter. As it's one of the major waterpolo venues in Budapest, this means one of its pools may be given over to the players on weekdays. 1700Ft. Daily 6am–7pm.

Gellért Gyógyfürdő XI, Kelenhegyi út 4 ☎ 1 466 6166, ⊚ gellertbath.com. The most popular of the city's baths, and also one of the oldest – although nothing remains of the medieval buildings – the Gellért has it all: a magnificent main pool for swimming, hot pools for sitting around in both inside and outside on the terrace, fabulous Art Nouveau steam baths, and a large outdoor area, including a wave machine in the main pool (May–Aug) and shaded terraces. To enjoy the waters you must first reach the changing rooms by a labyrinth of passages. At the far end of the pool are steps leading down to the separate thermal baths, with segregated areas and ornate plunge pools for men and women. The Gellért attracts a lot of foreigners, and many of the attendants speak German or English. Mon–Fri 3800ft with locker, 4100Ft with cabin; Sat & Sun 4000ft with locker, 4300Ft with cabin. Daily 6am–8pm.

Hajós Alfred Sport Uszoda XIII, southern end of Margit-sziget. One of the nicest places for proper swimming, this is a beautiful 1930s lido renovated for the 2001 European waterpolo championships. There's a small sauna, and two large outdoor pools against a backdrop of trees; one is normally given over to waterpolo. In the winter you can swim out along a channel to the larger of the pools

without walking outside. 1700Ft. Mon–Fri 6am–5pm, Sat & Sun 6am–6pm.

Király Gyógyfürdő II, Fő utca 84 ☎ 1 202 3688. Fabulous Turkish baths, in the Víziváros in Buda, easy to spot thanks to the four copper cupolas. This was formerly the most popular of the steam baths with the gay community, but is now mixed sex every day. The main pool under the cupola is surrounded by smaller – hotter and cooler – pools, with doors leading off to the steam massage rooms. 2200Ft with cabin. Daily 9am–9pm.

Lukács Fürdő II, Frankl Leó út 25–29 ☎ 1 326 1695. This spa complex just north of the Margit híd in Buda has four small but delightful open-air pools, as well as mud baths and a medical treatment section – its waters are said to be good for rheumatism, arthritis and other complaints. The open-air facilities, including a thermal pool, a cooler and smaller swimming pool, and a bubbling pool with whirling currents, are in two intimate courtyards. Enter via the folly-like drinking hall (where you can take a sample) and head round to the left (past plaques declaring gratitude in different languages from those who have benefited from the medicinal waters), following the signs for the *uszoda* (pool). The swimming pool and adjacent baths are mixed. Mon–Fri 2600ft with locker, 3000Ft with cabin; Sat & Sun 2700ft with locker, 3100Ft with cabin. Daily 6am–8pm.

Palatinus Strand XIII, Margit-sziget ☎ 1 340 4505. Set among a sprawling park halfway up the island on the west side, the Palatinus is the city's most popular pool, with a large outdoor set of pools, including a wave pool and children's pools, all set in a big expanse of grass. Other facilities include football pitches and volleyball courts, as

19

well as snack bars. The sunroof above the changing rooms is something of a gay centre. Mon–Fri 2200ft with locker; Mon, Tues & Thurs after 4pm 1500Ft; Sat & Sun 2500Ft. June–Aug daily 9am–8pm.

Rác Gyógyfürdő I, Hadnagy utca 8–10. One of the oldest baths – the medieval King Mátyás is said to have used the baths on this site in the Tabán – but nothing remains from those times. It was closed at the time of writing, pending redevelopment of the new *Rácz Hotel & Spa* complex.

Rudas Gyógyfürdő I, Döbrentei tér 9 ☎ 1 356 1322. One of the city's original Turkish baths, at the Buda end of the Erzsébet híd, this is at its best when the sun shines through the holes in the dome to light up the beautiful interior. The steam baths were for many years a male preserve, but women now get a day to themselves (Tues). There's an apron system in the steam section on single-sex days, but swimming costumes are compulsory on mixed days (Fri night, Sat & Sun). There is also a nineteenth-century swimming pool, open to both sexes, to the left of the main entrance – normal swimwear compulsory here. Mon–Fri 2800Ft, Sat & Sun 3000Ft, Fri & Sat night 3500Ft. Daily 6am–8pm, plus Fri & Sat night swimming 10pm–4am.

Széchenyi Fürdő XIV, Állatkerti körút 11 ☎ 1 363 3210, ⓦ szechenyibath.com. A magnificent nineteenth-century complex in the Városliget, with its entrance opposite the entrance to the Budapest Circus. There are sixteen pools in all, including the various medicinal sections, but you'll probably use just the three outdoor ones: the hot pool where people play chess (bring your own chess set if you want to play); a pool for swimming (bathing caps compulsory); and a whirlpool. Across the far side of the hot pool from the changing rooms is a mixed sauna with a maze of hot and cold pools. Mon–Fri 3100Ft for locker, 3200Ft for cabin; Sat & Sun 3350Ft for locker, 3500Ft for cabin. Daily 6am–10pm.

19

THE ZOO

Kids' Budapest

Budapest offers a healthy range of activities for kids, from adventure and roller-skating parks, to indoor play centres and state-of-the-art playgrounds. Moreover, the zoo – always a sure-fire hit with the little ones – is one of the most impressive anywhere in the region. There's plenty by way of artistic entertainment, too, and the capital retains a strong tradition of children's theatre – particularly puppetry – and dance. Don't expect anything too high-tech, however, as a lack of cash dogs many of the facilities, but many of the city's playgrounds have been refurbished in recent years, and plenty of places have activities specifically for children, from the Palace of Arts, which has events most weekends, to the Millenáris Park with its regular workshops. Concessions for under-14s are available at most attractions.

Budapest's public transport – under-6s travel free – will keep children happily entertained. Trams are an endless source of fun, the best ride being along the embankment in tram #2. Across the water, the Sikló (see p.101) is a great experience, rising up above the rooftops from the Lánchíd to the Royal Palace. A popular way for families to spend an afternoon in the Buda Hills is to go on the "railway circuit" – the Cogwheel Railway, the Children's Railway and the chairlift (see p.24) – though the last of these can be unnerving for smaller children. From April to October there's the added thrill of boat rides on the Danube – either short tours of the city up to Margit-sziget and back, or further afield to Szentendre and on to Esztergom – though for young children, boredom is less likely to kick in on the shorter rides. Throughout the summer there are lots of craft activities and children's entertainment at the Open-Air Museum in Szentendre, and a lot of the summer festivals also have craft stalls and activities for children, such as the August 20 festivities around the Royal Palace. If you want more ideas for keeping children occupied, you might want to track down *Benjamin in Budapest*, a very enthusiastic city guide for children that you can find in larger bookshops in Budapest.

PLAYGROUNDS, PARKS AND OUTDOOR ACTIVITIES

Caves Underground Buda is good fun for children as long as they aren't scared of the dark. The caves under the Várhegy (see p.94) offer some underground exploration, while the Pálvölgyi and Szemlőhegyi Caves (p.116) display dramatic geological formations. Note the Pálvölgyi doesn't admit children under 5.

Challengeland (Kalandpálya) XII, Konkoly Thege Miklós út 21 ⓦ kalandpalya.com. Up in the Buda Hills and offering some of the city's best in outdoor fun, this is a real adventure playground, where children over 100cm in height can go on ropewalks and swing from tree to tree. The shade of the trees makes this a good place to take kids on hot days. Safety is paramount here and all children have to go through a mini-course on how to work the safety harnesses. The website has films showing what's on offer: click on *belépés*. To get there, take the Children's Railway to Csillebérc Station, or catch the #21 bus from Széll Kálmán tér. Entry 2900–3900Ft depending on the height of child – this is for a 3hr 30min session. It is also worth renting gloves (200Ft). April–Oct daily 10am–6pm; Nov–March Sat & Sun 10am–5pm.

Görzenál Skatepark III, Árpád fejedelem útja ⓦ gorzenal.hu. Space to rollerblade, skateboard and cycle, with ramps and jumps, all to your heart's content. You can get here by taking the Szentendre HÉV to Timár utca. Entry is 400Ft, but 600Ft Fri–Sun and holidays. Mon–Fri 2pm–dusk, Sat & Sun 9.30am–dusk.

Kids' Park (Kölyökpark) II, Mammut 2 (shop 328), Lövőház utca 1–5 ☏ 1 345 8512. Indoor play area (for ages 1–11) in a city mall that comes into its own on wet days. You pay 800Ft for half an hour's use of slides, climbing walls and more – parents can leave the kids here while they go shopping. Mon–Sat 10am–9pm, Sun 9am–8pm.

Margit-sziget See p.116. The island in the middle of the Danube is a great open space where you can rent bikes, pedaloes and electric cars, leaving from the strange sculpture at the southern end of the island. The Palatinus lido (see p.117) has a wave machine and lots of small pools for kids – there have been issues about locker security here, so don't take all your valuables. The petting zoo across on the eastern side has been vastly improved, and the varied scenery and open areas for frisbee and ball games all create a very pleasant atmosphere.

Playgrounds Since central Budapest is still very residential, there are a lot of playgrounds in squares and parks, such as the Károlyi kert near the Astoria (Belváros), Szabadság tér (Lipótváros), Klauzál tér (Erzsébetváros), on the Margit-sziget and at several locations in the Városliget, one of the best being near Dembinsky utca, while in Buda you can find them at the Millenáris Park near Széll Kálmán tér (see p.104), on the Gellért-hegy and at the Feneketlen tó (see p.108).

Tropicarium See p.126. You can get close to the sharks, feed the stingray and experience the rainforests in this huge aquarium-terrarium in southern Buda.

Városliget See p.71. The park has the largest concentration of activities and attractions for children: playgrounds, the zoo (see p.73), a circus and a fairground. The Széchenyi Baths (see p.196) are popular with bigger children – especially the large outdoor hot pool and the whirlpool – but it's not a great place for splashing around in as the old ladies don't want their hairdos messed up. For those who prefer to stay above water level, there's also rowing in summer and ice-skating in winter (Nov–March Mon–Fri 9am–1pm & 4–8pm, Sat & Sun 10am–2pm & 4–8pm, depending on the weather) on the lake by Hősök tere.

Zoo (Állatkert) See p.73. With its visionary director, the zoo gets better every year. Kids can feed the camels and giraffes, watch the polar bears swimming or stroke the farm animals in the petting farm, and explore attractions such as the Palm House with its tropical birds and alligators, or the Crocodile House. There's also the **Zoo Funhouse** (Állatkert Játszóház; ⓦjatekmester.hu), a brilliant indoor playcentre for babies, toddlers and children aged up to 10. In addition to a well-constructed activity centre, there's also the chance to be taken by the zookeepers to see the animals being fed. You can enter from the zoo (600Ft/ hr in addition to the zoo ticket), or from the street entrance between the zoo and the circus (1200Ft/hr – includes visit to the zoo). Prices are higher at weekends. Daily 9am–8pm.

MUSEUMS

Hospital in the Rock See p.94. With gory waxworks, spooky Cold War bunkers and an excellent guided tour, this could be great fun for kids (especially boys) – but unfortunately you can't run around or touch anything and admission charges are steep.

Hungarian Open-Air Museum See p.134. Children's programmes every weekend, a playground and frequent folk-craft and folk-dancing displays in this museum outside Szentendre, north of the city.

Natural History Museum See p.84. Full of colour and activity, with interactive games and lots to look at, plenty of it at child height. Well thought out, it certainly grabs children's attention. Across the road is the Botanical Garden (p.84).

Palace of Miracles See p.104. This great interactive playhouse in the Millenáris Park has loads of activities for children which serve as a back-door way of explaining scientific principles, such as gravity. Good explanations in English.

Railway History Park See p.125. Strong child appeal here: lots of big old engines and carriages, and in summer you can even drive an engine yourself.

Telephone Museum See p.94. A hands-on museum, which is a rarity in Budapest; children enjoy sending faxes and calling one another on vintage phones.

Transport Museum Városliget; see p.72. Vehicles, trams, ships and trains of all kinds and sizes, plus model train sets that run every hour until 5pm. Across the way, on the first floor of the Petőfi Csarnok, is an Aviation and Space Flight display.

THEATRE, DANCE AND OTHER ACTIVITIES

20

The fact that successful music ensembles such as the Budapest Festival Orchestra and the folk group Muzsikás hold regular events designed specifically for children says a lot about Hungarian attitudes to young people. Members of the orchestra introduce children to their musical instruments, while Muzsikás invite children to take their first steps in Hungarian folk-dancing – both of these events are conducted primarily in Hungarian but non-Hungarian speakers will still enjoy them. Budapest also has a strong tradition in **puppetry**, and many big Hungarian writers have contributed to its children's repertoire. There are some English-language performances, but again, puppet shows are good visual entertainment even without the language. Morning and matinée performances are for kids. Tickets are available from the puppet theatres (*bábszínház;* see p.188) or the ticket offices listed on p.185.

Budapest Festival Orchestra Cocoa Concerts III, Selmeci utca 14–16, Óbuda ☎1 388 6538, ⓦbfz.hu; the website has details of dates. The ensemble, under its inspirational leader Iván Fischer, holds hour-long Cocoa concerts (*Kakaó koncert*) for children aged 5–12. Members of the orchestra introduce children to the music and the instruments – and give them a cup of cocoa, too. The concerts are usually every other month on either a Saturday or a Sunday at 2.30pm and 4.30pm; tickets cost 2500Ft.

Budapest Puppet Theatre (Budapest Bábszínház) VI, Andrássy út 69 ☎1 342 2702, ⓦbudapest-babszinhaz .hu (see p.188). One of the most established puppet theatres – it also does shows for adults.

Kalamajka Children's Dance House Aranytíz Club V, Arany János utca 10 ☎1 354 3400, ⓦaranytizhu (see p.187). Children can take to the dancefloor and learn Hungarian folk dance steps to music played by leading folk musicians. Afterwards it's the turn of the grown-ups. Late Sept to May Sat 5–6pm.

Kolibri Theatre (Színház) VI, Jókai tér 10 ☎1 353 4633 and **Kolibri Nest** (Fészek) VI, Andrássy út 74 ☎1 311 0870, ⓦkolibriszinhaz.hu. The Kolibri venues have shows for children of all ages, but those at the Kolibri Fészek are usually better for smaller children. Closed early June to Aug.

Millenáris Park See p.104. Regular children's programmes are put on in the *Fogadó* building here, including puppet shows, craft workshops and more.

Muzsikás Children's Dance House TEMI Fővarosi Művelődési Háza, XI, Fehérvári út 47 ⓦmuzsikas.hu. While members of the Muzsikás folk band – if they are not away on tour – play, two dancers take children (and their parents) through some basic steps, chanting Hungarian children's songs and rhymes – but non-Hungarian children will enjoy the dancing anyway. Sessions are held most Tuesdays at 5.30pm from Sept–May, and cost 400Ft for children, 700Ft for adults; you pay at the door. The Capital Cultural Centre, as the venue is called in English, is a couple of stops beyond Móricz Zsigmond körtér on trams #18 and #47.

Shopping

Budapest's shopping scene has been transformed in recent years by the mushrooming of international chain stores and the opening of modern shopping malls across the city. The malls have brought in long opening hours and a bright new style that sets the pace for other shops. Still holding their own, however, are numerous small backstreet shops, which continue to preserve local crafts and traditions. Budapest also has a set of distinguished market halls (*vásárcsarnok*) dating from the late nineteenth century, some of which still function as food markets; others have been turned into supermarkets, though you can still admire their structure. There are also some outdoor markets (*piac*), which are more lively affairs, with smallholders coming into town to sell their produce. Whatever you're after, Budapest has become an enticing proposition.

21

One feature of old Budapest that has survived is its **artisan shops**: whether it's the small jewellery workshops such as Wladis, the quirky brush shop in Dob utca and the old craftsmen and workshops in the backstreets inside the Nagykörút, or the growing number of young fashion designers whose work is deservedly attracting attention. Look out for Emilia Anda, Edina Farkas, Anikó Németh and Katti Zoób, whose clothes range from the trendy to the avant-garde and the eccentrically unwearable. One event not to miss is the Wamp design market (ⓦwamp.hu); taking place every month on Erzsébet tér, it showcases the work of emerging Hungarian designers, with some one hundred vendors selling everything from clothes and jewellery to home decor.

ESSENTIALS

Shopping areas The main shopping areas are located to the south of Vörösmarty tér in central Pest, in particular in and around pedestrianized Váci utca, which has the biggest concentration of glamorous and expensive shops, as well as branches of popular Western stores. It is also, however, full of tourist tat. The nearby Deák Ferenc utca has been jazzed up as "Fashion Street" and attracted names such as Sisley, Tommy Hilfiger and Benetton. The main streets radiating out from the centre – Bajcsy-Zsilinszky út, Andrássy út and Rákóczi út – are other major shopping focuses, as are the Nagykörút (especially between Margit híd and Blaha Lujza tér) and the Kiskörút. Shops in the Vár are almost exclusively given over to

providing foreign tourists with folksy souvenirs such as embroidered tablecloths, hussar pots and fancy bottles of Tokaj wine.

Opening times Most shops are open Monday to Friday between 10am and 6pm, and Saturday until 2pm, with food stores generally operating from 8am to 6 or 7pm. Some shops in the centre of the city have extended hours on Saturdays, while the malls are open roughly 10am to 8pm every day, but close around 6pm on Sunday. You can usually find a 24-hour outlet selling alcohol, cigarettes and some food in the centre of town. It's useful to recognize that "Azonnal jövök" or "Rögtön jövök" signs on shop doors both mean "back shortly".

MARKETS AND MARKET HALLS

Bio-piac XII, Csörsz utca 18; map p.87. Organic market behind the Mom Cultural Centre (Mom Művelődési Központ), up the road from the Mom Park Mall. Great range of produce, especially in summer – the peaches, tomatoes and peppers are so much better than supermarket fare. There is also a playground for children. The odd right-wing nationalist stalls should not bother visitors. Sat 6.30am–noon.

Fény utca II, at the back of the Mammut mall, by Széll Kálmán tér; map p.87. Popular market that has survived a transfer to a modern setting. Fruit and veg stalls on the street level floor, and meat and cheese counters on the upper floor, alongside one of the best *lángos* kiosks in town – a popular stand-up snack of fried dough eaten with garlic, sour cream, cheese or all three together. Mon–Fri 6am–6pm, Sat 6am–2pm.

★ **Great Market Hall** IX, Vámház körút 2; map p.77. By the Szabadság híd at the bottom end of Váci utca, the Nagycsarnok is the largest and finest market hall of them all, as well as being the most expensive. Fruit, veg, meat and cheese counters galore, as well as bakers, confectioners and endless paprika stalls, though it's all rather hammed

up for the tourists. Mon 6am–5pm, Tues–Fri 6am–6pm, Sat 6am–3pm.

Hold utca V, Hold utca 13; map p.48. Right behind the American Embassy, this fine nineteenth-century market hall still has some smaller holders selling their produce. Mon 6.30am–5pm, Tues–Fri 6.30am–6pm, Sat 6am–2pm.

Hunyadi tér VI; map p.58. Another of the old market halls, free of any modernization with stalls full of colourful produce spilling out into the square in front. Mon 7am–5pm, Tues–Fri 7am–6pm, Sat 7am–2pm.

Klauzál tér VII; map p.58. Pitched right in the heart of the old Jewish quarter, most of the fruit and veg stands have been squeezed out into the entrance passage by a supermarket, but it's still worth visiting if you're in the area. Mon–Fri 6am–5pm, Sat 6am–1pm.

Lehel Hall XIII, Lehel tér; map p.48. Large, popular market housed in a wacky, and rather ugly, market hall designed by the former dissident László Rajk – whatever you think of the exterior, it's a lively place inside with lots of small stalls. Mon–Fri 6.30am–6pm, Sat 6.30am–2pm.

FLEA MARKETS

Ecseri piac XIX, Nagykőrösi út; bus #54 (red) from the Határ út metro stop on the blue line, or bus #54 (black) from Boráros tér by Petőfi híd; map p.5. On the southeast edge of the city, this has become a well-known spot for tourists – and for ripping them off (you'll

need to bargain hard). Stalls sell everything from bike parts and jackboots to peasant clothing and hand-carved pipes, with a few genuine antiques among the tat. Mon–Fri 8am–4pm, Sat 6am–3pm, Sun 9am–1pm.

21

Petőfi Csarnok XIV, Zichy Mihály utca 14; map p.69. A weekend flea market in and around the "Pecsa", the ugly cultural centre in the Városliget, this is smaller than Ecseri, and less established. Lots of the wares are junk, but there are some good bargains too. Small entry fee. Sat & Sun 8am–2pm.

MALLS

Mammut II, Lövőház utca 2–6 ☎ 1 345 8020, ⓦ mammut.hu; map p.87. Close to Széll Kálmán tér, and next to Fény utca market, this is actually two malls linked by a pedestrianized bridge. Amid the 300 or so shops, there's a cinema, fitness centre, squash courts, children's play area and nappy-changing room. Mon–Sat 10am–9pm, Sun 10am–6pm.

Mom Park XII, Alkotás utca 53 ☎ 1 487 5500, ⓦ mompark.hu; tram #61; map p.87. One of the newer malls, up the road from Déli metro station, and with more than seventy shops, a cinema and a fitness centre. Mon–Sat 10am–8pm, Sun 10am–6pm.

WestEnd City Center VI, Váci út 1–3 (next to Nyugati Station) ☎ 1 238 7777, ⓦ westend.hu; map p.48. Past the grand indoor waterfall cascading down at the southern entrance, you'll find the city's busiest mall, with over 400 shops (including lots of familiar brand-name stores), cinema and a huge food court. Mon–Sat 10am–9pm, Sun 10am–6pm.

ANTIQUES

Falk Miksa utca, running south off Szent István körút, near the Pest end of the Margit híd, is known as Budapest's "Street of Antiques", and is where you'll find the biggest collection of **antique stores** and galleries. Three or four times a year the street holds an evening festival of music, entertainment and, of course, antiques. There are also a couple of outlets on Kossuth Lajos utca, between Ferenciek tere and the *Astoria Hotel*. Most antique specialists should be able to advise on what you can export from the country and how to go about it. Several shops organize **auctions**; the best months for these are April, May, September and December – check the free hotel magazine *Where Budapest* for dates. Another good source of antiques are the flea markets listed on p.201, though you'll need to be wary about parting with large sums of money, as stallholders can charge hugely inflated prices.

BÁV V, Bécsi utca 1–3 ☎ 1 429 3020; map p.38. The biggest of numerous BÁV outlets in the city, this store specializes in paintings, jewellery and other treasures. BÁV is primarily an auction house, and it holds regular auctions here. Mon–Fri 10am–6pm, Sat 10am–2pm.

Judaica VII, Wesselényi utca 13 ☎ 1 354 1560; map p.58. Down the road behind the Dohány utca synagogue, and offering Jewish books, pictures and artefacts. It also organizes occasional auctions. Mon–Thurs 10am–6pm, Fri 10am–3pm.

★ **Sóos Foto** VII, Wesselényi utca 10 ☎ 1 317 2341; map p.58. An excellent place to pick up some fine junk and secondhand photographic goods. Mon–Fri 9am–5pm, Sat 10am–1pm.

ART AND PHOTOGRAPHY GALLERIES

★ **ACB** VI, Király utca 76 ☎ 1 413 7608, ⓦ acbgaleria .hu; map p.58. Contemporary fine arts with a friendly, well-informed management, up the road from the Music Academy. Tues–Fri 2–6pm, Sat noon–4pm or by appointment.

Deák Erika Galéria VI, Mozsár utca 1 ☎ 1 201 3740, ⓦ deakgaleria.hu; map p.58. Contemporary Hungarian art gallery off Andrássy út. Wed–Fri noon–6pm, Sat 11am–4pm.

Dovin Galéria V, Galamb utca 6 ☎ 1 318 3659, ⓦ dovin .hu; map p.38. Elegant gallery in central Pest selling contemporary Hungarian art. Tues–Fri noon–6pm, Sat 11am–3pm.

★ **Ernst Galéria** V, Irányi utca 27 ☎ 1 266 4016, ⓦ ernstgaleria.hu; map p.38. Across from the Centrál Kávéház, this terrific shop keeps a superb stock of rare vintage posters, mostly of the Communist-era propaganda kind, but there are some choice film ones too – they don't come cheap, mind. Mon–Fri 10am–7pm, Sat 10am–2pm.

Knoll VI, Liszt Ferenc tér 10 ☎ 1 267 3842, ⓦ knollgaleria.hu; map p.58. Run by the Viennese gallery owner Hans Knoll, this was the first private gallery in the city when it opened in 1989. Since then, it has built up a strong reputation, with shows by Hungarian and foreign contemporary artists. Tues–Fri 2–6.30pm, Sat 11am–2pm.

★ **Mai Manó Galéria** VI, Nagymező utca 20 ☎ 1 473 2669 ⓦ maimano.hu; map p.58. Located on the first floor within the Hungarian House of Photography, this delightful little gallery/shop stocks contemporary and old Hungarian photographs, cards and books. Mon–Fri 2–7pm, Sat & Sun 11am–7pm.

Várfok Galéria I, Várfok utca 14 ☎ 1 213 5155, ⓦ varfok-galeria.hu; map p.87. The best known of the three small galleries just off Széll Kálmán tér, the gallery was founded in 1990 and displays work by the younger generation of Hungarian avant-garde artists. Tues–Sat 11am–6pm.

BOOKS AND MAPS

Hungarians love their books and Budapestis' homes tend to be crammed with literature – Book Week each June is a long-awaited event. Bookshops stock a good range of photographic albums, books about the city and foreign-language books. The English language is particularly well represented, to the extent that there are several bookshops selling books in English only. If it's old books and prints you want, one of the best places to head for is Múzeum körút, where there are numerous **secondhand bookshops** (*antikvárium*) clustered opposite the Hungarian National Museum – though the range of English books it stocks is variable.

Alexandra VI, Andrássy út 39 ☎1 484 8000, ⓦalexandra.hu; map p.58. Occupying the magnificent Paris Department store, this is the flagship store of the chain, with three vast floors of browsing; the English language section – with lots of good Hungarian fiction – is to the rear of the ground floor. While here, it'd be remiss not to visit the sumptuous coffee salon on the first floor. Its branch by the Dohány utca synagogue at Károly körút 3 has a secondhand section upstairs as well as a pleasant covered rooftop café. Both branches daily 10am–10pm.

★ **Bestsellers** V, Október 6 utca 11 ☎1 312 1295, ⓦbestsellers.hu; map p.48. Budapest's oldest and best English-language bookshop, with thousands of titles; English and Hungarian literature, travel and reference, academia and children's books, as well as newspapers and magazines. Staff are friendly and can order books in. Mon–Fri 9am–6.30pm, Sat 10am–5pm, Sun 10am–4pm.

CEU bookshop V, Zrinyi utca 12 ☎1 327 3096; map p.48. Just around the corner from Bestsellers, and attached to the Central European University, this has mainly academic books, though there is a comprehensive selection of Hungarian literature in English. Mon–Fri 10am–7pm, Sat 10am–2pm.

Földgömb-Térkép VI, Bajcsy-Zsilinszky út 37; map p.58. A well-stocked map shop, but you have to ask the staff for the maps you want, which makes browsing difficult. Mon–Fri 9am–5pm.

★ **Írók Boltja** VI, Andrássy út 45 ☎1 322 1645; map p.58. On the premises of the prewar *Japán* coffee house, the beautiful "Writers' Bookshop" has a wide range of Hungarian fiction in translation upstairs, and a good selection of photography, art and architecture books in the main part of the shop. You can drink coffee and read at the tables in the front. Mon–Fri 10am–7pm, Sat 11am–3pm (July & Aug closed Sat).

Központi Antikvárium V, Múzeum körút 17; map p.77. Large secondhand bookshop with some antiquarian books and prints, plus maps. Mon–Fri 10am–6pm, Sat 10am–2pm.

Libra VIII, Kölcsey utca 2 ☎1 483 0659; map p.77. Sectioned into two parts; the main shop specializes in English-language teaching books, and the other, across the road, offers general fiction, history and the like. There's also a small café here in which you can mull over a few books. Mon–Fri 9am–7pm, Sat 9am–1pm.

Libri V, Váci utca 22 and Rákóczi út 12; (map p.38). The *Stúdium* branch in Váci utca is a foreign language specialist store, and has a good stock of books on Hungary. The store on Rákóczi út has a large stock of English-language travel books, as well as some excellent hiking maps. Mon–Fri 10am–7.30pm, Sat–Sun 10am–3pm.

Red Bus V, Semmelweis utca 14 ☎1 337 7453, ⓦredbusbudapest.hu; map p.38. Next to the hostel of the same name, Red Bus is devoted to secondhand English-language books, from fiction and history to travel, sport, cooking and poetry. Mon–Fri 11am–6pm, Sat 10am–2pm.

Térképkirály VI, Bajcsy-Zsilinszky út 21; map p.58. Range of maps and guidebooks across the road from Arany János utca metro station. Also sells BKV public transport tickets. Mon–Sat 8am–8pm.

★ **Treehugger Dan** VI, Csengery utca 48 ☎1 704 6303 ⓦtreehugger.hu; map p.58. Tiny and easy to miss shop just off Andrássy út that's packed with secondhand English books; lots of classic fiction, history and travel, as well as a decent display of Central and Eastern European authors in translation. Good gay and lesbian section too. You can also loiter here over a smoke-free cup of organic Fairtrade tea, coffee or chocolate and use the wi-fi access. There's another branch in the Discover Budapest/Yellow Zebra office behind the Opera at VI, Lázár utca 16. Csengery branch Mon–Fri 10am–6pm, Sat 10am–4pm; Lázár utca branch Mon–Fri 9.30am–6.30pm, Sat & Sun 10am–4pm.

CLOTHES AND SHOES

Eclectick V, Irányi utca 20 ☎1 255 3341, ⓦeclectick .hu; map p.38. Vibrant streetwear and accessories designed by Edina Farkas, and a retro shop – toys and more – in the basement. Mon–Fri 10am–6pm, Sat 11am–4pm.

Emilia Anda V, Galamb utca 4 ☎1 337 2354, ⓦandaemi.com; map p.38. One of the most highly regarded Hungarian couturiers, Anda designs classy day and evening wear for women, and a range of jewellery including chunky rings and beautiful pendants. Mon–Fri 11am–6pm, Sat 11am–2pm.

Fleischer Shirts VI, Paulay Ede utca 53 ☎1 267 4756; map p.58. Old-fashioned shirt-maker selling handmade garments at good prices. On the corner of

21

Nagymező utca, 5min walk from the Opera House. Mon–Fri 10am–6pm.

Havalda Leather VI, Hajós utca 23 ☎1 30 361 5945, ⓦhavalda.hu; map p.58. Leather shop opened in 1938 by the grandparents of the present owner. Bags, belts and jewellery, as well as dog leads and collars, and loads more. Bespoke items made on site, for which there is a two- to three-day wait. Open Mon–Fri 11am–7pm.

Iguana VIII, Krúdy Gyula utca 9 ☎1 317 1627; map p.77. A packed, colourful shop selling all kinds of 1950s, 1960s and 1970s retro fashion – clothes, bags, music, sunglasses and jewellery. Mon–Fri 10am–6pm, Sat 10am–2pm.

★ **Katti Zoób** V, Szent István körút 17 ☎1 312 1865, ⓦkattizoob.com; map p.48. Among the band of young designers who've made a big splash with their products, Zoób is one of the most successful, and uses gorgeous fabrics. She has also collaborated with the porcelain company Zsolnay to produce jewellery. Her store is inside the courtyard to the right. Mon–Fri 10am–6pm, Sat 10am–1pm.

Manier VI, Hajós utca 12 ☎1 354 1878, ⓦmanier.hu; map p.58. Zany, appealing clothes by Anikó Németh; the designs have calmed down from the Baroque early days but they retain plenty of inventiveness. The first-floor shop/workshop is at V, Nyáry Pál utca 4, just off the lower half of Váci utca (appointment only). Mon–Sat 11am–7pm.

★ **Tisza Shoes** VII, Károly körút 1 ☎1 266 3055; map p.58. This Hungarian brand of trainers is an unlikely survivor of the Communist era, and the shop at the Astoria junction, Tisza Cipő, has won an international reputation for the hipness of the shoes. Mon–Fri 10am–7pm, Sat 9am–1pm.

Valéria Fazekas V, Váci utca 50 ☎1 337 5320; map p.38. Another of the more creative places on the lower part of Váci utca, this small shop produces delightful hats, some wacky and some very wearable. Mon–Fri 10am–6pm, Sat 10am–4pm.

Vass V, Haris köz 2 ☎1 318 2375; map p.38. One of several fine shoemakers along this street, this traditional outfit, just behind Ferenciek tere, produces handmade shoes to order and ready-to-wear. Mon–Fri 10am–6pm, Sat 10am–2pm.

POTTERY, JEWELLERY AND CRAFTS

Brush Shop VII, Dob utca 3; map p.58. A wonderful little place: every kind of brush you can think of in this very traditional artisan's shop. Mon–Fri 10am–6pm, Sat 10am–1pm.

★ **Haas & Czjzek** VI, Bajcsy-Zsilinszky út 23 ☎1 311 4094, ⓦporcelan.hu; map p.58. This lovely shop, dating back to 1792, offers a full selection of Hungarian porcelain, including Hollóháza, Alföld and Zsolnay, and some glassware. Mon–Fri 10am–7pm, Sat 10am–3pm.

Herend V, József nádor tér 11 (☎1 317 2622) & VI, Andrássy út 16 (☎1 374 0006) ⓦherend.com; (map p.58). Very fancy – some would say twee – and expensive porcelain from the Herend factory in western Hungary, as collected by the likes of Queen Victoria. Both shops Mon–Fri 10am–6pm, Sat 10am–2pm.

Holló Folk Art Gallery V, Vitkovics Mihály utca 10 ☎1 317 8103; map p.38. This beautiful early nineteenth-century shop near the Astoria is a very pleasant place in which to browse wares such as intricately iced gingerbread figures, and wooden furniture, boxes, eggs and candlesticks, all hand-painted with bird, tulip and heart folk motifs. Mon–Fri 10am–6pm, Sat 10am–2pm.

Intuita V, Váci utca 67; map p.38. Amid the tourist tat at the main market hall end of Váci utca, this shop stands out for its quality Hungarian pottery and jewellery. Intuita 2, just along the road, is the place to go for hats and bags. Both Mon–Fri 10am–6pm, Sat 10am–2pm.

★ **Ómama Bizsúja** V, Szent István körút 1 ☎1 312 6812; map p.48. A tiny treasure-trove of a shop – its entrance is tucked in to the left as you walk down the passageway that leads from the street at the Pest end of the Margit híd. Absolutely crammed full of jewellery – in among the more glitzy costume jewellery there are some stunning Deco-style pieces and good-quality paste. Mon–Fri 10am–6pm, Sat 10am–1pm.

Wladis Galéria V, Falk Miksa utca 13 ☎1 354 0834, ⓦwladisgaleria.hu; map p.48. Founded by a lecturer at the Applied Arts College the workshop produces very appealing chunky silver jewellery at a price: rings from 20,000Ft and earrings from 29,000Ft. Mon–Fri 10am–6pm, Sat 10am–1pm.

PHOTOS

Fotólabor VIII, Gyulai Pál utca 14; map p.77. Good black and white prints done very cheaply, and photos developed and enlarged. Mon–Fri 8am–6pm.

Fotolux VII, Károly körút 21; map p.58. Good-quality photographic developing and printing, and professional films. Mon–Fri 9am–9pm, Sat 9am–7pm.

RECORDS AND CDS

★ **Fóno** XI, Sztregova utca 3 ☎1 206 5300, ⓦfono.hu; map p.108. It's a 20min tram ride from Deák tér on #47 to get to the shop in the bar of this folk club, but it's worth the effort for the range of jazz, ethno-jazz blues and world music and, above all, Hungarian folk CDs. Mon & Tues 2–6pm, Wed–Fri 2–10pm, Sat 7–10pm.

Kodály Zoltán Zeneműbolt V, Múzeum körút 21; map p.38. Scores of CDs, tapes and secondhand Hungarian classical records, opposite the *Múzeum Cukrászda*. Good jazz and folk section too. Mon–Fri 10am–6pm, Sat 9am–1pm.

Lemezdokk VIII, Horánszky utca 27; map p.77. Quirky little den just off Krúdy Gyula utca, with lots of old vinyl as well as some CDs; they have blues, rock and some jazz. A jumble of secondhand equipment too. Mon–Fri 11am–7pm Sat 11am–2pm.

★ **MesterPorta** I, Corvin tér 7 ☎1 486 1189; map p.87. The outlet for Etnofon Records, one of the most active publishers of Hungarian and other folk music, and also sells instruments and sheet music. The shop is a tram stop down from Batthyány tér. Mon–Fri 10am–6pm.

Rózsavölgyi Zeneműbolt V, Szervita tér 5 ☎1 318 3500; map p.38. Long-established record shop with a knowledgeable staff, near Vörösmarty tér. Classical music on the ground floor, rock and folk downstairs. It has a concert ticket office at the back, and is good for sheet music as well. Mon–Fri 9.30am–7pm (Wed 10am), Sat 10am–5pm.

★ **Wave** VI, Révay köz 1 ☎1 269 0754; map p.58. Cool, independent shop off the bottom of Bajcsy-Zsilinszky út, with wall-to-wall vinyl and racks of CDs; mainly indie-rock, but also underground, folk and Roma. It also sells tickets to concerts. Mon–Fri 11am–7pm, Sat 11am–3pm.

TOYS

★ **Fakopáncs** VIII, Baross utca 46 ☎1 337 0992, ⓦfakopancs.hu; map p.77. A massive array of wooden puzzles, toys and models, and sweet little cotton finger puppets, in the wonderful "Woodpecker" shop, near the junction of Baross utca and the Nagykörút. It has smaller outlets at József körút 50 and Erzsébet körút 23. Mon–Fri 10am–6pm, Sat 9am–1pm.

★ **Játékszerek anno** VI, Teréz körút 54 ☎1 302 6234; map p.58. Gorgeous little shop with beautifully made reproductions of toys and games from the turn of the last century, including wooden tops, kaleidoscopes, and a spectacular wind-up duck on a bicycle. Mon–Fri 10am–6pm, Sat 9am–1pm.

Modell Makett VII, Erzsébet körút 51 ☎1 351 2335; map p.58. Small shop selling models and do-it-yourself kits of buses, cars, trams and trains. Mon–Fri 10am–6pm, Sat 10am–1pm (July & Aug closed Sat).

FOOD, WINE AND PÁLINKA

Bamo VII, Dob utca 16 ☎70 632 2771; map p.58. On the edge of the Jewish quarter, a couple of minutes' walk from the Dohány utca synagogue, this is one of the few shops in Budapest selling kosher Hungarian and imported wines and foods. Mon–Thurs 8am–8pm, Fri 8am–6pm, Sun 10am–4pm.

Bio ABC V, Múzeum körút 19; map p.38. Stacks of great organic products in this large store opposite the National Museum; natural oils, organic fruits, juices and teas, pastas, pulses and herbal medicines. Mon–Fri 10am–7pm, Sat 10am–2pm.

★ **Bor Bortársaság** V, Vécsey utca 5 ☎1 269 3286, ⓦbortarsasag.hu; map p.48. The largest branch of what's become the major distributor of Hungary's leading producers, with excellent wines and knowledgeable staff. There are three more outlets in the centre: Batthyány utca 59 (up the hill from Széll Kálmán tér), Lánchíd utca 5 and Ráday utca 7. Vécsey utca branch Mon–Fri 10am–8pm, Sat 10am–7pm.

★ **In Vino Veritas** VII, Dohány utca 58–62 ☎1 341 3174, ⓦborkereskedes.hu; map p.58. Friendly store close to Blaha Lujza tér, with an excellent range of wines, including a beautiful Baroque cabinet stocked with some vintage bottles of Tokaj. Mon–Fri 9am–8pm, Sat 10am–6pm.

Magyar Pálinka Háza VIII, Rákóczi út 17 ☎1 338 4219; map p.77. A vast and dazzling range of flavours going far beyond the conventional pear and apricot *pálinkas* to include elderflower, quince, paprika and many more. Mon–Sat 9am–7pm.

★ **Malatinszky** V, József Attila utca 12 ☎1 266 4397, ⓦmalatinszky.hu; map p.38. Tucked away just off the main street, this delightful small shop has a concentrated selection of excellent wines from Villány and Tokaj. Mon–Fri 10am–6pm, Sept–May also Sat 10am–3pm.

Monarchia IX, Kinizsi utca 30–36 ☎1 456 9898, ⓦmonarchiaborok.hu; map p.77. A handsome little brick cellar shop offering a solid range of Hungarian wines alongside some from California, in addition to a tempting selection of jams, chutneys, oils and vinegars. Free tasting sessions take place on two Thursdays each month. Mon–Sat 10am–6pm.

Sexardicum VIII, Krúdy utca 6 ☎30 229 4216, ⓦsexardicum.hu; map p.77. The rather fruity name of this cool cellar shop is a play on the wine region, Szeksard, which is where the (mostly red) wines here are from. Mon–Fri 10am–9pm, Sat 3–9pm.

STATUE OF MÁTYÁS CORVINUS ON THE MÁTYÁS FOUNTAIN

Contexts

History

Although Budapest has only formally existed since 1873, when the twin cities of Buda and Pest were united in a single municipality together with the smaller Óbuda – initially known throughout Europe as "Pest-Buda" – the locality has been settled since prehistory. Homo sapiens appeared here around 8000 BC, and a succession of peoples overran the region during the first Age of Migrations, the most important of whom were the Celtic Eravisci who settled on Gellért-hegy in about 400 BC.

In 35 BC the Danube Basin was conquered by the **Romans** and subsequently incorporated within their empire as the province of Pannonia, whose northern half was governed from the town of **Aquincum** on the west bank of the Danube. Ruins of a camp, villas, baths and an amphitheatre can still be seen today in Óbuda and Rómaifürdő. Roman rule lasted until 430 AD, when Pannonia was ceded to **Attila the Hun**. Attila's planned assault on Rome was averted by his death on his wedding night, and thereafter Pannonia was carved up by **Germanic tribes** until they were ousted by the Turkic-speaking **Avars**, who were in turn assailed by the Bulgars, another warlike race from the Eurasian steppes. Golden torques and other treasures from Hun, Goth and Avar burial sites – now on display in the National Museum – suggest that they were quite sophisticated rather than mere "barbarians".

The coming of the Magyars

The most significant of the invaders from the east were the **Magyars**, who stamped their language and identity on Hungary. Their origins lie in the Finno-Ugric peoples who dwelt in the snowy forests between the Volga and the Urals, where today two Siberian peoples still speak languages that are the closest linguistic relatives to Hungarian; along with Finnish, Turkish and Mongolian, these languages make up the Altaic family. Many of these Magyars migrated south, where they eventually became vassals of the Khazar empire and mingled with the Bulgars as both peoples moved westwards to escape the marauding Petchenegs.

In 895 or 896 AD, seven Magyar tribes led by Árpád entered the Carpathian Basin and spread out across the plain, in what Hungarians call the "**landtaking**" (*honfoglalás*). They settled here, though they remained raiders for the next seventy years, striking terror as far afield as France (where people thought them to be Huns), until a series of defeats persuaded them to settle for assimilating their gains. The runic-style writing the Magyar tribes used is increasingly visible today – often used by hardline nationalists to underline their Hungarianness. According to the medieval chronicler, known today simply as Anonymous, the clan of Árpád settled on Csepel-sziget, and it was Árpád's brother, Buda, who purportedly gave his name to the west bank of the new settlement.

8000BC	35BC	895	1000
Homo sapiens appeared in Budapest area	Danube Basin conquered by Romans	The seven Hungarian tribes enter the Carpathian Basin under Árpád	Pope Sylvester II sends crown for King Stephen's coronation

The Árpád dynasty

Civilization developed gradually after Árpád's great-grandson **Prince Géza** established links with Bavaria and invited Catholic missionaries to Hungary. His son **Stephen** (István) took the decisive step of applying to Pope Sylvester for recognition, and on Christmas Day in the year 1000 AD was crowned as a Christian king. With the help of the Italian Bishop Gellért, he then set about converting his pagan subjects. Stephen was subsequently credited with the **foundation of Hungary** and canonized after his death in 1038. His mummified hand and the crown of St Stephen have since been revered as both holy and national relics, and are today some of Budapest's most popular tourist attractions.

Despite succession struggles after Stephen's death, a lack of external threats during the eleventh and twelfth centuries enabled the **development of Buda and Pest** to begin in earnest, largely thanks to French, Walloon and German settlers who worked and traded here under royal protection. However, the growth in royal power caused tribal leaders to rebel in 1222, and Andrew II was forced to recognize the noble status and rights of the **nation** – landed freemen exempt from taxation – in the Golden Bull, a kind of Hungarian Magna Carta.

Andrew's son **Béla IV** tried to restore royal authority, but the **Mongol invasion** of 1241 devastated the country and left even the royal palace of Esztergom in ruins. Only the timely death of Ghengis Khan spared Hungary from further ravages. Mindful of a return visit, Béla selected the **Vár** as a more defensible seat and encouraged foreign artisans to rebuild Buda, which German colonists called "*Ofen*" after its numerous lime-kilns (the name Pest, which is of Slav origin, also means "oven").

Renaissance and decline

After the Árpád dynasty expired in 1301, foreign powers advanced their own claims to the throne and for a while there were three competing kings, all duly crowned. Eventually **Charles Robert** of the French Angevin (or Anjou) dynasty triumphed. Peacetime gave him the opportunity to develop the gold mines of Transylvania and northern Hungary – the richest in Europe – and Charles bequeathed a robust exchequer to his son **Louis the Great**, whose reign saw the population of Hungary rise to three million, and the crown territories expand to include much of what are now Croatia and Poland. The oldest extant strata of the Buda Palace on Várhegy date from this time.

After Louis' demise, the throne was claimed by **Sigismund of Luxembourg**, Prince of Bohemia, whom the nobility despised as the "Czech swine". His failure to check the advance of the Turks through the Balkans was only redeemed by the Transylvanian warlord **János Hunyadi**, whose lifting of the siege of Belgrade caused rejoicing throughout Christendom. Vajdahunyad Castle in the Városliget is a romantic nineteenth-century replica of Hunyadi's ancestral seat in Transylvania.

Hunyadi's nephew, **Mátyás Corvinus**, is remembered as the **Renaissance king** who, together with his second wife Beatrice of Naples, lured humanists and artists from Italy to their court. Mátyás was an enlightened despot, renowned for his fairness, but when he died in 1490, leaving no legitimate heir, the nobles took control, choosing a pliable successor and exploiting the peasantry. However in 1514 the peasants, led by **György**

1458	1541	1556	1686
Mátyás Corvinus accedes to the throne, ushering in a golden age	Ottoman armies occupy Budapest	Rudas Baths constructed on orders of Pasha Sokoli Mustafa	Habsburg armies capture Budapest from Turks

Dózsa, rebelled against the oppression. The savage repression of this **revolt** (over 70,000 peasants were killed and Dózsa was roasted alive) and subsequent laws imposing "perpetual serfdom" alienated the mass of the population – a situation hardly improved by the coronation of the 9-year-old **Louis II**, who was barely 16 when he had to face the full might of the Turks under Sultan Süleyman "the Magnificent".

The Turkish conquest: Hungary divided

The Battle of **Mohács** in 1526 was a shattering defeat for the Hungarians – the king and half the nobility perished, leaving Hungary leaderless. After sacking Buda, the Turks withdrew to muster forces for their real objective, Vienna. To forestall this, Ferdinand of Habsburg proclaimed himself king of Hungary and occupied the western part of the country, while in Buda the nobles put János Zápolyai on the throne. Following Zápolyai's death in 1541, Ferdinand claimed full sovereignty, but the Sultan occupied Buda and central Hungary and made Zápolyai's son ruler of Transylvania, which henceforth became a semi-autonomous principality – a tripartite division known as the **Tripartium**, formally recognized in 1568. Despite various truces, warfare became a fact of life for the next 150 years, and national independence was not to be recovered for centuries afterwards.

Turkish-occupied Hungary was ruled by a Pasha in Buda, with much of the land either deeded to the Sultan's soldiers and officials, or run directly as a state fief. The towns, however, enjoyed some rights and were encouraged to trade, and the Turks were largely indifferent to the sectarian bigotry practised in Habsburg-ruled Hungary. The Habsburg **liberation of Buda** in 1686 was actually a disaster for its inhabitants, as the victors massacred Jews, pillaged at will and reduced Buda and Pest to rubble. The city's Turkish baths and the tomb of Gül Baba were among the few surviving buildings.

Habsburg rule

Habsburg rule was a bitter pill, which the Hungarians attempted to reject in the **War of Independence** of 1703–11, led by Prince **Ferenc Rákóczi II**. Though it was unsuccessful, the Habsburgs began to soften their autocracy with paternalism as a result. The revival of towns and villages during this time owed much to settlers from all over the empire, hence the Serb and Greek churches that remain in Pest and Szentendre. Yet while the aristocracy commissioned over two hundred palaces, and Baroque town centres and orchestras flourished, the masses remained all but serfs, mired in isolated villages.

Such contradictions impelled the Reform movement led by **Count István Széchenyi**. His vision of progress was embodied in the construction of the Lánchíd (Chain Bridge) between Buda and Pest, which proved an enormous spur to the development of the two districts. The National Museum, the Academy of Sciences and many other institutions were founded at this time, while the coffee houses of Pest became a hotbed of radical politics. Széchenyi's arch-rival was **Lajos Kossuth**, small-town lawyer turned member of parliament and editor of the radical *Pesti Hirlap*, which scandalized and delighted citizens. Kossuth detested the Habsburgs, revered "universal liberty", and demanded an end to serfdom and censorship. Magyar chauvinism was his blind spot, however, and the law of 1840, his greatest pre-revolutionary achievement, inflamed

1800	1848	1849	1873
Beethoven plays in Budapest	Crowds gather on March 15 in front of the National Museum, the start of the War of Independence	Opening of István Széchenyi's Lánchíd, the first permanent bridge between Buda and Pest	Uniting of Buda, Pest and Óbuda to form Budapest

dormant nationalist feelings among Croats, Slovaks and Romanians by making Hungarian the sole official language.

When the empire was shaken by revolutions that broke out across Europe in **March 1848**, local radicals seized the moment. Kossuth dominated Parliament, while **Sándor Petőfi** mobilized crowds on the streets of Pest. A second war of independence followed, which again ended in defeat and Habsburg repression, epitomized by the execution of Prime Minister Batthyány in 1849, and the Citadella atop Gellért-hegy, built to intimidate citizens with its guns.

Budapest's Belle Époque

Gradually, brute force was replaced by a **policy of compromise**, by which Hungary was economically integrated with Austria and, as Austrian power waned, given a major shareholding in the Habsburg empire, henceforth known as the "Dual Monarchy". The compromise (*Ausgleich*) of 1867, engineered by **Ferenc Deák**, brought Hungary prosperity and status, but tied the country inextricably to the empire's fortunes. Buda and Pest underwent rapid expansion and formally merged. Pest was extensively remodelled, acquiring the Nagykörút (Great Boulevard) and Andrássy út, a grand approach to the Városliget, where Hungary's millennial anniversary celebrations were staged in 1896, marking a thousand years since the arrival of the Hungarian tribes in the Carpathian Basin. (In fact they arrived in 895 but preparations were late, so the official date was adjusted to 896.) New suburbs were created to house the burgeoning population, which was by now predominantly Magyar, though there were still large German and Jewish communities. Both elegance and squalor abounded, café society reached its apogee, and Budapest experienced a **cultural efflorescence** in the early years of the twentieth century to rival that of Vienna. Today, the most tangible reminders are the remarkable buildings by Ödön Lechner, Béla Lajta and other masters of Art Nouveau and National Romanticism – the styles that characterized the era.

The Horthy years

Dragged into **World War I** by its allegiance to Austria and Germany, Hungary was facing defeat by the autumn of 1918. The Western or Entente powers decided to dismantle the Habsburg empire in favour of the "**Successor States**" – Romania, Czechoslovakia and Yugoslavia – which would acquire much of their territory at Hungary's expense. In Budapest, the October 30 "Michaelmas Daisy Revolution" put the Social Democratic party of Count **Mihály Károlyi** in power, but his government avoided the issue of land reform, attempted unsuccessfully to negotiate peace with the Entente and finally resigned when France backed further demands by the Successor States.

On March 21, 1919, a **Republic of Councils** (*Tanácsköztársaság*) was proclaimed led by **Béla Kun**, which ruled through local Soviets. Hoping for radical change and believing that "Russia will save us", many initially supported the new regime, but enforced nationalization of land and capital and attacks on religion soon alienated the majority. After 134 days, the regime collapsed before the advancing Romanian army, which occupied Budapest.

1896	**1898**	**1905**	**1912**
Underground Railway inaugurated as part of Millennial celebrations in Budapest	Sisi, Empress Elizabeth, assassinated in Switzerland	St Stephen's Basilica is completed after 54 years' work	The magnificent Elephant and Giraffe Houses unveiled in Budapest's Zoo

Then came the **White Terror**, as right-wing gangs moved up from the south killing "Reds" and Jews, who were made scapegoats for the earlier Communist "Red Terror" – especially in Budapest, the Bolshevik capital. **Admiral Miklós Horthy**, self-appointed regent for Karl IV, who had been exiled by the Western allies ("the Admiral without a fleet, for the king without a kingdom") entered what he called the "sinful city" on a white horse, and ordered a return to "traditional values". Meanwhile, at the Paris Conference, Hungary was obliged to sign the **Treaty of Trianon** (July 4, 1920), surrendering two-thirds of its historic territory and three-fifths of its total population (three million in all) to the Successor States. The bitterest loss was **Transylvania** – a devastating blow to national pride. Horthy's regency was characterized by gala balls and hunger marches, revanchism and growing **anti-Semitism**, enshrined in law from 1925. Yet Horthy was a moderate compared to the **Arrow Cross** Fascists waiting in the wings, whose power grew as **World War II** raged, and the Hungarian Second Army perished at Stalingrad.

Anticipating Horthy's defection from the Axis in October 1944, Nazi Germany staged a coup, installing an Arrow Cross government, which enabled them to begin the massacre of the **Jews** of Budapest. It was only thanks to the valiant efforts of foreign diplomats like Wallenberg and Lutz that half of them survived, when ninety percent of Hungary's provincial Jews perished. In late December, the Red Army smashed through the defensive "Attila Line" and encircled the capital, held by German troops. During the seven-week **siege of Budapest**, citizens endured endless shelling amid a bitter winter, as street-fighting raged. In January the Germans withdrew from Pest, blew up the Danube bridges and holed up in Buda, where Várhegy was reduced to rubble as the Red Army battered the *Wehrmacht* into submission. Aside from the Jews in the ghetto – for whom it meant salvation from the Arrow Cross – the city's **liberation** on February 13, 1945 brought little joy to Budapestis, as the Red Army embarked on an orgy of rape and looting, followed by a wave of deportations to Siberia.

The Communist takeover and the 1956 Uprising

As Budapestis struggled to rebuild their lives after the war, the Soviet-backed **Communists** took control bit by bit – stealthily reducing the power of other forces in society, and using the threat of the Red Army and the **ÁVO secret police**, who took over the former Arrow Cross torture chambers on Andrássy út. By 1948 their hold on Hungary was total, symbolized by the red stars that everywhere replaced the crown of St Stephen, and a huge statue of Stalin beside the Városliget, where citizens were obliged to parade before Hungary's "Little Stalin", **Mátyás Rákosi.**

The power struggles in the Moscow Communist Party leadership that followed the death of Stalin in 1953 were replicated in the other Eastern European capitals, and in Hungary Rákosi was replaced by **Imre Nagy.** Nagy's "New Course" allowed Hungarians an easier life before Rákosi struck back by expelling him from the Party for "deviationism". However, society had taken heart from the respite and intellectuals held increasingly outspoken public debates during the summer of 1956. The mood came to a head in October, when 200,000 people attended the funeral of László Rajk (a victim of the show trials in 1949) in Kerepesi Cemetery, and Budapest's students decided to march to the General Bem statue near the Margit híd.

1919	1920	1944	1945
Admiral Horthy enters Budapest, marking the start of the anti-Semitic White Terror	Treaty of Trianon carves up old Hungarian kingdom	Budapest ghetto set up in Jewish quarter	Soviet troops capture Budapest from the Nazis

On October 23, demonstrators chanting anti Rákosi slogans crossed the Danube to mass outside Parliament. As dusk fell, students demanding access to the Radio Building were fired upon by the ÁVO, and a spontaneous **1956 Uprising** began, which rapidly took hold throughout Budapest and spread across Hungary. The newly restored Nagy found himself in a maelstrom, as popular demands were irreconcilable with realpolitik – independence and withdrawing from the Warsaw Pact were anathema to the Kremlin. It was Hungary's misfortune that the UN was preoccupied with the Suez Crisis when the Soviets reinvaded on November 10, crushing all resistance in six days. An estimated 2500 Hungarians died and some 200,000 fled abroad; back home, hundreds were executed and thousands jailed for their part in the uprising.

"Goulash socialism" and the end of Communism

After Soviet power had been bloodily restored, **János Kádár** gradually normalized conditions, embarking on cautious reforms to create a "**goulash socialism**" that made Hungary the envy of its Warsaw Pact neighbours and the West's favourite Communist state in the late 1970s. Though everyone knew the limits of the "Hungarian condition", there was enough freedom and consumer goods to keep the majority content. Decentralized management, limited private enterprise and competition made Hungary's economy healthy compared to other Socialist states, but in the 1980s it became apparent that the attempt to reconcile a command economy and one-party rule with market forces was unsustainable. Dissidents tested the limits of criticism, and even within the Party there were those who realized that changes were needed. Happily, this coincided with the advent of Gorbachev, which made it much easier for the reform Communists to shunt Kádár aside in 1988.

The **end of Communism** was heralded by two events the following summer: the ceremonial reburial of Imre Nagy, and the dismantling of the barbed wire along the border with Austria, which enabled thousands of East Germans to escape to the west while "on holiday". In October 1989, the government announced the legalization of other parties as a prelude to free elections, and the People's Republic was renamed the Republic of Hungary in a ceremony broadcast live on national television. Two weeks later this was eclipsed by the fall of the Berlin Wall, closely followed by the Velvet Revolution in Czechoslovakia and the overthrow of Ceaușescu in Romania on Christmas Day.

The post-Communist era

Hungary's first **free elections** in the spring of 1990 resulted in a humiliating rejection of the reform Communists' Hungarian Socialist Party (MSzP), and the installation of a centre-right coalition government dominated by the **Hungarian Democratic Forum (MDF)** under Premier **József Antall**. Committed to a total break with Communism, the MDF aimed to restore the traditions and hierarchies of prewar Hungary and its former position in Europe. While this appealed to many, not everyone wanted the Catholic Church to regain its earlier power, and Hungary's neighbours were quick to suspect a revanchist claim on the lost lands of Trianon. For most Hungarians, however, inflation, unemployment, crime and homelessness were more pressing issues.

1949	1953	1956	1958
First trolleybus line inaugurated, #70, on Stalin's seventieth birthday	Hungary's football team demolishes England 6–3	Hungarian Uprising breaks out on October 23	Imre Nagy executed for his role in the 1956 revolt

After Antall's premature death in 1993, his successor failed to turn the economy around and the 1994 elections saw the **Socialists** (under the **MSzP**) return to power. To allay fears of a return to totalitarianism, they included the **Free Democrats (SzDSz)** in government, and reassured Hungary's foreign creditors with austerity measures that angered voters who had expected the Socialists to reverse the growing inequalities in society. It soon became obvious that they were riddled with corruption; some party members became millionaires almost overnight.

The 1998 elections were narrowly won by the **Fidesz-Hungarian Civic Party** of **Viktor Orbán**, a Tony Blair-like figure who repositioned his party to the right, stressing the need to revive national culture and using the buzz-word *polgári* (meaning "civic", but redolent of bourgeois middle-class values) to appeal to a broad constituency. The youngest prime minister in Hungarian history, Orbán promoted a conservative Christian agenda with an acute understanding of national and religious symbolism. Like Admiral Horthy, he regarded Budapest with suspicion, trying to undermine its SzDSz mayor, Gábor Demszky, by halting the building of the National Theatre in Erzsébet tér (whose foundations had already been laid at vast expense), and cancelling the city's planned fourth metro line.

With an expanding economy, falling inflation and low unemployment levels – plus the achievement of steering Hungary into NATO – Orbán anticipated victory in the parliamentary elections of 2002. Instead, after a vitriolic campaign, his Fidesz–MDF coalition was ousted, the electorate preferring a return to the centre-left alliance of Socialists and Free Democrats, whose most important achievement was to preside over Hungary's accession to the **European Union** in 2004. While most Hungarians were fervently committed to membership, there was a widespread wish to limit foreign ownership – contrary to EU directives – and anxiety about the allocation of agricultural subsidies.

In August 2004, the premiership passed to the sports minister and millionaire businessman **Ferenc Gyurcsány**, who revitalized the jaded Socialists by appointing a cabinet of fellow millionaires who got rich during the privatization of state assets in the 1990s. Like previous governments, however, they faced the dilemma that Hungary was living beyond its means – its budget deficit of ten percent of GDP was the highest in the EU – while voters opposed further belt-tightening or reforms of the health system. By promising better welfare while secretly running up deficits, Gyurcsány managed to delay a reckoning long enough to win the April 2006 election – the first time a government had been re-elected since democracy was restored.

In September 2006, however, national radio broadcast a tape-recording of him telling his cabinet that austerity measures were inevitable "because we fucked up. Not a little, a lot... We lied in the morning, we lied in the evening." A furore ensued, with weeks of demonstrations outside Parliament led by Fidesz and the MDF, which boycotted the state ceremony marking the fiftieth anniversary of the Uprising, staging their own rally on October 23. That night, **rioting** erupted, protesters battling police around Kossuth tér and Nyugati station. In a throwback to 1956, they waved Hungarian flags with a hole cut out, and even managed to activate an old Soviet tank from a museum (which stalled before it reached Parliament).

Incredibly Gyurcsány clung to office but the government was robbed of all authority. Even after he resigned in 2009, the Socialists were a broken force, and in the elections

1978	1989	1990	1999
St Stephen's crown returned to Hungary from Fort Knox	The Iron Curtain is dismantled	First free elections after the fall of Communism	Hungary joins NATO

of 2010 Fidesz, led by a resurgent Orbán, stormed to a massive victory right across the country. With its minor Christian Democrat partners it captured 172 out of 176 constituency seats, and even under Hungary's complicated system, which combines constituencies with proportional representation, the Fidesz coalition still took more than two-thirds of the parliamentary mandates.

An even clearer sign of the change in Hungarian politics was the success of the **far-right** Jobbik (Movement for Better Hungary), which received sixteen percent of the vote, coming third. Jobbik is a media-savvy group under Gábor Vona that has a sizeable following among younger Hungarians – anti-Semitic nationalism is no longer the preserve of old embittered Magyars. Jobbik proudly waves its flags bearing the "Árpád stripes" of the Arrow Cross and openly flaunts its links with the banned Magyar Gárda (Hungarian Guard), the paramilitary group that parades through villages in eastern Hungary "restoring order" – ie terrorizing Gypsy villagers. With no sign of an economic upturn – the surest way to weaken Jobbik's appeal – and with both Fidesz and the Socialists happy to use the far-right to scare voters, Jobbik looks set to stay.

After the discredited Socialists and the extreme Jobbik, the next biggest party in parliament is the LMP (Lehet Más a Politika – Politics Can be Different), a new group trying to claim the centre-left ground but struggling to assert its political identity.

The new Hungary

Convinced that he had been defeated in 2002 by the cheating remnants of Communism, Orbán vowed that this time he would wipe them from power with his conservative Christian agenda. A two-thirds majority in parliament gave him the power to rewrite the Constitution and all the major laws, and he set about the task at a breakneck pace before that majority melted away.

However, the speed with which laws were passed and the lack of any coherent opposition did not always make for good legislation. Furthermore, all opposition was swept aside: when independent bodies such as the Constitutional Court made a criticism, they were stripped of powers, stuffed with government supporters or simply abolished. Diplomats, civil servants and the whole public sphere have all been targeted in a mass of new appointments.

Fidesz's targets to improve the economy, tackle corruption and stand up to foreign banks and the IMF have widespread support, though many find the means more debatable. The newly elected government ordered a proclamation to be put up in public offices declaring the dawning of a new order – in a manner very familiar from the worst Communist period. However, the government's belief that a new era has begun is clearly strong: when a Jewish cemetery was vandalized in 2010, Orbán seemed shocked that under his government people still felt the need to do such things.

Another revealing episode took place in 2011. With a visit by the Chinese premier pending and the potential for big economic deals, Orbán began to talk about the twilight of the liberal West (his hostility to liberals is a common theme) and how the future was in the East. Then, on the morning of the visit, all the Tibetans in Budapest were rounded up and detained all day – so that there would be no embarrassing protest. Even Fidesz supporters were shocked.

2001	2002	2004	2006
Gresham Palace restored to its 1907 glory	National stadium renamed after Ferenc Puskás, the legendary Hungarian footballer	Hungary joins EU	Riots after Prime Minister's admission of lies, lies, lies

These authoritarian tendencies led to alarmist talk about democracy being under threat. This seemed exaggerated, but Orbán's demagogic style was a concern to many, especially when the Socialists, with their talk of lying to the electorate, had already lowered the bar of honesty.

Just when Hungary's polarized society needed a touch of healing, Fidesz took the surgical approach. It talked about national unity but seemed intent on division, and its aggressive style spread a message of intolerance of others' opinion.

While governments came and went after 1990, **Mayor Gábor Demszky** steered the city forwards without any major upsets for twenty years, finally securing state funding for a **fourth metro line,** running from Keleti Station in Pest to Étele tér in Buda. However, he stepped down at the 2010 elections before he was engulfed by the Fidesz tide. His successor, **István Tarlós**, an engineer by trade and mayor of the Óbuda district for sixteen years until 2006, ran as an independent with Fidesz backing. He immediately stamped his mark on the city by changing several street names, offending both the Russians (by renaming Moszkva tér) and the Americans (by renaming Roosevelt tér), and vowed to make the city a leaner, cleaner place by tackling the corruption of the Budapest transport authority – particularly the soaring cost of the fourth metro line.

The city's intellectuals viewed Tarlós with suspicion: his attempt to ban a gay stall at the Sziget festival in 2001 when he was mayor of Óbuda did little to endear him to them. Their fears seemed confirmed when he overruled an appointment committee to put two anti-Semitic right-wingers in charge of the New Theatre, a move that provoked widespread protest.

2007	2010
The neo-fascist Magyar Gárda formed in Budapest	Viktor Orbán leads Fidesz to crushing electoral victory

Music

Hungarian classical music enshrines the trinity of Liszt, Bartók and Kodály: Liszt was the founding father, Bartók one of the greatest composers of the twentieth century, and Kodály (himself no slouch at composition) created a widely imitated system of musical education. When you also take into account talented Hungarian soloists such as András Schiff and ensembles such as the Budapest Festival Orchestra, it's clear that this small nation has made an outstanding contribution to the world of classical music. After classical, the musical genres most readily associated with Hungary are Gypsy and folk, both of which have some excellent exponents, the former led by the likes of the cimbalom player Kálmán Balogh, and the latter by Muzsikás and the wonderful singer Márta Sebestyén. The increasing popularity of jazz is manifest in the growing number of clubs in Budapest and other larger cities, as well as several terrific summer jazz festivals held around the country. Meanwhile, Hungarian popular music, while not exactly cutting-edge, is becoming more adventurous as a new generation of DJs and bands soaks up the influence of Western European and American artists.

Classical music

Franz Liszt (1811–86), who described himself as a "mixture of Gypsy and Franciscan", cut a flamboyant figure in the salons of Europe as a virtuoso pianist and womanizer. His *Hungarian Rhapsodies* and other similar pieces reflected the "Gypsy" side to his character and the rising nationalism of his era, while later work like the *Transcendental Studies* (whose originality has only recently been recognized) invoked a visionary "Franciscan" mood. Despite his patriotic stance, however, Liszt's first language was German (he never fully mastered Hungarian), and his expressed wish to roam the villages of Hungary with a knapsack on his back was a Romantic fantasy.

That was left to **Béla Bartók** (1881–1945) and **Zoltán Kodály** (1882–1967), who began exploring the remoter districts of Hungary and Transylvania in 1906, collecting peasant music. Despite many hardships and local suspicion of their "monster" (a cutting stylus and phonograph cylinders), they managed to record and catalogue thousands of melodies, laying down high standards of musical ethnography, still maintained in Hungary today, while discovering a rich source of inspiration for their own compositions.

Bartók created a personal but universal musical language by reworking the raw essence of Magyar and Finno-Ugric folk music in a modern context – in particular his six String Quartets – although Hungarian public opinion was originally hostile. Feeling misunderstood and out of step with his country's increasingly pro-Nazi policies, Bartók left Hungary in 1940, dying poor and embittered in the United States. Since then, however, his reputation has soared, and the return of his body in 1988 occasioned national celebrations, shrewdly sponsored by the state.

Kodály's music is more consciously national: Bartók called it "a real profession of faith in the Hungarian soul". His *Peacock Variations* are based on a typical Old Style pentatonic tune and the *Dances of Galanta* on the popular music played by Gypsy bands. Old Style tunes also form the core of Kodály's work in musical education: the

"Kodály method" employs group singing to develop musical skill at an early age. His ideas made Hungarian music teaching among the best in the world.

For others Kodály was a voice of conscience during the Rákosi era, writing the *Hymn of Zrínyi* to a seventeenth-century text whose call to arms against the Turkish invasion – "I perceive a ghastly dragon, full of venom and fury, snatching the crown of Hungary. . ." – was tumultuously acclaimed as an anti-Stalinist allegory. Its first performance was closely followed by the Uprising, and the *Hymn* was not performed again for many years; nor were any recordings made available until 1982.

Gypsy music

In recent years **Gypsy or Roma music** has really made a mark on the Hungarian music scene. Played on anything from spoons and milk jugs to guitars, Roma music ranges from haunting laments to playful wedding songs – as can be seen in French director Tony Gatliff's excellent film *Latcho Drom*, which explores Roma music from India to Spain. The most exciting artist around in the field of Gypsy music is **Kálmán Balogh**, one of the world's foremost exponents of the cimbalom, a hammer dulcimer (stringed instrument) played with little mallets. A mesmerizing virtuoso performer with a repertoire ranging from Gypsy tunes to Bach, Balogh also tours regularly with his Gypsy Cimbalom Band, who bring a strong, jazz-influenced sound to proceedings. The next generation of Hungarian Gypsy musicians is led by **Bela Lakatos and the Gypsy Youth Band**, a wonderfully talented five-piece collective whose predominantly vocal sound is complemented by guitar and mandolin, and a percussive element comprising sticks, spoons, metal cans and the like. Other well-established Roma artists in Hungary to keep an eye out for include Parno Graszt, Romano Drom, Andro Drom, the Szilvási Folk Band, and Kalyi Jag – all these groups tour extensively and are the focal point of most Roma festivals in Hungary and abroad.

Another internationally recognized figure is the wizard violinist **Roby Lakatos**, who tours extensively around the world. A seventh-generation descendant of János Bihari (aka "King of the Gypsy Violinists"), Lakatos hails from the tradition of "Gypsy music" that you will see advertised at touristy restaurants, known in Hungarian as **Magyar nóta**. Consisting of a series of mid-nineteenth-century Hungarian ballads traditionally played by Roma musicians, Magyar nóta is usually performed by one or two violinists, a bass player and a guy on the cimbalom. The more famous restaurants boast their own musical dynasties, such as the Lakatos family, who have been performing this sort of music for over a century.

However, with the growth in world music the musical divisions that used to split the different traditions are far less distinct now, as musicians from both traditions get together to move in new directions: the violinist and accordionist **Róbert Farkas** and bands such as the fusion group **Nomada** are busy reshaping Roma urban traditions. Catch any of them while you are in Budapest, in venues such as the *Gödör Klub* (see p.45, 187) and you'll see that the skills that fascinated Brahms are as strong as ever today.

Folk music

Hungarian folk music (*Magyar népzene*) originated around the Urals and the Turkic steppes over a millennium ago, and is different again from Gypsy or Roma music. The haunting rhythms and pentatonic scale of this "Old Style" music (to use Bartók's terminology) were subsequently overlaid by "New Style" European influences – which have been discarded by more modern enthusiasts in the folk revival centred around Táncház. These "Dance Houses" encourage people to learn traditional dances – with much shouting, whistling, and slapping of boots and thighs.

The two biggest names to emerge from the Táncház movement were **Muzsikás** and **Márta Sebestyén**, who have been regular collaborators for years. A four-piece ensemble comprising bass, violin and flute, Muzsikás (pronounced *Mu-zhi-kash*) started out in the early 1970s by exploring the musical archives of village folk music, from which they derived their own distinctive repertoire, combining traditional Hungarian music with the sounds of Transylvania, across the border in Romania – while their recorded output is not that prolific, they do tour regularly, both at home and abroad.

Unquestionably Hungary's finest folk singer, and one of the best in Europe, Sebestyén's gorgeous and distinctive voice has seen her become firmly established on the world music scene in recent years, a reputation that was sealed after she featured on the soundtrack to the film *The English Patient*. Aside from her regular appearances with Muzsikás, Sebestyén has also guested with **Vujicsics**, a marvellous seven-strong ensemble from Pomáz near Szentendre who specialize in Serbian and Croatian folk melodies. Another singer whose powerful voice has won her many fans is **Bea Pálya**, who spans Hungarian, Roma and Jewish music traditions. Other folk artists to watch out for include the Csík Ensemble, who also work with leading pop singers to produce an intriguing blend, the Magyarpalatkai Band and the Ökrös Ensemble, who both play folk music from Transylvania, and the superb Budapest klezmer outfit Di Naye Kapelye.

One big name to look out for is **Félix Lajkó**, a Hungarian virtuoso violinist from Vojvodina in Serbia, whose eccentric fusion of folk, Gypsy and jazz inspires a devout following.

Popular music and jazz

Budapest has undergone a **popular music** revival in the last few years: radio stations and music magazines have taken off and the city has become part of the international tour circuit – the Sziget Festival each August (see p.185) is now one of the premier music gatherings on the continent. This has all had a knock-on effect on local music, which ranges from instrumental groups (Korai Öröm and Másfél) to techno-inspired performers like Anima Sound System. Heaven Street Seven call their version of guitar pop Dunabeat, while Quimby's Tibor Kiss is the Hungarian equivalent of Tom Waits. The controversial, and one-time underground, local radio station **Tilos Rádió** has done much to promote **DJs**, and there are now a host of them around the country. Some like Tommy Boy and Schultz play run-of-the-mill **techno**, while others like Palotai and Mango do a lot of wild mixing using a mass of sources and sounds. Bestiák are a sort of Magyar Girls Aloud and Ganszta Zoli looks to LA gangster rap for his inspiration.

Jazz has always had a devout, but small, following in the country and more and more clubs and bars offer live jazz. Names worth checking out are Béla Szakcsi Lakatos, a jazz pianist who frequently plays in Budapest clubs, Mihály Dresch, the saxophonist who draws on folk traditions, and Nikoletta Szőke, a singer whose win at the 2005 Montreux Jazz Festival brought international recognition.

In recent years a decline in demand for Gypsy restaurant bands has sent younger Romungro musicians in a new direction: **Roma jazz**. Players in their early twenties or younger are taking the jazz world by storm; those in the know rate Gábor Bolla as one of the finest tenor saxophone players in Europe.

Discography

Many of the recordings listed below can be bought from Passion Music in the UK (Ⓦpassiondiscs.co.uk). In Hungary, good-quality **records and CDs** produced by Hungaroton (Ⓦhungaroton.hu) retail for half or a third of what you'd pay abroad, which makes it well worth rooting through record shops (*lemezbolt*). After Western and Hungarian **pop**, the bulk of their stock consists of **classical music**. A full discography of the works of Liszt, Bartók and Kodály, directors like Dohnányi and Doráti, and contemporary Hungarian soloists and singers would fill a catalogue, but look out for the following names: pianists András Schiff, Zoltán Kocsis (who also conducts) and Dezső Ránki; the Liszt Ferenc Chamber Orchestra, the Budapest Festival Orchestra and the Hungarian Radio and TV Symphony; conductors Iván Fischer and Tamás Vasáry; and singers Mária Zádori, Ingrid Kertesi, Andrea Rost, Adrienne Csengery, József Gregor and Kolos Kovats.

For those who like contemporary music, the grand old man of the modern Hungarian scene is György Kurtág, while Tibor Szemző produces meditative works, one of which, *Tractatus*, inspired by German philosopher Ludwig Wittgenstein, is quite extraordinary.

Folk and Gypsy music can be bought at all record stores, though you should be warned that a CD with a picture of a Gypsy orchestra all dressed up in red waistcoats is of the "*nóta*" variety – it's worth asking to listen before you buy. As well as the artists listed here, there are hundreds of great recordings in the above fields. The following simply offer an introduction; particular recommendations are marked with the ★ symbol.

INDIVIDUAL ARTISTS

★ **Kálmán Balogh** *Kálmán Balogh and the Gipsy Cimbalom Band* (Fonó). A superb collection of tunes from Hungary and the wider region, including the heart-rending version of the folk song "A csitári hegyek alatt". Recorded with artistic director Romano Kokalo, *Gipsy Colours* (Fonó, Budapest) is a fabulous selection of Gypsy dance tunes from the region.

★ **Félix Lajkó** *Remény*, *Félix* (both on Tilos), *Lajkó Félix and his Band* (Fonó). The best recordings so far of this Hungarian virtuoso violinist from Subotica in northern Serbia – *Remény (Hope)* is a marvellous record featuring previously unreleased concert recordings alongside pieces from the soundtrack to *Othello*, while *Lajkó Félix and his Band* is a highly charged set of recordings made in the woods near his home He also features with the Boban Markovic Orchestra, the fantastic Serbian Gypsy ensemble, on the CD *Srce Cigansko*, which combines typically rumbustious Serbian brass with Lajkó's violin to marvellous effect.

★ **Roby Lakatos** Earlier works include *Lakatos* (Deutsche Grammophon), which features new workouts of favourites by the likes of Brahms alongside traditional Hungarian folk songs; *Later with Lakatos* (Deutsche Grammophon), a homecoming concert in Budapest's Thália Theatre in 1999. More recent albums (all on the Avanti label) are *Firedance*, a sizzling record exploring Gypsy themes from around the world; *Klezmer Karma*, a funky, Jewish-influenced recording featuring performances by Miriam Fuks and the Franz Liszt Chamber Orchestra; and *Roby Lakatos with Musical Friends*, an all-jazz project boasting some stellar guests such as Stephane Grappelli and Marc Fossett.

Bea Pálya *Ágról ágra* (Orphea). Starting with a Hungarian folk prayer at dawn Pálya moves across borders to embrace Romanian and Persian songs with the same authority she brings to her own tradition.

Márta Sebestyén *Kismet* (Hannibal). On this wide-ranging album, Hungary's leading Táncház singer draws upon various folk traditions, with Bosnian, Hindi and Irish songs, among others; otherwise, Sebestyén is best known for her recordings with the folk group Muzsikás (see p.220), while her international star has risen thanks to significant contributions to the Grammy-award-winning Deep Forest album *Boheme* and the film *The English Patient*.

GROUPS

Bela Lakatos and The Gypsy Youth Project *Introducing* (World Music Network). Lively and refreshing debut album from this superbly talented outfit, with songs pertaining to rural Roma life. Wonderful vocals and some fabulous instrumental improvisation.

Besh o Drom Vibrant large ensemble that produces a feverish Balkan blend of dance music with its driving brass and whirling rhythms perhaps at its rawest on their first album, *Macsó Hímzés* (Fonó).

★ **Budapest Bar** *Volume 1* (EMI). The first album of the Robert Farkas cabaret band is their best, with the supreme opening song "Szivemben bomba van" (There's a bomb in my heart).

★ **Csik Ensemble** *Ez a vonat, ha elindult, Hadd menjen...* (Fonó). Rooted firmly in the folk tradition, the band also works with pop musicians such as Tibor Kiss of the band Quimby, to powerful effect.

★ **Di Naye Kapelye** The band's three albums to date are the eponymous *Di Naye Kapelye*, *A Mazeldiker Yid* and *Traktorist* (all Oriente Musik), all terrific, and typically exuberant, klezmer recordings, which make for immensely enjoyable listening. *Traktorist* features a wonderfully jolly Communist-era ode to the Yiddish tractor.

Jánosi Ensemble *Jánosi Együttes* (Hungaroton). A group performing "authentic" versions of some of the folk tunes that Bartók borrowed in his compositions – a record that makes a bridge between classical and folk music.

The Kalamajka Ensemble *Bonchidától Bonchidáig* (Hungaroton). This terrific Táncház enemble plays Transylvanian and Csángó ballads and dances.

★ **Muzsikás** *The Bartók Album* (Hannibal). Featuring Márta Sebestyén and the Romanian violinist Alexander Balanescu, this manages to set the music of Bartók in its original context – three of Bartók's violin duos are presented alongside original field recordings and recordings of his transcriptions by Muzsikás.

★ **Morning Star** (Hannibal) is another fine Muzsikás volume – interestingly, their record company recommended slight changes and a softening of edges for this foreign edition of *Hazafelé* (Hungaroton), the original Hungarian recording. Their latest release, 2004's *Live at the Liszt Academy of Music*, which again stars Sebestyén, is a compilation of recordings taken from successive appearances at the Budapest Spring Festival.

★ **Prímás Parade** *Rendhagyó Prímástalálkozó* (FolkEuropa). A fascinating supergroup that brings together folk musicians, a rock guitarist, a classical violinist, jazz saxophonist and more – but all rooted in Hungarian and Roma traditions. The result sparkles, never more so than when the electric guitar plays the role of the violin *primás*.

Transylvanians *Denevér* (Mega) and *Igen!* (Westpark). On these two recent albums, this exceptional group of young musicians showcase their full range of talents – the latter features the wonderful voice and terrific bass playing of the front woman, Isabel Nagy.

Vujicsics Ensemble *Serbian Music from South Hungary* (Hannibal). More complex tunes than most Magyar folk music, with a distinct Balkan influence. Two albums featuring Márta Sebestyén are *25 – Live at the Academy of Music* (R-E-Disc 005), a concert in Budapest celebrating the group's twenty-fifth anniversary, and *Podravina* (R-E-Disc 004), a selection of Croatian dance melodies.

János Zerkula and Regina Fikó *Este a Gyimesbe Jártam* (Hungaroton). Music from the Csángó region; sparser, sadder and more discordant than other Transylvanian music.

COMPILATION ALBUMS

Magyar népzene 3 (*Hungarian folk music*; Hungaroton). A four-disc set of field recordings covering the whole range of folk music, including Old and New Style songs, instrumental and occasional music, that's probably the best overall introduction. In the West, the discs are marketed as "Folk Music of Hungary Vol.1".

Magyar hangszeres népzene (*Hungarian Instrumental Folk Music*; Hungaroton). A very good three-disc set of field recordings of village and Gypsy bands, including lots of solos.

X. Magyarországi Táncház Találkozó. One of an excellent series, the *Tenth Dance House Festival* (Hungaroton) features a great mixture of dances, ballads and instrumental pieces from all over Hungary.

Rough Guide to Hungarian Music (World Music Network). Despite one or two obvious omissions, this is an otherwise excellent introduction to the many wildly differing sounds of Hungarian music.

Rough Guide to the Music of Eastern Europe (World Music Network). Although most of the songs on this CD are from the Balkans, there is a healthy representation from Hungary, featuring songs by Márta Sebestyén, Vízöntő and Kálmán Balogh and the Gypsy Cimbalom Band.

Rough Guide to the Music of Hungarian Gypsies (World Music Network). All the big-hitters are here on this marvellous and thoroughly comprehensive introduction to the many strands of Hungarian Gypsy music – the highlight is a ripping tune by Mitsou performed with the brilliant Romanian band Fanfare Ciocarlia.

Rough Guide Music of the Gypsies (World Music Network). From India to Spain, this is a fantastic introduction to Gypsy music worldwide, with Hungary represented by Kálmán Balogh and the Joszef Lacatos Orchestra. Also worth checking out is the *Rough Guide to Klezmer Revival* (RGNET 1203), which features a track by Di Naye Kapelye.

Tánczházi muzsika (*Music from the Táncház*; Hungaroton). A early double album of the Sebő Ensemble playing Táncház music from various regions of Hungary. Wild and exciting rhythms.

Books

There is a wide range of books on Budapest available in the city, particularly architecture titles, or translations of Hungarian literature. Books tagged with the ★ symbol are particularly recommended. For a gentle introduction to Hungarian current affairs and literature, look for the locally published *The Hungarian Quarterly* (ⓦhungarianquarterly.com). See p.203 for a list of Budapest's better bookshops, most of which can take orders.

ART, ARCHITECTURE AND PHOTOGRAPHY

Our Budapest. A very informative series of pocket-size books: written in Hungarian and English by experts in their fields, and published by Budapest City Hall, they cover the city's architecture, baths and parks, and are very cheap, though unfortunately the standard of English varies.

★ **Irén Ács** *Hungary at Home*. Excellent collection of photos covering all walks of life in postwar Hungary. Her other books, including *Rendezvous*, are also worth looking out for in bookshops.

★ **Bruno Bourel & Lajos Parti Nagy** *Lightscapes*. One of the most interesting collections of photos available. Taken around the city by Bourel, a sharp-eyed French photographer who has lived there for many years, they are accompanied by words from a leading contemporary Hungarian writer.

Györgyi Éri et al *A Golden Age: Art and Society in Hungary 1896–1914*. Hungary's Art Nouveau age captured in a beautifully illustrated coffee-table volume.

★ **János Gerle** *et al Budapest: An Architectural Guide*. The best of the small new guides to the city's twentieth-century architecture, covering almost 300 buildings, with brief descriptions in Hungarian and English.

Ruth Gruber *Jewish Heritage Travel: A Guide to Central and Eastern Europe*. The most comprehensive guide to Jewish sights in Budapest and elsewhere.

Edwin Heathcote *Budapest: A Guide to Twentieth-Century Architecture*. A useful and informative pocket guide to the city, though with some curious omissions.

Tamás Hofer et al. *Hungarian Peasant Art*. An excellently produced examination of Hungarian folk art, with lots of good photos.

Imre Móra *Budapest Then and Now*. A personal and very informative set of accounts of life in the capital, past and present.

★ **László Lugo Lugosi** et al. *Budapest – On the Danube; Walks In the Jewish Quarter; The Castle District; Jewish Budapest; Walks Around the Great Boulevard*. A series of small-format architectural guides – the last one is especially recommended.

Tamás Révész *Budapest: A City before the Millennium*. Excellent collection of black and white photographs of the city, though the text can be irritating.

Dora Wieberson et al. *The Architecture of Historic Hungary*. Comprehensive illustrated survey of Hungarian architecture through the ages.

HISTORY, POLITICS AND SOCIETY

Robert Bideleux & Ian Jeffries *A History of Eastern Europe: Crisis and Change*. An excellent and wide-ranging history of the region.

Judit Frigyesi *Béla Bartók and Turn-of-the-century Budapest*. Placing Bartók in his cultural milieu, this is an excellent account of the Hungarian intellectual world at the beginning of the century.

Jörg K Hoensch *A History of Modern Hungary 1867–1994*. An authoritative history of the country.

László Kontler *Millennium in Central Europe: A History of Hungary*. Another very thorough and reliable history of the country, although its archaic style lets it down somewhat.

Paul Lendvai *The Hungarians: 1000 Years of Victory in Defeat*. Refreshing and authoritative book on Hungary's complex and often tragic history, with particularly stimulating accounts of the Treaty of Trianon and the subsequent Nazi and Communist tyrannies – there are some fascinating pictures, too.

Bill Lomax *Hungary 1956*. Still probably the best – and shortest – book on the Uprising, by an acknowledged expert on modern Hungary. Lomax also edited *Eyewitness in Hungary*, an anthology of accounts by foreign Communists (most of whom were sympathetic to the Uprising) that vividly depicts the elation, confusion and tragedy of the events of October 1956.

John Lukács *Budapest 1900*. Excellent and very readable account of the politics and society of Budapest at the turn of the century, during a golden age that was shortly to come to an end.

John Man *Attila the Hun*. A beautifully written biography of the Magyars' mythical ancestor, illuminating horsemanship and warfare as practised by the Seven Tribes that later colonized the Carpathian basin.

★ **Michael Stewart** *The Time of the Gypsies*. This superb book on Roma culture is based on anthropological research conducted in a Roma community in southeastern Hungary in the 1980s.

Peter Sugar (ed) *A History of Hungary*. A useful and not too academic survey of Hungarian history from pre-Conquest times to the close of the Kádár era, with a brief epilogue on the transition to democracy.

Tony Thorne *Countess Dracula*. An intriguing biography of the sixteenth-century "Blood Countess" Erzsébet Báthory, which argues that she was framed by her uncle to safeguard the Báthory fortune.

BIOGRAPHY AND TRAVEL WRITING

Magda Dénes *Castles Burning: A Child's Life in War*. A moving biographical account of the Budapest ghetto and postwar escape to France, Cuba and the United States, seen through the eyes of a Jewish girl. The author died in 1966, shortly before the book was published.

Ray Keenoy *Eminent Hungarians*. Everything you always wanted to know about Hungary's most renowned historical and contemporary figures – from Lajos Kossuth and Attila József, to Harry Houdini and Ernő Rubik, creator of the Rubik's cube.

★ **Patrick Leigh Fermor** *A Time of Gifts; Between the Woods and the Water*. In 1934 the young Leigh Fermor started walking from Holland to Turkey, reaching Hungary in the closing chapter of *A Time of Gifts*. In *Between the Woods and the Water* the inhabitants of the Great Plain and Transylvania – both Gypsies and aristocrats – are superbly evoked. Lyrical and erudite.

Edward Fox *The Hungarian Who Walked to Heaven*. A brief account of the life of Sándor Kőrösi Csoma, the Hungarian who went in search of the roots of the ancient Hungarians and got sidetracked into making the first Tibetan dictionary.

John Paget *Hungary and Transylvania*. Paget's massive book attempts to explain nineteenth-century Hungary to the English middle class, and, within its aristocratic limitations, succeeds. Occasionally found in secondhand bookshops.

Giorgio and Nicola Pressburger *Homage to the Eighth District*. Evocative short stories about Jewish life in Budapest, before, during and after World War II, by twin brothers who fled Hungary in 1956.

Ernő Szép *The Smell of Humans*. A superb and harrowing memoir of the Holocaust in Hungary.

Rogan Taylor & Klára Jamrich (eds) *Puskás on Puskás*. Not only does this marvellous book depict the life of Hungary's – and one of the world's – greatest footballers, it also provides an intriguing insight into postwar Communist Hungary.

LITERATURE

Hungary's fabulously rich **literary heritage** has been more widely appreciated in recent years thanks to the success of authors such as Sándor Márai and the Nobel Prize-winning Imre Kertész. A useful starting point is *Hungarian Literature* (Babel Guides), an informative guide to the best Hungarian fiction, drama and poetry in translation, with selected excerpts. There are also numerous collections of short stories published in Budapest, though the quality of translations varies from the sublime to the ridiculous. Works by nineteenth-century authors such as Mór Jókai are most likely to be found in secondhand bookshops (see p.203).

ANTHOLOGIES

Loránt Czigány (ed) *The Oxford History of Hungarian Literature from the Earliest Times to the Present*. Probably the most comprehensive collection in print to date. In chronological order, with good coverage of the political and social background.

György Gömöri (ed) *Colonnade of Teeth*. In spite of its strange title, this is a good introduction to the work of young Hungarian poets.

Michael March (ed) *Description of a Struggle*. A collection of contemporary Eastern European prose, featuring four pieces by Hungarian writers including Nádas and Esterházy.

George Szirtes (ed) *An Island of Sound: Hungarian Poetry and Fiction Before and Beyond the Iron Curtain*. Superbly compiled anthology featuring the cream of Hungarian prose and poetry from the end of World War II through to 1989.

POETRY

Endre Ady *Poems of Endre Ady*. Regarded by many as the finest Hungarian poet of the twentieth century, Ady's allusive verses are notoriously difficult to translate.

George Faludy *Selected Poems 1933–80*. Fiery, lyrical poetry by a victim of both Nazi and Soviet repression. Themes of political defiance, the nobility of the human spirit, and the struggle to preserve human values in the face of oppression predominate.

Miklós Radnóti *Under Gemini: the Selected Poems of Miklós Radnóti, with a Prose Memoir; Foamy Sky: the Major Poems*. The two best collections of Radnóti's sparse, anguished poetry. His final poems, found in his coat pocket after he had been shot on a forced march to a labour camp, are especially moving.

Zsuzsa Rákovsky *New Life*. Well-received volume translated by the Hungarian-born English poet George Szirtes.

FICTION

Géza Csáth *The Magician's Garden and Other Stories; Opium and Other Stories*. Disturbing short stories written in the magic realist genre. The author was tormented by insanity and opium addiction, killing his wife and then himself in 1918.

Tibor Déry *The Portuguese Princess*. Wry short stories by a once-committed Communist, who was jailed for three years after the Uprising and died in 1977.

Péter Esterházy *Celestial Harmonies*. Written by a descendant of the famous aristocratic family, this is a dense and demanding book, chronicling the rise of the Esterházys during the Austro-Hungarian empire and their downfall under Communism. His latest novel (yet to be translated), was born of his shock at discovering that his father had been an informer for the Communist secret police.

★ **Tibor Fischer** *Under the Frog, A Black Comedy*. "Under a frog down a coalmine" is a Hungarian expression meaning "Things can't get worse", but this fictional account of the 1956 Uprising will have you in stitches. Fischer's parents fled to Britain in 1956.

Jenő Rejtő *The Blonde Hurricane*. Like Antal Szerb and Miklós Radnoti, Rejtő was a great Hungarian writer who was killed in the Holocaust for his Jewish descent: all three could have escaped, but they thought it would never happen in Budapest. He wrote a series of excellent romps – this translation succeeds far better than Rejtő's *Quarantine in the Grand Hotel*.

★ **Imre Kertész** *Fateless*. Drawing from the author's own experiences as an Auschwitz survivor, this Nobel prize

winning book tells the tale of a young boy's deportation to, and survival in, a concentration camp. A brilliant translation by Tim Wilkinson.

Dezső Kosztolányi *Skylark*. A short and tragic story of an old couple and their beloved child by one of Hungary's top writers of the twentieth century, in a masterly translation by Richard Aczél. Kosztolanyi's *Esti Kornél* is a Hungarian classic, a series of whimsical short tales that offers a wonderful portrait of prewar Budapest.

Gyula Krúdy *Adventures of Sinbad*. Stories about a gourmand and womanizer by a popular Hungarian author with similar interests to his hero.

★ **Sándor Márai** *Embers*. An atmospheric and moving tale about friendship, love and betrayal by one of Hungary's most respected pre-World War II writers; a beautiful read. His *Conversations in Bolzano* is another character study, but its didactic, declamatory dialogue doesn't ring true.

Zsigmond Móricz *Be Faithful Unto Death*. This novel by a major late nineteenth-century Hungarian author sheds light on how Hungarians see themselves – both then and now.

Péter Nádas *A Book of Memories*. This translation of a novel about a novelist writing about a novel caused a sensation when it appeared in 1998. A Proustian account of bisexual relationships, Stalinist repression and modern-day Hungary in a brilliant translation by Iván Sanders.

★ **Antal Szerb** *Journey by Moonlight*. This Hungarian classic, written in 1937, tells the story of a Hungarian businessman on honeymoon in Italy who embarks upon a mystical and dazzling journey through the country. The superb translation by Len Rix ensures that the atmosphere of the original is beautifully retained. *The Pendragon Legend* and *Oliver VII*, one set in Wales and the other mainly in Venice, are also brilliant, while Szerb's *Martians' Guide to Budapest* is a delightful introduction to the city.

FOOD AND WINE

Susan Derecskey *The Hungarian Cookbook*. A good, easy-to-follow selection of traditional and modern recipes.

Stephen Kirkland *The Wine and Vines of Hungary*. Authoritative and accessible guide with tips on what to order. Covers the different wines of the country's regions, and their wine-makers too.

George Lang *The Cuisine of Hungary*. A well-written and beautifully illustrated work, telling you everything you need to know about Hungarian cooking, its history and how to do it yourself.

Hungarian

Hungarian is a unique, complex and subtle tongue, classified as belonging to the Finno-Ugric linguistic group, which includes Finnish and Estonian. If you happen to know those languages, however, don't expect them to be a help: there are some structural similarities, but lexically they are totally different. In fact, some scholars think the connection is completely bogus and have linked Hungarian to the Siberian Chuvash language and a whole host of other fairly obscure tongues. Essentially, the origins of Hungarian remain a mystery and, although a few words of Turkish have crept in, together with some German, English and (a few) Russian neologisms, there's not much that the beginner will recognize.

Consequently, foreigners aren't really expected to speak Hungarian, and locals are used to being addressed in **German**, the lingua franca of Hungarian tourism. However, **English** is gaining ground rapidly, and is increasingly understood. That said, a few basic Magyar phrases can make all the difference. Hungarians are intensely proud of their language and pleased when foreigners make an effort to learn a few courtesies. Note that **signage** is mostly in Hungarian only, though multilingual signs can be found on the metro, in most museums and in many restaurants.

The Rough Guides' *Hungarian for Travellers* is a useful **phrasebook** and, if you're prepared to study the language seriously, the best available book is *Colloquial Hungarian* (Routledge). As a supplement, invest in the handy little *Angol–Magyar/Magyar–Angol Kisszótár* dictionaries, available from bookshops in Hungary.

BASIC GRAMMAR

Although its rules are complicated, it's worth describing a few features of **Hungarian grammar**, albeit imperfectly. Hungarian is an agglutinative language – in other words, its vocabulary is built using **root-words**, which are modified in various ways to express different ideas and nuances. Instead of prepositions "to", "from", "in" etc, Hungarian uses **suffixes**, or tags added to the ends of genderless **nouns**. The change in suffix is largely determined by the noun's context: for example the noun "book" (*könyv*) will take a final "*et*" in the accusative (*könyvet*); "in the book" = *könyvben*; "from the book" = *könyvből*. It is also affected by the rules of vowel harmony (which take a while to get used to, but don't alter meaning, so don't worry about getting them wrong!). Most of the nouns in the vocabulary section below are in the nominative or subject form, that is, without suffixes. In Hungarian, "**the**" is *a* (before a word beginning with a consonant) or *az* (preceding a vowel); the word for "**a/an**" is *egy* (which also means "one").

Plurals are indicated by adding a final "k", with a link vowel if necessary, giving -ek, -ok or -ak. Nouns preceded by a number or other indication of quantity (eg, many, several) do not appear as plural: eg *könyvek* means "books", but "two books" is *két könyv* (using the singular form of the noun).

Adjectives precede the noun (*a piros ház* = the red house), adopting suffixes to form the comparative (*jó* = good; *jobb* = better), plus the prefix *leg* to signify the superlative (*legjobb* = the best).

Negatives are usually formed by placing the word *nem* before the verb or adjective. *Ez* (this), *ezek* (these), *az* (that) and *azok* (those) are the **demonstratives**.

PRONUNCIATION

Achieving passably good **pronunciation**, rather than grammar, is the first priority (see below for general guidelines). **Stress** almost invariably falls on the first syllable of a word and all letters are spoken, although in sentences the tendency is to slur words together. Vowel sounds are greatly affected by the bristling **accents** (that actually distinguish separate letters) which, together with the "double letters" *cs, gy, ly, ny, sz, ty,* and *zs*, give the Hungarian **alphabet** its formidable appearance.

a o as in h**o**t
á a as in f**a**ther
b b as in **b**est
c ts as in ba**ts**
cs ch as in **ch**urch
d d as in **d**ust
e e as in y**e**t
é ay as in s**ay**
f f as in **f**ed
g g as in **g**o
gy a soft dy as in **d**ue
h h as in **h**at
i i as in b**i**t, but slightly longer
í ee as in s**ee**
j y as in **y**es
k k as in sic**k**
l l as in **l**eap
ly y as in **y**es
m m as in **m**ud
n n as in **n**ot
ny ny as in on**i**on

o aw as in s**aw**, with the tongue kept high
ó aw as in s**aw**, as above but longer
ö ur as in f**ur**, with the lips tightly rounded but without any "r" sound
ő ur as in f**ur**, as above but longer
p p as in si**p**
r r pronounced with the tip of the tongue like a Scottish "r"
s sh as in **sh**op
sz s as in **s**o
t t as in si**t**
ty ty as in **T**uesday
u u as in p**u**ll
ú oo as in f**oo**d
ü u as in the German "**ü**ber" with the lips tightly rounded
ű u as above, but longer
v v as in **v**at
w v as in "**V**alkman," "**v**hiskey" or "WC" (vait-say)
z z as in **z**ero
zs zh as in mea**s**ure

WORDS AND PHRASES

BASICS

Do you speak ...	beszél ...
... *English*	... angolul
... *German*	... németül
... *French*	... franciául
yes	igen
OK	jó
no/not	nem
and	és
or	vagy
I (don't) understand	(nem) értem
please	kérem
excuse me (apology)	bocsánat, or elnézést
excuse me (to attract attention)	legyen szives
two beers, please	két sört kérek
thank you (very much)	köszönöm (szépen)
you're welcome	szívesen
hello/goodbye	szia (informal)
good morning	jó reggelt
good day	jó napot
good evening	jó estét
good night	jó éjszakát
goodbye	viszontlátásra (formal)
see you later	viszlát (more informal)
how are you?	hogy vagy? (informal)
how are you?	hogy van? (formal)

could you speak more slowly?	elmondaná lassabban?
what do you call this?	ennek mi a neve? or ezt hogy hivják?
please write it down	kérem, írja le
today	ma
tomorrow	holnap
the day after tomorrow	holnapután
yesterday	tegnap
the day before yesterday	tegnapelőtt
in the morning	reggel
in the evening	este
at noon	délben
at midnight	éjfélkor

QUESTIONS AND REQUESTS

Hungarian has numerous interrogative modes whose subtleties elude foreigners, so it's best to use the simple *van?* ("is there?"), to which the reply might be *nincs* or *nincsen* ("there isn't"/"there aren't any"). In shops or restaurants you will immediately be addressed with the one-word *tessék*, meaning "Can I help you?", "What would you like?" or "Next!". To order in restaurants, shops and markets, use *kérek* ("I'd like ...") plus accusative noun; *Kérem, adjon azt* ("Please give me that"); *Egy ilyet kérek* ("I'll have one of those").

I'd like/we'd like	Szeretnék/szeretnénk
Where is/are ...?	Hol van/vannak ...?
Hurry up!	Siessen!
How much is it?	Mennyibe kerül?
per night	egy éjszakára
per week	egy hétre
a single room	egyágyas szoba
a double room	kétágyas szoba
hot (cold) water	meleg (hideg) víz
a shower	egy zuhany
It's very expensive	Ez nagyon drága
Do you have anything cheaper?	Van valami olcsóbb?
Do you have a student discount?	van diák kedvezmény?
Is everything included?	Ebben minden szerepel?
I asked for ...	Én ... -t rendeltem
The bill please	Fizetni szeretnék
We're paying separately	Külön-külön fizetünk
what?	mi?
why?	miert?
when?	mikor?
who?	ki?

SOME SIGNS

entrance	bejárat
exit	kijárat
arrival	érkezés
departure	indulás
open	nyitva
closed	zárva
push	tolni
pull	húzni
free admission	szabad belépés
women's toilet	női (or WC – "Vait-say")
men's toilet	férfi mosdó (or WC – "Vait-say")
shop	bolt
market	piac
room for rent	szoba kiadó or Zimmer frei
hospital	kórház
pharmacy	gyógyszertár
(local) police	(kerületi) Rendőrség
caution/beware!	vigyázat!/vigyázz!
no smoking	tilos a dohányzás/ dohányozni tilos
no bathing	tilos a fürdés/fürdeni tilos

DIRECTIONS

Where's the ...?	Hol van a ...?
campsite	kemping
hotel	szálloda/hotel
railway station	vasútállomás

bus station	buszállomás
bus-stand	kocsiállás
(bus or train) stop	megálló
inland	belföldi
international	külföldi
Is it near (far)?	Közel (messze) van?
Which bus goes to ...?	Melyik busz megy ... -ra/re?
a one-way ticket to ... please	egy jegyet kérek ... -ra/ re csak oda
a return ticket to ...	egy retur jegyet ... -ra/re
Do I have to change trains?	Át kell szállnom?
towards	felé
on the right (left)	jobbra (balra)
straight ahead	egyenesen előre
(over) there/here	ott/itt
Where are you going?	Hova megy?
Is that on the way to ...?	Az a ... úton?
I want to get out at ...	Le akarok szállni ... -on/en
please stop here	itt álljon meg
I'm lost	eltévedtem
arrivals	érkező járatok (or érkezés)
departures	induló járatok (or indulás)
to/from	hova/honnan
change	átszállás
via	át

DESCRIPTIONS AND REACTIONS

nothing	semmi
perhaps	talán
very	nagyon
good	jó
bad	rossz
better	jobb
big	nagy
small	kicsi
quick	gyors
slow	lassú
now	most
later	később
beautiful	szép
ugly	csúnya
Help!	Segítség!
I'm ill	beteg vagyok

NUMBERS AND MEASURES

In shops and markets, items are priced per piece (*darab*, abbreviated to *db*.) or per kilogram. Shoppers commonly request purchases in multiples of ten grams (*deka*); one hundred grams is *tíz deka*. The measure for fluids is the *deci* (abbreviated to dl.) – see "Drinks" (p.230) for how this applies in bars and restaurants.

1	egy	900	kilencszáz
2	kettő	1000	egyezer
3	három	half	fél
4	négy	a quarter	negyed
5	öt	each/piece	darab (db.)
6	hat	10 grams	egy deka
7	hét	100 grams	tíz deka
8	nyolc		
9	kilenc		

TIME, DAYS AND DATES

Luckily, the 24-hour clock is used for timetables, but on cinema programmes you may see notations like 1/4, 3/4, etc. These derive from the spoken expression of time which, as in German, makes reference to the hour approaching completion. For example 3.30 is expressed as *fél négy* – "half (on the way to) four"; 3.45 – *háromnegyed négy* ("three quarters on the way to four"); 6.15 – *negyed hét* ("one quarter towards seven"), etc. However, " ... o'clock" is ... *óra*, rather than referring to the hour ahead. Duration is expressed by the suffixes –*től* ("from") and -*ig* ("to"); minutes are *perc*; to ask the time, say "*Hány óra?*"

10	tíz		
11	tizenegy		
12	tizenkettő		
13	tizenhárom		
14	tizennégy		
15	tizenöt		
16	tizenhat		
17	tizenhét		
18	tizennyolc		
19	tizenkilenc		
20	húsz	**Monday**	hétfő
21	huszonegy	**Tuesday**	kedd
30	harminc	**Wednesday**	szerda
40	negyven	**Thursday**	csütörtök
50	ötven	**Friday**	péntek
60	hatvan	**Saturday**	szombat
70	hetven	**Sunday**	vasárnap
80	nyolcvan	**on Monday**	hetfőn
90	kilencven	**on Tuesday**	kedden
100	száz	**on Wednesday**	szerdán
101	százegy	**on Thursday**	csütörtökön
150	százötven	**on Friday**	pénteken
200	kettőszáz	**on Saturday**	szombaton
300	háromszáz	**on Sunday**	vasárnap
400	négyszáz	**day**	nap
500	ötszáz	**week**	hét
600	hatszáz	**month**	hónap
700	hétszáz	**year**	év
800	nyolcszáz		

HUNGARIAN FOOD AND DRINK TERMS

The food categories here refer to the general divisions used in menus. In cheaper places you will also find a further division of meat dishes: ready-made meals like stews (*készételek*), and freshly cooked (in theory) dishes such as those cooked in breadcrumbs or grilled (*frissensültek*). *Tészták* is a pasta-doughy category that can include savoury dishes such as *turoscsusza* (pasta served with cottage cheese and a sprinkling of bacon), as well as sweet ones like *somlói galuska* (cream and chocolate covered sponge). Two popular **snacks** which are nicer than they sound are *zsíros kenyér* (bread spread with lard and sprinkled with paprika; often sold in old-fashioned wine bars); and *lángos* (fried dough served with soured cream or a variety of other toppings, and available in markets).

BASICS		**egészségedre!**	Cheers!
borravaló	tip	**étlap**	menu
bors	pepper	**jó étvágyat!**	Bon appétit!
cukor	sugar	**kenyér**	bread
ecet	vinegar	**kifli**	croissant-shaped roll

méz	honey
mustár	mustard
rizs	rice
sajtos or vajas pogácsa	cheese or butter scones
só	salt
tejföl	sour cream
tejszín	cream
vaj	butter
zsemle or	bread rolls
péksütemeny	

COOKING TERMS

comb	leg
mell	breast
angolosan	(English-style) underdone/ rare
főtt	boiled
főzelék	creamed vegetable dishes – better than it sounds
jól megsütve	well done (fried)
jól megfőzve	well done (boiled)
paprikás	in a paprika sauce
pörkölt	stewed slowly
rántott	deep-fried in breadcrumbs
roston sütve	grilled
sülve	roasted
sült/sütve	fried
töltött	stuffed

SOUPS (LEVESEK)

bakonyi betyárleves	"Outlaw soup" of chicken, beef, noodles and vegetables, richly spiced
csirke-aprólék leves	mixed vegetable and giblet soup
erőleves	meat consommé often served with noodles (*tésztával* or *metélttel*), liver dumplings (*májgombóccal*), or an egg placed raw into the soup (*tojással*)
gombaleves	mushroom soup
gulyásleves	goulash in its original Hungarian form as a soup, sometimes served in a small kettle pot (*bográcsgulyás*)
halászlé	a rich fish soup often served with hot paprika
húsleves	meat consommé
jókai bableves	bean soup flavoured with smoked meat
kunsági	chicken soup

pandúrleves	seasoned with nutmeg, paprika and garlic
lencseleves	lentil soup
hideg	chilled sour cherry
meggyleves	soup
palócleves	mutton, bean and sour cream soup
paradicsomleves	tomato soup
tarkonyos	lamb soup flavoured
borjúraguleves	with tarragon
ujházi tyúkleves	chicken soup with noodles, vegetables and meat
zöldségleves	vegetable soup

APPETIZERS (ELŐÉTELEK)

These comprise both hot (*meleg*) and cold (*hideg*) dishes.

füstölt csülök tormával	smoked knuckle of pork with horseradish
hortobágyi palacsinta	pancake stuffed with minced meat and served with creamy paprika sauce
körözött	a paprika-flavoured spread made with sheep's cheese and served with toast
libamáj	goose liver
rakott krumpli	layered potato casserole with sausage and eggs
rántott gomba	mushrooms fried in breadcrumbs, sometimes stuffed with sheep's cheese (*juhtúróval töltött*)
rántott sajt, Camembert, karfiol	Camembert or cauliflower fried in breadcrumbs
tatárbeefsteak	raw mince mixed with an egg, salt, pepper, butter, paprika and mustard, and spread on toast
tepertő	crackling (usually pork, sometimes goose)
velőcsont fokhagymás pirítóssal	bone marrow spread on toast rubbed with garlic, a special delicacy associated with the gourmet Gyula Krúdy

SALADS (SALÁTÁK)

Salads are not Hungary's strong point; they are usually simple, and are often served in a vinegary dressing, although other dressings include blue cheese (*rokfortos*), yogurt (*joghurtos*) or French (*francia*).

csalamádé	mixed pickled salad
fejes saláta	lettuce
idénysaláta	fresh salad of whatever is in season

jércesaláta	chicken salad
paradicsom saláta	tomato salad
uborka saláta	cucumber; can be gherkins (*csemege* or *kovászos*) or the fresh variety (*friss*)

FISH DISHES (HALÉTELEK)

csuka tejfölben sütve	fried pike with sour cream
fogas	a local fish of the pike-perch family
fogasszeletek Gundel modra	breaded fillet of *fogas*
harcsa	catfish
harcsa paprikás	catfish in paprika sauce
kecsege	sterlet (small sturgeon)
nyelvhal	sole
pisztráng	trout
pisztráng tejszínes mártásban	trout baked in cream
ponty	carp
ponty filé gombával	carp fillet in mushroom sauce
rántott pontyfilé	carp fillet fried in breadcrumbs
rostélyos töltött ponty	carp stuffed with bread, egg, herbs and fish liver or roe
süllő	another pike-perch relative
sült hal	fried fish
tonhal	tuna

MEAT DISHES (HÚSÉTELEK)

baromfi	poultry
bécsi szelet	Wiener schnitzel
bélszin	sirloin
bélszinjava	tenderloin
csirke	chicken
fácán	pheasant
fasírt	meatballs
hátszin	rumpsteak
kacsa	duck
kolbász	spicy sausage
liba	goose
máj	liver
marha	beef
nyúl	rabbit
őz	venison
pulyka	turkey
sertés	pork
sonka	ham
vaddisznó	wild boar
vadételek	game
virsli	frankfurter

borjúpörkölt	closer to what foreigners mean by "goulash": veal stew seasoned with garlic
cigányrostélyos	"gypsy-style" steak with brown sauce
csikós tokány	strips of beef braised in bacon, onion rings, sour cream and tomato sauce
csülök Pékné módra	knuckle of pork roasted with potatoes and onions
erdélyi rakott-káposzta	layers of cabbage, rice and ground pork baked in sour cream (a Transylvanian speciality)
hagymás rostélyos	braised steak piled high with fried onions
pacal	tripe (usually in a paprika sauce)
paprikás csirke	chicken in paprika sauce
rablóhús nyárson	kebab of pork, veal and bacon
sertésborda	pork chop
sült libacomb tört burgonyával és párolt káposztával	grilled goose leg with potatoes, onions and steamed cabbage
töltött káposzta	cabbage stuffed with meat and rice, in a tomato sauce
töltött paprika	peppers stuffed with meat and rice, in a tomato sauce
vaddisznó borókamártással	wild boar in juniper sauce
vasi pecsenye	fried pork marinated in milk and garlic

SAUCES (MÁRTÁS OK)

bormártásban	in a wine sauce
ecetes tormával	with horseradish
fokhagymás mártásban	in a garlic sauce
gombamártásban	in a mushroom sauce
kapormártásban	in a dill sauce
meggymártásban	in a morello cherry sauce
paprikás mártásban	in a paprika sauce
tárkonyos mártásban	in a tarragon sauce
tejszínes paprikás mártásban	in a cream and paprika sauce
vadasmártásban	in a brown sauce (made of mushrooms, almonds, herbs and brandy)
zöldborsós	in a green-pea sauce
zöldborsosmártásba	in a green peppercorn sauce

ACCOMPANIMENTS (KÖRETEK)

galuska	noodles (though *Somlói galuska* is different – see introduction)
gombóc	dumpling
hasábburgonya	chips, french fries
krokett	potato croquettes
petrezselymes burgonya	boiled potatoes served with parsley
rizs	rice
zöldköret	mixed vegetables

VEGETABLES (ZÖLDSÉGEK)

bab	beans
borsó	peas
burgonya/krumpli	potatoes
fokhagyma	garlic
gomba	mushrooms
hagyma	onions
(vörös) káposzta	(red) cabbage
karfiol	cauliflower
kelkáposzta	savoy cabbage
kukorica	sweetcorn
lecsó	tomato and green pepper stew that's a popular ingredient in Hungarian cooking
padlizsán	aubergine/eggplant
paprika (édes/erős)	peppers (sweet/hot)
paradicsom	tomatoes
sárgarépa	carrots
spárga	asparagus
spenót	spinach
uborka	cucumber
zöldbab	green beans
zöldborsó	peas
zukkini	courgette
Rakott krumpli	layered potatoes with egg and sausage
Sólet	a superior baked beans (a Jewish speciality)
spenót főzelék	a garlicky creamed spinach (often served with a fried egg)
tök főzelék	creamed marrow with dill

FRUIT AND NUTS (GYÜMÖLCSÖK ÉS DIÓK)

alma	apple
birsalma	quince
bodza	elderflower
citrom	lemon
dió	walnut
eper	strawberry
földi mogyoró	peanut
füge	fig
(görög) dinnye	(water) melon
körte	pear
málna	raspberry
mandula	almond
meggy	morello cherry
mogyoró	hazelnut
narancs	orange
őszibarack	peach
sárgabarack	apricot
szilva	plum
szőlő	grape
tök (sütőtök)	marrow (pumpkin/squash)

CHEESE (SAJT)

Cheeses made in Hungary are a rather limited selection, the most interesting being the soft *juhtúró*.

füstölt sajt	smoked cheese
juhtúró	sheep's cheese
kecske sajt	goat's cheese
márvány	Danish blue cheese
trappista	rubbery, Edam-type cheese
túró	a cross between cottage and curd cheese

DESSERTS (ÉDESSÉGEK)

almás pite	apple pie
aranygaluska	golden dumpling cake
diós metélt	pasta with walnuts
fánk	doughnut
gesztenye puré	chestnut purée
Ggundel palacsinta	pancake with walnuts in a chocolate sauce
mákos or diós beigli	poppyseed or walnut roll
mákos guba	poppy seed pudding
palacsinta	pancake
párolt alma	stewed apple
rétes	strudel
szilva gombóc	dumpling stuffed with a plum
túrógombóc	cottage cheese dumpling

DRINKS (ITALOK)

The drinks list (*itallap*) is usually divided into wine, beer, spirits and soft drinks. **Wine** is often served by the *deci* (dl.), or 100ml, and may be charged as such, so that the sum on the drinks list may be multiplied by two or three times on the bill. To avoid ambiguity over glass sizes, you can specify *egy deci*, *két deci* or *három deci* (respectively, 100ml, 200ml or 300ml). **Pálinka** is a popular aperitif, distilled from apricots (*barackpálinka*), plums (*szilva*), William's pears (*Vilmoskörte*) or other fruit; and **Unicum** a dark, bitter digestif that Hungarians swear is good for the

SPRITZERS

Most bars serve **spritzers** – wine mixed with soda water – on request and increasingly you can see them on menus too. Given the quality of the wine in cheaper wine bars, it is a much nicer way to drink it, and very thirst-quenching. A popular drink among the younger generation is VBK, wine mixed with cola (see below).

Hungarians give their mixes curious names:

Kifröccs – small spritzer:	1dl. soda water, 1dl. wine
Fröccs – spritzer:	1dl. soda water, 2dl. wine
Hosszúlépés – long step:	2dl. soda water, 1dl. wine
Viceházmester – deputy janitor:	3dl. soda, 2dl. wine
Haziúr – landlord:	1dl. soda, 4dl. wine

stomach. Due to Hungary's abundant thermal springs there are numerous local brands of **mineral water**; it's sold with colour-coded bottle-caps for easy recognition of still (*szénsavmentes* – pink caps), mildly fizzy (*enyhe* – green) or sparkling (*szénsavas* or *buborékos* – blue).

ásányvíz	mineral water
bor	wine
borsmenta teá	peppermint tea
csapalt sör	draught beer
édes bor	sweet wine
fehér bor	white wine
félédes bor	medium-dry wine
gyümölcslé	fruit juice
kávé	coffee (espresso)
koffeinmentes kávé	decaffeinated coffee
korsó	half-litre of beer
menta teá	mint tea
narancslé	orange juice
pálinka	schnapps-like fruit brandy, in a range of flavours
pezsgő	sparkling wine
pohár	300dl. of beer, or a glass of wine
rosé	rosé wine
sima (csap) víz	ordinary (tap) water
sör	beer
száraz bor	dry wine
szódavíz	soda water
teá	tea
tejeskávé	coffee with milk
Traubiszóda	sparkling grape-flavoured soft drink
Unicum	a bitter medicinal *digestif*
üveg	bottle (of wine)
(csap) víz	(tap) water
vörös bor	red wine
vörösboros kola (VBK)	red wine mixed with cola

Glossary of Hungarian terms

ÁFA Goods tax, equivalent to VAT.

Állatkert Zoo.

Arrow Cross see Nyilas.

Áruház Department store.

ÁVO The dreaded secret police of the Rákosi era, renamed the ÁVH in 1949.

Barlang Cave.

Belváros Inner city.

Biedermeier Heavy nineteenth-century style of Viennese furniture that became very popular in Budapest homes.

Borkostoló Wine tasting.

Borozó Wine bar.

Botanikuskert Botanical garden.

Büfé Snack bar.

Cigány Gypsy/Roma (can be abusive).

Cigánytelep Gypsy settlement.

Cigányzene Gypsy music.

Csárda Inn; nowadays, a restaurant with rustic decor.

Csárdás Traditional wild dance to violin music.

Cukrászda Cake shop.

Diszterem Ceremonial hall.

Domb Hill.

Duna River Danube.

Egyetem University.

Erdély The Hungarian word for Transylvania, the region of Romania where a large Hungarian minority lives.

Erdő Forest, wood.

Étterem Restaurant.

Fasor Avenue.

Fogadó Inn.

Folyó River.

Forrás Natural spring.

Fürdő Public baths.

Gőzfürdő Steam bath.

Gyógyfürdő Mineral baths fed by thermal springs with therapeutic properties.

Hajó Boat.

Hajóállomás Boat landing stage.

Halászcsárda/halászkert Fish restaurant.

Ház House.

Hegy Hill or low mountain.

HÉV Commuter trains running from Budapest.

Híd Bridge.

Hídfő Bridgehead.

Honvéd Hungarian army.

Ifjúsági szálló Youth hostel.

Iskola School.

Kápolna Chapel.

Kapu Gate.

Kert Garden, park.

Kerület (*ker.*) District.

Kiállítás Exhibition.

Kiáltó Lookout tower.

Kincstár Treasury.

Kirakodó vásár Fair, craft or flea market.

Kollégium Student hostel.

Korzó Promenade.

Körönd Circus (road junction, as in Piccadilly Circus).

Körtér Circus (as *körönd*).

Körút (*krt.*) Literally, ring road, but in Budapest refers to the main boulevards surrounding the Belváros.

Köz Alley, lane; also used to define narrow geographical regions.

Kulcs Key.

Kút Well or fountain.

Lakótelep High-rise housing estate.

Lépcső Flight of steps.

Liget Park, grove or wood.

Lovarda Riding school.

Magyar Hungarian (pronounced "*mod*-yor").

Magyarország Hungary.

Malév Hungarian national airline.

MÁV Hungarian national railways.

Megálló Railway station or tram or bus stop.

Megye County; the county system was originally established by King Stephen to extend his authority over the Magyar tribes.

Mozi Cinema.

Műemlék Historic monument, protected building.

Művelődési ház/központ Arts centre.

Nádor Palatine, highest administrative office in Hungary in the Habsburg empire pre-1848.

Nyilas "Arrow Cross"; Hungarian Fascist movement.

Palota Palace; *püspök-palota*, a bishop's residence.

Pályaudvar (*pu.*) Rail terminus.

Panzió Pension.

Patak Stream.

Pénz Money.

Piac Outdoor market.

Pince Cellar.

Rakpart Embankment or quay.

Református The reformed church, which in Hungary means the Calvinist faith.

Rendőrség Police.

Repülőtér Airport.

Rév Ferry.

Rom Ruined building; sometimes set in a *romkert*, a garden with stonework finds.

Roma The romany word for gypsy, preferred by many Roma in Hungary.

Sétány "Walk" or promenade.

Skanzen Outdoor ethnographic museum.

Sor Row, as in *fasor*, row of trees, ie avenue.

Söröző Beer hall.

Strand Beach, open-air baths or any area for sunbathing or swimming.

Szabadtér Open-air.

Szálló or **szálloda** Hotel.

Szent Saint.

Sziget Island.

Szoba kiadó Room to let.

Tájház Old peasant house turned into a museum, often illustrating the folk traditions of a region or ethnic group.

Táncház Venue for Hungarian folk music and dance.

Temető Cemetery.

Templom Church.

Tér Square; t*ere* in the possessive case.

Terem Hall.

Tilos Forbidden; *tilos a dohányzás* means "smoking is forbidden".

Tó Lake.

Torony Tower.

Türbe Tomb or mausoleum of a Muslim dignitary.

Udvar Courtyard.

Uszoda Swimming pool.

Út Road; in the possessive case, *útja*.

Utca (*u.*) Street.

Vár Castle.

Város Town.

Városháza Town hall.

Vásár Market.

Vásárcsarnok Market hall.

Vasútállomás Railway station.

Vendéglő Restaurant.

Verbunkos Folk dance, originally a recruiting dance.

Völgy Valley.

Zsidó Jew or Jewish.

Zsinagóga Synagogue.

Small print and index

A ROUGH GUIDE TO ROUGH GUIDES

Published in 1982, the first Rough Guide – to Greece – was a student scheme that became a publishing phenomenon. Mark Ellingham, a recent graduate in English from Bristol University, had been travelling in Greece the previous summer and couldn't find the right guidebook. With a small group of friends he wrote his own guide, combining a highly contemporary, journalistic style with a thoroughly practical approach to travellers' needs.

The immediate success of the book spawned a series that rapidly covered dozens of destinations. And, in addition to impecunious backpackers, Rough Guides soon acquired a much broader readership that relished the guides' wit and inquisitiveness as much as their enthusiastic, critical approach and value-for-money ethos.

These days, Rough Guides include recommendations from budget to luxury and cover more than 200 destinations around the globe, as well as producing an ever-growing range of eBooks and apps.

Visit **roughguides.com** to see our latest publications.

Rough Guide credits

Editor: Ann-Marie Shaw
Layout: Ankur Guha
Cartography: Subhashree Bharati
Picture editor: Mark Thomas
Proofreader: Karen Parker
Managing editor: Keith Drew
Assistant editor: Jalpreen Kaur Chhatwal
Production: Rebecca Short
Cover design: Dan May & Ankur Guha
Photographers: Eddie Gerald & Michelle Grant
Editorial assistant: Eleanor Aldridge

Senior pre-press designer: Dan May
Marketing, Publicity & roughguides.com: Liz Statham
Design director: Scott Stickland
Travel publisher: Joanna Kirby
Digital travel publisher: Peter Buckley
Reference director: Andrew Lockett
Operations coordinator: Becky Doyle
Operations assistant: Jöhanna Wurm
Publishing director (Travel): Clare Currie
Commercial manager: Gino Magnotta
Managing director: John Duhigg

Publishing information

This fifth edition published May 2012 by
Rough Guides Ltd,
80 Strand, London WC2R 0RL
11, Community Centre, Panchsheel Park,
New Delhi 110017, India
Distributed by the Penguin Group
Penguin Books Ltd,
80 Strand, London WC2R 0RL
Penguin Group (USA)
375 Hudson Street, NY 10014, USA
Penguin Group (Australia)
250 Camberwell Road, Camberwell,
Victoria 3124, Australia
Penguin Group (NZ)
67 Apollo Drive, Mairangi Bay, Auckland 1310,
New Zealand
Rough Guides is represented in Canada by Tourmaline
Editions Inc. 662 King Street West, Suite 304, Toronto,
Ontario M5V 1M7
Printed in Singapore by Toppan Security Printing Pte. Ltd.
© Charles Hebbert and Dan Richardson, 2012

MIX
Paper from
responsible sources
FSC™ C018179

Help us update

We've gone to a lot of effort to ensure that the fifth edition
of **The Rough Guide to Budapest** is accurate and up-to-
date. However, things change – places get "discovered",
opening hours are notoriously fickle, restaurants and
rooms raise prices or lower standards. If you feel we've got
it wrong or left something out, we'd like to know, and if
you can remember the address, the price, the hours, the
phone number, so much the better.

Please send your comments with the subject line
"Rough Guide Budapest Update" to
@mail@uk.roughguides.com. We'll credit all contributions
and send a copy of the next edition (or any other
Rough Guide if you prefer) for the very best emails.

Find more travel information, connect with fellow
travellers and book your trip on Ⓦroughguides.com

ABOUT THE AUTHOR

Dan Richardson first visited Budapest in 1984, while researching what would become three separate guidebooks to Hungary, Romania and Bulgaria – and has since written other Rough Guides to Egypt, Moscow and St Petersburg. He is also the author of *Gog* – an apocalyptic thriller set in near-future Egypt – and works as a special-effects actor.

Charles Hebbert fell in love with Budapest in 1982 and lived there for more than ten years. He regularly visits the city with his family when he isn't working as an editor in London, playing his accordion or updating Rough Guides in northern Italy.

Acknowledgements

Charles Hebbert would like to thank Ann-Marie Shaw for her patient editing, Fazakas Péter and Makk Lili for their huge help and generosity, Lőrincz Anna, Bakonyi Ági, Rachel Appleby, Rozgonyi 'Rozi' Zoltán, Altorjai Anita, Pallai Péter, Helen and Yvette Teitelbaum (when Fergus got lost in the zoo), Kosa Judit, Celia Armand Smith, Richard Lim, Craigie Pearson, Evelyn and Alisdair Nicholas, Jean and Peter Hoare, Molly, Fergus and, as always, Caroline.

Norm Longley Thanks to Annie for her diligent and enthusiastic editing, as always. Very special thanks to Viktor Hajko and Karin Jones at the Hungarian National Tourist Office in London, and to Timea Major at Mellow Mood in Budapest. Thanks also to my colleague and good friend, Charles, for his support on this book. Above all, to Christian, Luka, Patrick and Anna.

Readers' letters

Thanks to all the readers who have taken the time to write in with comments and suggestions (and apologies if we've inadvertently omitted or misspelt anyone's name):

Darcy R Fryer, Jon Johnson, Richard Koss, Ruth Swirsky, Jenny Feng Wong

Photo credits

Index

Maps are marked in **grey**

Maps

Index

Listings key

■ Accommodation

● Restaurant/cafés/bars

● Shops

■ Clubs

City plan

The **city plan** on the pages that follow is divided as shown:

N

0 ——————— 500
metres

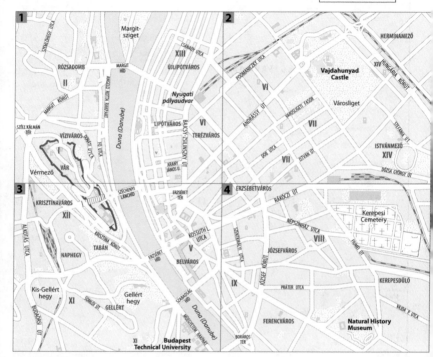

Map symbols

✈ International airport	∩ Arch	▓ Building
Ⓜ Metro station	🏛 Monument	⊐ Church
Ⓗ HÉV station	✝ Church (regional)	▢ Market
🅿 Parking	⚓ Swimming pool	○ Stadium
✡ Synagogue	⊤ Gardens	▢ Christian cemetery
♛ Castle	)(Bridge	▱ Jewish cemetery
⚠ Campsite	★ Bus stop	▢ Park/forest
⌒ Cave	⚓ Ferry docks	- - Chairlift
∴ Ruins	♦ Point of interest	- - - Ferry route
☇ Viewpoint	⊠ Post office	— Wall
▲ Peak	ⓘ Tourist office	
⊙ Statue	@ Internet access	
⊠ Gate		

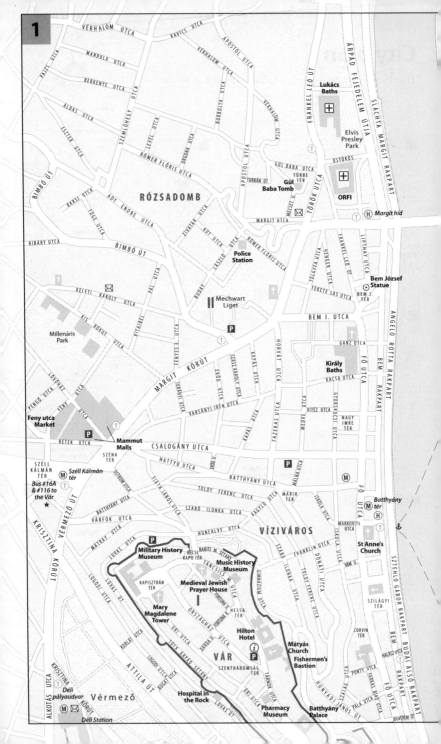

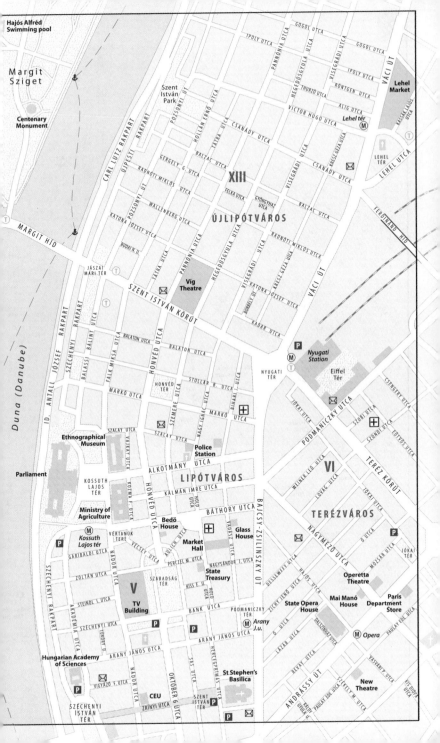

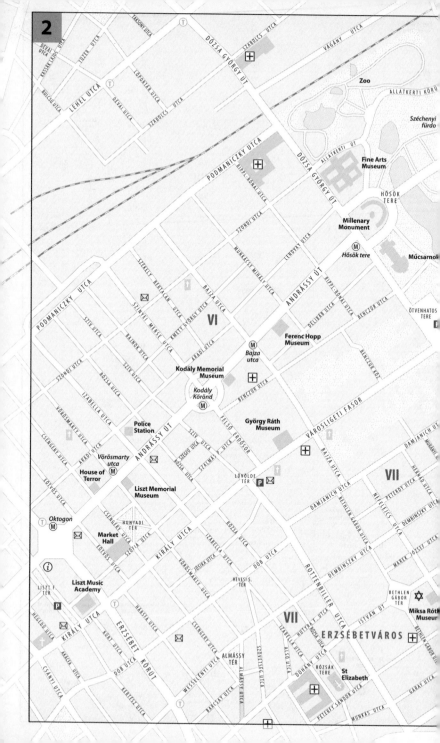

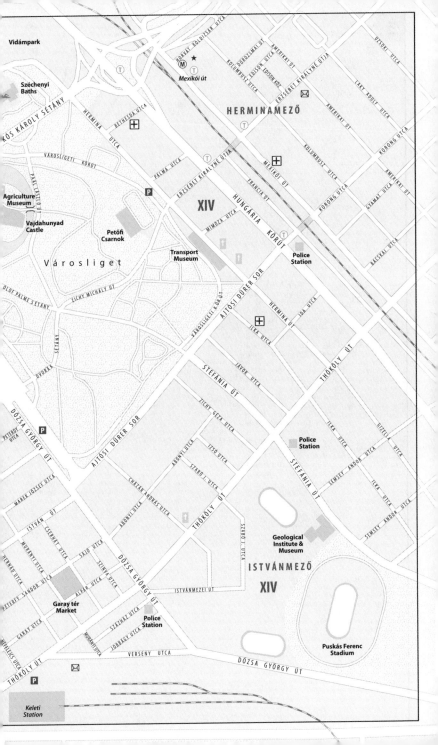

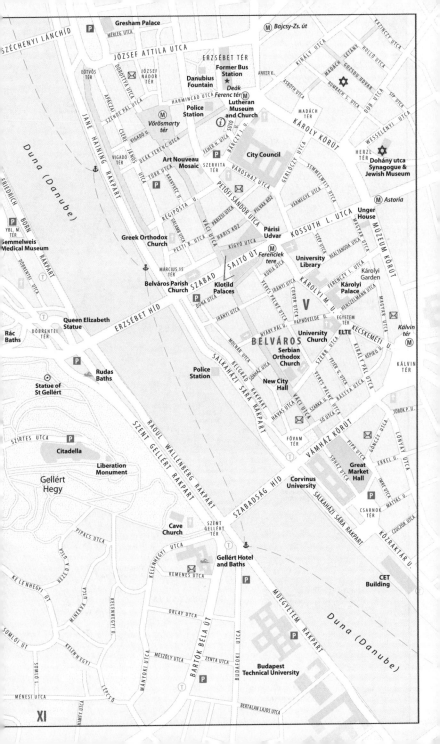

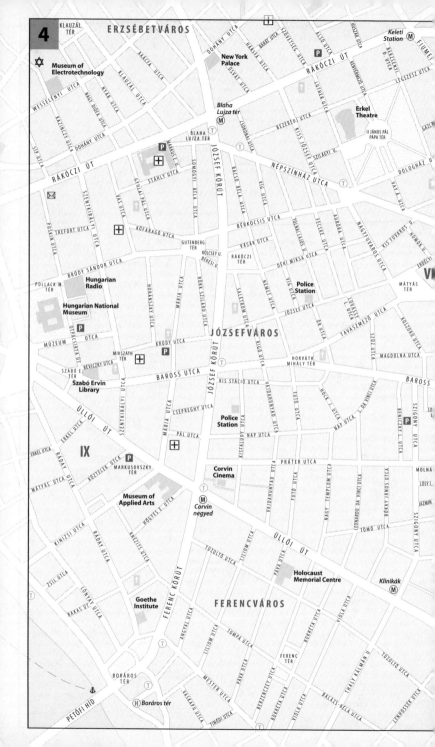

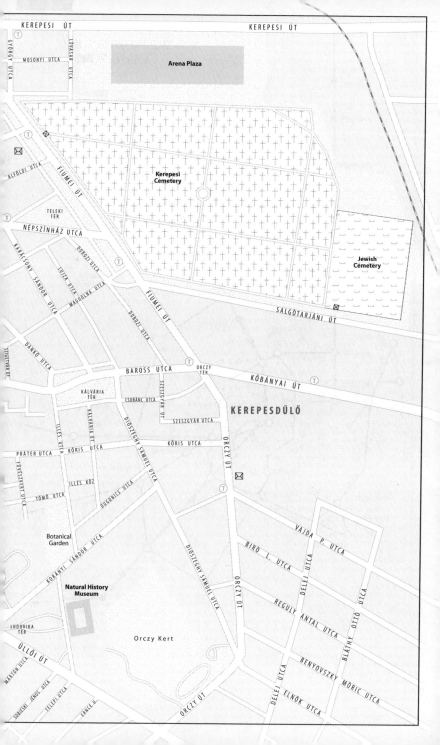

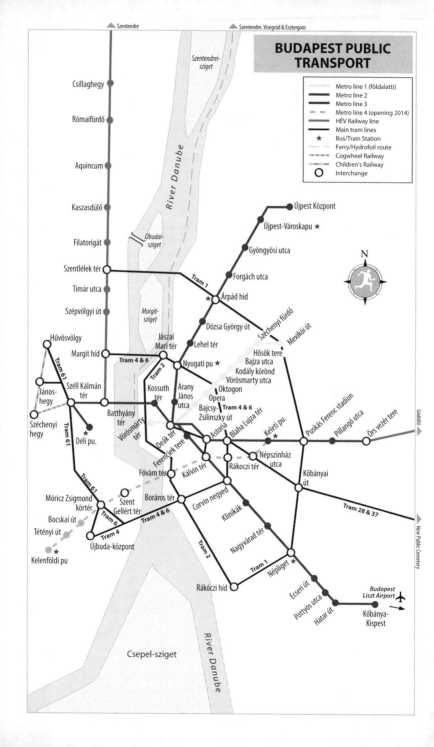

BUDAPEST PUBLIC TRANSPORT

MAKE THE MOST OF YOUR CITY BREAK

BARCELONA

LONDON

NEW YORK CITY

PARIS

ROME

FREE PULL OUT MAP WITH EVERY SIGHT AND LISTING FROM THE GUIDE

THE ROUGH GUIDE to
Las Vegas

Rome
ROUGH GUIDES

ROUGH GUIDES

ESSENTIAL ITINERARIES AND RELIABLE RECOMMENDATION